NORTH AFRICA 1800–1900

Magali Morsy

NORTH AFRICA 1800–1900

A SURVEY FROM THE NILE VALLEY TO THE ATLANTIC

Longman, London and New York

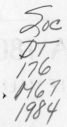

Longman Group Limited
Longman House,
Burnt Mill, Harlow
Essex CM20 2JE
England

Published in the United States of America
by Longman Inc., New York

Associated companies, branches and representatives
throughout the world

First published 1984

ISBN 0 582 78376 3 cased
ISBN 0 582 78377 1 paperback

British Library Cataloguing in Publication Data
Morsy, Magali
  North Africa 1800–1900.
  1. Africa, North–History–1882–
  I. Title
  961'.03   DT176

ISBN 0 582 78376 3
ISBN 0 582 78377 1 Pbk

Library of Congress Cataloging in Publication Data
Morsy, Magali.
  North Africa, 1800–1900.

  Bibliography: p.
  Includes index.
  1. Africa, North–History–1517–1882. 2. Africa,
North–History–1882–   I. Title.
DT176.M67   1983   961'.03   82–23959
ISBN 0-582-78376-3
ISBN 0-582-78377-1 (Pbk)

Set in 10/11 pt Linotron 202 Baskerville
Printed in Singapore by
Kyodo Shing Loong Printing Industries Pte Ltd

To Charles-André Julien, this book owes everything except its defects

CONTENTS

LIST OF MAPS

LIST OF FIGURES

Map 1.1 *North Africa in the 19th century*

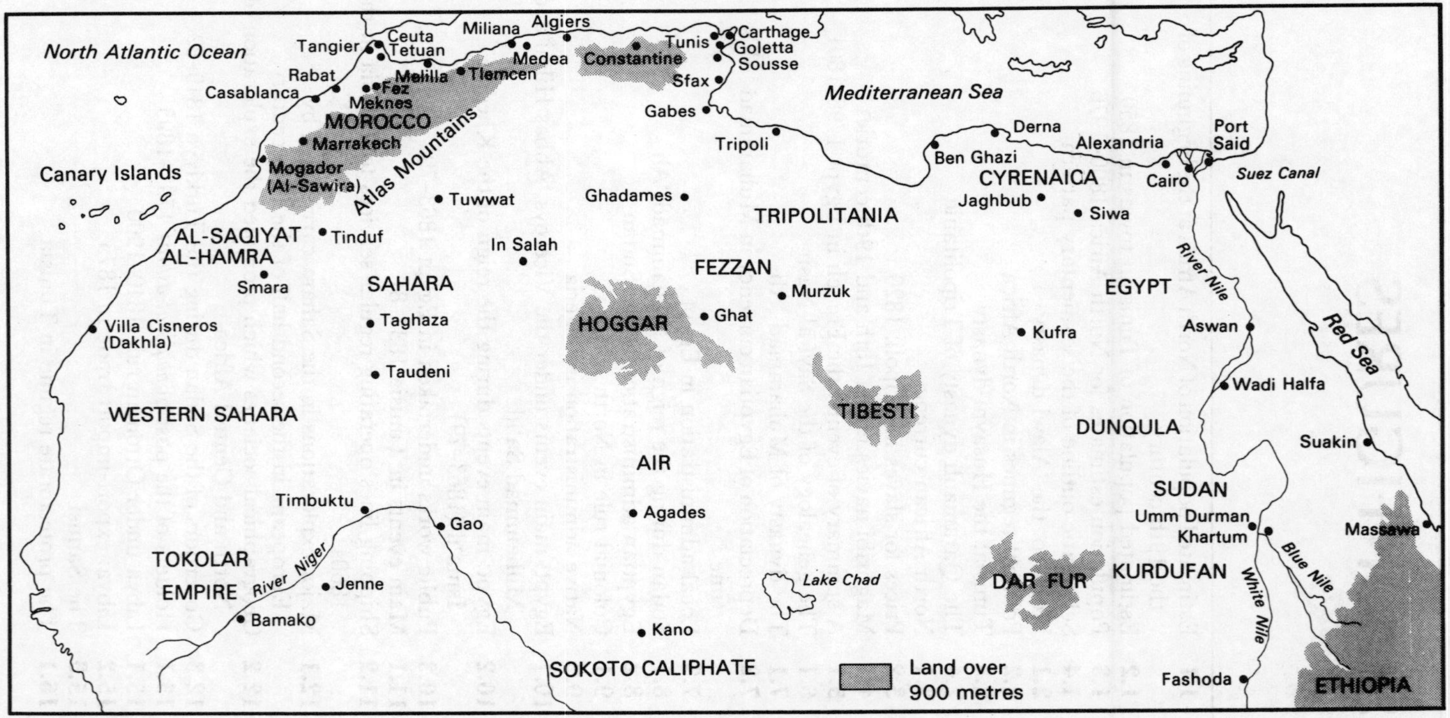

A NOTE ON TRANSLITERATION

Any book dealing with a different cultural and linguistic idiom from that in which it is written is faced with the problem of translating concepts and specific cultural factors. This is particularly obvious when dealing with as distinct and sophisticated a civilization as that of the Arabs. However debatable in theory may be the correspondences a translation somewhat artificially establishes, these are nonetheless a necessary means of communication and the difficulty with which an author is faced is, in fact, a practical one: where is the line to be drawn between exactitude and intelligibility?

This book, which is intended for a wide reading public and one not necessarily specialized in the study of the Muslim world or the Arabic language, will necessarily make greater concessions to the foreign reader. Few Arabic terms are used here and, where they are, they are always explained. Concepts, terms for social or political institutions and cultural facts are, as far as possible, rendered by their counterparts in Western civilization, even if these are often inadequate renderings. Thus, to mention but one example, dates are given here in *anno domini* and not according to the Muslim *hijra* calendar.

The rendering of Arabic proper names (both personal and place names) involves the problem of transliteration, i.e. the use of letters of the Latin alphabet instead of the Arabic one. The fact that the latter is more complex leads to a further dilemma: should one add special signs for letters which do not exist in Indo-European or bring the Arabic alphabet down to the Latin script by using a single letter for two distinct phonemes? For reasons of convenience and to make the book more easily readable, we have generally preferred to simplify. The letter *s*, for example, will be used to render both the Arabic *sin* and *sad*. The same rule will apply for the two *t* and two *h* phonemes.

On the other hand, *ayn* which has no equivalent in English will be indicated by an apostrophe. It should further be pointed out that the *hamza* is not noted and *ta marbuta* only where it is pronounced. Grammatical problems will be avoided, and we shall consequently indicate the plural by adding *hyphen s* to the singular. Even so a number of problems occur especially in view of the fact that accepted systems of transliteration have varied in different countries and periods and in some cases usage, however inaccurate, has made one form prevail over another. The names of President Bourguiba of Tunisia or President Gamel Abdel Nasser of Egypt, for example, would be unrecognizable were they to be transcribed according to academic standards. In such cases it has been deemed more practical to stick to these generally accepted versions. The same problem occurs with place names, which are strongly influenced by local dialects and whose etymology is often uncertain. Here too we shall often give words as they are found on European maps.

The following system of transliteration will nonetheless be used, except in the above-mentioned cases:

ا	a	ض	dh
ب	b	ط	t
ت	t	ظ	zh
ث	th	ع	ʿ
ج	j	غ	gh
ح	h	ف	f
خ	kh	ق	q
د	d	ك	k
ذ	dh	ل	l
ر	r	م	m
ز	z	ن	n
س	s	ه	h
ش	sh	و	u or w
ص	s	ي	y or i

PART 1
BACKGROUND TO 19TH CENTURY HISTORY

INTRODUCTION

Thinking about history is a complex process involving awareness of the past as such – that is as a state of things different from that which prevails today and which must be interpreted in its own terms – but also as a background to the present, part of a collective heritage to which contemporaries have both a claim and a duty. It is merely pushing this a step further to say that the past not only informs the present, but is part of history in the making, and this may help explain why an historian's account, however full and adequate, will nonetheless have to be rewritten by successive generations who will be asking different questions or seeing things from a different angle. This is underscored today by the speed and complexity of changes underway throughout the world, further emphasizing the need for a more consistent stand from which to see society in perspective and from which the fundamental and contradictory tendencies of progress – namely change and continuity – can be appreciated. This has special significance for those countries which were until recently subject to foreign domination. The writing of history is generally a privilege of the conqueror denied to the conquered, and this was well illustrated by the type of outlook which prevailed in the 19th century and which has persisted well into our time. It has tended to see the world in terms of Europe and Europeans. Are we not told that explorers 'discovered' Africa, blandly ignoring the people who for centuries have lived there and who often had continent-wide relations? The societies of those regions were too often seen as merely passive elements in history, and described in terms of unconnected responses to European stimuli. This approach to historical reconstruction was, of course, part of the will to dominate which implied not only bringing people into subjection but also depriving them of their identity and therefore of their right to a history of their own.

The long struggle of colonized peoples on the road to independence and development has led to new awareness among such groups, not only in terms of their social or economic characteristics, but also with respect to those long-term traits through which cohesion is built up and self-identity is put over. This, of course, places special emphasis on culture as the means through which a group's identity is maintained through a process of historical change. It is this which a contemporary historian has to bring out. His capacity to do so is determined both by awareness of the more significant aspects of the world in which he lives, and by his correct appreciation of the material which can be used to illustrate these. This involves a professional aptitude to ask the right questions in the right context. The 'right' questions are those which are fundamental to our own times, but the right answers are those which are provided by adequate historical material. This has to be rediscovered, correctly interpreted and taken fully into account even if and when it does not appear immediately relevant. This is not merely a question of intellectual honesty. History, as a complex process of interaction between past and present, has its own power of backlash.

What we shall try and define in the course of this book is what history meant in 19th-century North Africa and what its inhabitants have to say for themselves and to us today. It will also, however, be an attempt to bring to light the forgotten pages of time, or those which have been blotted out by European preponderance in what was for North Africa a largely negative context of economic and political imbalance, because we believe that the men and women of those times clung to their personalities, continued to uphold their social and cultural traditions, and showed their determination to live up to the challenge of history. This was their legacy not only to the nations which struggled and are still struggling to achieve effective independence, but to the men and women of tomorrow.

CHAPTER 1

THE SCOPE OF THIS BOOK: BASIC FACTS AND TENETS

The historical import of any given study is to a large degree determined by the outline of the subject and by the basic tenets referred to. This chapter will therefore define those involved in this book, but the question the reader probably has in mind at the outset concerns the scope of this book. Why have we chosen to give an account of nation-states in a regional context, that of North Africa? The reader is all the more likely to ask this in view of the fact that a division inherited from the Colonial Age still largely prevails in this context, dividing the area into two separate entities: a *Maghrib* (West of the Muslim world) seen as comprising Algeria, Tunisia, and Morocco which were formerly part of the French Empire, and a more eastern zone which, though not part of the Muslim *Mashriq* (or East), was seen in terms of a British sphere of influence. Libya, between the two, was only too often until recently a vague area, the mere shore of what Italians called *mare nostrum*. People are, moreover, even less clear as to the southern limits of the North African states, the latter being essentially defined as a coastal strip. This is further emphasized by present-day frontiers although these result from 20th-century political decisions which have little meaning in the long-term historical context as present-day tensions in the Sahara and in Sudanic Africa show. Moreover the loss of control by North African states over the southern hinterland, which was part of the colonial process, was paralleled by the creation of new political entities connected to central Africa which did away with the Muslim principalities or kingdoms which in the former period had interacted with their powerful northern neighbours. The contention in this book is that there exists a regional entity defined by common historical, social, ethnic, economic, cultural and religious factors. In spite of local or national differences, and even more characteristically of differences in the respective balance of common factors involved, the region, its populations and historical evolution point to the unity of the area which expresses itself in a common historical pattern and a specific identity within the dominant framework of Islam. Since the 16th century, changes in the Mediterranean and the growing role of nation-states emphasize the importance of the latter in terms of boundaries within which societies are historically operative. The kind of isolation which later resulted from European pressures in the region, acquired positive significance during the struggle for independence. It is thus fashionable today to write national histories. Whilst not underestimating the role of nation-states in the modern period – indeed the very layout of this book in terms of chapters of national histories will stress the latter's importance – we shall also point to regional interaction as part of the historical process underway, one which will be illustrated both by developments that showed parallel features occurrent within separate historical frontiers and by currents that cut across frontiers and promoted the sense of a common involvement in the wider issues of the Muslim Maghrib.

THE LAND AND THE PEOPLE

The physical background

A glance at the map reveals an outline of North Africa in terms of what are generally called 'natural frontiers'. These are constituted on three sides by seas which are also major routes of communication and trade, namely the Atlantic Ocean in the west, the Mediterranean in the north and the Red Sea in the east. Moreover the Sahara Desert, which constitutes the southern boundary of the region plays a similar role which may explain why Arab geographers often refer to it metaphorically as a sea. Within the area bounded by these 'seas' we find three ecological zones combined in different proportions. The first of these is a coastal plain of variable extent in the northernmost part where adequate rainfall has promoted agriculture whilst the proximity of the sea has encouraged trade. This zone of easy access has over the centuries been characterized by immigration, either on a large scale or on an individual basis. Major migrations took place overland, from east to west. This was the case with the Berber migration, possibly as early as the second millennium BC, and that of the Arabs from the second half of the 7th century AD. Other groups have come by way of the sea. They include the Phoenicians from about 1200 BC, the Romans from 146 BC, the Vandals in the 5th and 6th centuries AD, and, in the modern period, Europeans. It is in this northern zone, through a combination of local factors and foreign influences, that an elaborate form of society developed, promoting among other things urban growth. It was here too that the state institutions came into their own.

The second zone runs parallel to the first from east to west at a higher altitude. It is constituted by a mountain range which reaches to high snow-clad peaks in the west while bare plateaux and a steppe vegetation are more characteristic of Algeria and the eastern areas. The difficulties of maintaining subsistence there has led to a greater emphasis on pastoralism and a low population density.

Further south begins a third zone, a desert area characterized both by sand dunes and high, bare rocky peaks. In some parts of North Africa and notably in central Libya and western Egypt, the absence of the mountains of the Atlas range brings the desert zone up to the coastline. Characterized in general by a low density of population and a lack of resources, the Sahara is the homeland of nomads who, besides raising livestock, notably camels, derive profit from the trans-Saharan trade. Even in such unfavourable circumstances, however, we also come across a settled population, having a concentrated habit, living off agriculture and trade. This is typical of the oases and certain other physically more privileged areas such as part of the Tibesti mountains, south of Libya. With respect to the Sahara, it should also be borne in mind that a long-term process of desiccation has been underway since around 1000 BC, and the arid, uncultivated parts of the zone have constantly tended to increase. In the modern period, the desert extends between two roughly parallel lines, in the north between Wad Nun on the Atlantic and the

Egypto-Libyan frontier and, in the south, at the level of the Niger and Agades Bend.

North Africa between sea and desert is further characterized by the fact that the river network is on a north-south axis. This is particularly evident in the west where the Atlas mountains constitute a watershed from which rivers flow north into the well-irrigated Atlantic plain, or south through narrow, densely populated valleys and oases before disappearing in the sands of the desert. It is less obvious in central North Africa, and Libya, for example, has no permanent rivers. At the eastern end of the continent, the long Nile valley is the most cultivated area of the region, besides constituting a highroad of communication pushing deep into the heart of the continent. This river system together with more adequate rainfall in the north has promoted interaction between the three ecological zones and has led to state formation on the basis of a necessary but uneasy balance between different types of economy. Even this cursory glance at the map and at the consequences of geographical factors points to the fact that natural frontiers only become meaningful in terms of people, and the kind of society built up on the basis of the ecological environment.

Demography

North Africa was until very recent years a sparsely populated area. Estimates for the precolonial period are vague and often contradictory. Such figures as we have apply essentially to the northern zone and are the result of somewhat impressionistic estimates made by European observers. On the basis of these, modern historians conclude that the population of North Africa at the beginning of the 19th century was probably around 14 million, no estimates being made for the Sudan or the Sahara.

Fig. 1.1 Estimated population of North Africa at the beginning of the 19th Century

Morocco	4 million
Algeria	4 million
Tunisia	1.5 to 2 million
Libya	no estimates available
Egypt	4 million
Sudan	no estimates available
Sahara	no estimates available

Though further research may well prove these figures to be too low, they nonetheless point to relative underpopulation. This is further emphasized by uneven distribution and great regional disparity. Thus fertile river valleys, notably the Nile, are densely populated if not overpopulated, whereas the desert is hardly inhabited. Local disparity is further emphasized if one takes into account concentrated human settlement, although towns in the precolonial period were few in number and small in size. Only Cairo, with its 300 000 or so inhabitants in 1800, would be considered a metropolis by modern standards. The population of most towns did not, in fact, exceed 10 000.

Fig. 1.2 Estimated population of Tunisian Towns in 1850

Tunis	80 000 to 90 000
Qairawan	15 000
Sfax	10 000
Sousse	3 000
Bizerta	5 000
Monastir	5 000

But other forms of concentrated inhabitation implying a permanent population several thousand strong also exist in North Africa, even if not generally reckoned as towns. Among these are fortress villages in some regions of the Atlas and several oases; Awjila, for example, on the Libyan caravan roads whose population was estimated at around 9 000 in the 19th century. Mention should also be made of less permanent concentrations of population including the religious fairs which for short periods attracted people from far and wide. Such major fairs as that of Tanta in Egypt, were attended by hundreds of thousands.

Another and no less significant feature is the great stability in population figures throughout the modern period at least up to the last quarter of the 19th century. It was not until the late 1870s that any distinct upward demographic trend became apparent and even by the end of the 19th century the increase was no more than 0.5 per cent per annum. In other words the type of expansive demographic trend today associated with underdeveloped countries is a recent phenomenon which, in North Africa, only began to take off relatively slowly between the two World Wars, the increase then being between 1.7 per cent and 1.8 per cent, whilst the present 3.2 per cent rate was only reached in the middle of the 20th century. The stability of former times should not necessarily be seen as a positive factor. The absence of evolution characteristic of 'traditional' societies is probably to some degree the result of lack of manpower. The fact that there was no significant change in the pattern of human distribution, either in terms of physical location or of the age composition of the population, also meant an absence of stimuli to change. Stability further implies social fragility. This was true in individual terms with a short life expectation and a high child mortality rate, but also of society as a whole since the great majority of people lived at mere subsistence level. With only 5–7 per cent of the population living and working in towns, economic resources came essentially from agriculture and this was characterized by archaic methods of production. A closer look at the demographic trend thus shows up considerable irregularity.

In a country dependent on agriculture, climatic conditions were important and in the Mediterranean these were generally characterized by ten-year cycles – roughly seven years of adequate rainfall and therefore good harvests, followed by three years of more or less severe drought. This, combined with irregular water supply (including floods) and such calamities as locusts, periodically upset the balance. People rarely had enough resources to tide them over prolonged bad periods (even though one should not

Years	Egypt	Sudan	Libya	Tunisia	Algeria	Morocco	Sahara
1800	Between 3 and 4 million			Around 2 million	Around 4 million	Around 4 million	
1810							
1820							
1830							
1840	4 323 000		750 000	1.5 to 2 million	4 million	4 million	
1850	4 750 000						
1860				1 500 000			
1870				1 500 000			
1880							
1890	10 million (1897)						
1900			800 000		4 138 742		Mzab and Wargla: 48 000
1910			523 176 (1911 census)				
1920	14 million (1927)			1 986 000 2 160 000 (1926)	4 999 000 6 201 000 (1936)	5 487 000 (Fr. Prt. only) 7 558 000 (1936)	
1930							
1940	19 million (1947)			2 800 000 (1946)	7 729 618 + 120 000 Jews (1948)	7 800 000 (1946)	Mazb: 55 000
1950 1960	30 075 858 (1966 census)	10 262 536 (1956 census) 14 148 000 (1967)	1 564 369 (1964 census) 1 869 000 (1969)	4 500 000 (1966)	12 096 347 (1966 census)	11 626 470 (1960 census)	
1970	34 million (1971)	15 675 000 (1971)		5 100 000 (1971)		14 million	Sp Sahara: 117 000 Mauritania: 1 320 000 (1976)

underestimate the regulating role of food storage, whether by the government – since most taxes were paid in kind – or by communities which, amongst other techniques, kept stores of cereals in large plastered holes where they could remain fresh for several years). Nonetheless, prolonged periods of drought created hardship and sometimes actual starvation. Undernourishment favoured outbreaks of rampant diseases, including the bubonic plague, which could spread over vast areas, sometimes the whole of North Africa, with incredible violence. Two severe cases of this occurred in the last quarter of the 18th century, around 1775–80, and in the early 19th century, between 1817 and 1820, besides a no less violent but limited outbreak around 1800. Such epidemics created extensive depopulation, both in urban and rural areas, and rent apart the social fabric. It took several years and much reorganization for North African society and governments to recover from the effects of the early 19th-century epidemics and this may help us to understand why reactions to early colonial aggressions were limited. Other diseases, including cholera and typhus, continued periodically. Tunisian historians record such epidemics in 1836, 1849–50, 1856 and 1866–9, whilst the French authorities in Algeria noted similar outbreaks after the worst recorded famines, those of the 1870s and 1920s.

Life in Upper Egypt in 1927–8, described by a contemporary Egyptian author

At Manfalut, for the first time in my life, I was face to face with the victims of bilharziasis and malaria – all those young men in full manhood whose faces disease had rendered deathly pale. Hypertrophy of the spleen had swollen their stomachs. They had become monsters of whom it was impossible to say whether they were youths or old men. Their exhausted gaze was nonetheless turned towards one as if to escape from the iron grip which held them in mortal throe as they expressed their innermost feelings, seemingly merry, gay, and carefree. I noted that often peasant women, as soon as they had been married and had given birth once or twice, could hardly be distinguished from their mothers. All alike were tanned by the heat of the sun and the flames of the oven. They bore the mark and odour of their cow-dung bricks, the stamp of their continuous, monotonous, and exhausting work. In our people, the peasant woman is the person who passes most quickly from youth to old age. But those for whom I feel sorriest are the young, the children who, in the country and in the towns, toil away: peasant children working on the land, tiny pedlars in the streets, pickers-up of cigarette ends, waifs and strays hanging on to tramways, boy and girl servants. All that they have to endure to survive gives them the experience of mature men, the cruelty, the cunning, and the language of adults. They have been deprived of one of the finest periods of life, that of childhood with its games and illusions, the carefree world of play acting and creativity. The betrayal of childhood is the tragedy we live with and ignore. Of course, we are not the only ones in this case. It is the loss of all nations struggling against poverty.

Translated from *Khalliha 'ala Allah*
by Yahya Haqqi

This further suggests that contrary to a prevalent notion that if colonial rule had some advantage, it was precisely in the medical field, no general improvement in North Africa is perceptible until a very recent period. The fact that infant mortality remained high and life expectancy short points to the fact that few sanitary measures were introduced and medical care was essentially for the settler community and did not reach native society, except such individuals as had close contacts with the colonists. Moreover, European requirements, notably in the matter of cereals, both in the precolonial and colonial periods, led to the authorities more or less forcibly buying up, or collecting by way of taxation, local produce which had formerly been put by for hard times. This, together with growing dependence on modern commodities and therefore on cash-crop production to pay for them, made people more subject to daily hazards. One should further take into account the hardship and toll on human lives which resulted from the system of colonial exploitation: for example, native troops were recruited and sent out to foreign battlefields. New diseases came in the wake of new economic activities: we thus find North Africans working in the mines and falling victims to tuberculosis, others, notably in Egypt, increasingly suffered from such illnesses as bilharziasis which became prevalent when perennial agriculture based on irrigation was developed.

The peoples of North Africa

Having outlined the general characteristics of life in North Africa one is led to a more fundamental question: who were or are the North Africans? Can one speak of 'ethnic unity' with any degree of relevance? The latter in fact generally has little significance in practice although dominant groups can contribute to the overall pattern of any given society. This also applies to North Africa whose inhabitants are of mixed origins but where a number of major migrations have played a leading role in establishing a prevalent social and cultural pattern.

The earliest recorded inhabitants of the region were themselves of mixed origins. We thus find such groups building up village communities in the Nile valley and promoting the highly elaborate civilization of Pharaonic times. Various Nilotic groups of the south-east, including the Nubians of the Upper Nile, came under its influence. Further west we find traces of a dark-skinned but non-negro population which was progressively overrun and driven southwards by new immigrants. The descendants of this population of early times can still be found on the northern outskirts of the desert where they are known as *haratin* and generally have a servile status. Others have survived as more or less independent communities with their own social organization and dialects (generally grouped under the name of Central Saharan languages) as for example the Tubus of Tibesti. Others contributed to the building up of village communities and states in Sudanic Africa. Their descendants have often come under the influence of the Arabs and even more of the religion the latter brought to the region, namely Islam, but they themselves have not significantly contributed to the development of the northern states.

Of far greater importance – both ethnically and socially – was the arrival in North Africa of the Berbers, a population of Caucasian origin which had migrated south through Arabia before crossing over to Africa from the 2nd

11

millennium BC onwards. They swept through the continent as far west as the Atlantic. The Berbers can be said to constitute the basic population in North Africa, west of the Nile valley. More important still is the fact that they provided the dominant social pattern of the region. The Berbers were – and to some degree still are – organized in tribal units built up on a segmentary pattern involving balanced opposition of groups through a complex hierarchized system seen as reflecting consanguinity. It is probably no mere coincidence that the definition of the principle of segmentation by the British anthropologist E. E. Evans-Pritchard should have been the result of field work in North Africa, first among a non-Berber people, the Sudanese Nuer, and later among the Berbers and Arabs of Cyrenaica. In economic terms, the smallest unit of production is that constituted by an extended family, generally living under a single roof or in a small group of tents. The head of the household classifies relations in the extended family with immediate neighbours defined as cousins claiming descent from a common ancestor three to five generations removed and this cousinship can be extended to adopt members of the clan. The need to find a solution for a wider range of problems – for example agreements for the share-out of water in a river valley – involves agreements between groups worked out by chosen representatives and these . can, once again, be justified in terms of consanguinity, all claiming a common, distant, and sometimes mythical ancestor.

Reference to family ties as justifying help given to kin against 'strangers' are, of course, a more or less universal trait, even if tribal organization uses the pattern of consanguinity in a more formal and systematic way, and, moreover, gives it institutional backing. This is merely one reason for which there is a tendency today to avoid using the term tribe as a historical concept. Another even more obvious reason is the unfounded but nonetheless prevalent belief that the term implies essentially primitive forms of social organization, incapable of development. This is, in many ways, the legacy of the past and of the imperialist use to which anthropological interest in primitive societies was put. Historical research on the structural and ethical principles on which tribal societies have based their development is, as yet, at an early stage. It has still not sifted the material which distinguishes between non-European societies as different as sub-Saharan village communities, Indian empires in America, or North African tribal confederacies and according to which some would be classified as tribes and others not. Even those which would be classified as tribes have been subject to different structural and economic factors in the course of historical development.

This book which deals with the modern period cannot, of course, undertake a systematic description or definition of the Berber tribe in antiquity, by which time it was already a highly sophisticated polity, but special mention must be made of what is probably the key institution which is built up to become operative at a political level: arbitration. Arbitration can be defined in basic abstract terms as the set of connecting links between levels of segmentation (family units, lineages having a common ancestor three to five generations removed, whether real or supposed, and the tribe, i.e. people who could all claim to descend from a common mythical ancestor). Links between these levels which one might call vertical, as also 'horizontal' relations between entities within or outside the tribe, involve tensions through which each unit maintains its autonomy, and alliances by means of which each unit can ensure its independence by appealing to a larger entity to neutralize the aggressive instincts of other groups.

Arbitration involved not only channelling conflicts through various levels of segmentation but an element of decision-making: 'should a particular conflict be moved to a higher level of involvement, or should an attempt be made to underplay the issue and ultimately work out a negotiated compromise acceptable to both parties?'. In contrast to automatic appeal to solidarity through the various strata, this involved not only a personal appreciation of

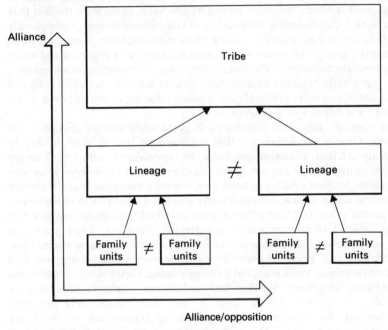

Fig. 1.4 *Schematic outline of the segmentary pattern*

the nature of the conflict, but also a higher principle, that of the collective weal: was it in the interest of the community as a whole to uphold the claims of a given group or did circumstances make it preferable to work out a compromise and avoid full-scale involvement? This, from early times, involved recourse to mediators (generally called arbiters by modern anthropologists) who were posed as neutral third parties. These arbiters who conveyed requests for help and presided over negotiations often did so in special places set apart for this and where direct confrontation or threatening attitudes were forbidden, discussion alone being tolerated. The development of the arbiter institution and of a specialized personnel was part of the political development of Berber tribes in antiquity. Arbiters were defined as non-tribal. They could be actual strangers called in to work out harmonious relations between groups, or they could be persons considered as neutral: old men, for example, who were respected for their wisdom and experience, and who were seen as far removed from the passions and ambitions of younger men. In traditional Berber society

13

where men and women seem to have had a more equal status than that which prevailed in the later Islamic period, women also sometimes acted as arbiters. As the institution became more sophisticated, arbiter functions were increasingly the privilege of hereditary lineages, not only because it was useful to know whom to contact in any crisis and what authority the arbiter could command, but also because rulings themselves required ever greater knowledge of the history of any given tribe, of its complex organization, and of tribal lore. The particular emphasis placed by Berbers on the central institution represented by authorized arbiters expressed itself in the aura of reverence which surrounded the latter. The shamanistic or supernatural 'priestly' powers which they were considered to have, came from the fact that they embodied the collective personality of the tribe and were consequently expected to act in this capacity in dangerous circumstances. These involved mediating the group's relations with its environment: of a supernatural order was the mediation between the community and its ecological environment, seen by these early societies as involving contact with the powerful forces at work in nature; of a more political nature was mediating relations between the tribe and rival entities or strangers.

It is through the early contact of Berbers with foreign groups – the Egyptians, Greeks, or Romans – that we have an insight into the highly sophisticated tribal organization with its specialized arbiters. Foreign observers, though they have not given full descriptions of the type of society which existed in North Africa in antiquity, nonetheless prove that the system of arbitration was complex, both politically and culturally. Historical evidence further points to the fact that arbiters constituted a hierarchical network and that top arbiters could command an extended following. Thus, over and beyond the apparently autonomous status of small tribal groups, taking their own decisions and being responsible for their own management, we find reference to common rules accepted by large confederacies of tribes which the Romans called 'kingdoms'. We thus find the Libyans – the term is used to refer to Berbers in general in antiquity – not only collectively resisting encroachments, but undermining neighbouring states such as the latter Pharaonic dynasties. One of these (the 22nd dynasty, *circa* 954–730 BC) was itself of Libyan origin and the role played in Egypt by the god Amon, symbolized by a ram's head, may have been itself borrowed from the Libyans who had made of his shrine at Siwa a holy centre where the shamanic arbiters practised divination.

The tribal ideal has always been to obviate power accruing to any one individual or group. In Berberland, this democratic tendency has as far as possible been maintained both by the common will to break individual ambitions and the collective respect for decisions taken in common. We also find there such egalitarian principles as the annual election of the tribal chief chosen in turn from different groups, periodic reallocation of land, etc. Many of these practices have survived up to the present in outlying areas, notably in the Moroccan Atlas. There is, however, one potential danger which in particular circumstances such as difficult historical conditions or outside pressures, has not always been obviated, namely the constitution of a warrior class having a privileged and dominant position. Thus control of Pharaonic Egypt by the Libyans was effected through the growing influence their warriors had in the Egyptian army. In later Roman times, the need to make a stand against a common enemy brought to the fore Jugurtha, the Numidian hero of Algerian resistance, who was chosen as leader by the soldiers. In more modern times, we find the Tuareg Saharan Berber tribes, because of difficult ecological conditions, making of the warrior class a dominant element in a stratified society. It should nonetheless be pointed out that they shared decision-making with the saintly or scholar class of tribal mediators. Less often, and under the impact of modern circumstances, and notably foreign rule, feudal lords whose power is based on their military force have come to the fore, but these dominant positions tended generally to be short-lived as the Berber mechanisms of what one might term primitive communism reasserted themselves.

By contrast, arbitration was privileged and built up into the central political institution of the Berbers precisely because it did not constitute a position of power. 'Holy men' of former times theoretically had no tribal involvements and therefore could not appeal to a particular sector of society to uphold them. They were not allowed to take part in those activities from which they could derive wealth or influence, whether warfare or agriculture, work being carried out for them by the tribesmen. They were expected to confine themselves to their social, cultural and religious activities. Such authority as they had ultimately depended on tribal consent. We find the institution of arbitration providing the underlying principle of social organization throughout North Africa, even though different forms of economy, including more intensive forms of agriculture and urban growth, have tended to break down tribal structures and remodel society on different lines. Even in such circumstances, however, holy men have not been eliminated and often continue to be the pillars of society. Their influence should not therefore be underestimated, nor indeed the resilience of the tribal organization in general, even under new political and economic conditions.

Having stressed the importance of Berbers in the ethnic makeup of North Africa and their contribution to the basic social organization of the region, it should be pointed out that the term Berber as generally used today, has a more limited application. It has come to have a purely linguistic and by extension cultural meaning: those referred to as Berbers are people who still speak Berber, a language related to the Semitic group. As a result of the Arab invasion which we are going to describe and of the prevalence in North Africa of Arabic, the language of the Quran, Berbers have, in the course of the centuries, progressively identified themselves with a new dominant civilization, that of the Arabs. Not only have they often switched over from the Berber to the Arabic language but have tended to see themselves and be seen as Arabs. Only a minority today still continues to speak Berber and even among this minority more extensive schooling in recent years has led to bilingualism, in Arabic and Berber. Berber today is still the mother tongue of nearly half the population of Morocco, but its importance wanes as one moves eastwards. In Algeria there are still a number of large Berber-speaking areas including the Kabylies, the Aures, and the Sahara where the large Tuareg confederacy (which extends over into present-day Mali, Niger, northern Nigeria, Chad and Libya) is Berber. In Tunisia, Berber survives only in isolated localities, notably the island of Djerba. Attachment to traditional ways including the local language is upheld there by specific religious factors since the inhabitants of Djerba do not belong to the orthodox Sunni rite but are Ibadhites, members of a religious minority group descended from the *khariji* (literally 'those who go out') movement which arose from the first major quarrel among Muslims as to who was to lead the community after the Prophet's death. This is also the case of the oases which make up the Mzab region in southern Algeria and of the Nafusa mountain region in Libya which are both Ibadhite and Berber-speaking. The easternmost point where Berber is still spoken is the Egyptian oasis of Siwa.

Leaving aside the contribution of successive waves of invaders who came to North Africa by way of the sea – the Phoenicians who founded the flourishing city of Carthage which the Romans destroyed in 146 BC, and the Romans themselves who stayed in the region for about 650 years, and others who played an important role in North Africa and set on foot the Mediterranean trade relations – we shall now turn to what is probably the major force to have influenced the history of the northern part of the continent, namely the arrival of the Arabs in the 7th century AD. There is ambiguity as to what is actually meant by the term Arab just as there are problems with the term Berber, since different levels of meaning are ambiguously fused. If by Arabs we mean people who actually came from Arabia or their descendants, it should be stressed that the first Arab *mujahidin* (religious warriors) who came to North Africa in the 7th century, were few in number, but their zeal and the conversions they affected were impressive. In less than 50 years, they overran the continent as far as the Atlantic and reached Spain. The first Arab military camp in North Africa was set up at Fustat, now Cairo (al-Qahira in Arabic) in 639. Alexandria was conquered in 642, Qairawan in 670. The Atlantic was reached in 681 and Spain invaded in 711. This does not imply a massive impact in ethnic terms and the very fact that these early Arabs came without wives or children implied intermarriage from the start. On the other hand it underlines the importance of Islam to which the Arabs were seen as having a privileged relationship. It also brings out the importance of a new dominant social, political and cultural pattern legitimized by religion, with which, from the start, people began to identify themselves. Thus the new Berber converts played an important role in the early military camps set up by the Arabs and they were progressively integrated into the ruling class until such times as they came to see themselves, and be seen as authentic Arabs.

The Arab strain such as it is, is due not as much to this initial expansion, which was basically religious and by extension political, as to the subsequent arrival in the region of Arab tribes, the Banu Hilal and Banu Sulaym, which had taken part in the Prophet's early campaigns and in the subsequent expansion of the Muslims. These troublesome nomads had begun to settle on the banks of the Nile at the end of the 9th century and it was in order to get rid of them that the Fatimid sovereign of the time encouraged them to move westwards, which they did from 1050 onwards. They may have been about 150 000 strong and they swept through the region, component units dropping off on the way. Thus in Cyrenaica the rural population sees itself as divided along ethnic lines, consisting of the *Mrabitin* and the *Sa'di*. The former are descendants of conquered local tribes who submitted to the invaders and were integrated into the new dominant pattern, whereas the Sa'di-s give themselves out to be the nine Arab tribes who hold the country by right of conquest. They further see themselves as being related and claim descent from a common ancestor, a woman of the Banu Sulaym whose name was Sa'da. In the desert region between Cyrenaica and Tripoli, the Awlad Sulayman whose history will be referred to in the course of this book, are also of Banu Sulaym stock, so too are the Mahamid of the Nafusa mountains and the Jawari around Tripoli. On a similar though less extensive scale, Arabs have contributed to the Beduin or pastoral population of Tunisia and Algeria. In northern Morocco they merged into what is now a mosaic of disintegrated tribes in the Atlantic plain. A last wave of Arab expansion was constituted by the Ma'qil-s of southern Arabia who in the 13th century took part in the political conflicts of Morocco and were driven out into the desert. There they had to wage a long struggle against the Berber tribes of the Sahara to obtain right of place. The fighting lasted up to the 18th century and progressively made of them the dominant population of the western Sahara, from Wad Nun in the Moroccan Sus as far south as the River Senegal. They constituted large complex tribal confederations in which the warrior class was an important and constantly feuding element, whilst the influential scholar class (often recruited from former vanquished tribes) regulated the social order and tried to maintain peace between conflicting parties.

To be complete on the subject of Arab infiltration into the region, one should also mention a reduced but persistent tendency for Arabs to continue to move into Africa. This was sometimes provoked by political events, chief of which was the expulsion from Spain in the 15th and 16th centuries of the descendants of the early Muslim invaders, but was more generally an individual trend bringing merchants and preachers to North Africa. Such men often travelled far into the south. Their influence was particularly important in the *bilad al-sudan* (literally, 'the land of the blacks') which for Arab geographers covers the whole southern fringe of the Sahara as far west as the Atlantic. They made major contributions to the conversion of sub-Saharan African states to Islam and we find African political elites often adopting Islam as the official state religion, without their subjects necessarily converting. In the process these African rulers sometimes came to claim Arab origins for themselves, thus further highlighting the fact that self-definition as an Arab is in fact a religious claim and one which can further imply more or less complete identification with Arab values and the use of Arabic as a cultural language.

NORTH AFRICA IN A SOCIO-RELIGIOUS CONTEXT

This leads us to a reappraisal of the frontiers of North Africa as we have just delineated them in terms of interaction between a dominant civilization seen as having a privileged status because of its link with the Prophet's early community, and a local society whose degree of acceptance of or identification with this pattern will constitute the objective test by which we shall be led to consider them as part or not of our regional pattern. Three somewhat distinct lines of Arab Islamic penetration must be examined:
1) the eastern frontier, integrating Egypt and the Upper Nile into North Africa, but excluding the Christian kingdoms, notably Abyssinia, which is now part of the modern state called Ethiopia;

2) the extensive northern zone, including most of the Sahara, where coexistence of Berber and Arab tribes within a common Islamic pattern is to be found;

3) the southern frontiers which impinge on the Sudanic states of sub-Saharan Africa, which we shall classify as being distinct socially, culturally, and politically, even if in many cases Islamic and Arab influences are evident and interaction with the north must be taken into account.

The Arab conquest in the east

The first stage of the Arab conquest involved Egypt which had up to then been part of the Byzantine Empire and had converted to Christianity on a large scale. Arab Muslim rule was nonetheless welcomed and seen as freeing the country from an oppressive regime. Two factors contributed to this. On the one hand the Arab rulers, here as elsewhere, limited themselves to overseeing local communities without actually interfering in their running. On the other they applied the *dhimma* pact which the Prophet had established as the guiding rule with respect to 'People of the Book' (i.e. Christians and Jews). Such people were encouraged but not forced to convert, and should they refuse, were to be allowed (as *dhimmi*-s) to practise their religion and keep their own customs but, in exchange for this right, were to pay heavier taxation. They would then be considered not as full members of the Muslim community, but as a protected minority. On this principle, Arab dominion was established over Egypt. Conversion to Islam of the Christian Egyptians was a gradual but nonetheless continuous process, one which has continued up to the present. At the beginning of the period covered by this book, the number of those who had remained Christian was estimated at about 16 000 out of a total population of between 3.5 million and 4 million. The term Copt was and still is used to refer to this Christian minority, the Muslim Egyptians being generally referred to as Arabs.

Expansion of the newly dominant Arab and Islamic influence southwards was apparent from the start but was, here again, a gradual and generally peaceful process even if, at a more political level, it sometimes involved strife-ridden relations between the Egyptian Arab province and neighbouring Christian kingdoms. This was particularly true of relations between Egypt and Nubia (now part of northern Sudan), and as early as 651–2 a treaty was concluded between them, marking respective limits of sovereignty. Nonetheless a process of erosion had been set underway which was later, around 1300, to lead to the disappearance of the Christian civilization in Nubia and with it, the Christian kingdom. Changes set in motion by intermarriage between Arab immigrants and Nubians led to the appearance of new or redefined tribal groups identifying themselves with the Muslim community. Thus in the area where the Blue and White Niles meet, the Ja'ali-s became an important group. Among them the Dunqula were to be at the fore of the *jallaba* or trading community which, in a later period, continued to spread Islam southwards whilst, at the same time, establishing the trading network of the north with the *bilad al-sudan*. By the 16th century a new political centre had emerged which can be considered the foundation of the modern republic of Sudan although it lacked much of the latter's territory. Thus, in the north, the region between the First and the Third Cataracts was nominally

Egyptian, and in the west Kurdufan and Dar Fur were independent entities; these and the southern provinces of the modern republic were only annexed in the late 19th century. The new organization involved a local state, the Funj sultanate, which set up its capital at Sennar in the early 16th century. At the height of its power in the 17th century the sultanate extended from the foothills of Abyssinia northwards to the Third Cataract, and westwards across the Jezira to the White Nile. Not only did this state identify itself with Arab values (and with this went claims to an Arab origin), but it also promoted use of Arabic. With Islamic scholarship came Sunni Islam and the Funj sultanate not only accepted this but also the Maliki *madhhab*, one of the four official schools of thought in Sunni Islam which is adhered to by the great majority of North Africans.

The limits of Sudan as defined by the Funj sultanate also mark the limits of what in the pre-modern period was the Arab-Muslim sphere of influence in the east of the continent. Southwards, difficult communications made for absence of contact with the pagan tribes of the Bahr al-Ghazal and of the Great Lakes. To the east, Abyssinia as a Christian theocracy resisted Arab and Islamic penetration. It was thus led to sever relations and turn in upon itself, maintaining only a tenuous connection with the Muslim west.

The Arab conquest of Berber North Africa

In the Berber areas along the African coast from the Nile to the Atlantic, the initial Arab conquest was characterized by the rapid and wholesale conversion of the population to the new religion. This does not mean that there was no armed resistance to the conquerors, nor that a number of important revolts did not subsequently take place, but these must be seen as political opposition, and even more as a reaction against the often overbearing ways of the Arab warriors rather than as opposition to the new religion, which continued to spread over and beyond those regions where Arabs were actually present.

The Berbers, who had up to then been largely pagan, gave up their deities and non-Islamic practices, or else reinterpreted these on Muslim lines. In the coastal area, Christianity had also to some degree spread among the Berbers who had been influenced by the Church which had developed in North Africa in the later Roman period. Other Berbers had adopted Judaism, while the influence of exiles from Palestine preaching the Old Testament was even earlier. One might here mention the case of the Kahina, an Algerian woman who seems to have had typical shamanic arbiter powers and who led the initial resistance of the Berber tribes to the Arab invaders. Early documents suggest contradictorily that she was either Christian or Jewish. In the face of Islam, Christianity disappeared rapidly and totally. The Jewish faith, however, survived to a limited degree and some Berbers who had resisted conversion to Islam founded small communities, generally in isolated mountain or desert areas, and continued to cling to their faith until modern events connected with the founding of the state of Israel led them to emigrate there. These Berber Jews should not however be confused with more important urban-based communities which have a different origin: these were founded in the 15th and 16th centuries by Jews fleeing persecution in Spain who found refuge in North Africa.

From the start the spread of Islam went well beyond the limits of the coastal strip where the Arabs had established their dominion, and though it took some time for the new faith to reach isolated areas, we can nonetheless consider the process as over by the 10th century, by which time Islam had been accepted even by the Saharan nomads.

Indeed this set on foot a new movement underscored by the religious zeal of the southern converts which influenced the subsequent history both of the northern states and sub-Saharan Africa. Chief of these movements was that of the al-Murabitun ('Almoravids') which developed among the Saharan Berber Lamtuna tribes which had been converted in the 9th century. In the middle of the 11th century, under the influence of a religious leader called 'Abd Allah bin Yasin, they surged out of the western desert. With their leader, Abu Bakr, they conquered Morocco and founded the city of Marrakech. Abu Bakr then passed over command to one of his lieutenants, Yusuf bin Tashfin (1060–1106) who founded a new Maghribi empire which included most of western North Africa and Spain, and which lasted until the middle of the 12th century when it was itself overrun by a new religious movement set on foot among the Masmuda Berbers of the Atlas above Marrakech by the puritan Ibn Tumart (*circa* 1083–1130). The al-Murabitun Abu Bakr did not himself stay in North Africa but returned to the desert to extend his crusade southwards. He and his followers contributed to the conversion to Islam of kingdoms in West Africa. Thus Abu Bakr made alliance with Takrur – already a Muslim state around the estuary of the river Senegal – to attack Ghana, then the major kingdom of the region, which was conquered in 1076–7. Though the political control of the al-Murabitun was short-lived, they nonetheless set on foot a trend which brought about the acceleration of the conversion to Islam of the savanna states which generally adopted Islam as the official religion, promoted Arab scholarship and developed trade relations with North Africa and the Middle East. Such was the case in the three major kingdoms of the western and central southern borders of the Sahara: in the west Ghana and Mali, formerly a tributary of Ghana, and in the centre Kanem-Bornu around Lake Chad which up to the beginning of our period was the major and most prosperous of the Sudanic trading states with which North Africa had constant relations.

This defines the political limits of the North African states. Outside these limits the border sultanates were built up out of contradictory but coexisting tendencies: a savanna civilization with its own persistent traits including social organization, language and religious practices, and sometimes a claim to Arab status upheld by the ruling class and by certain dependent nomad tribes. This went hand in hand with an official Islamic identity and a promotion of Arabic and literacy. This, of course, does not exclude constant interaction, notably in the cultural and religious fields, prosperous trade relations, and tension-fraught political relations with North African states. However, these semi-Saharan, semi-savanna sultanates must be considered as belonging to the Sudanic context and as such outside the detailed scope of this book.

Nonetheless, here too, the ambiguity of the situation is indicated since reference to a common Islamic identity largely overlaps the political and economic boundaries and creates the sense of a wider sphere of interaction. The expansion of Islam southwards or to isolated desert communities was a persistent trend characteristic of the region up to the 15th and 16th centuries, by which time conversion of Kanem-Bornu's neighbours had been effected. By the 18th century not only had an official Muslim stand been taken by many of the Sudanic African states, but new impetus had thus been provided which, in the 19th century, stirred up powerful movements based on reformist zeal. They were based on the belief that non-Islamic practices should be eliminated and that the community should be rebuilt on the model of that of the Prophet and his companions. They were also characterized by a revolutionary levelling tendency and, in some cases, a growing awareness of the dangers of European penetration. South of the desert and impinging on the border amirates which were the North African states' traditional trading partners, *jihad*-s developed and spread over extended areas, bringing new states into being. Chief of these movements was that launched by 'Uthman dan Fodio in 1804 which led to the setting up of the Sokoto Caliphate, the largest regional entity in the first half of the 19th century. Also important, particularly from the point of view of the Moroccan colony of Timbuktu which it overran, was the *jihad* of Seku Ahmadu, west of the Niger Bend, which led to the founding of the Macina state. A few years later, al-Hajj 'Umar Sa'id Tall started a *jihad* which had considerable impact over a wide region stretching from Upper Senegal to Timbuktu. The Mahdist movement in Sudan, in the late 19th century, may itself be seen in terms of this new backlash of Islam, even if it can also be connected with the north and interpreted as a reaction against Egyptian rule. One may contradictorily appreciate these developments of the 19th century both as part of a new and greater Muslim self-awareness, involving ideological interaction of north and south, east and west, and also as a contraction and isolation of the northern states whose attention and efforts in any case were increasingly concentrated in the coastal areas where European pressures were particularly forceful. This will make an appreciation of relations with the south particularly difficult to estimate during the period covered by this book.

Whereas in Sudanic Africa one sees different social patterns coexisting and contributing mingled cultural references, North Africa, on the other hand, strongly puts over a single self-view, explicitly defined as Islamic and Arab. Both society and state identify themselves with this model. This leads us back to the question posed by the massive and indeed enthusiastic acceptance of Islam by the North African tribes and the apparently well accepted if sometimes difficult relationship of Berbers and Arabs.

The Berber reception of Islam
Why should the tribal societies of North Africa and notably the Berbers, who make up the majority of the population of the region, have so readily accepted Islam? Historians have given a number of generally unconvincing answers to this question. Thus they point to the fact that by converting, Berber pagans avoided the risk of being made slaves, whilst those of them who were Jews or Christians freed themselves from the inconvenience and extra taxation that went with the *dhimma* pact. Others point to the conquest of Spain as an added inducement. It is probably more meaningful to look for an answer in the parallel social structures of the Berber and Arab tribes. This leads us back to the basic social pattern of the region, namely the tribal order and its political evolution through the development of an institution in the hands of hereditary holy lineages having shamanic powers and specialized in overseeing and

providing mediation for the social order. A fact of capital importance, which may help us to understand how and why Berbers adopted Islam and many features of the Arab civilization to define their view of themselves as a community, is the fact that Arabian society was organized on a similar model and had probably reached a similar stage of evolution, both economically in terms of interdependence of nomads or pastoralists and settlers in trading communities such as those of Mecca and Medina, and politically as a society committed to tribal organization which felt a growing need for a transcendental ideal cutting across the ties of kinship, supposed or real. In Arabia as in Berberland, arbiters had played a central role in society and it is not irrelevant at this point to note that the Prophet himself had been considered a *hakam* (mediator) and, in his prophetic period, divine injunctions binding on all coexisted with Muhammad's practice of advising and recommending peaceful settlement of conflicts.

The rapid, wholesale conversion of the Berbers to Islam would probably not have been possible without the support of the traditional pillars of society: the local holy lineages. The fact that the Prophet himself provided a justification for their functions and gave them enhanced prestige does not explain sufficiently the zeal shown by local holy men. Up to then these holy men had been Berber-speaking, part of a largely oral civilization, ruling by virtue of precedent and tribal lore. They now went to considerable trouble, often travelling far afield and in difficult conditions, to acquire the new religious language, Arabic, a new tool – the written word – and knowledge connected with the Quran and religious law. The fact that they were highly successful in this is indicated both by the spread of Islamic knowledge and practices, and by the fact that traditional arbiters remained the uncontested masters of the tribal scene and indeed even gained a foothold in the new Arab centres as they developed. It would not be possible to understand this if one did not take into account the advantages they as a group derived from converting their stance to an Islamic one.

What Islam gave the arbiters was something they had conspicuously lacked in the former period: power. As persons in the tribe specialized in the cultural field and over which, with the need to learn Arabic and religious knowledge, they now had a monopoly, their relationship to their illiterate Berber-speaking clients was subtly modified since instead of merely advising, they could now back up their decisions by reference to a Quranic ruling which Muslim Berbers could neither contest nor check. The arbiters were thus able to claim a more central position for themselves. They were no longer seen as mere strangers but as holy intermediaries whose connection with Islam was increasingly represented as a personal relationship with the Prophet's first community of Muslims. It soon became an accepted fact that holy lineages were sharifian, i.e. they consisted of descendants of the Prophet himself (*sharif*-s). The group's personality came to be identified with the tomb of the ancestor of the local holy lineage. Arbiter activities were less often carried out at some accepted neutral meeting place. Clients came to the *sharif* and it was at the tomb of the ancestor that such ceremonies as oath-taking took place, Islamic sanction being provided by recitation of the *fatiha*, or first chapter of the Quran.

Moreover the holy lineages were able through Islam to extend their involvement in society and their control over various activities. Thus in the complex set of buildings which often surround the holy tomb and the arbiters' private buildings (generally referred to in Maghribi dialects as *zawiya*-s), we find guest rooms, the tribal mosque and school as also, in a somewhat more recent period, a fraternity lodge where people could be initiated to Sufi doctrines by a *shaykh* (i.e. a leader in a wide variety of contexts) who was either a member of the holy lineage or had its patronage. These buildings are to be found throughout North Africa. Also characteristic of a more recent development which seems to have spread in the 15th–16th centuries, was the training of legal specialists in these *zawiya*-s. They were either members of the holy lineages or students attached to the *zawiya* and would draw up deeds, which now became commonplace, whereas in former times oral agreements between parties had sufficed. We thus find land deeds, tribal pacts, rules and regulations for such institutions as granary citadels being placed on written record.

The building up of the arbiter's power is paralleled in the growing sophistication of the communications network of the holy men. This, of course, also reflects social and economic changes with increasing inter-tribal relations upheld by extended trade relations and awareness of a transtribal community involving the coexistence of populations of different origin (Arab/Berber, Muslim/*dhimmi*) or social type (farmer/nomad, city/country dweller). These were all part of an Islamically defined community which was actualized not only in the layout of holy lineages throughout the country, but in its own hierarchy. Interaction was largely controlled by the *sharif*-s who had the necessary authority to ensure safe travelling or peaceful commerce by means of weekly *suq*-s or religious fairs. In addition, they came to have specialized functions within the network, some having purely local functions, whilst the solving of conflicts of a more extended nature was passed on to a higher level of arbitration. At the top of the pyramid we find *sharif*-s whose authority extended over several regions and over populations having no ties of consanguinity. At the highest level one may ultimately see such personalities achieving nation-wide recognition and becoming state rulers. As an example of this one may point to Morocco which even as recently as the 16th century promoted the Sa'di dynasty which had originated in a southern *zawiya* of the Dra' region which for centuries had settled inter-tribal conflicts and protected trade between the Atlas and the desert. They were replaced in the middle of the 17th century by a dynasty of similar origin, the 'Alawi-s, a sharifian family of the Tafilalt, also connected with the trans-Saharan trade and relations between the desert Ma'qil and more northern populations. The 'Alawi dynasty still reigns today.

One of the things Islam brought to societies that had reached a stage of evolution such as that of the North African and Arabian tribes was a more clearly identified social hierarchy in which leadership took on the position of intermediary between the Divine plan and human society. The institutional and legal expression of this leadership was not however on the rudimentary level of the early Muslim community of the Prophet and his *ansar* ('companions'). Rather, the Arabs borrowed elements from the more sophisticated empires that they conquered in the initial phase of their expansion, notably the Persian Sassanid Empire and that of Byzantium. Whilst enhanced significance was given to holy men who, because of their religious knowledge and their will to make peace prevail, were natural counsellors, the idea of a head arbiter and community leader was also brought to the fore. He was to be the successor of the Prophet and imitate his example. He was the *imam* (leader of community prayers) and as religious leader was the head of an increasingly complex institution involving *mufti*-s (legal advisers), *qadhi*-s (religious judges) and *'ulama* (teachers). He also had responsibilities with respect to the general welfare and order of society. This involved a civil administration the chief function of which was collecting Quranic dues to be spent for the good of the community. This became increasingly complex both with respect to state prerogatives – minting money for example – and in terms of personnel: the *sultan* (which signifies 'the one who has power'), for example, appointed *wazir*-s (ministers) to whom he delegated his responsibilities in various fields. The welfare and good order of society also had moral aspects which imposed on him the task of 'doing away with evil and doing good', if necessary by force. He moreover had to increase the capacity for self-defence of the *dar al-Islam* (land in which Islam is established) in a non-Muslim environment. This made the *sultan* not only the head of a religious and civil administration, often referred to as 'the men of the pen', but also of a military force, the 'men of the sword'.

This background helps us to understand the type of relationship which was established between the largely autonomous but now Muslim communities of North Africa and the Arab invaders whose capacity and right to take charge of the state institution and exercise its responsibilities was largely accepted. It also helps us to understand future developments when, during the 'Abbasid period (750–1258), Morocco became an independent Muslim state under the leadership of an Arabian *sharif*, Idris, who presided over a tribal kingdom from 788 to 791, whilst the Fatimid-s (909–1171) set up an independent province in Ifriqiya, that is in what is now Algeria, Tunisia, Libya and Egypt.

In the modern period we find the political and social order largely overseen and mediated by sharifian arbiter lineages throughout North Africa, but only in one instance there, in Morocco – other examples being available elsewhere such as the Zaydi dynasty of Yemen – do we find the arbiter body establishing its control over the state institution. This long-term pattern illustrated both by Yemen and Morocco from the 9th and 8th centuries respectively to the 20th century, has, in Morocco, been constantly reasserted and even if not all dynasties were on this model, it has nonetheless prevailed up to the present. On the other hand, elsewhere in North Africa, for historical reasons which we shall be led to examine in a subsequent chapter, the state institution passed into the hands of an administrative body, strongly military in its organization, foreign in origin, and legitimized by its formal recognition of the authority of the Turkish sultan seen as legitimate heir to the leadership of the *Dar al-Islam*. This, for example, was the situation in Egypt, notably during the Mamluk sultanate and under the 19th-century rule of Muhammad 'Ali and his descendants, as also in the Regencies (namely Algeria, Tunisia and Libya) which were Ottoman provinces.

It would be wrong, however, to consider these two tendencies as contrary or mutually exclusive. In fact, both are necessary features of the political system. Thus Morocco which promoted the arbiter system to state level during the short reign of Idris I, saw his son and heir, Idris II (803–829) both maintain traditional arbiter practices and strive to make himself independent, both with respect to the tribes and to the holy lineages, by setting up the type of personally defined administration which could make his authority and control effective. He appointed a *wazir* and other state personnel, and recruited a private (i.e. non tribal) army from among the Arabs of the Maghrib and Spain. Conflict between the tribes and the sovereign could in the last resort, if traditional forms of negotiation broke down, be solved by force. This was the case in Morocco in 807–8 when tribal opposition was repressed and its leader executed. Conversely the rule of a foreign military group such as prevailed in the rest of North Africa was largely dependent on the cooperation of the holy lineages, and acceptance of the state's authority and decisions was mediated through their network.

The role of sufism

Above and beyond the competition of holy men and state institutions for control of society, yet another field of confrontation must be pointed to: sufi fraternities which are indeed the main force channelling socio-religious intercourse in the Muslim world, more particularly in North Africa where the great majority of people are affiliated to one of several prevalent orders.

Sufism can be defined as the deep-seated mystical urge of union with God which is to be found in the major religions and which, though it attracts only a limited number of exceptional people, is nonetheless generally opposed by the religious establishment since it undermines the rational foundations of established belief and institutions. Islam from early times has had its great mystics whose heightened spiritual awareness has been passed down from generation to generation through *shaykh*-s (in this context spiritual guides) initiating *ikhwan* (disciples). As institutionalized orders – and such orders have had a wide following since the 11th century – they must be assessed in more mundane terms since few *shaykh*-s fall into the category of great mystics. What they provide is a *tariqa* ('way') which is a graduated building-up of religious self-awareness, most disciples rarely passing beyond the stage where recitation of daily prayers (often a religious formula repeated over and over) and occasional religious ceremonies, often of a trance-like nature, provide them with spiritual satisfaction. The organization of fraternities, besides providing affiliated members with a trans-historical view since a common link binds them to other members whatever their social or national origins and, through a complex chain of transmission refers them back to the great mystics of the past and to the Prophet and his companions, also involves a more immediate commitment to the *shaykh* and the fraternity. The sufi is connected to his order by respect of its practices, by ties with a given *zawiya* (lodge) and by his relationship to the *shaykh* whom he consults and to whom he owes absolute obedience. Though most North African fraternities claim descent from early sufi-s, notably 'Abd al-Qadir al-Jilani (died 1166) and Abu Madyan Shu'aib (died 1197) whose teachings were passed on by Abu al-Hasan 'Ali al-Shadhili (died 1258), and indeed refer to this by including the term Qadiriyya or Shadhiliyya in their description of themselves, the orders in fact developed more particularly from the 15th century onwards and can be seen historically as a Muslim response to an increasingly complex situation. The fact that the 15th century was marked by a Spanish onslaught on North Africa, and that fraternities played a leading role in the organization of defence, as governments tended to compromise, highlights this.

It is thus both in terms of a new world order marked by imperial pressure and of an inner development of Muslim society characterized by capitalist influences and increasingly apparent class stratification that we must appreciate the development of the network and influence of sufi orders from the middle of the 18th century onwards. They can be seen as themselves reflecting a dialectical tendency. On the one hand, they express the will to cut across national or class barriers by spreading through North Africa and setting up *zawiya*-s where all members whatever their origins and status were on an equal footing. On the other hand new orders or offshoots of major fraternities were created which provided an adapted organization for specific clienteles. In line with the first tendency, we find that one or two major orders tended to be dominant in any given period, both by spreading a new message attracting a large following and by converting to this message *zawiya*-s formerly affiliated to another order now on the wane. Thus the 19th century marked the rise of the Darqawiyya fraternity to which many *shaykh*-s converted their stand and which spread to *zawiya*-s which, notably in Morocco, had formerly been affiliated to the Nasiriyya. The two major orders of the 19th century were both founded in the late 18th century. The Darqawiyya resulted from the teaching of al-'Arbi al-Darqawi (1760–1823) who was born in a rural district of Morocco just north of Fez. His impact was particularly strong in rural areas but he also obtained a following in the towns where people held *hadra*-s (fraternity ceremonies) in private homes, reciting the *dhikr* (fraternity prayers) and indulging in more irrational practices sometimes involving trances. The order was also open to women. The Darqawiyya, some of whose more dedicated members move around the country dressed as dervishes with a rosary of wooden beads, apparently oblivious of modern comfort or material welfare, embodies a popular reaction against the wealth and complexities of modern life and its irreligiousness. A strong levelling tendency in the movement was brought out by its connection with various forms of rural protest. This did not prevent the Moroccan sovereign, Mulay Sulayman, from encouraging the order since its impact in western Algeria seemed to favour his policies. The Tijaniyya – the other dominant order in the 19th century – was, on the other hand, largely connected with the upper classes. It had a following among people having political or economic power and its stand was more generally pro-governmental. It was founded by Ahmad al-Tijani (1737–1815) at 'Ayn Mahdi in south-western Algeria, but the order's headquarters were later set up in Fez. Al-Tijani, who was in the Shadhiliyya tradition, had first been initiated to the Khalwatiyya (a popular fraternity in the Ottoman Empire which went back to the 14th century) but he later founded his own *tariqa* which involved a simple message but a strict rule. Tijani-s were not allowed to be affiliated to any other order than that of Ahmad al-Tijani who claimed to have been in direct communication with the Prophet himself. Obedience to established authority led the Tijani-s to refuse leadership to opposition groups and movements of social protest, which is generally the role of fraternities. In Morocco they upheld the sovereign even when Mulay

Sulayman advocated Wahhabi reformism which tried to do away with heterodox practices encouraged by sufi-s. In French-dominated Algeria, the Tijani stand was particularly ambiguous and they were often allies of colonial power. Their importance in the 19th century was particularly brought out in the Sahara and in Sudanic Africa. Many members of the scholar class of nomad Arab tribes joined the order, as did many Muslims of the Sahel. The Tijaniyya became a major political force south of the desert when al-Hajj 'Umar (1794–1864) spread its message among the Tukulor and set up a Caliphate extending from the upper Senegal river and Gambia to the Niger Bend. He had been appointed the order's representative in the Western Sudan by the Tijani *shaykh* of the Hijaz and, in the middle of the 19th century, he led a major *jihad* with a double objective: reforming the Islamic community of the region and opposing French encroachments. The Tijaniyya whose message was spread by Maghribi pilgrims, had a strong following throughout North Africa, including Egypt and the Sudan. It did not, however, spread beyond the frontiers of the continent, although it had a lodge in Arabia.

In contrast with these dominant orders, the late 18th century also saw the proliferation of fraternities adapted to specific groups. Particularly catered for by these orders were new depressed categories resulting from modern capitalist evolution, notably in the towns. Thus craftsmen who had lost much of their trade and whose guilds were no longer influential social organizations, and rural immigrants who constituted a new urban lumpenproletariat, promoted such popular fraternities as the Moroccan-founded 'Isawiyya and Hamadisha which, in the 19th century, spread to most of the major towns of North Africa where its members expressed their feelings in often spectacular public ceremonies and processions.

Though these associations largely led and organized public life and opinion, they were also pressure groups which constituted authorities tried to manipulate and control. They were moreover wealthy and derived profit from the Islamic institution called *waqf* or *habus* by means of which property could be given or left after death for religious purposes and thus become pious endowments. State governments were very wary of fraternities and a general policy of alternative blandishments and threats was used to bring *shaykh*-s to subservience. Rulers would often be members of orders, perhaps out of conviction, but more often out of political necessity. The religious establishment had also, from early times, established partial control over fraternities. *'Ulama* were thus often fraternity *shaykh*-s and taught mystic doctrines as part of the university syllabus. It is also part of the general evolution of the modern period, from the late 18th century onwards, that *'ulama* should progressively have lost their hold over the living social tissue of the sufi orders, whilst *shaykh*-s having a strong social, often rural-based impact, were promoted to leadership. The connection of holy lineages and fraternities was of long-standing and in many ways promotion of fraternities was their doing. Fraternity lodges were founded within the precincts of rural *zawiya*-s (indeed the term in North African dialects applies indifferently to lodges and the buildings wherein holy lineages operated). Holy men were themselves fraternity leaders or gave their official protection to a *shaykh* who would have found it extremely difficult to preach if unsupported or opposed by the holy men. One may further see in the promotion of sufi affiliation the means through which holy lineages attempted to build up a specific clientele of their own, one which cut across tribal commitments and which, as state power grew, also provided them with a pressure group by which the traditional balance between arbiters and military or political leaders could be maintained.

Sufi fraternities, whose activities will be brought in various sections of this book, can thus be seen as one of the chief social forces in an increasingly political and national context, expressing public opinion on trans-national and trans-political lines, upholding the common response of Islam to the challenge of modern times.

SELECTED READING LIST

General works
Gibb, H. A. R., *Mohammedanism, An Historical Survey*, (Oxford, 1953).
Julien, Ch.-A., *Histoire de l'Afrique du Nord*, (Paris, 1931), reprinted in 1956, into English by J. Petrie and ed. by C. C. Stewart in *History of North Africa: Tunisia, Algeria, Morocco: from the Arab conquest to 1830*, (London, 1970).
Levy, R., *The Social Structure of Islam*, (Cambridge, 1969).
Lewis, B., *The Arabs in History*, (London, 1970).
Lewis B. (ed.), *The World of Islam. Faith, People, and Culture*, (London, 1976).

Demography
Ganiage, J., 'La Population de la Tunisie vers 1860', *Etudes Maghrébines: Mélanges Charles-André Julien*, (Paris 1964).
Rouissi, M., *Population et Société au Maghreb*, (Tunis, 1977).
Valensi, L., 'Calamités démographiques en Tunisie et en Méditerranée orientale aux XVIIIe et XIXe siècles', *Annales*, 24, 1969.

Islam
Gellner, E., *Saints of the Atlas*, (London, 1969).
Geertz, C., *Islam observed. Religious Development in Morocco and Indonesia*, (Chicago and London, 1968) reprinted in 1971.
Hopkins, J. (trans.), *Corpus of Early Arabic Sources for West African History*, (Cambridge, 1981).
Keddie, N. R. (ed.), *Scholars, Saints, and Sufis. Muslim Religious Institutions*, (Berkeley and Los Angeles, 1978).
Kritzek, J. and Lewis W. H. (eds), *Islam in Africa*, (New York, 1969).
Lewis, I. M. (ed.), *Islam in Tropical Africa*, (Oxford, 1966).
Martin, B. G., *Muslim Brotherhoods in 19th Century Africa*, (Cambridge, 1976).
Naqar, N. al-, *The Pilgrimage Tradition in West Africa*, (Khartum, 1972).
Stewart, C. C. & Stewart E. K., *Islam and Social Order in Mauritania*, (Oxford, 1973).
Trimingham, J. S., *The Sufi Orders in Islam*, (London, 1971).

Religious Minorities
Hirschberg, H. Z., *A History of the Jews in North Africa*, tr. from Hebrew, (Leyden, vol. I, 1974; vol. II, 1981).
Lane, E. W., *Manners and Customs of the Modern Egyptians*, (London,1836; New York, 1954).
Miege, J. L. (ed.), *Les Relations entre Juifs et Musulmans en Afrique du Nord, XIXe-XXe siècles*, (Paris, 1980).

Society
Crapanzo, V, *The Hamadsha: A Study in Moroccan Ethnopsychiatry*, (Berkeley, Los Angeles, London, 1973).

28

THE SCOPE OF THIS BOOK: BASIC FACTS AND TENETS

Eickelman, D., *Moroccan Islam*, (Austin and London, 1974).
Fahmi, N., *Turuq al-Tijara al-Duwaliyya wa Mahattahuha bayn al-Sharq wa al-Gharb*, (Cairo, 1973).
Gellner, E., *Muslim Society*, (Cambridge, 1981).
Gellner, E. & Micaud Ch. (eds), *Arabs and Berbers*, (London, 1973).
Holt, P. (ed.), *Political and Social Change in Modern Egypt*, (Oxford, 1968).
Marsot, A. al-Sayyid Lutfi, 'The Political and Economic Functions of the 'Ulama in the Eighteenth Century', *Journal of the Economic and Social History of the Orient*, 16, 1973.

CHAPTER 2

POLITICAL HISTORY AND STATE FORMATION

The geographical and religious unity of North Africa no less than its characteristic physical zones running parallel to the coast are belied by state formation which cuts across those lines successively with, from west to east, Morocco, Algeria, Tunisia, Tripoli (Tarabulus al-Gharb), the name by which Libya was formerly known, and Egypt. These states – though their limits and specific characteristics were to be emphasized by colonial rule – are in fact political divisions of long standing which were redefined in modern terms in the 16th century.

MOROCCO: A SHARIFIAN KINGDOM

Our survey of the North African coastal states begins at the western end of the continent because, as was earlier pointed out, Morocco has in many ways remained closest to the indigenous system of tribal states. It is the oldest of the present-day regimes of North Africa and the only one which does not result from foreign rule.

Though the Romans have little to say about 'Western Mauritania' as Morocco was then called, it seems to have been a well-organized tribal kingdom having at its head a hereditary 'royal' lineage connected both politically and by family with the ruling family of Numidia in Algeria. A few centuries later, when Islam came to Morocco, the tribes of Fez reasserted the traditional pattern and ultimately chose as their collective leader a sharifian arbiter of Arab origin, Idris I (788–91) who was able to equate this with the Muslim conception of the state, creating a political model which has prevailed to the present.

The Sa'di dynasty
It is obviously not the purpose of this book to sketch out the whole of the political history of Morocco before 1800 although aspects of this, such as the Saharan influence of the 11th–12th century al-Murabitun dynasty have been mentioned. Special emphasis must however be placed on the Sa'di dynasty (16th to first half of the 17th century) which marks the beginnings of modern Morocco within the frontiers of the nation-state of today. It also marks the heyday of Moroccan involvement in international relations, a position which from then on it gradually lost as trade routes increasingly bypassed it, and a change of European strategy with respect to North Africa increased the importance of the eastern end of the Mediterranean. It was in the Sa'di period that the expansion of the Ottoman Empire came to a halt with Algeria as its

westernmost province and through a long succession of political intrigues and minor armed conflicts, a definite frontier was established between Algeria and Morocco seen as distinct areas of national sovereignty. This further emphasizes the specific identity of Morocco, the only state of the region not to have come under Ottoman influence.

The Sa'di-s did not only consolidate their frontier with Turkish-ruled Algeria, they also expanded southwards. Their active policy in this direction can be connected with the Moroccan-Ottoman rivalry since by reactivating traditional Muslim relations with the Sudanic zone, they could and did pose as potentially legitimate leaders of the Muslim community, at least as far as an African caliphate went. In line with this policy, we find Sa'di emissaries travelling to various parts of Sudanic Africa and ambassadors from there being received at court, at Marrakech. The range and extent of these relations can best be illustrated by the distant Sultanate of Bornu whose ruler during the period of maximum contact with Morocco was the Mai Idris Alaoma (*circa* 1564–1612), one of the better-known kings of the Banu Sayf dynasty claiming Arab origins which ruled over one of the most powerful states of the region for some 800 years, until its downfall in the 19th century. Bornu, whose trade was carried out mainly with the Turkish province of Tripoli, felt itself threatened by the latter's irredentism when Ottoman troops invaded the Fezzan in 1576–7. The Mai wrote at the time to the Turkish Sultan, Murad III, seeking his help and protection. The latter replied favourably to Idris who was referred to in an official letter as *'malik'* (king) of the 'Province (*wilaya*) of Bornu'. Murad III sent instructions to the Governor of Tripoli that Bornu's independance and sovereignty were to be respected. Not content with these assurances, however, the Mai also wrote to the king of Morocco, Al-Mansur (1578–1603), who promised his aid if his nominal and religious suzerainty over Bornu were recognized. This would seem to have been agreed to but as the Bornu ambassador died on one of his journeys, it is difficult to know what decision, if any, had actually been taken.

Sa'di policy also involved building up Morocco's economic power as a Mediterranean trading state. In the context of the time when the traditional commerce of the 'inner sea' as the Arab geographers called the Mediterranean, was increasingly coming under the influence of new trading routes turned towards America, Morocco was strategically placed and was an important partner in its own right since it commanded the trans-Saharan trade routes of West Africa. A gold-starved Mediterranean economy underscored Morocco's capacity to provide a precious and much needed commodity. This not only gave new importance and prosperity to the southern trading outposts of Morocco, it also favoured the rise to power of the Sa'di dynasty itself which passed from its former position of being an influential holy lineage of the Dra' valley to one of national supremacy. The Sa'di-s further established *makhzen* (governmental) control over other trading centres of the south from the Atlantic coast to Tuwwat, a prosperous inland oasis market to which even Europeans had recourse. The importance of Tuwwat was due to the fact that it commanded what was then the major caravan route to the Central Sudan, leading to the salt mines of Taghaza – salt being a basic commodity traded in the south – and from there to the Niger bend where gold and slaves could be obtained. However, this involved coming to terms with a powerful and well-organized kingdom – Songhay – which from the second half of the 15th century had developed into the major state of the region. At the height of its power in the early 16th century, Songhay stretched from modern Senegal in the west, north to Taghaza and east as far as Kanem-Bornu. It had established its rule both over the Hausa states and the Tuareg sultanate of Aïr, besides taking control of the former Berber-Tuareg trading centres of Timbuktu, Jenne and Agades. From their capital Gao (conquered in 1529), the *askiya*-s as the rulers of Songhay were called, had established flourishing markets further characterized by a strongly emphasized Islamic identity

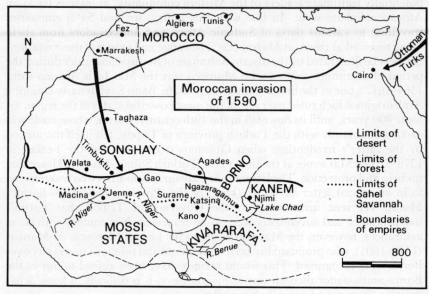

Map 2.1 *North Africa and the Central Sudan (source: M. Crowder, West Africa, An Introduction to its History)*

which had acquired a more official status after *askiya* Muhammad had made the pilgrimage to Mecca in 1496 and had been appointed *khalifa* (deputy) of the Western Sudan by a descendant of the 'Abbasid dynasty. *Askiya* Muhammad further upheld his claim to being a devout Muslim by waging the *jihad* (holy war) against his non-Muslim neighbours. Less than a century later, though still largely unchallenged, the authority of the *askiya*-s over their extended kingdom had begun to decline. Drought and various calamities had undermined their power no less than the assertive personality of some of their subjects, including the Tuareg who were in a phase of territorial and political expansion in the Aïr (Sultanate of Agades). Al-Mansur's imperial aims were to materialize in this context.

In 1598, al-Mansur made his first claim on the region by asking the *askiya* to pay the Moroccan government taxes on salt leaving Taghaza. These taxes, he declared, were to be used for military purposes since the Moroccan army was the bulwark of resistance against the irreligious spirit of the age characterized by idolatry (the term ambiguously referring here both to Christian encroachments in the north and to pagan practices in Sudanic

Africa which the *askiya*-s had failed to eradicate). To his own councillors, hostile to a dangerous and immoral expedition against a Muslim community, al-Mansur further justified his claims on the Songhay kingdom by pointing out the need to unite Muslims of Africa under a single leader and drawing attention to the profit Morocco would derive from 'a country richer than Ifriqiya'. The *askiya*'s refusal was to be pretext for war.

The crossing of the desert was a lengthy, perilous and well nigh impossible undertaking for a large army, and yet this feat was achieved, though not without considerable hardship, by some 3 000–4 000 soldiers under the leadership of a Spanish convert to Islam, Pasha Judar, who left Morocco on 30 October 1590, and reached the Niger 60 days later. On 12 March, 1591, the inevitable battle took place and the *askiya*'s forces were routed by an enemy whose equipment was far superior. Gao and other settlements were conquered and a Moroccan dominion founded. As a kingdom Songhay had disappeared, even if the *askiya* escaped and, locally, many features of the former social and political order were maintained under a military ruling class of Moroccan origin. Local governors continued for a while to be appointed by the Sa'di sovereigns (until 1604), and reinforcements were sent out from the mother country until 1618, but, as the Sa'di-s in turn declined, the *arma* (Moroccan garrison) of the Niger bend was left to fend for itself. Through intermarriage and the defence of its prerogatives as a dominant warrior class, this community survived in the Timbuktu region, though increasingly hedged in and dominated by powerful neighbours, including the 19th-century Macina state to which the last *arma* Pasha of Timbuktu was forced to submit in 1833. The sense of belonging to Morocco nonetheless persisted among the *arma* and when, in 1892, French invasion of the region appeared imminent, they made a desperate and unavailing attempt to obtain help from Mulay Hasan, King of Morocco, on the grounds of their traditional links with the mother country.

Two conclusions can be drawn from this Moroccan imperial venture at the end of the 16th century. First, it represented an important economic penetration into the heart of Africa to establish control over both ends of the Saharan trade. It made Morocco an important purveyor of gold in a gold-starved economy and thus a prosperous country: during the reign of al-Mansur, some eight to ten tons of gold were estimated to have been brought into the kingdom. This new wealth essentially benefited the trading bourgeoisie and the dynasty, and made Morocco an important commercial and political partner on the world scene. Second, the Marrakech-Timbuktu axis must also be appreciated in a wider African context, as the Sa'di-s claimed for themselves a rival caliphate to that of the Turks, one which also involved claims both east and west of Songhay from Kanem-Bornu to the estuary of the Senegal, where Moroccan troops irregularly patrolled and where holy lineages often helped to promote pacts of tribal alliance with, or actual allegiance to the Moroccan ruling *sharif*-s, both the Sa-di's and the later 'Alawi-s. A somewhat insubstantial 'Greater Morocco' was thus outlined which faded into the background under the stress of colonial pressures in the 19th century, but which never entirely disappeared, as more recent Moroccan claims in the region have shown.

Morocco's successful policy of expansion in the south should not however lead us to forget its position in North Africa with respect to the age-old confrontation of Islam and Christianity – now an uneasy triple confrontation involving the Turks, the Spanish, and the Moroccans. Morocco's position on the Mediterranean scene was neither as stable nor as strong as its short-lived commercial prosperity in the 16th century might lead one to believe. Portugal and Spain as powerful imperial nations had ambitions both in America and Africa and saw in Morocco a base of operations. The *reconquista* policy with respect to the Muslims had led, prior to the advent of the Sa'di dynasty, to the conquest of a number of Moroccan ports: Ceuta (Sebta in Arabic) in 1415, Arsila and Tangier in 1471, al-Jadida in 1502, Agadir in 1505, besides outlying islands. The inroad on Moroccan sovereignty was pursued as the Sa'di dynasty grew weaker. An ill-mastered economy with strong inflationary trends, widespread and catastrophic epidemics, and changes in the tribal layout, led the Sa'di dynasty to avoid confrontation with Spain and ultimately to compromise with the hereditary enemy.

This led the holy lineages and tribal chiefs brought together because of the impact of a redefined national and international context, to launch an onslaught on a dynasty discredited by its incapacity to resist foreign encroachments. Ultimately, in the middle of the 17th century, this brought to national leadership another holy lineage of the south, the influential *sharif*-s of the Tafilalt who had for centuries mediated relations between the Saharan nomad Arabs and their northern neighbours, besides themselves taking an active part in the Timbuktu trade.

The 'Alawi dynasty

Under the leadership of one of the first kings of the new 'Alawi dynasty, Mulay Isma'il (1672–1727), the Moroccan offensive against the European invaders met with success: Arsila, Larash (al-'Araysh) and Tangier were reconquered (the latter having in the meantime become part of British Crown possessions as a result of the marriage of Charles II and Catherine of Braganza). Some fortresses however held out. They included al-Jadida (generally called Mazagan in European sources) which was not evacuated until 1769, Ceuta and Melilla which are still today under Spanish control. Mulay Isma'il also maintained Moroccan control over the Saharan trade, but the inflow of gold was greatly reduced and because of its high price no longer attracted European merchants. Mulay Isma'il confirmed the traditional pattern of the Moroccan state as a religious and nationally defined institution superimposed on largely self-sufficient tribal entities which were however woven into a national community by the network of hereditary arbiter lineages. At the same time he reaffirmed the personal powers of the sovereign as head of state and to this end he created a strong professional army of slave soldiers, the 'abid-al-Bukhari, who were obtained from Sudanic Africa by means of slave raids. This army was responsible for many administrative functions, including tax collecting. It maintained peace and order between tribes, and between the tribes and the monarchy through a military layout which included fortresses in strategically located points, in or around the main towns and along the trade routes. Among royal prerogatives figured foreign policy. Under Mulay Isma'il this was extended to trade relations with other countries and notably Europe. These were carried on by the king's agents, or by men who obtained monopoly rights.

Morocco was thus built up into a cohesive state but one in which excessive

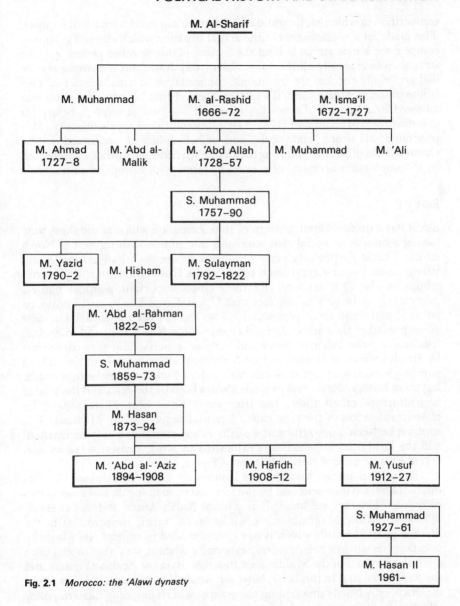

Fig. 2.1 *Morocco: the 'Alawi dynasty*

central government control over the interplay of local social groups progressively built up tensions behind the orderly facade of state authority. These were to break out in the form of revolts characterized by the irredentism of newly powerful tribes at the expense of their weaker neighbours at the first opportunity and indeed on the traditional occasion, namely the death of the sovereign. The fact that a successor was not automatically the eldest son or heir designate but was chosen from among the close members of the deceased sovereign's family – one of his sons or brothers – left the road open to competition in which each candidate tried to obtain maximum tribal support. This made for a reassessment of the actual situation which allowed groups to compete for a new status behind the banner of one or other pretender. The struggle was generally all the more violent and drawn out if a strong regime had artificially checked the traditional confrontation of tribal segments. This is illustrated in Mulay Isma'il's case by the fact that his powerful reign was followed by a quarter of a century of unrest and *fitna* (anarchy), before his grandson, Sidi Muhammad (1757–1790), re-established royal authority. This pendulum of strong state rule and tribal upheaval continued to be characteristic of Morocco throughout the 19th century, further complicated by the unpleasant necessity of coming to terms with European states.

EGYPT

Egypt has a quite different pattern of state formation whilst at the same time having a number of social characteristics in common with the rest of North Africa. This is particularly evident in areas where the tribal pattern is still strong, as in Upper Egypt. Such tribes as the Huwwara were still powerful groups in the 19th century and their chiefs important political figures, particularly so in view of the fact that Upper Egypt traditionally provided political asylum to those personalities who had not been able to make their views prevail in the capital. On either side of the Nile Valley and in Sudan, tribes were very much in evidence and *'asabiyya* (group solidarity) as described by Ibn Khaldun, continued to justify political alliances or enmities. These parallels with other parts of North Africa should not however be overstated. Egyptian history, dominated as it has always been by the delta and the kind of agriculture practised there, has from early times been characterized by class-stratification of the type called 'oriental despotism' by Marxists. The contrast between a powerful and wealthy ruling class, often of foreign origin, and the local *fellah*-s (peasantry) exhausted by work, conscript labour and taxation, is an almost eternal feature of Egypt.

Egypt's political history has moreover been determined by its international environment and by the fact that it, so to speak, looks out in two directions. On the one hand, it is part of North Africa and is extremely influential on the Maghribi scene whilst on the other, it opens out to the *Mashriq* (East) towards which it has always tended to expand. Its Mashriqi vocation has always been evident, especially when it was able to establish control over parts of the Middle East (notably Syria) or Arabia (Yemen, and the Red Sea coast). In this book, however, we shall be concentrating on Egypt in Africa, only briefly mentioning those aspects of its outgoing Eastern policy which directly impinge on our subject.

It is nonetheless in Middle Eastern terms that Egypt became politically meaningful in the Islamic age. Egypt was the first military base from which the newly converted Arab warriors planned their conquest of North Africa and Spain. As early as 640 AD – a mere eight years after the Prophet's death – Egypt became a Muslim and Arab dominion. With the development of a Muslim empire based on the Middle East, Egypt became a frontier province which commanded relations with the West, both North Africa and Muslim Spain. By the middle of the 9th century it had gubernatorial dynasties of its own and later, under the Fatimid-s (969–1144), it became the seat of a Maghribi empire of *shi'a* doctrine. Sunni orthodoxy and local independence were re-established under the Ayyubi dynasty whose founder was the famous Kurdish general Salah al-Din, better known as Saladin.

The Ayyubi-s introduced the *mamluk* system, that is one based on large retinues of soldiers who, when children, had been bought in distant provinces of the Ottoman Empire, converted to Islam, and educated in lordly households where they were trained as warriors in a spirit of exclusive loyalty to their masters. This system, based on a military ruling class of foreign origin, was to persist in Egypt up to the 20th century. On the death of the last effective ruler of the Ayyubi dynasty in 1250, the *mamluk* guards seized power and administered the state as an independent Mamluk sultanate which under the strong leadership of Baybars (1260–77) extended to Syria and exercised suzerainty over the Arabian Hijaz.

The first phase of the overthrow of the Mamluk sultanate was signalled by the Ottoman reconquest of Syria in 1516, followed a year later by the invasion of Egypt. The Turks re-established three distinct provinces – Northern Syria, Southern Syria, and Egypt – without, however, doing away with the *mamluk* ruling class: thus they maintained a bulwark against Portuguese encroachments in the Red Sea. A local *mamluk*, Khayr Bey – the term *bey* being one of the Turkish titles in use in Egypt and other countries connected with the Ottomans – was placed in command, but two political checks on *mamluk* power were instituted: the authority of the governor was to be periodically reconfirmed by the Sultan in Constantinople (the town which came to be known under the name of Istanbul) and Ottoman troops were left to garrison Egypt. These troops, who were themselves recruited in much the same way as the *mamluk*-s, competed with, but increasingly shared power with the *mamluk*-s who themselves continued to recruit new retainers from the slave markets of the East. Egypt was considered as a vassal state farmed out by the Ottoman Sultan. The governor had full responsibility for administering the province and collecting taxes and he himself extended this right to other officers of the military ruling class under his command. A yearly tribute was sent to Istanbul. Egypt was also a strategic military base from which the Ottomans could launch expeditions to ensure control of the Red Sea and of the Arabian coast. They were thus able to conquer Yemen in 1515–17 and Aden.

The decline of the Ottoman Empire soon set in, however, and two dates are often mentioned as landmarks: the Turkish defeat at Vienna in 1529 and at Lepanto in 1571. They were interpreted as forebodings of evils and even disaster to be expected of the millennium which, in the *hijra* calendar, was to begin in 1591. It is however more important to stress inner structural causes of decline. They include cultural stagnation, inefficiency and corruption in the running of the state, and an unfavourable economic situation characterized by a strong inflationary trend and the growing importance of European trading nations. A sure sign of this is the prevalent use of European coins, and notably the Maria-Teresa thaler, in trade throughout the Muslim world.

The Ottoman Empire's decline created the conditions under which Egypt re-established its effective independence. By the 17th century the powerful *mamluk* warlords and their households had succeeded in shaking off the shackles of control. The military aristocracy – foreign with respect to indigenous Egyptians but local with respect to the Turkish appointed personnel – concentrated all administrative functions in its hands. Not only were the *bey*-s able to build up their strength and wealth through heavy taxation imposed on the peasantry, but they also made alliances with the local bourgeoisie, thus sharing control over the religious establishment and more profitable forms of trade. The 18th century, which was marked by a progressive reorientation of the world economy in terms of European mercantilism, favoured the interests of the Egyptian upper class, with Cairo as a major international trading centre at the crossroads of the African commercial network: European imports came by way of the sea, coffee from Yemen, spices from the Far East, slaves and various African commodities from the Sudan, Moroccan leather or Tunisian *shashiya*-s (hats known in Europe as fezes) from the Maghrib.

The prosperity of the ruling class in 18th century Egypt made for political change. This was illustrated by the career of 'Ali Bey who seized power in 1760 and established an autocratic form of government which did away with the collegial rule of the *bey*-s. By a series of tactical or military moves, he was able to deprive the grandees of much of their power and wealth. At the same time he undertook to bring the outlying tribes under control. Independence with respect to the Ottoman suzerain became ever more marked as 'Ali Bey emphasized the function of the *shaykh-al-balad* (the local governor), as opposed to the viceroy appointed by the Turks. The viceroy was not only reduced to an honorary position but was further weakened by 'Ali Bey's initiative in deposing the Ottoman nominee. 'Ali Bey ultimately came to assume the position of *qaim-al-maqam* (or acting viceroy), thus taking a further step to total autonomy if not actual independence. 'Ali Bey also had an expansive military policy and was able to re-establish the old frontiers of the Mamluk Sultanate by imposing Egyptian over-rule in Arabia and the Holy Places, and by reconquering Syria in 1770–1. 'Ali Bey's efforts were, however, historically premature and opposition from the former ruling elite soon brought about his downfall. He was beaten and fatally wounded in battle in 1773.

The career of 'Ali Bey at the end of the 18th century is a milestone in the historical evolution of Egypt both with respect to the previous independent Mamluk Sultanate which he largely succeeded in re-establishing, and with respect to the reign of Muhammad'Ali in the 19th century which his own in many ways prefigures. Some 30 years, however, separate the two autocrats, and in this short lapse of time at the end of the century the general problems of the age reasserted themselves. The former military ruling class reclaimed power whilst at the same time giving rise to factional oppositions among the leading *bey*-s. In 1786, the Ottomans made an effort to restake their claim by sending a fleet to Egypt to set up a viceroy. In 1798, the French army under Napoleon Bonaparte occupied Egypt. Thus our account of 19th-century Egypt opens on a typically modern scene of colonial invasion.

THE BARBARY REGENCIES

The Barbary Regencies (as they used to be called by Europeans) were Algeria, Tunisia, and Tripoli whose territories were initially limited in extent and characterized by the ports (Algiers, Tunis and Tripoli) which gave the

Fig. 2.2 Political regimes in North Africa

EGYPT	THE BARBARY REGENCIES			MOROCCO	SUDAN
	Tripoli	Tunisia	Algeria		
Egypto-Turkish rule	Qaramanli dynasty (1711–1836)	Dynasty of the Husayni Beys (1705–1957)	Turkish appointed deys until the French invasion (1830)	Sharifian empire under the 'Alawi-s (1672 to the present)	Funj dynasty in the north (16th to early 19th century) Independent sultanate of Dar Fur
Beys at the head of Mamluk households. After 1805 a hereditary royal family of Albanian origin.	A hereditary ruling family, recognized by the Ottoman authorities. The Kulughli-s were an important group upholding Qaran:anli authority.	A growingly independent dynasty ruling over a well-knit national community.	A military regime maintaining close links with Turkey.	An independent kingdom ruled over by a sharifian dynasty.	A royal family whose origins are not clear, ruling over largely autonomous principalities and tribal groups. Dar Fur was a Muslim state whose hereditary ruling family claimed descent from the 'Abbasid-s. The court was highly literate and trade important.

Regencies their names. The Ottomans, on the other hand, called them *garb odjaklari*, 'the western provinces', and it is the political significance of this which we shall now consider, not neglecting to recall that North Africa has, in fact, a much older institutional history, whether in terms of tribal kingdoms in antiquity, of Phoenician or Roman colonies, or as the Muslim province of Ifriqiya.

The Ottoman western provinces have a common origin. They are the result of the struggle between two rival and ideologically opposed blocks: the Muslim empire of the Turks and the Christian states of Europe. The struggle had begun with the Crusades and was to continue in the modern age with, at first, Venice bearing the brunt of the fighting until it gave in and concluded a humiliating peace treaty with Sulayman the Magnificent in 1540. On the continent, Austria and Hungary were directly involved in the confrontation and successfully withstood the siege of Vienna in 1529. They too, in 1547, accepted unfavourable peace terms. It was in fact Pope Pius V who, banking on Spanish ambitions, organized a united Christian front in the Mediterranean. This led to a joint naval expedition which succeeded in destroying the Muslim fleet off Lepanto on 7 October 1571. This is often seen as the European breakthrough which created a new balance of power detrimental to the Muslims.

One expression of the struggle was the fight between the Spaniards and the Turks for mastery of the ports of North Africa. Here, in spite of successive victories and defeats, Muslim efforts were ultimately to prove successful. We have already mentioned Christian conquests in Morocco. The same process was under way all along the Mediterranean. In Algeria, Oran was captured by the Spanish in 1509 and occupied until 1708, and again between 1732 and 1792. The rocky island off Algiers was occupied between 1511 and 1529. Throughout the 16th century efforts were made to maintain or establish Spanish control over the coast. They include Charles V's ill-fated attempt on Algiers in 1541. Bougie was occupied between 1509 and 1555. Goletta and Tunis were taken in 1535 and though freed by the Muslims in 1569, Tunis fell again briefly in 1573–4. Sousse Mahdiya (captured in 1550) and the island of Djerba were all at one time or another under Spanish fire. In Libya, Tripoli fell in 1510.

The creation of the Regencies was the result of a combined Ottoman and local stand against the invaders. The Turkish fleet included a number of enterprising *rais*-es (captains) who needed North African harbours as fortified ports of call. Among these famous sea-wolves who are part of the legendary history of the Mediterranean, we find four brothers: 'Urudj, Ishaq, Iliyas and Khayr al-Din (*circa* 1483–1546) who is better known by his nickname, Barba Rosa. Though more interested in sea-fighting than in anything else, the *rais*-es were also loyal Muslims even though many of them were of Christian origin and mere converts to Islam. They were determined not only to uphold Turkish political interests but also to come to the help of those who in North Africa were subject to Christian attacks. In 1514, 'Urudj answered a call for help from the people of Algiers whose resistance he helped to organize. However he soon quarreled with his protégés who rose up in arms against him and he crushed the uprising with great brutality in 1516. That same year he inflicted a severe defeat on the Spaniards. He then set about establishing his effective control over the harbour and its hinterland. At the same time his brother Khayr-al-Din was active elsewhere along the coast. Fighting against the Spanish continued and 'Urudj himself was killed in 1518 after being besieged for six months in Tlemcen. Khayr al-Din took command.

At this stage a new step was taken, one of considerable import. Khayr al-Din sent an envoy to the Ottoman Sultan, Salim I, acknowledging the latter's sovereignty. The Sultan sanctioned the *rais*'s position by naming him *beylerbey* (governor) and making Algiers a province of the Empire. A little later he went still further and granted Khayr al-Din the title of *pasha*. Two thousand *janissaries* (Turkish soldiers) were sent out to enable him to rule effectively. Thus was established the first of the Barbary Regencies.

Khayr al-Din was however first and foremost a sea-wolf and in 1536 he handed over command to one of his officers, Hasan Agha (the term *agha* indicates officer rank in the Turkish army) and returned to sea. He continued to fight the Christians along the northern coast and later in other parts of the Mediterranean at the head of the Turkish fleet of which he had been named Grand Admiral in 1533.

The story of the other two Regencies, namely Tunis and Tripoli, follows the same pattern. Tunisia in the early 15th century was in a state of confusion under the weak leadership of a local dynasty, and was submitted to fierce Christian attacks. Khayr al-Din had begun to reverse the trend by freeing Bizerta and Tunis in 1534. He expelled the local ruler Mulay Hasan who sought the help of the Spanish. Charles V, who was much worried by the efficient line of defence being set up in North Africa, sent out a combined Spanish and Italian force which took the Gulf of Tunis in 1535. A Spanish garrison occupied Goletta and Mulay Hasan was re-established in his capital. In spite of this, Muslim resistance remained active and strategic harbours were successively reconquered, including the island of Djerba in 1560. Here too Turkish sovereignty was recognized and military organization set up. By the turn of the century, the European invaders were very much on the defensive, holding on to their last outposts which included Tunis. Conquered in 1569 by *rais* 'Ulj 'Ali Pasha, it fell again after the battle of Lepanto and was finally freed in 1574 by Kilidj 'Ali Pasha and Sinan Pasha.

Tripoli, an independent municipality, had fallen to the Spaniards led by the energetic Pedro Navarro in July 1510, but in 1530 Charles V had handed it over for better security to the warring order of monks known as the Knights of Malta. In 1545 or 1546, the Libyans had appealed to the Turks for help and a naval force under the command of Murad Pasha had been sent to them. The Knights nonetheless held out in Tripoli until attacked by Darghut, the famous sea-captain whom Europeans know under the name of Dragut. He conquered Tripoli in August 1551 and was named *beylerbey* of the province which comprised most of Tripolitania. To this was added in 1577 the southern district of Fezzan. This does not mean that the Fezzan (which was an autonomous sultanate and remained so until the 19th century) passed under full control of Tripoli, but following on the military expedition into the region in 1576 – a move which as we saw earlier had caused considerable agitation in Bornu – the Sultan of Fezzan was led to accept the suzerainty of Tripoli and payment of an annual tribute. One may thus consider that a new frontier in the south had been established with the official assent of the Sublime Porte

(Turkish government), which was recognized by the surrounding Muslim states or principalities. Libya's present day eastern province, Cyrenaica, was more slowly and vaguely integrated into the Regency and its nomad tribes remained largely beyond the bounds of administrative control. Nonetheless the Governor of Tripoli set about strengthening the harbours of the coast and establishing some governmental and notably military personnel in Derna, Misurata, and Ben Ghazi. The desert zone between Egypt and Cyrenaica was largely unclaimed although Egyptian sovereignty extended over part of what is now Libyan territory.

Thus between 1514 – the year in which 'Urudj had set up in the citadel of Algiers – and 1574 when the Spanish were finally expelled from Tunis, a Muslim line of defence had been established along the coast with most of the region – with the exception of the independent kingdom of Morocco – passing under Ottoman control.

The political regime which resulted from this consisted of a Turkish province under the rule of a *beylerbey*. This gave way in 1574 to three distinct provinces and the title of *beylerbey* was given up. Each province thereafter followed its own path. The political organization of the Regencies nonetheless remained the same. It was based on *odjak*-s (military units) recruited in distant provinces of the Ottoman Empire. The soldiers or *janissaries* continued for some time to receive new contingents from the East, but by the 16th century they were largely autonomous. Power was vested in the officer corps which also constituted the *diwan* (ruling assembly) of the Regencies. Also part of the ruling class were the *rais*-es and members of the religious establishment. Another category but not necessarily one having political power, was that of the *kulughli*-s (descendants of Turks on the male side but having local mothers). Native men were generally excluded from governmental office. The *janissaries* jealously upheld their privileges and absence of social integration with the native population was the rule. Even intermarriage was looked down upon and Turkish women or slave-girls were preferred to local women. The barriers were further underscored by the fact that the military overlords made little attempt to settle inland or share in local activities, except those connected with seafaring. This political pattern common to the three Regencies persisted until confrontation with Europe in the 19th century. There were, however, specific local evolutions which go to explain the different stands made by each province with respect to imperial encroachments.

Algeria: local developments

Algeria which was the first of the Regencies to be conquered, and which put up little resistance to the French in 1830, should be examined in this light. Its structural weakness was due at least partly to the fact that the Turks had made little effort to forge the unity of the central province, but rather emphasized divisions by creating three distinct districts, that of the west which extended as far as Tlemcen with, from the end of the 18th century, Oran (evacuated by the Spanish in 1792) as its regional capital. The western district continued to have close links with Morocco, notably in the religious and cultural fields. The eastern district with Constantine as local capital, was traditionally turned towards Tunisia. Algiers was the capital of the Province, but also part of the central district which extended as far south as Tuggurt, Wargla and Biskra.

The ruling class continued to be alien to the masses. Its Turkish origins were in greater evidence here than elsewhere, especially as recruits continued to arrive from the East. The *janissaries* were however no more than 15 000-strong at any time so that they were led in the 17th century to open up their ranks to *kulughli*-s. Power was vested in the *dey* who after the 17th century was no longer appointed by the Sublime Porte, but chosen from among the *janissary* corps by the officers who formed the *diwan*. The decision was however ratified by the Sultan who sent the new governor a *firman* (decree of investiture) which was periodically reconfirmed (every three years). The *rais*-es also constituted a pressure group and had their own *taifa* (assembly). Although their importance was considerable, notably in the matter of seatrade, they avoided involvement with the military and did not fill the function of *dey*. The strife-ridden relations of the *janissaries* dominated the political life of Algiers and this is well illustrated by the fact that of 28 *dey*-s who succeeded each other between 1671 and 1830, 14 came to power as the result of the assassination of their predecessors. The *dey*-s thus came to live in fear and isolation, shut up in their citadels and only communicating with the outside world through their personal guards and servants.

The political class remained alien to the mass of the population which, though self-administered, paid heavy taxation to the central government and had to put up with the overbearing ways of the Turkish soldiery. Revolts of which we know little seem to have occurred frequently and were generally cruelly repressed. A limited form of feudalism was introduced by large grants of land being made to pensioned officers. It was only in the towns that some form of social interaction took place: members of the religious class were to a limited degree involved in the administration of the country, whilst the wealthier merchants derived profit from seafaring activities.

We cannot therefore consider national unity to have been in any way promoted by the Turkish regime in Algeria. Indeed revolts highlight opposition to the regime even if lack of social cohesion prevented them from being successful. On the other hand by the end of the 18th century some forms of collective self-awareness and attempts at developing social cohesion can be detected in Algeria. In tribal areas, families having political or religious influence came to the fore and we find mention of the Muqrani family, the Bin Habyles of Djidjelli, the Bin 'Azdin of the Zuwagha tribe and the Bin Zamun of Western Kabylie who were to continue to be rallying points in the 19th century. Of more considerable import was the role of sufi fraternities, some of which were older well-established orders such as the Qadiriyya whilst others were newer orders, often founded in the 18th century, either in Algeria itself such as the Rahmaniyya, or, more typically, set up in Algeria as an offshoot of a Moroccan fraternity. The two major North African orders of the 18th–19th centuries, the Darqawiyya and the Tijaniyya, had a strong following in western Algeria. It would be a shortsighted view to overstate on the fact that the 'Alawi sovereigns encouraged this expansion into Algeria in order to neutralize Turkish influence and promote Moroccan interests. The local lodges also identified themselves with their new clientele and a militant anti-Turk stand seems also to have reflected the latter's political views. We thus find Darqawi involvement in at least two revolts in the early 19th century: those of a man called Bin Ahrash and, in 1803–9, of Bin Sharif.

One might conclude from this that the Turkish regime as applied to Algeria was essentially a governmental facade which did little to promote social integration and indeed probably retarded Algeria's development both in the economic and political spheres.

Tunisia: local developments

In Tunisia an initially identical situation led to different results. Though here too power was Ottoman-defined with a *diwan* of army officers and a *taifa* of sea-captains, headed by a *pasha* appointed by Istanbul, the whole history of the political institutions is marked by an interplay of Turkish-sponsored and local factors with an ever more marked identification of the political establishment with national objectives.

The evolution of the state institutions was determined by the role of the military ruling class which in this case was limited in the early period to 40 *odjak*-s of 100 men with at their head officers known as *dey*-s. From early times, local contingents were recruited. A Kabylie tribe settled in Tunisia, the Zuwawa, thus provided a regiment known as the *spahi*-s. Their importance grew as they were used to counterbalance the *janissaries*. Seditious tendencies and personal rivalry among the officers brought about political changes. In 1590, the *janissaries* revolted and massacred a number of their officers. The *dey*-s now chose their own leader, the *agha* who at first shared power with the Turkish-appointed *pasha*, but progressively the latter came to have a merely honorary role. A tendency to more autocratic and personal rule became apparent as the *agha* appointed his own candidates to two major functions: that of *qabtan* (head of the navy), and *bey*, an officer who acted as tax-collector. The *bey* as head of the armed forces and of the treasury was in a key position and this led to a military *coup* with the *bey* assuming full powers. Murad Bey (1612–31) had his position sanctioned by the Ottoman suzerain who sent him a *firman* appointing him *pasha* on a hereditary basis. Thus, in the early 17th century, a local dynasty was created which was largely independent with respect to the nominal sovereign, the Turkish Sultan.

The Muradi dynasty reigned for nearly a century and developed the independence and cohesion of Tunisia by a better integration of the tribes, by defending the country against encroachments from its neighbours, and notably from Algeria which at various times tried to expand territorially and politically. It was under the Muradi dynasty that the island of Djerba passed definitely under Tunisian sovereignty. The Muradi-s also strengthened coastal defences to withstand foreign attacks, notably those launched by the Knights of Malta. Among significant expressions of autonomy and national identity was the re-establishment of Arabic as the official language of the Regency, although Turkish continued in use as a cultural idiom to enhance the prestige and aloofness of the ruling class. Turkish also continued to be a means of international communication with the Middle East and notably in relations with the Sublime Porte.

After reaching its peak under a powerful and autocratic ruler, Murad Bey (1659–79), the dynasty declined and, in the course of a civil war which lasted some 20 years during which both the Algerians and the Ottomans attempted to take advantage of the situation, a new dynasty came to power with Husayn bin 'Ali (1705), an officer not of the *janissary* corps which had by then lost much of its power, but of the *spahi*-s. Husayn bin 'Ali was the founder of a dynasty which continued to reign until 1957 when Tunisia became a republic. Though the dynasty still defined itself as Turkish, this must be seen for what it is, namely a ruling class style, as links with the Eastern Empire became more distant. The dynasty itself could hardly substantiate its claim to Turkish origin since Husayn bin 'Ali's father came originally from the island of Crete and his mother was Tunisian.

It is therefore of greater interest to try and see why in Tunisia the state pattern should have evolved towards national self-identification. The nature of the country, its economic resources, and the kind of society this upheld, all

Fig. 2.3 Tunisia: the Husayni dynasty

Husayn bin 'Ali.	1705–1735
'Ali Pasha.	1735–56
Muhammad bin Husayn.	1756–9
'Ali bin Husayn.	1759–82
Hammuda bin 'Ali.	1782–1814
'Uthman bin 'Ali.	1814
Mahmud bin Husayn.	1814–24
Husayn bin Mahmud.	1824–35
Mustafa bin Mahmud.	1835–7
Ahmad bin Mustafa.	1837–55
Muhammad bin Husayn.	1855–9
Muhammad al-Sadiq.	1859–82
'Ali bin Mahmud.	1882–1902
Muhammad al-Hadi.	1902–6
Muhammad al-Nasir.	1906–22
Muhammad al-Habib.	1922–9
Ahmad bin 'Ali.	1929–42
Moncef bin Muhammad al-Nasir.	1942–3
Lamin bin Muhammad al-Habib.	1943–57.

form part of the explanation. Tunisia is a small country – a mere 164 000 sq km within its present-day boundaries – closely hemmed in by expansionist neighbours: the Algerians in the west, Tripoli in the east, and the European states of the Mediterranean, notably Italy, in the north, and Sicily, a mere 100 km off the Tunisian shore. In spite of the importance of semi-nomad Beduins, often of Banu Hilal stock – about half the total population of Tunisia – important sectors of the rural and urban economy had developed on early capitalist lines. The making of red felt hats, of the type known in Europe as the fez and in Tunisia as the *shashiya*, was on these lines; about 2 million hats were produced a year, providing work for at least 1 500 persons. In the field of agriculture special mention must be made of the extensive planting of olive groves in northern Tunisia in the 16th century by Andalusian refugees who introduced a complex system of irrigation. Vegetable oil once again became the main export commodity, as it had been during the Roman period, with cereals coming close behind. Sea trades were also active, chiefly coral fishing. Thus, 18th-century Tunisia was prosperous, in spite of such natural calamities as drought, locusts, and epidemics. Moreover, its privileged position on the Mediterranean made it a commercial partner both of Europe and the Middle East. Tunisia thus tended to have a well-knit society and this was further upheld by the importance of its urban centres. In Tunisia the proportion of city dwellers was far higher than in the rest of the Maghrib and in addition it had a number of large villages. Urban centres were of great antiquity and had been particularly influenced by the sophisticated Arab *madina* pattern. Qairawan had cultural and religious prestige as the first town founded by the Arabs when they conquered the West. It was later outshone by Tunis as a capital and intellectual centre. Tunis's Zaytuna Mosque, founded in 734, became one of the most famous universities of the Muslim world. The complex set of religious buildings surrounding the Zaytuna and providing places of prayer and study, besides hostels for the students, attracted scholars from all over Tunisia and from further afield still. This established contacts between the capital and the hinterland, promoting interaction between town and country and spreading a dominant ideology and culture, that of the religious establishment. In this interrelated pattern we do not have as clear a break between town and tribe as in Morocco, nor the kind of distortion which existed in Egypt between the Nile peasantry, the desert tribes and the towns. In fact we have something which comes closer to a European-type urban development based on a bourgeoisie dependent on the countryside, where it had its lands and from which it obtained raw materials in exchange for services and goods.

These trends culminated under the reign of an able and energetic *bey*, Hammuda, who ruled from 1777 to 1814 (although he only came officially to power in 1782 on his father's death). The latter part of Hammuda Bey's reign belongs to the history of the 19th century and will be studied in that context. At this stage it is more important to point to new social and political trends promoted by Hammuda who tried to combat social disintegration for which the plague was responsible and the dramatic decline of agriculture which was one of its consequences, by strengthening the regime which increasingly tended towards autocracy. This was very similar to the tendency which was apparent in Egypt under 'Ali Bey but whereas the latter had failed because of powerful opposition from his fellow officers, Hammuda Bey was successful because the *janissary* corps could not effectively oppose him, and its mutinies – notably that of 1811 – were severely crushed. Hammuda Bey also instituted a new form of recruitment for military and administrative personnel with a view to counterbalancing both the *janissaries* and tribal levies. This was the *mamluk* system which was developed in Tunisia on much the same lines as in Egypt, except that the young Christian slaves bought in the east were not attached to lordly households, but to the *bey* himself. They were trained as soldiers and those who showed aptitude often received in addition a good scholarly education. Their origins were no social handicap since they could occupy the highest functions and married into the best families, including that of the *bey*. As an example of such high fortunes one might mention Hammuda Bey's Keeper of the Seal: Yusuf Sahib al-Tabi'. He had been bought as a child in the slave market of Istanbul by a Tunisian of high rank who had given him to Hammuda in 1777. Yusuf Sahib al-Tabi' was to dominate the political scene throughout Hammuda Bey's reign but was executed in 1815, the year following his master's death.

Another factor which goes a long way to explaining why Hammuda Bey should have succeeded where 'Ali Bey in Egypt failed was the political alliance and working partnership established by the Tunisian ruler at the end of the 18th century with influential families of local origin who had religious prestige, tribal authority, or wealth derived from trade or agriculture. Their connection with Hammuda brought to the fore those families who became a hereditary ruling class playing an active role in 19th- and 20th-century Tunisia such as the Bin 'Ayyad of Djerba, the Jalluli of Sfax, the Mrabit of Qairawan, and the Nuira of Monastir. Hammuda Bey enabled them to share in the benefits of the state; moreover, with a view to strengthening the ties between the central government and rural populations, he had the country divided into administrative districts which, from 1787 onwards were, so to speak, privately put up for auction. Candidates for office would obtain the post of *qaid* (governor) after negotiating the cost with the *bey* or one of his representatives (generally Yusuf Sahib al-Tabi'). They were then responsible for law and order in their districts and the regular payment of government dues. This was on the model of the *iltizam* (tax-farming system) practised in other parts of the Ottoman Empire including Egypt. It gave the *qaid* considerable opportunities to oppress the people and make a private fortune, but the system was partially kept in check by close government supervision and courts of justice open to all. The scholar class, whether of urban or rural origin – the two were closely connected in Tunisia – also had its privileges upheld. Its traditional functions had government support and in the doctrinal field the *bey* condemned both more popular forms of devotion which undermined the authority of the religious establishment and Islamic fundamentalism which had begun to spread in the Muslim world in the wake of the Arabian Wahhabi reformist movement.

In many ways, as we can see, the Tunisian Regency evolved rapidly in the period before the 19th century, passing from subservience to Turkish rule to national self-affirmation with a growing tendency, apparent in the reign of Hammuda Bey, to class stratification. How this was to be affected by growing European pressures, will be considered in a later chapter.

Tripolitania: local developments

The third Ottoman province of the West, namely Tripolitania, presents a still different picture. The Turkish *pasha* who from his citadel, or at the head of the *diwan* and *janissaries*, ruled over the town and province, soon saw his powers counterbalanced by the growing number of *kulughli*-s. In 1711 rivalry between Khalil Pasha and his Admiral of the Fleet gave the *kulughli*-s an opportunity to seize power. The coup was carried out by Ahmad Qaramanli whose ancestor, a Turk from Caramania, had come to Tripoli with Darghut and married a Libyan. He had settled in the *kulughli* community of the Menshiya, an oasis on the outskirts of Tripoli. The French consul noting the change of regime, wrote: 'Qaramanli Bey is now reigning Bey, placed on the Throne by the mountain Arabs. He is a Kulughli and a very pleasant man'. But Ahmad Qaramanli proved to be far more than that.

Having an extensive popular following and strong support from the Menshiya, Ahmad Qaramanli undertook to win over the *diwan* and was sufficiently successful in this for them to refuse to restore the former Turkish governor, Khalil Pasha, when a Turkish flotilla brought the fugitive back. Ahmad Qaramanli was not, however, prepared to openly defy the Ottoman Sultan: he had it given out that the Sultan's *firman* had been rejected not as an act of rebellion *per se* but on the technicality that it had been signed merely by the Grand Wazir of the Sublime Porte, and not by the Sultan himself. The

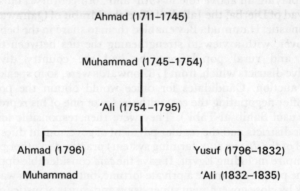

Fig. 2.4 *The Qaramanli dynasty of Tripolitania*

Turkish government itself accepted the *status quo* and for the time being made no further attempt to oust Ahmad Qaramanli, who set about consolidating his authority. He encouraged seafaring and concluded treaties of his own with foreign countries, including Holland and Genoa (1712). By these means he was able to obtain modern equipment and stores for his navy and armed forces. In 1712 and 1721, the Ottomans made two further abortive attempts to impose a governor of their own but finally decided to countenance the situation: in 1722 they sent out a *firman* recognizing Ahmad Qaramanli as hereditary *pasha* of Tripolitania. The legitimization of authority by the Ottoman Sultan still had political and religious import and the *firman* was welcomed.

Ahmad Qaramanli and his descendants were from then on to reign as independent sovereigns, the accession of each sovereign being confirmed by the Sultan. The rulers varied in their personalities and capacities, but Ahmad Qaramanli remained the greatest of them all. Even his death was marked by grandeur as the old Pasha who had for some time succeeded in covering up the fact that he was sick and blind, decided to hand over the government to his younger son, Muhammad whose mother was Libyan, eliminating the elder, Mahmud, whose mother was Turkish. Having made the *diwan* ratify his decision, he withdrew to his private apartments, recited a verse of the Quran and shot himself. Muhammad Qaramanli, however, proved a weak ruler and in the course of his reign which lasted from 1745 to 1754, he was easily manipulated by the various pressure groups: the Arab tribes of the interior, the trading class, and the army. Political decline was even more obvious under his successor, 'Ali Qaramanli (1754–95), who lived shut up in his palace, leaving the actual government to his entourage which included a number of Christian renegades. This reflected an incapacity to face up to the economic problems with which the Regency was faced. Its traditional role in the Mediterranean trade waned as European control over the sea routes was established. Even piracy, which will be defined in the next chapter as the last struggle of the Muslim states of North Africa to keep up their presence at sea, was itself threatened by the more powerful navies of Europe, and the profits accruing from roving declined. Tripoli's no less traditional trans-Saharan trade was disrupted by the political weakness of its partners in Sudanic Africa, notably Bornu. A troubled situation in the south including civil wars was to change the traditional pattern of Sudanic Africa before bringing new states to the fore. At the northern end of the Saharan routes social unrest also prevailed as a result of periods of drought followed by epidemics. Thus, in the 1780s, the plague made one of its deadliest onslaughts. In the capital, according to contemporary accounts, 90 per cent of the Christian community died or fled, as did half of the Jews, and 40 per cent of the Muslims. In the Regency some 27 000 persons were said to have died.

By the end of the century, a more or less total disruption of the social and political order was apparent. Tribal groups were either too hard hit by economic difficulties to pay the increased taxation the government tried to levy, or else had reacted positively, reforged tribal unity, and now stood out against the government. This was particularly so in the case of the Awlad Sulayman, a major Arab nomad tribe of Syrtica (between Tripoli and Cyrenaica), which gave up the feuding which had undermined it in the middle of the 18th century, and united under an able leader, Sayf al-Nasir, who was now a force to be reckoned with. Dissensions prevailed throughout the political establishment, culminating in the Pasha's family where the aged 'Ali Qaramanli was unable to keep in check the rival ambitions of his three sons Ahmad, Hasan and Yusuf. This led in 1790 to a scene of Shakespearean horror when Hasan and Yusuf met in their mother's presence for what was supposed to be an official reconciliation. Yusuf seized on the occasion to shoot his brother, wounding his mother in the process. The bloody event shocked the Regency and led to the realignment of various pressure groups behind one or other of the surviving princes, especially when it became evident to all that 'Ali Pasha was incapable or unwilling to bring the murderer to account. The only punishment inflicted on Yusuf was his appointment to the governorship of Misurata but the inhabitants of that city refused to allow the prince to take up his office. Sayf al-Nasir and the Awlad Sulayman sided with Misurata, thus creating a bitter and long-lasting feud between Yusuf Qaramanli and the tribal chief. But a new danger was at hand: the Turks saw the unsettled state of the country as an occasion to restore their sovereignty and in 1793 they sent out a Georgian renegade, 'Ali Efendi al-Jezaily, more commonly called 'Ali Burghul, as Pasha. He landed in Tripoli and wreaked havoc on the town whose population had been psychologically disarmed by the flying of the prestigious Ottoman colours. All past quarrels forgotten, the Qaramanlis hastily sought refuge in the *kulughli* home of the Menshiya, and they appealed to Tunis for help. The latter sent out a relief force (1795) which, with the Qaramanli-s at its head, drove out the invaders. Family relations had not, however, improved, and pressure was put on the old Pasha to abdicate which he did in 1796, appointing Ahmad as his successor. Not deterred, the energetic and ambitious Yusuf forestalled his brother by setting himself up in the citadel. Ahmad was forced to seek safety in flight. He went first to Derna in Cyrenaica and from there sailed to Tunis.

The reign of Yusuf Qaramanli, the last great Pasha of the dynasty was to last from 1796 to 1832. It is thus part of the history of the 19th century. It should nonetheless be pointed out that Yusuf Qaramanli was faced with a situation which is basically that of all the North African states at the end of the 18th century, but whereas in Egypt and Tunisia this was already being met by new responses which one may consider as characteristic of the modernizing trend, Yusuf Qaramanli met it inadequately, by military rather than political means, and by attempting to re-establish a former order of things which was already part of what one might term the *ancien régime* of Muslim states in North Africa. Though as we shall subsequently see he was more successful in his Saharan strategy than in his European policy, the preponderance of the Imperial factor ultimately brought about the fall of the Qaramanli dynasty and, with it, the end of Libyan independence, even though this was not due to the intervention of a European power but of the Ottomans.

SELECTED READING LIST

General Works
Abun-Nasr, J., *A History of the Maghrib*, (Cambridge, 1971).
Fischer, G., *Barbary Legend: War, Trade, and Piracy in North Africa (1415–1830)*, (Oxford, 1957).
Mantran, R., 'Khayr ed-Din Barberousse et l'implantation ottomane en Afrique du Nord', *Les Africains*, vol. III, (Paris 1977).
Valensi, L., *Le Maghreb avant la prise d'Alger*, (Paris, 1969).

Morocco
Brignon *et al.*, *Histoire du Maroc*, (Paris, 1967).
Morsy, M., 'Mulay Isma'il ou l'état 'alawite', *Les Africains*, vol. IV, (Paris, 1977).
Yahya, D., *Morocco in the Sixteenth Century*, (London, 1981).
Zayyani, A. al-, *Al-Turjuman al-Mu'arib 'an Duwal al-Mashriq wa al-Maghrib*, (Paris, 1886 and Amsterdam, 1969).

Egypt
Gran, P., *Islamic Roots of Capitalism, Egypt 1760–1840* (Austin, 1979).
Holt, P. M., *Egypt and the Fertile Crescent. 1516–1922. A Political History*, (Ithaca and London, 1966 and 1969).
Hourani, A. H., 'The Changing Face of the Fertile Crescent in the XVIIIth Century', *Studia Islamica*, 8, 1957.
Raymond, A., 'Ali Bey le Grand et le premier éveil de l'Afrique moderne', *Les Africains*, vol. II, (Paris, 1977).
Shaw, S. J., *Ottoman Egypt in the Eighteenth Century*, (Harvard, 1964).
Staffa, S. J., *Conquest and Fusion. The Social Evolution of Cairo A.D. 642–1850*, (Leyden, 1977).

Algeria
Barnby, H. G., *The Prisoners of Algiers*, (London, 1966).

Laugier de Tassy, *Histoire du Royaume d'Alger*, (Amsterdam, 1725). English translation under the name of J. Morgan, *A Compleat History of the Piratical States of Barbary*, (London, 1728).

Grammont, H. de, *Histoire d'Alger sous la domination turque (1516–1830)*, (Paris, 1887).

Venture de Paradis, *Alger au XVIIIe siècle*, (Paris, 1898).

Tunisia

Ben Dhiaf, A., *Ithaf ahl al-Zaman*, (Tunis, 1963–6).

Broadley, A. M., *Tunis Past and Present*, (London, 1882).

Chérif, M. H., 'Hammuda Pacha Bey et l'affermissement de l'autonomie tunisienne', *Les Africains*, vol. VII, (Paris, 1977).

MacGill T., *An Account of Tunis*, (Glasgow, 1811).

Mantran, R., 'L'évolution des relations entre la Tunisie et l'Empire Ottoman du XVIe au XIXe siècle', *Cahiers de Tunisie*, 7, 1959.

Sebag, P., 'La peste dans la Régence de Tunis aux XVIIe et XVIIIe siècles', *Ibla*, 109, 1965.

Libya

Dearden, S., *A Nest of Corsairs*, (London, 1976).

Féraud, Ch., *Annales Tripolitaines*, (Paris, 1927).

Ibn Ghalbun, M., *Al-Tadhkar fi man Malaka Tarabulus wa ma kana bihi min al-Akhbar*, (Cairo, 1930).

Tully, R., *Narrative of Ten Years' Residence at Tripoli*, (London, 1819).

Vansina, J. and Ayoub, A., *Histoire du règne d'Aly Caramanly, Pacha de Tripoli de Barbarie*, (Tripoli, 1978) (in Arabic and French).

CHAPTER 3

SAHARAN LIMITS

Underlying the history of the North African states is their involvement in Saharan issues. The southern dimension of North African politics is therefore important, but it is also difficult to assess, one reason for this being the fact that the kind of criteria used with respect to Mediterranean history are distorted in the desert context.

A DEFINITION OF THE SAHARA AND ITS INHABITANTS

The immensity of the Sahara and the relationship of men to environment in it are sometimes difficult to appreciate. The desert zone – about 8 million sq km – involves the whole width of the continent from the Atlantic to the Nile valley, and parts of all the North African states. The desert is a barrier and a very sparsely populated area – the central part, the home of the Berber Tuareg, has about 1 inhabitant per sq km and the figure must have been barely higher in the 19th century – and these characteristics have meant that it has developed a society which, though of mixed origins with Arab predominance in the west, a Berber block in the centre and more mixed African and Arab populations in the east, has common social characteristics developed in order to meet the challenge of the environment. Moreover the desert is crossed by a network of trails marked out by wells and these have always been used both by the Saharans and by travellers, chief of whom were the merchants. Variety and unity must therefore both be taken into account, as must also permanence and mobility. Indeed the latter factor is uppermost in any description of the Sahara and its inhabitants. The desert must be defined less in terms of its land area than in terms of the trails that cross it. These always ultimately lead out of the desert to more privileged ecological zones, either to the north or to the south. The permanent inhabitants are also mobile with nomadism as a common rule (even if some areas such as parts of the Tibesti or the oases have a settled population) and the social structure, though promoting the autonomy of groups for purposes of self-defence, is also directed towards the north or south since these non-desert areas are indispensable to the nomads, whether in terms of raiding or peaceful trading.

Desert conditions have further tended to emphasize the tribal pattern with solidarity pacts promoting powerful confederacies which maintain harmony within the group whilst upholding its predatory activities with respect to other groups or outlying districts. In this tribal society, political organization based on chiefs and religious advisers has sometimes brought into existence cohesive sultanates. Significantly, however, identification with Islam has often led them to seek legitimization from the Muslim empires of the

52

Maghrib or Mashriq. We thus find the Agades Sultanate (east of the Niger Bend) obtaining from the 'Abbasid *khalifa* in Cairo and later from the Turks, delegated powers of sovereignty which led the Sultan of Agades in his turn to sanction the authority of other rulers including that of the *amenokal* (or 'king') of the Tuareg Iwillimedden. This right, later and for a time, passed to the Moroccan *pasha* of Timbuktu. The Arab tribes of western Sahara had a similar relationship with the Moroccan Sa'di and later 'Alawi *sultan*-s. Another feature of Saharan society promoted by its difficult way of life is the special importance of warriors. Society in the desert has tended to evolve towards marked stratification, with the soldiers and holy men at the top of the social hierarchy. Various degrees of inferiority characterize different dependent groups such as serfs (often remnants of defeated tribes), pariahs (such as blacksmiths) and slaves. Slavery is indeed a typical feature of Saharan society and one which has persisted up to the present in spite of legislation to the contrary; Mauritania only abolished slavery in 1981. The capture of pagans as slaves was not only sanctioned by Islam but for many centuries was the main commodity which the Saharan nomads could obtain by raids and sell profitably in the north, thus obtaining in exchange indispensable goods.

Slaves were the chief commodity of the trans-Saharan trade. Trade integrated nomad groups into the overall pattern of North Africa. For the North African nations involved, the caravan trade required a working partnership with the nomads who were the masters of the desert and were therefore necessary for safe travelling. They protected caravans and acted as guides and camel drivers. Their military capacity could further be put to good use for the promotion of Arab trade in the south, all the more so in view of the fact that Muslim governments could not openly transgress the law by attacking black African Muslim states. The predatory nomads who would ignore such finer points were therefore necessary agents. We thus find a general policy of the northern states with respect to desert confederacies tending to uphold their institutions and autonomy as the best way of guaranteeing successful trading relations with the south.

Though the Saharan nomads were seen by the northerners as predatory, uncouth, and potentially subversive, a working partnership with them in the context of the desert trade was therefore a well-established practice. From a Sudanic point of view a different assessment would have to be made. The nomads were seen as foreign and as a constant source of danger. This did not exclude some settled and peaceful relations since more favourable agricultural areas and free access to markets was also a necessity for the nomads, whilst the Sudanic states could sometimes make use of the latter's military strength. Indeed the more powerful Sudanic states integrated nomads and proved able to keep their unruly instincts in check. Even powerful nomad confederacies were sometimes under the dominion of the Muslim Sudanic kingdoms. The trans-ethnic common bond of Islam could moreover be brought into play to further the policy of a ruler or uphold a *jihad*.

In this constantly evolving political pattern, the trade routes, which though themselves changing, have a long-term relevance, will help us define more concretely the situation which prevailed around 1800 and was to persist throughout the 19th century.

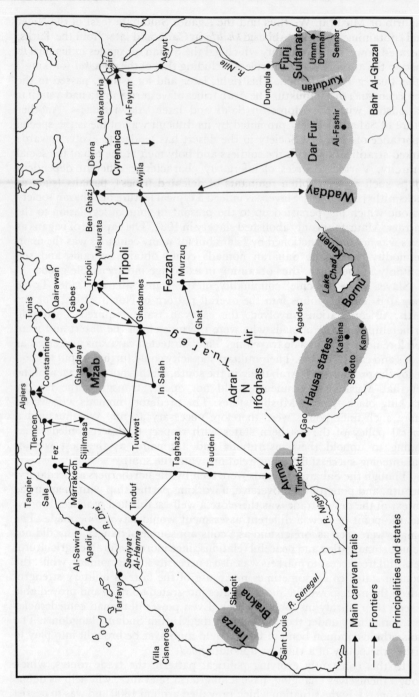

Map 3.1 Trans-Saharan trade routes

TRADE ROUTES AND NOMAD INVOLVEMENT

The expansion of Islam and the development of the Muslim empire cannot be dissociated from the trade over which the Arabs established their control and which promoted a flourishing urban merchant economy. This had led to Arab interest in the *bilad al-sudan* from an early period and, by the 10th century, well established caravan routes made the latter a synonym for luxury commodities, notably ivory, gold, and slaves. The flow of caravans from as far off as Takrur, on the Atlantic, to Cairo and the Middle East was to be progressively affected by the new trade routes established and controlled by European nations. First on the scene in the late 15th century were the Portuguese who established strategic control over the eastern and western coasts of Africa. The appearance of the modern North African states was a riposte to the economic challenge of Europe, characterized both by the will to maintain North Africa within the Muslim imperium and to play a role in the new trading circuits.

This had direct repercussions on the trans-Saharan trade routes as the traditional east to west network was increasingly counterbalanced by caravans crossing the desert from south to north, bringing Sudanic goods ultimately to the coast where international trade promoted the development of harbour-cities. Control of the intermediary phase of Sudanic trade with the Mediterranean and the Atlantic became of paramount importance to the modern North African states in terms of strategy and national power. A clear instance of this – namely Sa'di foreign policy and the Moroccan conquest of Timbuktu – has already been pointed to.

European expansion progressively extended the range of action of the new trading states of Europe. Thus Morocco at the end of the Sa'di dynasty was progressively bypassed by the merchants who set up outposts along the coast of West Africa where they exercised a powerful attraction if not actual domination. The most significant example, from the Moroccan point of view, was the settlement of St. Louis at the mouth of the Senegal where, in spite of international rivalry at first between France and Holland and later between Britain and France, a French colony was established in 1816.

Penetration inland and up the main rivers combined with coastal trade to attract goods to the western coast, although the European slave trade which in an earlier period had badly hit West Africa was progressively abandoned, France abolishing slavery in Senegal in 1848. One of the more perceptible results of a redefined world commerce based on the preponderance of states engaged in a process of industrialization was the break-up of the long Takrur route as two contradictory poles of attraction appeared. In a somewhat schematic way, one might say, for our purposes, that Timbuktu marks the dividing line between the western and eastern-orientated trades. In the former case, most of the commerce went to the coast, with Morocco having only a limited stake; in the latter, much of 19th-century traffic northwards still passed through Muslim Mediterranean harbours such as Tunis, Tripoli, and Alexandria where European merchants or their agents were active. Another characteristic feature of the new European-dominated trade is the fact that whereas in the pre-modern period goods taken south by the Muslim merchants had been local goods including semi-manufactured products such as copperware, leather, cloth, and weapons, these were progressively replaced in the precolonial period by European imports: the cloth came from Britain as did also the copperware, once a traditional Moroccan production, soon replaced by Manchester ware. Commodities imported from the south remained traditional for the local markets, including slaves, but included increasingly export commodities such as gum and ostrich feathers. Though the general pattern of trans-Saharan trade persisted throughout our period, it was geared to a new European-dictated world economy. This underscores and explains the specific economic and political changes apparent along the main trade routes.

Morocco and the western Sahara

Moroccan reaction and adaptation to a new situation of imbalance is apparent from early 'Alawi times as the pretension to a Western Caliphate was given up and even the privileged connection with Timbuktu was more or less abandoned in favour of a more limited western radius of action. Under the energetic rule of Mulay Isma'il at the end of the 17th century, this involved political alliances with the Ma'qil Arabs and their allegiance to the Moroccan sovereign. *Makhzen* authority over the region was affirmed by military and administrative outposts, notably at Shinqit in the middle of western Sahara and at Tuwwat on the eastern frontier. Annual military expeditions in the desert, in the course of which the soldiers would push out as far south as the right bank of the Senegal, enabled the Moroccan sultans to obtain recruits for the slave army. These official expressions of sovereignty became rare occurrences after Mulay Isma'il's death in 1727. This should not be taken to mean that Moroccan influence disappeared but rather that this was now largely indirect, and through Moroccan involvement in tribal politics, the major groups of the region continued to pay allegiance to the 'Alawi sovereign and reciting prayers in his name (this being a traditional expression of recognition of sovereignty in the Muslim world). Royal influence in the Sahara was made possible by the persistent connection of arbiter lineages with the north. The network of holy men, which was particularly influential among the nomad tribes, was closely knit through religious education and fraternity ties. It was customary for these lineages to send their children to be educated in neighbouring tribes where a good school or reputed master functioned. Children from the scholar class who showed aptitude or came from particularly influential families were sent out for further education, often to the reputed *zawiya*-s on the northern edges of the desert. Such establishments in the Sus (extreme west), in the Dra' valley, or in the Tafilalt thus had an important Saharan clientele. Fraternity ties further justified such journeys, the Qadiriyya being the most powerful of these sufi orders in the western Sahara where its network extended considerably under the influence of Sidi Mukhtar al-Kunti (1729–1811), and influential *shaykh*-s in the north would give their patronage to Saharan *talib*-s (students). They would also often help them make arrangements to carry out the Pilgrimage. It was not uncommon for such patrons to introduce their protégés at court and even obtain for them an audience from the Sultan. We thus find Shaykh Sidiyya (1775–1868), a disciple of the Kunta *shaykh*-s and one of the chief Qadiri personalities in West Africa in the mid-19th century, being received by Mulay 'Abd al-Rahman at Marrakech in the 1830s. The later correspondence between Shaykh Sidiyya and Mulay 'Abd al-Rahman's son and heir, Mulay Muhammad, indicates a spirit of collaboration. Shaykh Sidiyya's subsequent dominant influence on the social and economic order of the Moors or Arab tribes of present-day Mauritania, in a wider context involving French expansion in Senegal and the Islamic *jihad*-s of the Sahel, demonstrates the keen awareness in western Africa of the need for solidarity. Through the king's personal involvement in the network of holy men, Morocco played a key role in the defensive system of the west which throughout the 19th century attempted to repulse European penetration in the region, whether that of merchants along the coast, of political agents or, ultimately of a military force moving in on Morocco from Senegal. The effectiveness of this organization will be demonstrated in discussions in a later chapter on developments in the latter part of the 19th century, notably under the leadership of another holy man, Shaykh Ma al-'Aynayn (1831–1910) who was also a visitor of Mulay 'Abd al-Rahman's and of his successors.

This was the militant religious and tribal infrastructure which continued to uphold not only Moroccan sovereignty but also its necessary trade with the south, although this was drawn ever nearer to the western coast and was increasingly defined in terms of the European market. Goods were now generally sent to the Sus and from there to the chief European trading centre, al-Sawira, then called Mogador. Goods to the south were those mentioned earlier as the typical European products intended for the African market. We shall have occasion later to mention the value of these in the overall balance of payments of Morocco in the 19th century. It is here more important to stress the social and political impact this had. Trade continued to be in the hands of the Muslim merchants or rather of a limited number of powerful trading families to whom the sultans granted the title of *tajir al-sultan* ('royal merchant'). They were generally from the city of Fez and the same names occur throughout the 'Alawi period up to the present – al-Fasi, Benjelun, Bennani and Kohen for example. In the 18th and 19th centuries they established their control all along and at both ends of the trade route. We thus find their agents not only in Timbuktu, St. Louis, but also in Cairo and Manchester. Though they showed a remarkable spirit of adaptation both with respect to their clientele and to new commercial techniques such as the banking system, they continued to run affairs on a family basis, even junior employees being relations. Their prosperity throughout the 19th century was manifest, as also was their hold on the intermediary phase of the trade between the Sahel and the Moroccan ports, where European firms had their agents. This very monopoly which made them prosperous and influential up to 1900 at least, can also be seen to have had negative features, since it discouraged them from investing locally or providing incentive for those changes which would have made Morocco a producer country. In this way the Sahara can be seen to have played an essential part in Moroccan history but also provides part of the explanation for many aspects of home policy, whether in the political or economic fields.

The Regencies and the central Sahara

The central Saharan routes led off from two particularly favourable areas in terms of resources and trading possibilities: the Niger Bend and Lake Chad.

From the former the desert track crossed the Sahara to reach Algiers, Tunis, or Tripoli; from the latter, it led due north to Fezzan and from there either to Tripoli or to Cairo via the oasis of Awjila in Cyrenaica.

The central Sahara is the home of the Berber Tuareg who are a striking people having at the same time kept up many traditions characteristic of ancient Libyan society, including a Berber dialect, and developed a cohesive warlike society. Popular pictures of the Sahara and its inhabitants have in fact given a dominant position to this particular group whose men rather than women wear veils, the dark blue cloth they use having given rise to the expression 'the Blue People'. Their powerful confederacies – although they have complex local and lineage histories – have developed as four or five major political entities: the Tuareg of the Niger Bend, with, to the north of these, a long drawn out Tuareg area bordering on the western Arab tribes, the Tuareg of Agades and the Aïr, those of the Hoggar in the middle of the desert, and the Ajjir Tuareg around what is now the common frontier of Libya, Algeria and Tunisia. These powerful groups often had a recognized status as sultanates. The cohesive structure of the confederacies was upheld by discipline: that of the desert, that of the tribal leaders including a supreme chief or *amenokal*, and that of the holy men, *inselmen*, who promoted Islamic and tribal order. Here as among the western Arabs, fraternity affiliation was widespread, especially in the holy lineages where in the 19th century the Qadiriyya was increasingly supplanted as the dominant order by the Tijaniyya. The fact that the latter also inspired al-Hajj 'Umar, founder of the Tukulor caliphate, points to Muslim interaction between the Tuareg and their Sudanic neighbours.

Around 1800, two of these Berber principalities are particularly in evidence. The first is that of the Niger Tuareg who in the 17th century, as Sudanic kingdoms including their own Agades Sultanate declined, had entered into a phase of expansion and unification which brought into existence the kingdom of the Iwillimmeden which, at the height of its power between 1770 and 1816, occupied the whole of the Niger Bend region, including the main trading centres, notably Timbuktu and Gao. It had strong political and ideological leadership, the latter being in Kunta hands. Though the kingdom declined after 1816 with the rise of new Muslim African states in the region, and notably the Tukulor caliphate, it was nonetheless a force to be reckoned with as the French found when they fought their way into the region around 1900. The Iwillimmedden derived considerable wealth from their control of the Niger area. Thus the capture of Timbuktu in 1787 brought in a *gharama* (tribute) of 71 000 *mithqal*-s, partly in gold. Moreover they established control over the main sources of North African trade in the region and received regular dues from merchants besides themselves taking an active part in commerce, including participation in slave raids. On the northern edge of the desert, the Tuareg were also well organized and a necessary support to the trans-Saharan trade. The French conquest of Algiers in 1830 was to lead not so much to the decline of the trade as to its reorientation towards the east, thus enhancing the position of the Ajjir Tuareg and their trading centres of Ghat and Ghadames which remained active and prosperous throughout the 19th century.

A closer look at the type of effective economic partnership established by the Regencies with the Ajjir Tuareg points to the importance of this confederacy in parallel to that of the Iwillimmeden. Ghat and Ghadames were the two trading centres where arrangements between northern merchants and their Tuareg associates could be made. According to Duveyrier, the first European to have visited the region in 1860 and described it extensively, the caravans were organized on the spot, and never in Tunis or Tripoli. They were escorted into the desert by the Tuareg who acted as caravan guides and in a more general way accepted to protect the long caravan of camels. They were scrupulously honest, but their honesty had a price which had to be negotiated both with those directly involved and the tribal chiefs. The trading post of Ghat was under Tuareg control and merchants for a fee of 10 *riyal*-s could settle there to carry out their business. They could moreover rent a house there for 6 *riyal*-s, irrespective of the length of their stay. Ghadames, on the other hand, was a non-tribal town though in Tuareg territory, and an independent municipality where the authorities of Tripoli were officially represented, although this had to be periodically reaffirmed by military expeditions, as in 1810 when Yusuf Qaramanli occupied the town. It had both a permanent community and a floating population of merchants, and its inhabitants were collectively referred to as 'people of Ghadames' whatever their origins. All around stretched Tuareg territory and a standard pattern of relations existed between the nomads and the citizens. They were in fact complementary to each other since the traders needed the Tuareg to carry out their trade and the latter depended on the town for their livelihood and certain essential commodities. Moreover, there were accepted practices such as charity for destitute nomads. The Tuareg went in and out of town freely, but avoided spending the night within its walls. The trans-Saharan trade involved a higher strata of traders using sophisticated techniques as Laing, a British traveller who was to die on his way through Tuareg territory, noted in 1825: 'they calculate with profound nicety the expense of carriage to distant countries, duties, customs, risk, trouble, the percentage that their goods will bear, and even do business by means of bills and unwritten agreements and promises'. The merchant families here too had agents at both ends of the route, notably in Tripoli, Tunis, Awjila, and Cairo. They played a leading role and, through education, their children would become part of the northern urban elite.

Of greater importance from the 17th century onwards and notably in the 19th century, both with respect to the value of merchandise (particularly slaves) and its political implications was Bornu and later Kanem trade with Tripoli or Egypt, via the Fezzan. This had up to the end of the 18th century involved indirect Qaramanli control, the trade being based on the collaboration of two sultanates: that of Bornu which extended from Lake Chad to the border of Fezzan, and that of the Sultanate of Fezzan, now the southern province of Libya. The powerful rulers of the Banu Sayf dynasty of Bornu controlled Arab nomads on their territory and involved them in a trade based on raiding on peripheral pagan areas. The Sultanate of Fezzan which had an autonomous status whilst recognizing Tripoli's suzerainty, also had a local hereditary ruling family. Murzuq was the chief trading centre organized on somewhat similar lines to Ghadames, besides having a prosperous annual religious fair. Though the trade in question persisted and indeed was particularly flourishing throughout the 19th century, it was carried out in a changing political context, both with respect to north and south. In the south, the early 19th century was a period of decline for the former powerful Bornu sultanate which saw its former dependencies – Kanem, Borku and Bagirmi – become independent and hostile, whilst 'Uthman Dan Fodio's *jihad* undermined the kingdom to the west and in the south. The caliphate he founded was partially carved out of Bornu territory; moreover it became commercially competitive in its own right with such centres as Kano producing cloth which was sold throughout West Africa, and as far off as the Atlantic and southern Morocco. Around 1800 Bornu's decline was only staved off by recourse to a holy man, Muhammad al-Amin (*circa* 1775–1837), a Kanemi on his father's side, a Fezzani on his mother's. He proved an able statesman and military leader, and was to all intents and purposes the real ruler of the country between 1811 and 1835, the Banu Sayf being reduced to the role of puppets before being eliminated by Muhammad al-Amin's descendants in 1846. To protect the threatened kingdom, Muhammad al-Amin appealed to Yusuf Qaramanli in 1817. This led to more direct Libyan involvement in the region.

The early 19th century, characterized by increased European pressures on North Africa, does not therefore exclude – and indeed it perhaps explains – Libya's attempt to extend its influence southwards and increase its control over the trans-Saharan trade. This will be studied in the context of Yusuf Qaramanli's reign; but, in a long-term perspective of Saharan politics, one may well see the expansion of the Sanusiyya, a Cyrenaican militant sufi fraternity, in the Sahara as a reaffirmation, in a different period and on different ideological lines, of the Qaramanli riposte to the loss of influence in the Mediterranean. The answer, they would both seem to say, is expansion southwards, towards Lake Chad.

Egypt and the eastern Sahara

The eastern trade of North Africa followed a trans-Saharan route leading to Upper Egypt by the famous '40 days' road' (*darb al-arba'in*) and from there to Cairo, or by way of Awjila in Cyrenaica. This, the most active route of the Sudan, was commanded by Dar Fur. The independent sultanate of Dar Fur had become a trading state under a ruling class claiming Arab origins which had seized power in the 17th century. It had converted the inhabitants to Islam and imposed its suzerainty on neighbouring principalities including Wadday. Wadday was itself a trading sultanate ruled since the 17th century by the descendants of 'Abd al-Karim who claimed to be of the 'Abbasid family. The fact that in the 19th century it was able to capitalize on Bornu's growing weakness both politically and commercially further contributed to Dar Fur's power. The latter's prestige was also upheld by a high degree of literacy which included the use of slaves as official secretaries, and by a policy of military expansion which led the Dar Furi Sultan to conquer Kurdufan in the 18th century. The sultanate's main trade was slaves. It was there that men, women and children from the surrounding regions and notably from the Bahr al-Ghazal were brought together. The sultanate was open to North African traders, men from all parts of the continent but notably from the Upper Nile, who migrated along the trade routes and who under the collective name of *jallaba* carried out most of the transactions. They were, however, kept apart from the political institution of the sultanate which, from the 18th century onwards had al-Fashir as its capital, whilst the merchants lived in a town of their own: Qobay, some 40 km north of al-Fashir. The town which was later abandoned had some 6 000–8 000 inhabitants in the 18th century.

Trade remained strictly controlled by the Sultan himself from whom permission for exports had to be requested. It was the Sultan who organized the caravans to Awjila or Asyut in Upper Egypt. This was no small matter since something like 5 000 men and as many camels were generally involved. The journeys had to be well planned and the convoys disciplined. They further had to take into account the sovereignty of states crossed – the Funj dynasty of Sudan prior to 1820 and the Egyptian government authorities. It thus became an elaborate enterprise having its own traditional protocol scrupulously respected all along the road. The caravan was under the leadership of a *khabir* who was the Dar Furi's representative. The number and size of caravans varied according to needs and circumstances, but some were regular traditional features. They included a caravan of pilgrims going to the Holy Places via Cairo. This was sponsored by the Dar Furi Sultan and took with it gifts to be handed over in Mecca. This caravan left every year in time to join the main Egyptian-sponsored pilgrimage which left Cairo every year at the end of the month of Shawwal (the 10th month of the Muslim calendar). There were also two major annual trading caravans which left respectively in February and November. The importance of the Dar Furi trade is indicated not only by the respect shown by the northern states for the Sultan, and his representatives accompanying the caravans, but also by the role of Dar Fur in 19th-century irredentist policies, both of Egypt and of European states.

THE NATURE AND VALUE OF THE BILAD AL-SUDAN TRADE

The kind of trade carried out between the southern principalities and the northern states still has to be defined and its value tentatively assessed. We shall concentrate here on the trade of the east which, in the 18th and 19th centuries was more important than that of other areas. On a smaller scale, the western trade followed the same pattern.

The goods taken south by the northern merchants were already by the 18th century dominated by European products. First came cloth, especially cheap cottons. The Red Sea trade further introduced a colonial commodity: Indian muslins. Cloth represented up to 50 per cent of total southbound exports. We also find metalware, firearms, tea, coffee and sugar. Some North African goods were also sent south including luxury articles such as perfumes, rose-water, coral (from Tunisia), embroidered shawls and some finer cloth including woollen material. Even these, however, tended to be replaced by European products. From the East came beads and cowrie shells (which were used as currency) and from the Maghrib horses – a luxury export commonly bartered for 15 slave women. Sudanese goods taken north included alum, whips, rhinoceros horns, *shishem* (a plant used as an eye-ointment), tamarind, natron, waterskins and gum. These were sometimes exported to the Middle East, whilst gum was in demand in Europe. More important still were African luxury commodities, either destined for the North African ruling class or for export. As gold decreased in importance, ostrich feathers and ivory replaced it. Ivory was of particular importance and in the last years of the 18th century, it represented about 12 per cent of the total value of Sudanic imports entering

Egypt. The main commodity for local use or for export to other parts of the Muslim world was slaves.

Fig. 3.1 North African Currency

Morocco
Bi-metallic (copper and silver). In the 19th century the copper *uqiya* (ounce) became increasingly depreciated whilst the silver *dirham* disappeared. Foreign coins were most often used for trading purposes, notably the Maria Teresa thaler, later replaced by the silver French five-franc coin which was integrated into local currency under the name of *riyal*. Gold coins were rare.

Algeria
French currency after 1830, including the French gold franc worth 9.6 British pence.

Tunisia
The silver *piastre* or *riyal* (worth 52 *nasri*-s). It became increasingly depreciated and by 1873 was worth 0.62 French francs. Foreign coins used including the French 5-franc called locally *riyal duro*.

Libya
The *piastre* which at the beginning of the century was worth roughly a French franc. In 1837, the country reverted to Ottoman currency which became increasingly depreciated. In 1875, the Turkish *piastre* was worth only 0.22 French francs.

Egypt
The Egyptian *piastre* was constantly depreciated. It was worth 1 French franc in 1805 but only a quarter of a franc in 1843. At the end of the century the Egyptian pound (100 *piastres*) was worth about £1.

Sudan
Egyptian currency, except during the *Mahdiyya* when money was minted, though rarely used in trading transactions.

European currency
European coins were largely used for purposes of trade. In the early part of the century, the Maria Teresa thaler was favoured, but was eventually replaced by French and British coins. The stable rate of exchange of the pound was 25 French gold francs, the Maria Teresa thaler being worth a quarter of this.

It has been estimated that in the precolonial period at least 10 000 slaves were exported annually through the Sahara to the various North African markets. Early 19th-century records mention 2500 coming every year to Tunis. In Cairo, in spite of variations, the figure is generally put at 5000–6000 by way of Dar Fur, an extra 500 coming by way of Sennar from Abyssinia. The value of slaves varied considerably according to demand, but also in terms of such criteria as age and sex. Among the more expensive were Abyssinian girls and, most expensive of all, were the eunuchs who were used by wealthier families to guard female abodes. The barbarous custom of mutilating young males was generally carried out in the southern trading outposts, often by burning the testicles between red-hot coins. Slaves represented over 30 per cent of the total value of imports, but the actual figure at which they were sold is not always available in view of the fact that more beautiful girls were rarely put up for auction but were sold privately. Nonetheless early 19th-century records tend to prove that the average price for a slave was 100 Spanish piastres. The Spanish piastre, a silver coin weighing 9 drachmes, was much favoured by Arab traders who imported it in great quantities. It went locally under the name of *riyal*.

Fig. 3.2   Prices for Slaves in Tripoli: 1820s

(Figures given by Gräberg de Hamsö, Swedish consul in Tripoli from 1822 to 1828)

A black eunuch	650 to 700 Spanish piastres
An adult male	90 to 100 Spanish piastres
A youth	70 to 80 Spanish piastres
A boy under 10	40 to 50 Spanish piastres
A woman	120 to 150 Spanish piastres
A girl	90 to 100 Spanish piastres
A girl (under 10)	50 to 60 Spanish piastres

The import of slaves was also profitable for the state since, as merchandise, the slaves were subject to taxation. Thus in Ghadames where Yusuf Qaramanli had appointed officers, dues collected on incoming trade amounted to 9 per cent according to some sources, 13 per cent according to others. In Fezzan, also in the early 19th century, yearly military expeditions brought in between 1000 and 1500 slaves. A quarter of these were for the Sultan, the others were sold. Prices there were much lower than in Tripoli, thus a young girl would fetch about 35 piastres, a boy between 15 to 20. Taxes were paid on all transactions. In Egypt, inventories of the Dar Furi caravan were made by government officials near Asyut and duty was paid on each camel load at the rate of 240 *nisf*-s. Slaves, however, were taxed individually at the rate of 480 *nisf*-s. In the 19th century Muhammad 'Ali increased this to 60 piastres or 2400 *nisf*-s. Taking into account depreciation of local currency in the meantime, this, in fact, represents a doubling of the tax.

A final question on the subject still has to be answered: what variations in the volume of trade and prices took place between 1800 and 1900? Statistics have been brought to light, notably by Terence Walz in his book *Trade between Egypt and Bilad as-Sudan 1700–1820* which show a sharp increase in prices over the years. A male African slave in Cairo was worth on an average 2000 *nisf*-s in 1700, 16 000 in 1800, 40 000 in 1850. One must however here again take into account the constant depreciation of local currency as well as the higher dues imposed by the Egyptian government with a view to discouraging domestic slavery. One can only therefore tentatively interpret these figures which would in fact seem to indicate relatively stable prices. Evidence that would enable an assessment of how far these figures also apply to Morocco (the only country not to have officially forbidden slavery in the latter part of the 19th century) and to the persistent though illegal commerce elsewhere is not at present available.

Slavery is part of the social order in North Africa and has deeply influenced it, as domestic slaves were generally integrated into households where they were often trusted retainers whilst slave women who were concubines would be automatically freed if they bore their master a son. The latter, according to Muslim law, was on an equal footing with other legitimate children. In a more general way, the Prophet's recommendation that slaves should be given their freedom was generally practised by more pious Muslims. This having been said, it should also be recognized that people from the Sudan constituted much of the labour force in North Africa, both in rural areas where they were used to work the land and in towns where they were family servants or trained as craftsmen. Their contribution to the national economy as well as to popular culture should not be forgotten.

These aspects of trans-Saharan relations make it clear that the south constituted a major dimension of North African politics, one which to a large degree determined the prosperity and power of northern states, and this should be borne in mind even if and when, as in the 19th century, international strategy tended to concentrate attention on the North African coast.

SELECTED READING LIST

Abitbol, M., *Tombouctou et les Arma*, (Paris, 1979).
Boahen, A. A., *Britain, the Sahara, and the Western Sudan, 1788–1861*, (Oxford, 1964).
Bovill, E. W., *The Golden Trade of the Moors*, (2nd edition, London, 1958).
Duveyrier, H., *Les Touareg du Nord*, (Paris, 1864).
Fisher, A. and H., *Slavery and Muslim Society in Africa*, (London, 1970).
Folayan, K., 'Tripoli–Bornu political relations, 1817–1825', *Journal of the Historical Society of Nigeria*, V, 4, 1971.
Hopkins, A. G., *An Economic History of West Africa*, (London, 1973).
Lampen, G. D., 'The History of Darfur', *Sudan Notes and Records*, 1950.
Malowist, M., 'Le commerce d'or et d'esclaves au Soudan occidental' *Africana Bulletin*, 4, 1966.
Martin, B. G., *Muslim Brotherhoods in 19th-Century Africa*, (Cambridge, 1976).
Marty, P., *L'Emirat des Trarzas*, (Paris, 1919).
Marty, P., *Etudes sur l'Islam et les tribus maures, les Brakna*, (Paris, 1912).
Meinardus, O., 'The Upper Egyptian practice of the making of eunuchs in the XVIIth and XVIIIth century', *Zeitschrift für Ethnologie*, Band 94, Heft 1, 1969.
Norris, H. T., 'L'amenokal Kawa ou l'histoire des Touareg Iwillimmeden', *Les Africains*, vol. XI, (Paris, 1978).
O'Fahey, R. S., 'Slavery and the Slave Trade in Dar Fur', *Journal of African History*, 14, 1973.
Schultze, A., *The Sultanate of Bornu (1913)*. Translated from the German by P. A. Benton, (London, 1970).
Shinqiti, A. al-, *Al-Wasit fi barajim udaba Shinqit*, (Cairo, 1911).
Stewart, C. C. and Stewart, E. K., *Islam and Social Order in Mauritania*, (Oxford, 1973).
Vernier, B., 'Histoire d'un pays saharien: le Fezzan', *Orient*, 14, 1960.
Walz, T., *Trade between Egypt and Bilad as-Sudan 1700–1820*, (Cairo, 1978).
Zeltner, J. C., *Pages d'histoire du Kanem*, (Paris, 1980).

CHAPTER 4

CONFLICTS AT SEA

The fourth chapter of this introductory part will deal with the northern sea-boundary of the continent, namely the Mediterranean and, with respect to part of Morocco, the Atlantic. That the sea is closely bound up in the history of the region has already been demonstrated by our discussion of the history of the Regencies which were founded as the result of a sea-based conflict between the Ottoman Empire and the Christian states. In a more general way the problems of export trade underlie the economic, social and political trends of the various countries of North Africa, including their trans-Saharan relations. The interrelationship of sea and land must therefore be pointed to although, as we shall see, it is largely obscured by ideological factors, including the persistence up to the early 19th century of corsair activity and the largely unfounded terror this inspired in the naval community at large.

NORTH AFRICAN ROVERS

In an historical context piracy, as practised by the Maghribi states up to the early 19th century, can be seen as an aftermath of the Mediterranean rivalry which had led to the battle of Lepanto and the setting up of a Muslim line of defence by the Turks in North Africa. That the Ottomans had been beaten in their efforts to maintain a balance of power in the Mediterranean was from then on evident. Muslim ships increasingly gave way before those of European states who took command of the major sea-routes and developed new trading relations. As Muslim navies were driven from the sea and were excluded from a share in its more peaceful activities, the Regencies and Morocco increasingly compensated for their losses by piracy. The latter can thus be defined as rearguard tactics of resistance or, to use a more modern idiom, as a terrorist movement aimed at staking a claim in unfavourable political circumstances. Moreover a distinction should be made between *pirates* who are 'freelance' sea-thieves, and *corsairs* who commit similar acts, but by order of their governments. The North African *rais*-es were corsairs, not pirates.

ea-fighting and its result – namely prisoners, commonly called slaves, as indeed they were considering how difficult it was to get them freed – were a traditional feature in the long struggle between Muslims and Christians. In many ways it maintained, well into the modern age, the crusading spirit and part of its appeal to public imagination even today comes from this secular religious and historical tradition. It was not, therefore, one-sided even in the 18th and 19th centuries, although European historians tend to play up the theme of Christian captives in Muslim lands and underplay, or even hide the fact that there were just as many Muslims in slavery in Christian countries. In

Muslim countries, there were a number of such captives including, as we saw earlier with respect to *mamluk*-s, those captured in the outlying provinces of the Ottoman Empire which were frequently raided, but as victims of sea-fighting they constitute a category specifically connected in our period with the Regencies and Morocco. By the 18th century in Christian Europe, Protestant states had formally abolished the practice of holding Muslim slaves; but in Catholic countries, notably those of the Mediterranean, Turks and Moors (two terms generally used at the time when referring to the inhabitants of North Africa) continued to be enslaved. This was further sanctioned by Papal rulings. The Christian Knights of Malta had specialized in the capture of Muslims either in sea-fights or coastal raids, and their island was probably the chief slave-market of the Mediterranean, one which up to the end of the 18th century provided oarsmen and galley-slaves to all neighbouring Catholic countries.

In North Africa Christians captured at sea or on land – and the majority of slaves acquired in the 17th century came from the capture of Spanish fortresses rather than from actual sea-fighting – were generally and increasingly the property of North African sovereigns. In Morocco from 1782 onwards, all European prisoners went to the King. In the Regencies, they were sometimes privately-owned and constituted a kind of speculative investment for wealthier merchants and sea-captains, but even there, slaves generally came to be reserved for the head of state because they were pawns in terms of international bargaining between governments. Christians were kept in special quarters and were put to work on building sites or in the arsenal, besides being used as domestic servants. They had, however, the solace of religion since chapels were to be found in their quarters where priests could freely minister. One should further mention the fact that women and priests were exempted from work, and this was also generally true of ships' captains. Life, of course, was hard even if actual ill-treatment was rare and forced conversions the exception, except with respect to women and children; but even so, the plight of people subjected to an uncertain and often long drawn out captivity was sad. This should not however lead us to accept prevalent popular images of Christian suffering and Muslim cruelty which, to a large degree, were part of the propaganda carried out by religious orders in the 16th–18th century with a view to collecting funds to pay ransom money for poorer captives. Whilst bearing in mind that a captive's lot could rarely be a happy one, we should also remember that experiences could vary and that some men and women not only adapted to local conditions but found these more pleasant than their former lives. There were converts, for example, although such seemingly scandalous facts were kept from the public eye by the European authorities or by the Church and only mentioned in passing as a form of moral depravity. Christians too, though retaining their faith, sometimes chose to stay on in the Regencies. One might mention, among other examples in the 18th and 19th centuries, an American John Cathcart who, as a captive in Algiers, became relatively wealthy by running taverns (which Christians, though prisoners, were allowed to do) and who, when freed, asked to be posted to North Africa. He thus became the United States' first consul in Tripoli in 1799. The American consul named that same year in Algiers, Richard O'Brien, had also been a slave there for ten years. Simon Lucas,

British consul in Tripoli (1793–1801), had been a captive in Morocco.

What were the political and economic facts which the largely lengendary theme of Christian captivity tends to overshadow? From the early 17th century onwards, corsair raiding appears as merely one side of the coin. The other was trade. Thus we find European consuls with regular diplomatic privilege in all the North African states. In Tripoli the first European consul, that of France, was appointed in 1630 and here as in all the other Muslim ports, they were chosen by the Marseilles Chamber of Commerce which also paid their salaries. The Chamber upheld trade whatever the diplomatic relations between France and the countries concerned might be. Periodically war broke out. The *rais*-es were always given strict instructions as to which nations were fair game and which were not, and they themselves were always careful to collect passports from the various consuls in case they should be stopped at sea. Strange as it may seem to us today, war never interrupted trade and complex arrangements were made to prevent incoming ships from being seized once they were in view of the harbour.

How then did war and roving fit into the overall pattern implied by these more peaceful activities? From the point of view of Barbary politics it was a useful and indeed necessary way of upholding trade. Corsair activity provided the navy with a possibility of holding its own in the face of opposition by the European powers. This is indicated by the fact that when the ferocious Knights of Malta were disbanded after Napoleon captured their island in 1798, Tunisian trading ships reappeared in Mediterranean waters – 19 such passages being recorded at Malta in 1800. Raiding by Corsairs was also a useful complement to trade. Part of urban and state revenue came from the sale of the contents of captured ships, the latter being converted for local use. Even this, however, should not loom too large in the context of the 18th century, considering the gradual decline of the Muslim navies. Yearly captures in each of the states were between four and ten, rarely more, and they were generally ships of small tonnage. Thus, to take but one example, the long war between Algiers and the USA (1785–95) brought all told 13 ships and 131 captives.

More important was the use of raiding as a diplomatic threat. The presence of European captives in Muslim lands was a blow to national prestige and this inevitably led sooner or later to diplomatic overtures. An ambassador would be sent out after a preliminary round of negotiations. In cases where Catholic enemy states having permanently bad relations with Morocco or one of the Regencies were involved – this was notably the case of Spain – the authorized mediators were the religious orders such as the Franciscans. They and other missionary orders were specialized in ministering to the captives and arranging for ransom money to be paid in exchange for their liberty. Arrangements led to the Muslim state's obtaining the following advantages:

  a) the freeing of Muslim captives;
  b) ransom money for the slaves (these ranged from 300 to 600 Spanish piastres per head);
  c) and, most important of all, the wherewithal to equip the army and the navy. Collective ransoms were generally paid in this way.

In exchange Europeans obtained a lasting truce (thus the 100-year-truce obtained by Spain from Algiers in 1785) or a regular peace treaty, increasingly accompanied by important trading and consular privileges. Some of the less powerful states (notably Denmark, Sweden, Venice and the USA) further agreed to pay regular subsidies for maintaining peaceful relations.

How powerful were the navies which had this important role in international relations? They were, in fact, surprisingly small and got smaller as the years went by.

Fig. 4.1 Maghribi Navies in the 18th and early 19th Centuries	
Morocco	1716 – 10 ships (10 to 24 guns), 5 row-boats, 1 half-galley. 1764 – 2 frigates, 1 unspecified ship, 2 chebeks, 10 row-boats. 1818 – 1 ship.
Algeria	1724 – 24 ships (unspecified). 1788 – 2 galleys, 8 row-boats.
Tunisia	15 to 30 ships and row-boats throughout the century.
Tripoli	1754 – 2 frigates (26 guns), 2 galleys (24 guns) 10 chebeks (10 to 15 guns). 1829 – 1 corvette, 9 brigs or brigantines.

These fleets were nonetheless the tools used by the Maghribi states to uphold their diplomacy in the face of growing European power which could, and often did resort to blockading and shelling the Barbary harbours.

CORSAIRS AND FOREIGN POLICY

Some of the most important events, and the sequences of treaties connected with them, should be mentioned because, as we shall see, they set the background and in many ways characterize the specific evolution of each of the Maghribi states during the 19th century.

Morocco and the sea

In Morocco, 'Alawi rule and policy had developed on the basis of two apparently contradictory principles: the development of a strong army to control Morocco, expel the Christians, and ward off the threat of foreign invasions, and, at the same time, the need to obtain from Europe the wherewithal to do this, both in terms of revenue and equipment. The dynasty was, in fact, able to reconcile the two by well-nigh absolute royal control over foreign affairs. Here as elsewhere, roving and trade went hand in hand, although from the early 18th century, corsair activity had already begun to decline in view of the growing pressure of Europe, and notably of the British from their base in Gibraltar. Dependence on foreign trade rose in parallel. Mulay Isma'il and his successors, however, kept a strict control over European merchants who were only allowed to settle in government-let houses in the harbours, and their trade was mostly through royal agents. In the troubled period which followed Mulay Isma'il's death in 1727, a privileged partnership was set up with Great Britain which provided Morocco's sovereigns with weapons and gunpowder in exchange for fresh stores for the British colony of Gibraltar. Moreover Gibraltar was an international trading centre to which Moroccans (most of them Jews) had access by agreement between the Governor of Tangier (acting in the King of Morocco's name) and the Governor of Gibraltar. The 1721 treaty signed between Great Britain and Morocco became a permanent agreement which, in spite of periods of tension (and even war in the 1730s), was renegotiated and confirmed throughout the century.

Under Sidi Muhammad bin 'Abd Allah (1757–90), trading rights such as those Britain had obtained were extended to other nations. Thus Denmark (1767), Sweden (1763, 1777), Venice (1765), Austria, Portugal and the USA agreed to pay annual subsidies in order to ensure peace at sea. The more powerful nations – Holland which had signed treaties in 1752 and 1757, Spain in 1767, and France in 1767 – did not pay such humiliating peace-tokens. These numerous diplomatic agreements indicate Morocco's awareness that the confrontation was now no longer at sea but part of the struggle for international trade. The Sultan was already being led to make important concessions, notably with respect to the export of cereals which was forbidden by Muslim law. At the same time, Sidi Muhammad attempted to strengthen the *makhzen*'s control over foreign trade by creating a new port on the Atlantic in the 1760s: al-Sawira. He intended to make this the chief and if possible the sole place where foreign transactions could take place. He therefore ordered the consuls to establish themselves there and had a number of Jewish trading families called in from Tangier, Tetuan, and Agadir. Tariffs were lowered to 2 per cent *ad valorem* and efforts were made to put a ban on exports from other Moroccan harbours. By 1780, there were already 12 European firms established at al-Sawira and the town continued to develop throughout the 19th century. This, however, did not reduce exports from other harbours as their parallel development shows.

A peaceful trading policy required that an official end be put to the by now obsolete problem of the capture of European prisoners which had been abandoned, whilst even shipwrecked mariners were released by virtue of existing treaties. Sidi Muhammad consequently suggested that an international agreement be reached formally abolishing the practice. This did not at the time suit those governments he contacted and the project fell through. It was finally Mulay Sulayman (1792–1822) who took a unilateral decision in this respect in 1816.

The imbalance of the situation was already apparent and was to become clearer in the 19th century. Morocco had by now lost much of its strategic importance as a trading partner; moreover, if Morocco signed treaties and granted commercial advantages, it was in no position to counterbalance these by the threat represented by a powerful navy and a strong foreign policy. By 1820, it had only a single ship left and this was given as a present to Algiers. European threats consequently had a compelling effect as was shown when the French attacked in 1765 or when the Dutch carried out a naval demonstration in 1774. Even the Sublime Porte could now bring pressure to bear on Morocco and it did so in 1779 to obtain the release of a Greek ship. Morocco, by the late 18th century, was already faced with the choice between accepting an unequal trading partnership with Europe or isolation. As we shall see, it practised both and favoured the second without, however, being able to control the issue.

Algeria and the sea

The decline of the fleet and of commercial activity in general in the course of the 18th century also characterized Algeria. Once famous for its six slave-prisons, five hospitals for captives, and for its thousands of prisoners, Algiers, by 1785, had only three prisons and one hospital left. In spite of efforts to put up a brave show on the international scene as, for example, when its fleet was sent out to help the Ottomans against Russia in 1770, Algiers was forced to resign itself to a decline which had economic rather than military causes. The Atlantic sea-routes were increasingly important and consequently much trade bypassed the Mediterranean, such traffic as there was being concentrated at the eastern end of the sea. On land Algeria could still defend itself and the disaster the Spanish met with after their abortive landing in 1775, although much helped by the weather, seemed to prove this even if, a few years later in 1785, the Dey was led to accept a 100-years' truce with his country's traditional and permanent enemy. The French, by a combination of naval demonstrations and privileged agreements – Algiers was increasingly dependent for its foreign trade on Marseilles – had a dominant position. Under the protection of the Marseilles Chamber of Commerce, the Compagnie d'Afrique had already established three trading posts: La Calle, Bone, and Collo whose privileges were confirmed in 1714. The company had coral fishing rights and increasingly bought up cereals for export to France. In Algiers itself, a small minority of traders was acquiring a pre-eminent position, namely the Livornian Jews. In the 18th century Leghorn acted as an entrepôt from which Maghribi and other Eastern goods were redistributed all over Europe, furnishing in return those products in which the Muslim world was interested (Venetian glass, spices, sugar, and coffee).

At the end of the century, in the wake of the European wars which followed the French Revolution, Algiers tried to consolidate its position as a Mediterranean power. This led to a revival of corsair activity and to a number of conflicts, not only with the smaller Italian states, but also with the USA. War with the latter began in 1785 when the Algerians captured a schooner, the *Maria*, and only ended in 1795 after difficult negotiations. The peace settlement contained a number of clauses which were highly profitable for the Dey, including the gift of a frigate, military stores, and other presents. It is already a sign of new times that these arrangements should have been worked out by a Leghorn Jew, Micaiah Bacri and a European bank, the highly respected Baring & Baring firm of London.

As a closing picture of 18th-century Algiers, one may recall the final spurt of corsair activity which led to the capture of 1500 Europeans between 1802 and 1815, but even here the fact that times were changing is clear. Not only in 1815 did the USA obtain a revision of their treaty with Algiers by pointing guns on the town, but the European captives were all released in 1816 when an international fleet of 18 warships bombarded the city. The imbalance was not only patent, it could not be more clearly signified.

Tunisia and the sea

Tunisia, too, had begun as a corsair state and in the 18th century followed the same pattern of military-cum-trading activities, interrelated by means of complex negotiations in which references to treaties concluded with other Barbary states played a leading role. The Great Powers tended to deal at one and the same time with all the Regencies. Thus the 1816 naval demonstration undertaken by Lord Exmouth (Great Britain) and Admiral Van Cappellen (Holland) went successively from Algiers to Tunis, to Tripoli, whilst the American peace treaty with Algiers was paralleled by similar agreements with Tunis and Tripoli. The difference between Tunis and Algiers lay in the former's greater trading prosperity which can be illustrated by the following figures: out of 311 ships which sailed from North Africa to Leghorn between 1794 and 1798, 228 came from Tunisia. The relationship with Leghorn was a close one, and by its means Tunisia exported its products, including *shashiya*-s, and imported such luxury goods as Kashmiri shawls, white slaves and dyes, besides more indispensable commodities such as rice and wool. Some of these goods were for the Tunisian market, but Tunisia itself had an entrepôt function with respect notably to the Sahara. Here too economic imbalance is nonetheless apparent as Tunisia increasingly exported raw materials and imported manufactured products. The former included cereals and olive oil, Tunisia's chief trading partner being Marseilles.

The situation which prevailed in Europe at the end of the 18th century was characterized by food shortage and wars. As growing demands were made on Tunisia, the appearances of prosperity returned and with it optimism as to the nation's economic capacity. Illustrative of this was the arrival in Tunis of European immigrants who, for the most part, came from equally poor parts of the Mediterranean, but also included a number of active merchants who sometimes went into partnership with local men, often Jews from the rising urban trading class. This partnership was soon to come into its own as part of Tunisia's relations with the outside world, and notably Europe.

Tripoli and the sea

Most people would tend to see Tripoli in a different light, forgetting that up to the early 19th century, it was, in fact, typical of the cosmopolitan world of the Mediterranean. Of course Tripoli had been founded as a Muslim naval state and *rais*-es, here as elsewhere, were a typical feature. Indeed the Regency was involved in the same sort of problems as its neighbours: captures at sea and the presence of Christian captives whose liberation was obtained by a combination of naval demonstrations and political bargaining; but this in no way belies a non-fanatical atmosphere in which foreigners were tolerated and even well accepted.

This was true in the first place at official level since Tripoli of all the Barbary states was probably the one where foreign flags and consular privileges were most scrupulously respected. Agreements of long standing could be reached as is proved by Great Britain's signing a treaty with Tripoli as early as 1675, after which no British captives were ever made. The French obtained the freedom of their nationals by bombarding the town in 1685 and their last prisoners were sent home in 1698. Few French prisoners were taken after that date and their liberation was always easily obtained. Holland,

Sweden and Denmark signed treaties in the course of the 18th century, with the further advantage for Tripoli of regular subsidies. Relations with the USA, however, proved difficult, especially when in 1794 Congress authorized the building of a navy to protect its shipping, and this ultimately led to an actual war between the two countries, lasting from 1801 to 1805. Tripoli was also on a bad footing with its immediate neighbours, namely the various states of the Italian peninsula, and more or less continual raiding was the rule with respect to Sicily, Naples, Sardinia, the Papal States, and sometimes Venice and Genoa.

In spite of these warlike activities Tripoli was as pleasant a Mediterranean port as any and it is perhaps important to note this before going on to consider a period which was to bring to the fore power-based relations, mutual hate and fear, and to remember that the Mediterranean had in the past also inclined to cosmopolitan tolerance. European merchants and consuls often spent long and happy years there as is proved by consul Tully, *en poste* from 1768 to 1793, and his sister who left a picturesque account of Tripoli under Qaramanli rule, *A Narrative of Ten Years' Residence at Tripoli*. Europeans, both Christians and converts to Islam, coexisted with Muslims on a friendly footing, and exceptional though such cases were, they nonetheless go to show that east and west sometimes meet. But here as in the other Regencies, a new stage was already set when Lord Exmouth and Admiral Van Cappellen's warships turned their guns on the citadel of Tripoli to obtain from the Pasha, together with the liberation of 500 captives, an official statement declaring that the corsairs had had their day.

CORSAIR-RAIDING WITH EUROPEAN PERMISSION

This account of international relations between the Barbary states and the European nations, not to mention the USA, leaves one tantalizing question unanswered. If, as suggested here, the Barbary corsairs were a limited factor in the history of the Mediterranean in the precolonial period, why were they so much feared? Why did the 17th-century legend surrounding them survive into the early 19th century? Why did the obviously more powerful forces of the European states allow the corsairs to maintain a minimal activity? A closer look at the facts has only served to highlight the contradiction. The North African fleets were a negligible phenomenon. Indeed insurance premiums – a practical test – did not take corsair risk into account. Yet popular clamour was loud, and, at the highest level, the problem was discussed quite seriously. In 1816, the international conference of London debated on common European action. The plan was vetoed by the French, but nonetheless led to Lord Exmouth's show of strength. In spite of this, the French, 15 years later, were to put forward as their official motive for invading Algiers the need to put an end to piracy.

To understand this peculiar situation, we must consider different levels of public opinion and the way they interrelated. The fear of Barbary corsairs had been instilled in the 17th century into popular culture, and notably in regions where poverty drove men out to sea. These sailors characteristically worked the smaller traditional Mediterranean ships, carrying goods from one port to another, and having on board crews of between 10 and 20 men. These were easy prey for corsairs. In the 18th century, this was still the case for smaller ships, especially when they belonged to weak states, not only those which had traditionally carried out the Mediterranean trade but new northern countries such as Denmark, Sweden, and even at the time the USA. It was not the case for the new dominant states and for their faster and more powerful fleets. The trading convoys that France, Great Britain, or Holland sent across the seas were rarely or never attacked. That these powerful nations, who in addition had warships stationed in the region, could have put an end to what remained of corsair activity is obvious. That they did not choose to do so in the 18th century is equally obvious. In fact a climate of insecurity, real or artificial, probably suited their purposes. It reduced both Muslim trade and that of the smaller Latin states. With respect to the former the French chargé d'affaires in Malta quite cynically stated in 1790 that the piratical knights helped promote the trade of Marseilles for, as he put it, 'our principal interest lies in preventing the Turks from loading goods on their own ships and maintaining them under our dependence'. The same attitude prevailed with respect to smaller Christian shipping. Both Great Britain and France had refused to afford protection to American vessels when the latter appeared in European waters in the 18th century. In fact, they welcomed their capture by corsairs as a way of eliminating a possible rival. Lord Sheffield made the point quite clearly in a House of Commons debate in 1783: 'The Americans cannot pretend to a navy, and therefore the great nations should suffer the Barbary pirates as a check on the activities of the smaller Italian states and America.'

Not only did the great powers, who in the 18th century were busy promoting their own trade and establishing their monopoly rights over trade routes, tolerate Barbary corsairs, but they actively helped to maintain them in existence by furnishing the North African states with naval and military equipment. As long as it served their policy, it was therefore discreetly encouraged. When the new world strategy of imperialism involved direct Anglo-French confrontation, as it did during the Napoleonic wars, the Barbary states found a last loophole to maintain their claim to being naval states, but quite logically, when direct confrontation between the Great Powers was replaced by economic rivalry, it was by imperialist agreement decided that piracy had had its day. It disappeared and with it disappeared the old order of things in the Mediterranean.

SELECTED READING LIST

Barnby, H. G., *The Prisoners of Algiers. An Account of the Forgotten American-Algerian War 1785–1797*, (London, 1966).

Bono, S., *I Corsari Barbareschi*, (Turin, 1964).

Cathcart, J. L., *The Captives*, (Indiana, 1899).

Clissold, S., *The Barbary Slaves*, (London, 1977).

Dan, P., *Histoire de Barbarie et de ses Corsaires*, (Paris, 1637).

Dearden, S., *A Nest of Corsairs*, (London, 1976).

Fisher, G., *Barbary Legend. War, Trade and Piracy in North Africa (1415–1830)*, (Oxford, 1957).

Julien, Ch.-A., *Histoire de l'Afrique du Nord*, (Paris, 1931).

Lane Poole, S., *The Barbary Corsairs*, (London, 1890).

Masson, P., *Histoire des établissements et du commerce français dans l'Afrique Barbaresque*, (Paris 1903).

Mathiex, J., 'Trafic et Prix de l'homme en Méditerranée aux XVIIe et XVIIIe siècles' in *Annales*, 9, 1954.

NORTH AFRICA

Playfair, R. L., *The Scourge of Christendom*, (London, 1884).
Riggio, A., 'Relazioni della Toscana granducale con la Reggenza di Tunisi (1818–1825)' *Oriente Moderno*, 20, 1940.
Valensi, L., *Le Maghreb avant la prise d'Alger*, (Paris, 1969).

PART II
THE COLONIAL OPENING 1800–48

INTRODUCTION

In sketching out the background to 19th-century history, we have already pointed to many aspects of a changing world context leading dominant nations to adopt an aggressive stance towards the Muslim world. The period covered by this section, namely 1800 to 1848, though generally termed precolonial, in fact saw a build-up of economic and political pressures to which the North African states in particular were subjected. Their history shows that the process referred to as imperialism was in fact well under way.

The century indeed opens on a typically imperial scene: the conquest of Egypt by Napoleon Bonaparte in 1798, followed by a military occupation which lasted until 1801. The French were only driven out by a combined Anglo-Turkish force and the British troops stayed on in Egypt until 1803. In 1830, Algiers was attacked by the French and an expeditionary corps occupied the town. What was supposed to be a mere punitive raid in fact turned into a full scale occupation and a colonial regime which lasted until 1962. In various ways all the North African states found themselves involved in the situation resulting from these invasions, although the attitudes of the governments involved were not always clear-sighted with respect to the major threat of European intervention. Tunisia took some part in the initial period of the conquest of Algeria, not on the Regency's side but in support of the French who had promised territorial and political concessions to the ruling Bey. Egypt which toyed with a similar idea was led instead to invade Sudan in 1820. In Algeria itself initial resistance was weak although a powerful reaction soon set in under the leadership of 'Abd al-Qadir. In Morocco, support of 'Abd al-Qadir was given up when the French shelled the Moroccan ports of Tangier and al-Sawira and defeated the royal army in 1844. In the ensuing negotiations (treaty of Tangier, 10 September 1844), the Moroccan delegates were led to agree to no further help being given to 'Abd al-Qadir. This largely contributed to his downfall in 1847.

The period is therefore one of military and naval aggressions, besides diplomatic pressures which must be examined in the light of the strategy of what were now the Great Powers, namely France, Russia, and Great Britain, and must further be defined with respect to their main Muslim partner and victim, the Ottoman Empire. This was part of what was a little later to be called the 'Eastern Question'. The decision-making centres were now the European capitals and the fate of the world was something decided upon by the Great Powers, notably in such international meetings of statesmen and diplomats as the Congress of Vienna, held in 1815. We shall therefore be led to ask what the objectives of the Great Powers were, especially as these, though involving foreign conquests, were, in fact, in this period characterized by an armed neutrality known as the 'balance of power policy'.

This in no way means that the Muslim states were not directly involved in the momentous events taking place in the world, and notably in industrial Europe. Indeed Muslim reaction was evident throughout North Africa. The form which heightened awareness of danger took was, however, more complex than one might imagine. The ruling classes, whilst resentful, often tried to promote their interests and to this end sometimes attempted a policy of cooperation with the aggressors, whilst among the people more marked opposition came out which expressed itself either in a military or ideological fashion. In a more general way one may point to a nascent self-awareness through an experience of what to a Muslim was an unacceptable situation, namely Christian dominion over a part of the *dar al-Islam*.

CHAPTER 5

THE INTERNATIONAL SETTING

The first and in many ways the most spectacular of the early colonial wars of the 19th century was Napoleon Bonaparte's invasion of Egypt in 1798. It heralded a new age of European preponderance with Paris or London as the decision-making centres of oriental policy. This is well illustrated by Bonaparte (not as yet the Emperor Napoleon I) whose motives for leaving Paris where bourgeois rule fought its last battles against what remained of the popular aspirations of the 1789 revolution, were essentially national. His stay in Egypt was itself an episode of the long European war which lasted from 1792 to 1815. The occupation of Egypt was to some degree the result of an accident: the fact that Nelson who had set up a blockade in the Mediterranean, caught up with Napoleon's fleet off Abukir and, on 1 August 1798, destroyed it. The army, much dismayed, found itself prisoner in Egypt. Just as he had come to the East for reasons connected with the political situation in the French capital, so Bonaparte left it for the same reason a year later: in August 1799, he secretly re-embarked, giving his officers and troops the impression that he was abandoning them to their fate. Whilst he was in Paris making his bid for power, the French army in Egypt, cruelly harassed, set about negotiating conditions for evacuation which, with British help, it was able to effect in 1801. And yet, though an event of European import, with the Great Powers playing out their rivalry in the Mediterranean, Napoleon's invasion of Egypt was also momentous for Muslims in general and for North Africa in particular; but to appreciate this one must take into account the implications of the situation in international relations and in the balance of power in the Mediterranean.

THE EGYPTIAN CAMPAIGN

Bonaparte's expedition, whatever the fortuitous circumstances which may have surrounded it, was no mere historical accident, but rather part of a European strategy characteristic of the 19th century. The fact that Great Britain in 1795, three years before the French landed in Egypt, had had similar plans drawn up for the conquest of Alexandria, Cairo and Suez, is in itself proof of this. Britain felt the need to protect its prized possession: India. At the very time that the French occupied the northern end of the Red Sea, the British took over the southern end by setting up a military base on the island of Perim in 1799, this being transferred to Aden in 1802. At various times throughout this period, moves were made by France, independently or conjointly with Russia, to contest British control of the route to India. Russia, besides attempting to obtain for itself right of way to the Mediterranean, tried to advance overland to Afghanistan. This was part of 'the Great Game' which even the establishment of a British Protectorate over Afghanistan in 1879 did not bring to an end. The Eastern Question was dominated by the problem of the Ottoman Empire which not only extended over a large strategic zone, but which further had suzerainty over various other Muslim states including Egypt and the Regencies. The Ottoman Sultan moreover was accepted by Muslims throughout the world as the legitimate descendant of the early leaders of the Muslim community. Involvement in the Mediterranean thus implied a policy largely determined by the attitude taken with respect to the Ottoman Sultan.

Bonaparte's invasion of Egypt marked a reversal of France's traditional policy of friendship and alliance with the Sublime Porte which went back to the reign of Francis I (1515–1547). The break with the Sultan by a direct attack on a province over which he had suzerain rights was therefore of some concern to the French who ambiguously tried to put over the idea that their landing was in fact an attempt to bolster up Ottoman authority by punishing rebellious *mamluk* officers in Egypt. The view was expressed by Napoleon himself in a famous proclamation issued in French and in Arabic on his landing in Alexandria. It was, however, contradicted by the Sultan, Salim III, who sent out *firman*-s to all parts of the Empire declaring Holy War against the French because, as he put it, Muslims could not tolerate the main Pilgrimage road being under foreign control. Further, in September 1798, he formally declared war on France. The story of the campaign and of French policy in Egypt marks the progressive breakdown of secular amity and the setting on foot of a colonial policy at Turkey's expense.

In Egypt Napoleon had been at great pains to pose as a liberator come to free the oppressed natives from the tyrannical rule of the foreign *mamluk*-s. He at the same time expressed respect for Egypt which had had a great civilization, and for modern Egyptians whose religious convictions he professed to share. Indeed, in the course of his stay in Egypt, he expressed his willingness to convert to Islam, and some of his officers sometimes more genuinely did so. In what we would today consider as a modern-type colonial attitude, he respected local society, upheld the prestige of notables and religious leaders, and went out of his way to be popular by encouraging local traditions. He also posed as the protector of the annual caravan to the Holy Places. This was of considerable importance, not only for Cairo which, with much ceremony, provided the *mahmal*, a splendidly decorated empty litter, and the *kiswa*, an embroidered cloth, which were sent out every year to the Holy Places, but for Muslims from all parts of North and Sudanic Africa who traditionally joined the other pilgrims in the Egyptian capital. Bonaparte even wrote to the *sharif*-s of Mecca posing as protector of the *hajj*.

In spite of this, Napoleon's pro-Islamic policy failed, first and foremost because it was never accepted or taken seriously by the Egyptians themselves. The presence of the French was, at best, tolerated. As the French army moved in from the coast to Cairo in July 1798, it was constantly attacked by the Beduins. The French were only able to maintain their hold over the country by campaigns marked sometimes by heavy fighting and casualties. Moreover local conditions and diseases, including a severe outbreak of the plague, took their toll and the Egyptians made a point of showing satisfaction at the sight of maimed or wounded soldiers. The Egyptians, though formerly critical of the

An Egyptian 'Abd al-Rahman al-Jabarti who was in Cairo during its occupation by Napoleon, describes French behaviour after riots in the town . . .

After the first watch of the night, the French entered the city like a torrent rushing through the alleys and streets without anything to stop them, like demons of the Devil's army. They destroyed any barricades they encountered. They went and came as they pleased and brought the wrath of God upon their heads. A group of them entered Bab al-Barqiyya and crossed to al-Ghuriyya, rushing about in all directions without taking rest. And they knew for sure that there was no defender or ambush awaiting them, so they had free scope and did whatever they felt like, moving about freely on horse and on foot. Then those wild goats rode into the mosque on horses, entering through the big gate and going out from the other to the place where the donkeys were tied. And the French trod in the Mosque of al-Azhar with their shoes, carrying swords and rifles. Then they scattered in its courtyard and its main praying area and tied their horses to the *qibla*. They ravaged the students' quarters and ponds, smashing the lamps and chandeliers and breaking up the bookcases of the students, the *mujawirun*, and the scribes. They plundered whatever they found in the mosque, such as furnishings, vessels, bowls, deposits, and hidden things from closets and cupboards. They treated the books and Quranic volumes as trash, throwing them on the ground, stamping on them with their feet and shoes. Furthermore they soiled the mosque, blowing their spit in it, pissing, and defecating in it. They guzzled wine and smashed the bottles in the central court and other parts. And whoever they happened to meet in the mosque they stripped. They chanced upon someone in one of the *ruwaqs* and slaughtered him. Thus they committed deeds in al-Azhar which are but little of what they are capable of, for they are enemies of the Religion, the malicious victors who gloat in the misfortune of the vanquished, rabid hyenas, mongrels obdurate in their nature.

Tarikh Muddat al-Faransis bi-Misr
Translated by S. Moreh, *Al-Jabarti's Chronicle of the First Seven Months of the French Occupation of Egypt*, Leiden, 1975.

mamluk-s, now showed loyalty to them. The leading *bey*-s who had fled (Ibrahim to Syria, Murad to Upper Egypt) found local support to engage in rearguard actions against the French. Even in the conquered cities, including Cairo, people made a point of looking after *mamluk* families and the womenfolk who had been left behind. Correspondence was kept up with the *mamluk*-s and with Istanbul. The French hunted down those they considered as Turkish agents: some were executed, others fined or imprisoned. To establish their control over a hostile population, a strong police force was set up and local auxiliaries were recruited. Spying was rife. In spite of iron rule and martial law, the French were left with no illusions and even a minority of collaborators could not hide the fact that they were unwelcome. Indeed this was shown up on many tragic occasions: in October 1798 Cairo rose up in arms. On 14 June, 1800, Bonaparte's successor General Kleber was murdered. In 1800 Cairo again revolted.

Fig. 5.1 A summary of events: the French in Egypt 1798–1801

1798

July 2	French fleet lands at Alexandria
July 21	Battle of the Pyramids
July 24	Cairo occupied
August 1	Nelson destroys French fleet at Abukir
September	Popular discontent grows
October 21	Cairo revolts
November	Execution of prominent citizens
	The 'ulama forced to declare themselves in favour of French rule

1799

January	Fighting continues around Cairo
Feb–June	Bonaparte in Syria. Meets with defeat
June	Napoleon back in Cairo
July	Execution of prominent citizens
August	Bonaparte leaves Egypt secretly
	General Kleber takes over as Commander-in-Chief
Sept.–Dec.	Growing tension in Egypt. Turks invade Egypt. The British asked to mediate between France and the Ottomans

1800

January	French and Turks negotiate
March	French evacuate Cairo. Riots
April	French reconquer Cairo
June 14	Kleber killed by Sulayman al-Halabi
	General 'Abd Allah Menou takes over
Aug.–Dec.	French rule becomes ever more oppressive

1801

January	Efforts by Menou to bring the *Diwan* to collaborate are unavailing
February	The plague spreads
March	The French prepare to leave Egypt
April	Rosetta taken by Anglo-Turkish troops
	Fighting continues between French and Anglo-Turks
June 18	The Ottomans recapture Cairo
September 3	Menou surrenders in Alexandria

How indeed could alien oppressive control by a foreign army of occupation be anything but unacceptable, whatever official policy might be and however much more distinguished officers and orientalists might attempt to make it palatable? Not only did the soldiery behave as might be expected in the circumstances, but the army, receiving no money or stores from abroad because of the blockade, was forced to live off the land. Taxation and even such useful measures as sanitary regulations to prevent the plague spreading, created resentment. Tensions led to numerous incidents and these could only bring out the real nature of the regime. Thus when the Cairo riots took place, al-Azhar was occupied by the army and horses were stabled in the mosque which was defiled.

Colonial rule has an inner logic of expansion and the Egyptian campaign was no exception. Early in 1799, Bonaparte took the major part of his army to Syria with a view to gaining a foothold in the Middle East, besides crushing *mamluk* opposition on the way. The ultimate aim of the campaign was the capture of Acre. Scenes of great cruelty took place during the army's forward march, but the essential objective was not reached. Acre successfully withstood the siege and Napoleon was forced to retreat. The return journey proved a disaster with the plague taking many victims. In spite of optimistic communiqués, the Egyptians were in no doubt as to the outcome and when, in August 1799, news of Napoleon's clandestine departure spread, this was seen as the beginning of the definite withdrawal of the French forces. Throughout 1800 and up to September 1801, the French Commander-in-Chief, Kleber and, after the latter's death, General Menou made efforts to keep the situation under control. The fact that Menou had himself converted to Islam under the name of 'Abd Allah and married a local woman from Damietta in no way implied a less repressive regime.

Menou's chief task was to obtain satisfactory conditions for evacuation. His position became increasingly difficult as Turkish troops moved in on the eastern frontier whilst throughout the country people rose up against the oppressors. Muslims from Arabia had crossed to Upper Egypt and together with the *mamluk*-s were fighting their way north. Even in Cairo the situation became difficult and even dramatic when riots forced the French momentarily to evacuate the town in March 1800. Great Britain had come out openly in support of the Ottomans. Troops were sent out from India and, having landed on the Red Sea coast, progressed up the Nile Valley. A joint Anglo-Turkish expeditionary force was organized and the British fleet provided the ships to transport the troops to Rosetta. By Spring 1801, the French were in a hopeless situation: nonetheless negotiations dragged on a further three months. In June, Menou and his men withdrew to the coast, Cairo being retaken by national forces on the 18th. On 3 September, Menou surrendered and, with the remnants of his army, embarked on British ships.

THE EASTERN QUESTION

Napoleon's campaign in Egypt with its somewhat humiliating conclusion highlights a new pattern of tension in the Mediterranean which was a direct threat to Ottoman sovereignty. The champion of Ottoman independence and major opponent of the dismemberment of its empire was Great Britain, in spite of a few encroachments of its own on Turkish territory. Britain upheld this in the face of the powerful threat not only of Napoleon's Eastern policy, but also of Russian irredentism. This was particularly evident in Crimea and Georgia leading Turkey to declare war in 1787 to uphold its claim on Crimea. Austria sided with Russia (1787–90). A settlement was ultimately worked out, Britain and Austria mediating the treaty of Yassy in 1792 confirmed Russia's advance in the region. The Great Powers, after the conquest of Egypt by France, were led to work out a provisional solution to the situation created by rival European ambitions. This was to be the preservation of the Ottoman Empire, though in a weakened form allowing for peripheral encroachments. Egypt was thus to have a semi-independent status under the rule of *bey*-s recognizing the suzerainty of the Ottoman Sultan. The agreement which was worked out by Britain and Russia, was accepted by France (Treaty of Amiens, 27 March, 1802) and later included in a treaty signed by France and Turkey on 25 June, 1802.

This inconclusive arrangement marked an intensification of the unjustified claims of each of the Great Powers. Britain clearly showed its unwillingness to give up tactical advantages obtained through the support it had given the Ottomans, and it was only under considerable international pressure that it agreed to withdraw its troops from Egypt in accordance with the stipulations of the Treaty of Amiens. It flaunted the latter with respect to the island of Malta which had been taken by Nelson and which Britain now refused to give back to the Knights as promised. Indeed this was to be one of the causes for the resumption of hostilities with France in 1803. Russia continued to show an active interest in the northern provinces of the Ottoman Empire and in the overland route to the Far East. France, though increasingly involved on the continent, did not forget Egypt or the route to India, besides considering the possibilities of an eventual invasion of other parts of North Africa. Napoleon I sent out to Morocco and each of the Regencies remarkable officers to give a military account of the region: Burel to Morocco, Boutin to Algiers (and it was, in fact, his project for a landing at Sidi Ferruch which was used by the French in 1830) and Sebastiani to Libya.

In the years which followed the settlement of the Egyptian campaign, European rivalries were transferred to home ground. This ultimately led to Napoleon's invasion of Russia and his signal defeat there in 1812. European realignments and the coalition against France brought about his abdication in 1814 after a defeat at Prussian, Austrian, and Swedish hands. A last effort to re-establish his authority failed at Waterloo on 18 June 1815, and brought the Napoleonic saga to an end. The Eastern Question, however, remained open. This was apparent at the Congress of Vienna convened in 1815 to draw conclusions from France's defeat and establish post-Napoleonic Europe on a sounder footing. Under Britain's influence, a new principle of international relations was put into operation: the balance of power. This implied that France maintain its status as a Great Power and that the irredentism of other nations be subordinated to an overall equilibrium. The Congress deliberately avoided making clear its position with respect to the Ottoman Empire, and the few references made to the Eastern Question already pointed to future imperial expansion. Thus Britain obtained confirmation of its possessions in the Mediterranean, including Gibraltar, Malta, and the Ionian Islands which, though independent, were placed under its protection.

European peace can thus be seen as a prelude to imperial aggression on the Ottoman Empire. Russia was the first to illustrate this as, in the wake of the Congress of Vienna, it began massing its forces on the Balkan frontier. At the same time the Great Powers began showing a not disinterested sympathy for resistance movements in the Turkish provinces, notably Greece. European involvement in the region was discussed in the chanceries thus making it plain that the solution of problems within the Muslim empire was now to be worked out by the European nations and to their advantage. This was exemplified in Greece where the nationalist uprising against the Turks created a critical situation in the 1820s. Great Britain and Russia decided that the country was to become independent whilst paying the Sultan an annual indemnity. A European conference was held in London in 1827 to which France was invited and the decision with respect to Greece was part of the agreement known as the Treaty of London which was signed on 6 July 1827. The agreement also reaffirmed the balance of power principle by stating that no single European state was to make a direct move in the region. When the Sublime Porte refused to accept the treaty's recommendations, a combined naval force was sent out to the region and, as a result of what was described as an 'unfortunate event', the Turkish fleet was utterly destroyed in Navarino Bay. Russia attacked on land and the Ottomans were forced to accept Greek independence at Poros (1828) and later at the London Conference (1830) which further provided that the Great Powers were to have a free hand in the matter of 'peaceful political and economic penetration in the Balkans'. Russia acquired protectorate rights over Moldavia and Wallachia, indirect control over Serbia and Greece, besides becoming the official protector of all Christians in the region. Not only had the dismembering of the Ottoman Empire begun, but the threat to Turkish sovereignty in the Balkans was from then on to mobilize the efforts of the Sublime Porte whose military forces were concentrated in Central Europe and along the Russian frontier. It further had to avoid antagonizing any of the Great Powers for fear of creating the occasion for more direct interventions. The situation largely explains the incapacity of the Turks to protect their western flank. Attacks in that direction were not slow to follow: in 1830, France invaded Algiers.

THE FRENCH ATTACK ON ALGIERS

The raid on Algiers is generally described in terms of subsequent history as the beginnings of colonial rule in North Africa. From a contemporary point of view, its significance was somewhat different and its ultimate ends unclear. The French King, Charles X, took an international risk by launching an attack which was bound to stir up European fears, but it was nonetheless a calculated one in view of Ottoman weakness since the Sultan could only depend on the lukewarm support of Britain and Austria; moreover Britain's defence of Turkey was subordinated to its own Mediterranean strategy which included control of the naval bases and the protection of India against Russian encroachments. It therefore wished to avoid a showdown which would lead to a coalition of France, Russia, and Prussia. The attack was also dictated by French home policy: it was a means of upholding the authority of Charles X and his right wing government headed by Polignac in the face of mounting opposition. A feat of arms would, it was felt, bring the king personal glory and little more than that was envisaged at the time.

Of course, before making such a move France had to neutralize eventual foreign opposition. Initially Polignac envisaged Egyptian participation in the attack. This, he believed, would limit French responsibilities and divide Muslim opinion. Would it not further show that France had special interests in

North Africa? The ruler of Egypt, Muhammad 'Ali, was not averse to staking a claim on Algiers and the Regencies. His motives were not merely political but also economic: the fact that because of high taxes in Egypt much of the trans-Saharan trade was now going to Tripoli made him wish to extend his influence westwards. However Britain refused this and the Duke of Wellington, then Prime Minister, made it clear that he would oppose Egyptian participation in the expedition at the cost of war if need be. The idea was consequently given up. Britain further advocated a minimal formal recognition of Ottoman suzerainty over Algiers. France was thus led to write to the Sultan asking for permission to launch a raid on Algiers to punish the Dey Husayn (1818–1830) who, it was claimed, had encouraged piracy and shown disrespect to the French consul. The fact that the French ambassador in Constantinople at the time was informed that Polignac would go ahead with his plans, whether or not the Sultan agreed, shows up the insignificance of this diplomatic move. Moreover the Great Powers, and notably Britain, though they felt that the situation did not permit the actual dismembering of the Ottoman Empire, were nonetheless prepared to accept limited forms of encroachment. Pressure was consequently brought to bear on the Sultan to make him adopt a conciliatory attitude to French claims. The Sultan gave in and at Britain's request named a mediator to examine French causes of complaint against Algiers. European disregard of international law when a Muslim state was involved was shown up by the fact that the Sultan's envoy, Tahir Pasha, who had commanded the fleet at Navarino and who was now travelling with a passport delivered by the French Embassy in Istanbul, was stopped on the way and sent under French naval escort to Toulon where he was detained on the pretext of quarantine regulations.

Whilst the European chanceries were insisting on the need to maintain peace in the Mediterranean, in France preparations for the expedition got under way, both in the military and diplomatic fields. For the latter a *casus belli* had to be devised and the arguments put forward, though futile, bear witness to European attitudes of the time. The first was the now outdated pretext of punishing corsairs. Not only was this bound to appeal to public opinion, but it was also carrying out one of the recommendations of the Congress of Vienna. France could thus claim it was acting in Europe's name. Moreover, since the accusation applied indifferently to the three Regencies, it opened the door to European political expansion not only in Algiers, but also in Tripoli and Tunis. The second reason put forward was a sordid dispute involving French non-payment of bills for cereals provided by Algeria to the French during the Napoleonic period by a trading firm already mentioned, that of Bacri, in partnership with Busnach, another important Jewish concern. They come here into their own as models of devious dealing and dishonest practices such as will characterize a great many transactions in 19th-century North Africa. Bacri's business deals in general and sale of cereals in particular, are complex but can nonetheless be brought down to the following uncontroverted facts: Bacri and Busnach had sent wheat to France's southern provinces and to Napoleon's army in Italy and later Egypt between 1793 and 1798. Their bills were high and their credit expensive but they had succeeded in getting the contracts by means of their influential protectors including Talleyrand who, in 1797, became the French Minister of Foreign Affairs. Their bills in this period amounted to 8 million French francs, of which only 3 million had been paid. Talleyrand and the traders then had what seemed an ingenious idea: the Dey should be encouraged to write himself to Napoleon claiming that the money was due to him personally. Expecting some sort of profit, the Dey agreed. He was not however told that part of the money had already been paid, Bacri and Busnach being all the more loath to mention this in view of the fact that they themselves owed the Dey money and preferred to be considered impecunious. Nothing at the time came of the Dey's initiative nor of regular reminders as to other money owing to him.

In 1815, the monarchy was restored in France and Talleyrand once again became Foreign Minister. Jacob Bacri who was now at the head of the firm contacted his protector who gave orders to the French consul in Algiers to help in every way. The consul was a man named Pierre Deval, well-known throughout the Mediterranean for his ill-manners and dishonesty. Jacob Bacri produced his accounts which were not only unsatisfactory in themselves but which had increased the claims, the money owing being now estimated by him at 24 million French francs. They were examined by a French commission which brought this down to 7 million francs. This was accepted as fair settlement by all parties including the Dey. What the latter did not know, however, was that the unscrupulous traders had used third parties to lodge prior claims which far exceeded the settlement. The Dey's own bills were simply waved aside. He justifiably considered Deval an accomplice to the act and consequently asked for a new consul to be sent to the Regency. The French, once again, turned a deaf ear. On 29 April 1827, a discussion took place between the Dey and the consul in the course of which Husayn complained of the French government's attitude in general and Deval's behaviour in particular. The scene which followed cannot be authenticated as it was a private meeting and we only have for it the word of each party and their accounts do not entirely match. It would seem that Deval was his own usual ill-behaved self and that the Dey lost patience and struck him with the fan he had in his hand. Although Deval's claim that he had been insulted was not taken seriously in Algiers and other parts of the Mediterranean where he was well known, the French government decided to make the incident a question of national honour. A squadron of four ships appeared in the Bay of Algiers demanding a public apology from the Dey Husayn. The Dey refused to apologize, and on 16 June 1827, diplomatic relations were broken off and trade partially interrupted. It was this diplomatic incident which, some three years later, was turned to account. In the meantime the French had put forward a view, which they were from then on to hold, according to which conflicts with the Regencies did not imply a quarrel with the Sublime Porte. As Charles X's minister of Foreign Affairs put it: 'The Dey cannot be considered a subject of the Sultan', the latter having only 'the vaguest and most tenuous claims to suzerainty over Algiers'. Britain, whilst officially upholding Turkish rights, ultimately accepted this appreciation since when it appointed a successor to the British consul St. John in 1851, it applied for *exequatur* to the French government rather than the Sultan. The Sultan on the other hand refused to admit the loss of his province and official lists of the country's dependencies always subsequently included Algiers, although the name of its Pasha was left out. The divergence of opinion led, as we shall later see, to persistent skirmishes between the French Foreign Office and the Sublime Porte.

The French government made the necessary military and naval preparations for the punitive raid – for the French had promised their European partners it would be no more than that – and officially announced its intention of attacking Algiers on 31 January 1830. Did a punitive raid warrant such preparations? Possibly not, but European nations for various reasons were not prepared to do anything about the matter. Moreover it looked as if France was building up its military capacity for political reasons connected with opposition at home and the coming elections which imperilled Charles X's authoritarian rule. When assembled, the fleet consisted of 675 ships, 103 of the Royal Navy and 527 requisitioned trading vessels. The army under the command of General Bourmont amounted to 37 000 men.

The armada sailed from Toulon on 25 May, 1830, and reached the coast of Algeria on the 31st. The landing was effected at Sidi Ferruch, a few miles from Algiers, on 14 June. Resistance proved largely ineffectual. The 7 000 *janissaries* were under the Agha Ibrahim, the Dey's son-in-law, who did not prove equal to the task. We know from French records that the landing took place in unsatisfactory conditions which the Muslim forces could have turned to their advantage. The Dey Husayn himself seems to have allowed his fear of local troops to predominate, and it was only at the last minute that he called in contingents from Constantine, Oran, and the Kabylies. This army nonetheless put up a brave show but it was sadly lacking in military equipment, including artillery. The French won the day and overran the Algerian camp which had been set up at Staweli. The French then marched on without meeting with opposition as far as the Emperor's Fort (whose name recalled Charles V's ill-fated landing in 1541). It was shelled and taken on 4 July. Opinion in Algiers was divided. The Dey was for calling the people to arms, but his advisers favoured negotiation. They carried their point. The result was that Algiers surrendered almost without resistance on 5 July and the Dey and his entourage realised too late that their own fate was involved since French conditions included the expulsion of all the Turks. The measure was immediately put into effect, followed a little later by a similar decision with respect to the *kulughli*-s.

Turkish rule in Algiers was done away with by a stroke of a pen and conveyed to the people by a proclamation in Arabic which General Bourmont had had drawn up on similar lines to that issued by Bonaparte in Egypt. Bourmont further ordered that the solemn Friday prayers no longer be said in the Sultan's name. Defeat was even more patently brought home by the presence of the French army which undertook the systematic looting of the town. Even the contents of the state archives were thrown out and precious documents used by the soldiers to clean their shoes or light their pipes. The Treasury was ransacked and its contents served to pay the cost of the expedition, besides making of many officers wealthy men.

In Europe there was little reaction to the event beyond a few vague assurances of goodwill to the Sultan. Britain still insisted that a raid was a raid and should not be turned into permanent occupation and it was generally believed that some negotiated settlement could be reached. The Sultan was further made aware of his weakness on the international scene when, in 1831, Egypt encouraged by France, invaded Syria. The Sultan appealed to Britain for help but received a negative reply. As for Russia, it had openly come out in favour of the French and the Czar Nicholas I had sent Charles X a message of congratulations. It moreover capitalized on Ottoman weakness by sending the Russian fleet to the Dardanelles in 1833 to obtain a permanent right of access to the Mediterranean. Turkey's incapacity to defend its sovereignty was here again shown up since Russian preponderance was formally recognized by the Treaty of Unkiyar Skelessi (8 July 1833). Paradoxically it was in France itself that the expedition proved fruitless, even if it assuaged national pride still smarting from defeat at Waterloo. Not only was criticism of the expedition rife from the start, but it did not even influence election results which turned massively against Charles X and his supporters. The King was forced to flee the country and leave his throne to Louis-Philippe, a prince of the Orleans branch of the royal family. This liberal uprising sparked off similar movements in Europe (Belgium, Germany, Italy, and Poland). In the change of regime, Algiers came close to being forgotten.

Peripheral encroachments on the Turkish Empire thus appear at this stage less the result of a deliberate policy, with respect to the provinces involved, than as moves on the chessboard of European rivalry. For Muslim states, as we shall now see, they were of far greater consequence.

SELECTED READING LIST

Barlett, C. J., *Great Britain and Sea Power (1815–1953)*, (Oxford, 1963).

Caillé, J., *La Mission du Capitaine Burel au Maroc en 1808*, (Paris, 1953).

Crawley, C. W., *The Question of Greek Independence: a Study of British Policy in the Near East*, (Cambridge, 1930).

Douin, G., *Mohamed Ali et l'expédition d'Alger*, (Cairo, 1930).

Gorianov, S. M., *Le Bosphore et les Dardanelles; étude historique sur la question des détroits, d'après la correspondance diplomatique déposée aux archives centrales de Saint-Pétersbourg et à celles de l'empire*, (Paris, 1910) (translated from the Russian original).

Grant, A. J. & Temperley, H., *Europe in the Nineteenth and Twentieth Centuries (1789–1939)*, (London, 1927).

Holt, P. M., *Egypt and the Fertile Crescent, 1516–1922. A Political History*, (Ithaca & London, 1966).

Julien Ch.-A., *Histoire de l'Algérie contemporaine. Conquête et colonisation*, (Paris, 1964).

Jabarti A. al-, *'Ajaib al-Athar*, (Bulaq, 1879–1880).

Marriott, J. A. R., *The Eastern Question: an Historical Study in European Diplomacy*, (Oxford, 1917).

Plantet, E., *Correspondance des Deys d'Alger avec la Cour de France* (1579–1833), (Paris, 1889).

Phillips, W. A., *War of Greek Independence, 1821 to 1823*, (London & New York, 1897).

Sabry, M., *L'Empire Égyptien sous Mohamed-Ali et la Question d'Orient, 1811–1849*, (Paris, 1930).

Serres, J., *La Politique Turque en Afrique sous la monarchie de Juillet*, (Paris, 1925).

Temimi, 'A., *Sommaire des Registres Arabes et Turos d'Alger*, (Tunis, 1979).

CHAPTER 6

NORTH AFRICAN REACTIONS

The situation which prevailed in Egypt in 1800 was described in the previous chapter from the invaders' point of view. Let us now try and see what it meant for the Egyptians themselves, as also for their North African neighbours, both in terms of individual experiences and of national policies. At the start it should be stressed, however, that what we are dealing with is not just the kind of unpleasantness which results anywhere from foreign occupation, but with a deeper sense of shock. Muslims as True Believers in a world of infidels and pagans, considered their superiority obvious and their triumph inevitable, sanctioned by God's plan for the universe. In political terms the problem now facing them was both simple and fundamental: if the Muslim polity fell to the infidels, how could it continue to fulfil its historical destiny as the privileged *umma*? This was probably all the more acutely felt because ever since early Muslim expansion had been checked, people had largely given up outgoing attitudes, had turned in upon themselves, mentally building up seclusion within the *dar al-Islam*, a comfortable world of intellectual stagnation from which Christians, as independent actors of history, were mentally if not materially excluded. It was this self-confidence which Napoleon's landing in Egypt undermined.

EGYPTIAN REACTIONS TO FRENCH RULE

The way in which the shocking experience of invasion was not only felt by people but forcibly integrated into the pattern of their daily lives can best be illustrated by the situation in Egypt during the occupation, especially since a good insight is provided by contemporary accounts, including that of the Egyptian historian 'Abd al-Rahman al-Jabarti (1754–1825) who was an eye-witness of events.

The first point that comes out in al-Jabarti's description of the French landing at Alexandria in 1798 is Muslim unpreparedness. The landing itself created panic. Institutionalized power, namely the *bey*-s and their *mamluk*-s, had paid little or no heed to forewarnings of the attack, including information provided by the British, and made no attempt to organize an effective defence. The Turkish Sultan was himself manifestly incapable of upholding Muslim independence. Criticism of the incapacity of rulers was therefore rife, and Napoleon himself banked on this as also on complaints concerning the tax system, to make French rule palatable. His first proclamation stated that he had come to free the oppressed Egyptians from *mamluk* tyranny. French optimism was to have a setback. People in fact showed more resilience than might have been expected in the circumstances. This was true both of the army which rallied round and made a gallant though ineffectual stand on the road to Cairo (Battle of the Pyramids, 21 July 1798), and of ordinary people. In Alexandria, resistance was organized and though it was soon crushed by disciplined French forces and their superior equipment, it showed civilian capacity to fight back. The Beduins of the northern desert, moreover, moved in in support. This community of feeling persisted when the *mamluk*-s withdrew to Upper Egypt and organized guerilla warfare, and was also evident during the Cairo revolts. Tribesmen from outlying areas moved up to the capital, ready to help. The fact that insecurity also provided Beduins with occasions for looting does not necessarily contradict the fact that they also felt concerned. Even more characteristic of people's attitude was the well-established practice of urban passive resistance which was here particularly evident as people pretended to ignore the presence of foreigners and ostensibly refused to celebrate public holidays.

Nonetheless some sort of pattern of coexistence had to be devised, all the more so in view of Napoleon's policy which placed particular emphasis on social interaction. The commander-in-chief set up his headquarters in Cairo and recruited local aid. Trade flourished, servants and craftsmen worked for the army, and taverns were full. Napoleon's officers themselves aped the *mamluk*-s whose palaces and property they confiscated. Forced collaboration was underscored in a way which was particularly upsetting for Muslims, namely intercourse with local women. This included a few instances of actual marriages, but more often involved concubines or slave women, the ordinary soldiers making do with lower-class prostitutes. The scandal was brought home by the non-Muslim custom of showing women off in public. Equally distressing were French claims on Arab culture and religion. People resented the use of Arabic by Bonaparte in official texts and the setting up of a printing press in Bulaq, near Cairo. Well-meaning efforts by more distinguished orientalists to promote interaction by means of learned societies and archeological or scientific reports were seen as a more subtle form of aggression, particularly resented by those scholars who visited the French Library and saw non-Muslims fingering manuscripts of the Quran. As for conversions to Islam elicited by Bonaparte's pro-Muslim policy, they were seen not only as mere pretence, but as adding insult to injury.

In spite of this, collaboration was for many an unpleasant necessary duty. The first to be called upon by the French were the notables and religious leaders who were traditional intermediaries between foreign rulers – Turks in former times and now French – and local society. Moreover Bonaparte's sophisticated and indeed very modern colonial approach led him to promote indirect rule through elite collaboration. The material interests and social status of notables were upheld in exchange for their help in making French domination acceptable. This was institutionalized in assemblies (*diwan*-s) which the French convened, promising Egyptians they would have a say in the running of affairs. The fact that in practice they were merely to underwrite French decisions was an inevitable part of the colonial process. Compromise was accepted, albeit unwillingly by such personalities, and we find many well-known names in the *diwan*, including that of al-Jabarti himself. A line of least resistance was taken, even if notables made minor stands against the French, such as refusal to be seen in public wearing the French red, white and blue badge or *cocarde*.

Collaboration was up to a point a personal decision and though we may suppose that the majority of people behaved in a dignified way, we nonetheless find in every circle of society people who went out of their way to work with the French. Some merchants did good business and the head of their powerful guild, Ahmad al-Mahruqi, not only kept his post but was appointed to the *diwan*. Defeated *janissaries* were enrolled in the army. Not all scholars were averse to friendly relations with the French as Hasan al-'Attar's poems, warm with praise for the young officers he met, show. Even leading religious families came out in their favour. Chief of these were members of the al-Sadat, one of Cairo's major holy lineages, and the descendants of Abu Bakr al-Siddiq whose leader, Khalil al-Bakri was in 1798 appointed *naqib al-ashraf* (custodian of the Sharifian families) in replacement of 'Umar Makram who had preferred voluntary exile to French rule. More scandalous still for many Egyptians was the presence at the head of the *diwan* of 'Abd Allah Sharqawi, rector of al-Azhar university.

Collaboration should not however be seen as a purely individual matter since it also reflects the positions and interests of social groups. The merchant class, with the exception of major traders involved in international circuits, maintained a passive attitude. This is particularly the case of craftsmen and their once powerful guilds and probably reflects a decline in their economic capacity which had already set in by the end of the 18th century. By 1800, their apprentices were often out of work and constituted the rank and file of urban masses whose attitude could not be depended upon since they both provided the work force the occupiers required and upheld the city revolts. French requirements further modified the respective balance of groups in the overall pattern of society. This was particularly evident with the promotion of minority groups which had traditionally had an inferior status. Thus Jews and Christians from the Middle East (often referred to as 'Syrians') or from outlying parts of the Mediterranean arrived in Egypt in growing numbers. Their adaptability made them privileged auxiliaries for the French whilst former humiliations made them overbearing dignitaries or petty tyrants for the Egyptians. Some indeed acquired infamous reputations by their conduct, none more so than a man from the island of Chio known to contemporaries as Barthélemy who, at the head of the police force, did much of the dirty work for the French authorities. The staple divide and rule policy further led to the promotion of Egyptian Christians whose traditional capacities as traders or as tax-collectors were exploited to the full. The French went further in encouraging a more assertive Copt stand. Though as *dhimmi*-s the Copts were exempted from warfare, the French set up a Copt legion under the command of a man known as Ya'qub. When he fled from Egypt with the French army in 1801, he aired projects concerning a Copt uprising in order to pave the way for an independent state which would have European support. As Ya'qub died on board the ship carrying him to France, nothing more was heard of the plan, but the part he and other members of the Christian community had played created resentment which was later to express itself in racial hostility, which was only with difficulty kept under control by Egyptian authorities.

The social changes were in many ways the result of France's imperial views on Egypt and involved creating a native personnel to uphold it. This was particularly to be the case with the army, although the short-lived nature of the venture brought this to a premature end. Napoleon had set up various local regiments, including a camel-corps, and had further recruited former *janissaries*. Some left for France with the army and subsequently we find them at court where they added a touch of oriental pageantry to imperial glory as official portraits testify. Some indeed continued to promote France's colonial policy, as, for example, their commanding officer, 'Abd al-'Al, who served with the rank and title of *agha* and whose son later became General after taking part in the French invasion of Algeria. This, however, was the mere outline of a plan which had also envisaged recruitment of slaves, and Bonaparte had contacted the Dar Furi Sultan to this end.

French administration in Egypt also introduced structural changes and a new outlook on such problems as army recruitment, which was later to be conceived on Napoleonic lines. France's successful campaigns moreover made of military power a national status symbol which future sovereigns were to try and acquire at any cost. A new economic order was coming into its own, adapted to European mercantilism, as also a new conception of the state. Bonaparte's bureaucratic mania introduced in Egypt a number of new procedures such as censuses, registration of property, and death certificates which were to become commonplace a few years later. Also set up by Bonaparte were some of the technical means by which state ideology could become dominant. The setting-up of a printing press at Bulaq and the publishing of an official gazette were part of this. That such changes had come to stay was further reflected by the fact that the men promoted under the French regime often kept their positions in independent Egypt, even if more compromised individuals were called to account. Shaykh al-Sadat remained an influential personality whilst leadership of the sharifian lineages reverted to the Bakri family, though not to descendants of the *shaykh* of Bonaparte's time. Hasan al-'Attar was Muhammad 'Ali's nominee for the rectorship of al-Azhar. George Jahwari, a Copt appointed by Bonaparte Collector-in-Chief of taxation, acted in the same capacity for Muhammad 'Ali and with him those of his co-religionists who served in the Finance Department. Ahmad al-Mahruqi, head of the guild of merchants, was later in charge of municipal affairs in Cairo.

Behind the spectacular and oppressive facade of foreign rule, a modernizing trend was on foot which independent Egypt of the post-Napoleonic era was to make largely its own. This goes some way to explaining the somewhat ambiguous attitude of Arab historians when dealing with this first experience of colonial rule which is also seen as the foundation of modern Egypt.

CHANGES UNDER WAY ELSEWHERE IN NORTH AFRICA

Though, in Egypt, the process of change was emphasized by the invasion and French impact, it should also be seen in terms of a more general situation to which North Africa as a whole was reacting.

The lack of political foresight shown by the ruling class in Egypt with respect to European aggression also characterizes other Muslim states. This is true of the Sublime Porte whose vacillatory attitude persisted. Though the

Sultan had declared war on France, he did little to build up on this and it was only with active British encouragement that he was led to send out an army to reoccupy Egypt. The Regencies, though called upon by the Ottoman Sultan to break with France, avoided doing so. A few purely formal concessions were made to the suzerain, whilst, in practice, cooperation with the French continued. Not only did the North African states provide the army in Egypt with stores, thus reducing the effect of the blockade, but also sometimes provided political help: thus the Qaramanli Pasha contributed to Bonaparte's safe return to France by giving information as to the whereabouts of the British fleet and by allowing Bonaparte to sail close to the Libyan shore. At governmental level, it was obvious little solidarity with Egypt was shown.

With respect to social categories, our appreciation will be very similar to that made with respect to Egypt, thus pointing to the fact that structural changes underway in Egypt were in fact characteristic of North Africa as a whole. Thus the depressed status of formerly prosperous crafts and trades was underscored throughout the region by economic difficulties both in the agricultural and commercial sectors. In Fez, the creative capacity of the Jewish silversmiths disappeared in the late 18th century, as did such other traditional arts as leather-work in Marrakech or copperwork in the Sus. In Tunisia the silk-weaving industry was on the wane and everywhere cloth was being imported in growing quantities from Europe. As a pressure group or in terms of public opinion, the urban class now played an insignificant role. Only the higher strata of merchants, those involved in international or trans-Saharan trade, continued to be active, although their growing dependence on the European market did not make them leaders of protest against Imperial encroachments. Closely connected with the merchant class were the scholars who, in the 18th century, also began to lose much of their importance as traditional leaders of society. 'Ulama decadence in this period was shown up by a narrower outlook and more material preoccupations leading to greater subservience to temporal rulers. Their rulings often exemplify this, including the fetwa-s (legal decisions) provided by Moroccan mufti-s to the sovereigns to justify export of cereals to Christian countries.

Difficult economic conditions were leading to growing unrest and these in turn could lead to political stands involving overt criticism of existing governments, especially when these were considered as not filling the chief duty of the community leader, the defence of the dar al-Islam. However, these economic difficulties were unevenly spread out and new responses to new conditions were at the same time promoting certain sectors of society. Cities, in general, demonstrated this uneven spread, as inland towns were depressed whilst coastal towns developed. Again, individuals having incentive and a capacity for adaptation could make a name and a fortune for themselves under new conditions. This was particularly evident where minority categories were concerned – namely here urban-based Jews (generally referred to as Andalusians, Granas, or Livornians, because they had come to North Africa after the 15th century from Christian countries and notably Spain). They provide examples of highly successful business careers, sometimes at an international level. Some of these modern traders were often prepared to travel widely; by the late 18th century there were some ten Moroccan Jewish families settled at Saint-Austin in the USA. One of the more famous examples of such careers is that of a Mogador family called Belisha. Moses Belisha (1788–1851) had traded in Gibraltar and later gone to Manchester. His son Baruk (called Barrow in England) maintained trading connections between Mogador and Manchester besides extending these to various parts of the Mediterranean. In 1872 another member of the same family, Isaac, became President of the Jewish community of Manchester whilst his grandson, Leslie, a British citizen, went into politics, and was a Minister in several British governments between 1932 and 1940 and in 1945. Leslie Belisha who added Hore to his name, was made a peer in 1954. Another such prominent family and one which has already been mentioned on several occasions was the Algerian Bacri-s. The family fortunes date back to Micaiah who had opened a small grocery and hardware store in Algiers in 1774. By the 1880s he had family trading partners not only in Leghorn but in Marseilles, and had acquired control of the cereal trade. A few years later he was sufficiently rich and influential to be used as chief negotiator between Algiers and the USA, and he worked out the peace settlement which put an end to the war between the two countries. In 1827 his unpaid bills for cereals were the official cause of the breakdown of relations between France and Algiers. Such prosperous careers, though exceptions, are nonetheless representative of the way in which those with more self-assertive attitudes, particularly apparent in groups which had formerly had a depressed status, took advantage of new trends involving an acceptance of and adaptation to a new world-order which was largely dominated by European capitalism and industry.

Where then do we find consistent attitudes of resistance? Contemporary accounts of Egypt provide little insight into this because scholars and historians, whether Arab or European, tend to consider with elite superciliousness popular reactions with which they have little sympathy. It is nonetheless obvious that it is at that level opposition came out most strongly. Moreover it cut across national boundaries. We thus find Maghribi-s actively supporting Egyptian resistance. Maghribi soldiers – mercenaries in the army – put up as stiff a resistance to the French as did the *janissaries*. Maghribi immigrants in towns such as Cairo where they were workmen or apprentices, are mentioned by al-Jabarti as taking part in the uprising. The political awareness which they were to take home with them not only helped uphold feelings of Muslim solidarity throughout North Africa but could sometimes spark off new movements of the opposition there. Thus one of the anti-Turk revolts in precolonial Algeria was led by a man called Bin Ahrash who had been involved in the resistance to Napoleon in Egypt.

We also find impassioned preachers, many of them referred to as 'Westerners' finding a ready hearing in the Egyptian countryside. They called on people to fight the infidels. In line with this one should recall that one of the reasons given by Bonaparte for abandoning the siege of Acre was the fighting force of a 'Moroccan sharif called Muhammad'. A common commitment to Islam was further upheld by social structures, not least of which was the function of the Holy Pilgrimage which brought out the feeling of Muslim unity. The French in Cairo quite justifiably feared the arrival of the Maghribi pilgrims and made special arrangements to prevent them coming into town or having contact with the population. In spite of this, hopes were high among the Egyptians who, as al-Jabarti noted in April 1799, spread the rumour that

'20,000 Maghribi-s had come to free Egypt'. The fact that these men were able to take stock of the situation and took their indignation with them to the Holy Places led that same year to riots in Mecca and in the Ka'aba itself where a Maghribi called Shaykh al-Kilani called on pilgrims to go to Holy War. At least 600 men of all origins flocked to his side and a fighting force was set up which crossed the Red Sea to Upper Egypt and fought there throughout the period of occupation. Even those pilgrims who did not answer the call inevitably spread news of the Christian invasion when they returned home and even though this had no direct impact on governmental action, it nonetheless spread a new spirit of self-criticism which was later to take shape in fundamentalist movements such as those of the Sanusiyya in Libya or of the *jihad*-s of Sudanic Africa. As collective reactions, these did not take shape immediately and the overall assessment of Muslim involvement in the situation created by the French in Egypt is perhaps best rendered by an event which had almost symbolic value: recourse to an individual and suicidal expression of revolt, that of Sulayman al-Halabi, a man come from Aleppo, who went up to the French Commander-in-Chief, General Kleber, and stabbed him to death on 14 June 1800. Cross-examination revealed that he had no motive other than commitment to his religion. It might here be further added that though his trial is often quoted by colonial historians as an example of the advanced form of justice introduced by Europeans in North Africa, it is rarely if ever mentioned that he was neither shot nor guillotined, but impaled. His slow, long drawn-out death was intended to strike terror into the hearts of Muslims. Sulayman al-Halabi was one of North Africa's many tragic heroes whom official history tends to bypass with embarrassment, not so much because their acts were bloody, as because they are an implicit indictment not only of foreign oppression, but also of the betrayal of political leaders engaged on the path of compromise.

STATE POLICIES IN THE FACE OF THE EUROPEAN THREAT

Popular Islamic-based reactions against infidel aggressions contrasting with the opportunism of the ruling classes, underscore the lack of real political awareness with respect to events which marked the first stage of European penetration to which all North African states in turn were to be subjected. As this will concern us more particularly in this book, it is not irrelevant at this stage to look more closely at the respective policies of the nation-states during this period marked by two colonial conquests, that of Egypt and that of Algiers.

Moroccan responses

As the westernmost state of North Africa, Morocco was, of course, furthest from the scene, although this was not the feeling among pilgrims and other travellers. Morocco's apathy however had other causes. Economic conditions were dramatic around 1800 after nearly a quarter of a century of hard times for agriculture. There had been long and severe periods of drought, notably between 1776 and 1782, and these had led to considerable hardship. The plague which spread throughout the country between 1797 and 1800 was a particularly serious epidemic which left Morocco with a population of perhaps a bare three million.

These fundamental problems created a situation characterized by social and political unrest. As towns declined for reasons also connected with international trade, and agricultural production reached record low figures, tribal agitation spread, taking the form of resistance to government authority, notably when it came to paying taxes. Most of the Berber mountain areas were up in armed opposition and military repressions were unable to bring them under control. During this difficult period, which lasted throughout the reign of Mulay Sulayman (1792–1822), fighting was constant. Campaigns took place in the Rif mountains in 1793, 1803, and 1811–13. The Ait 'Atta tribes of south-east Morocco were overrun by the army between 1805 and 1808, whilst the Central Atlas which commands the strategic network of communications through Morocco, held out permanently.

The situation implied nationwide tensions which expressed themselves along traditional Moroccan lines of tribal alliances or enmities, upheld by the network of holy lineages. Thus the resistance of northern Berber tribes to the *makhzen* was sanctioned by pacts solemnly made at the sanctuary of Mulay 'Abd al-Salam bin Mashish. Many *zawiya*-s in this period became active centres of opposition and used fraternities to preach resistance. The king counterattacked, not only by putting pressure on religious leaders but also by openly breaking with some religious establishments considered as rebellious. Thus the famous *zawiya* of Buja'd which mediated relations between the plain and the Atlas mountains east of Marrakech, and which in addition had well-established links with the royal family, was attacked and partially destroyed (1785). Even the traditional use of some lineages to counter others proved fruitless as was shown when the highly venerated holy men of Wazzan in northern Morroco who were traditionally pro-'Alawi, passed into opposition. In spite of this, royal policy continued to operate on largely traditional lines involving the use of military force to restore order, and holy lineages to try and manipulate public opinion. Mulay Sulayman was consequently to encourage Ahmad al-Tijani's recently founded sufi order, and the *Tijaniyya* which upheld existing rulers and had *makhzen* following was the only sufi fraternity to officially side with the king.

With the involvement of traditional peace-makers, the conflict was ultimately to lead to dissension at the top, within the royal family itself. Between 1775 and 1797, various princes became pretenders to the throne by virtue of tribal support. Though Mulay Sulayman was able to uphold his position as rightful ruler of the kingdom, he could not put an end to an opposition which had popular origins. Indeed the first quarter of the 19th century brought this out on an unprecedented scale. A unity in opposition was achieved under the moral leadership of Mulay al-'Arbi al-Darqawi (1760–1823) whose fraternity spread extensively throughout the country, establishing its hold over a great number of rural *zawiya*-s. Between 1811 and 1820, the Berber tribes of the Central Atlas with Darqawi encouragement launched a general offensive which the royal army endeavoured to stop with little success. Not only was it repeatedly beaten, but the king himself fell into his adversaries' hands in 1818. His sharifian prestige made for his liberation four days later, nonetheless the blow was a serious one. Unable to restore his authority either politically or militarily, the king fell back on ideological warfare. He officially put over the rigorist Wahhabi views which had been communicated to him in 1811 by Sa'ud ibn 'Abd al-'Aziz, the Wahhabi ruler of the Hijaz. These condemned the cult of saints and more popular forms of religious worship which were traditional in Morocco and part of the aura surrounding holy men and fraternities.

Peace only returned after the death of Mulay Sulayman in 1822. His successor, Mulay 'Abd al-Rahman, went back on measures taken, both with respect to tribes and holy men, and Wahhabi puritanism which the Tijaniyya had supported, faded into the background. At that price the traditional order of things in Morocco was reestablished. In these circumstances one may well imagine that Morocco was not prepared to face up to the shock and challenge of the European conquest of Algiers. It is nonetheless noteworthy, even taking local circumstances into account, that Morocco's king and government should have had so little sense of Muslim solidarity, or even awareness of the fact that the situation in which Algiers found itself would inevitably, in some form or other, impinge on Morocco. This lack of political acumen expressed itself in what was a by now outmoded assessment: the Turkish rulers of Algeria had traditionally been Morocco's enemies and there was no reason, it was felt, for Morocco to go to their help. But even more important for an understanding of Mulay 'Abd al-Rahman's attitude during his long reign (1822–59), is the link between the recent past and the fragile social peace on which his sovereign power depended. His main, if not his sole objective, was to maintain order and underscore the legitimacy of sharifian authority. Mulay 'Abd al-Rahman's indifference to the fate of Algiers was in fact a mere show, covering up his deep-rooted fear of the consequences of social protest with respect to a government incapable of defending the Muslim community. He well knew that, as the French consul of the time put it, 'the whole country had its gaze fixed on the Algerian expedition', and yet, on 7 May 1830, he gave the French assurances that he would remain neutral. This marked not only his will to avoid a conflict with a powerful foreign power, but also his opposition to the subversive situation the latter had created.

The response of the Regencies

The Regencies, though their respective positions differed, were similarly involved in political difficulties leading to generally short-sighted strategies. The causes were the same. The Mediterranean no less than the Atlantic suffered a decline in trading importance in spite of the short-lived boom during the European wars. The Regencies of Tripoli and Tunis to some degree benefited from the situation prevailing in the Mediterranean which encouraged renewed corsair activity which had its last hour of fame during the Napoleonic wars. This, however, was not without sorry consequences, involving as it did conflicts with various states including the USA with which Algiers and Tripoli were at war, and a dangerous situation at sea. Moreover the resurgence of roving, whilst momentarily serving European interests, could only attract unfavourable attention, implying that common action would be taken once the European wars were over. England, for example, noted with considerable irritation the support that Tripoli provided the French in Egypt, and Nelson had threatened the Qaramanli Pasha with retaliation. The Regencies thus found themselves involved to some degree in the situation created in the Mediterranean. The Tunisian fleet was thus sent to help Turkey during the Greek War and was destroyed with that of the Ottomans and Egyptians in Navarino Bay in 1827. Recourse to piracy was also intended to compensate for financial losses due to the deteriorating economic situation of the last quarter of the 18th century. In the Regencies as in Morocco this had begun with a long period of drought which had led to epidemics, including serious outbreaks of the plague in the 1780s, around 1800, and again in 1815. The resulting decline in agricultural resources and the development of political agitation could only be met by military campaigns, and these required money. As revenue from taxation and piracy fell, governments increasingly had recourse to exports. Europeans were interested essentially in basic commodities, notably cereals, and the continental blockade did not apply to exports of foodstuffs from the Regencies. The latter were thus led to buy up local produce, thus further reducing the capacity of rural populations to put by for hard times. Against this common background, we find the three Regencies reacting differently during the first quarter of the 19th century.

Algiers, secure in its belief that it was the ally of France to which it had not only provided stores but lent money free of interest for the Egyptian campaign, was blind to Napoleon's expansionist views which took in the strategic importance of the North African coast. Nor was France the only nation to show its aggressiveness: on 27 August 1816, the United States navy shelled the town, as did the British fleet under Lord Exmouth's command in March and August 1816. Another attack took place after the Congress of Aix-la-Chapelle in 1818, and, in 1825, Admiral Neal was sent out on a similar mission. In spite of this, no effort at rearmament was undertaken, even after the breakdown of relations with France in April 1827. Here again, fear of the people was uppermost in the ruling class and tribes were not given weapons to strengthen the country's defensive capacity. In fact, when the French actually landed, the Dey and his entourage refused tribal involvement to the last minute. The town was thus to fall an easy victim to the French in July 1830.

In Tunisia, Hammuda Bey (1782–1814) has already been described as an efficient and able statesman who built up the effective independence of Tunisia. He was however concerned with doing this essentially at the expense of now obsolete European nations – notably Venice on which, after a long war which lasted from 1784 to 1792, he imposed harsh peace terms – or of his immediate Muslim neighbours. This was particularly the case with respect to Algeria which had established a kind of tutelage over Tunisia against which Hammuda Bey energetically reacted. Decisive victories in the field in 1808 and 1813 reaffirmed Tunisia's independence. Hammuda Bey was also closely involved in Tripoli's affairs since he had supported the Qaramanli Pashas, notably against 'Ali Burghul, the Turkish-appointed governor. Though not prepared to break openly with Turkey as is shown by the fact that he sent an ambassador to Istanbul to obtain pardon for himself and the Qaramanli-s, he nonetheless stressed Tunisia's autonomy on various occasions, and notably by refusing to break with France as the Sultan had requested in 1798. In the context of international relations in the early 19th century, this can be seen as leading to an egotistical policy at home and a pro-French attitude abroad.

Hammuda Bey's views on the subject of commerce and belief in mercantilism were further to uphold this. Tunisia's Mediterranean trade was promoted by him and he also encouraged Tunisian craftsmen or shopkeepers to settle abroad – in 1798, they were about 600 settled in Egypt. At the same time he made efforts to protect the national economy, notably by increasing import tariffs. As in Morocco, the will to protect the country from the disruptive effects of growing international trade led Hammuda Bey to exercise strict personal control in this domain, thus partially excluding the local merchant class and, at the same time, promoting the involvement of government officials in relations with foreign countries. The latter, in many cases, considered immediate interest rather than long-term assessment of the dangers of economic inbalance.

Hammuda Bey's belief in the need to build up Tunisia into a strong mercantile state was also held by his successors 'Uthman Bey (1814) and Mahmud Bey (1814–24) but the situation of inferiority of the older Mediterranean states with respect to the new powerful states of northern Europe, was by now apparent, and Tunisia was led to make a number of major trading concessions. Britain thus obtained privileges which included fishing rights at Tabarka.

The conquest of Algeria by France was seen by the Husayni Bey-s in terms of their national policy and as offering them the possibility of increasing Tunisia's potentialities through political expansion, even if this involved cooperation with France. Husayn Bey (1824–35) had been informed of French plans by Consul Mathieu de Lesseps and he had expressed satisfaction at the idea that France was to free Tunisia from the pressures exerted by the neighbouring Regency. This led him to side openly with the French not only against the Regency but also against its Ottoman suzerain. The Bey promised the consul fresh stores for the French army. French ships calling on their way to Algiers were not submitted to quarantine and were exempted from paying duty. On the contrary, Turkish soldiers sent out by the Sultan had to submit to quarantine and were thus prevented from taking part in the Regency's defence. When Algiers submitted to General Bourmont, the Bey sent an officer to congratulate the latter, a public reception for the Tunisian envoy being organized at the *qasba* (citadel). A different reception met the Turkish envoy, Tahir Pasha, who received a cold welcome in Tunis and was not allowed to have contacts with the local *janissaries* whose anti-French feelings were suppressed by military means.

In spite of this privileged treatment, France showed little respect for its Tunisian ally as was demonstrated early in July 1830 when, in the wake of the invasion of Algiers, a new treaty was negotiated granting France a privileged nation status and a number of commercial advantages. The treaty was forced on the Bey by a threatening naval squadron. The Bey gave in and signed the text on 8 August 1830, including its secret clause providing a building site for a Catholic chapel in honour of St. Louis, King of France and leader of the 7th Crusade, who had died of the plague in Tunis in 1270. In spite of a manifestly hostile public opinion, Husayn Bey was led to cooperate by the hope of territorial aggrandizement.

General Clauzel, the French commander-in-chief appointed to Algiers after the fall of Charles X, entered into secret negotiations with the Bey promising a share-out of the spoils in exchange for active help: if Tunisian troops were sent out to Oran in western Algeria and if help were to be given with respect to the conquest of Constantine, both would be placed under Tunisian control. An agreement was made and a Tunisian envoy was sent to Algiers at the end of 1830 to sign a convention. It had further been decided that Mustafa, the Bey's brother and heir, was to be appointed Governor of Constantine and Mustafa's son, Ahmad, Governor of Oran. Tunisia was to pay France a tribute of one million francs for each, the sum being later reduced to 800 000 francs. Early in 1831, 200 Tunisian soldiers landed in western Algeria and took control of Oran where their brutal behaviour caused considerable scandal even in French army circles. By now, the government in Paris had been informed of the agreement which it refused to ratify. This was signified to the Bey in May 1831, and though negotiations were resumed, it was obvious that the Bey's hopes of expansion at Algeria's expense had been dashed. This was further demonstrated by the evacuation of the Tunisian garrison of Oran in July. The Bey complained bitterly of what he considered to have been French double-dealing, all the more so in view of the fact that he had publicly compromised himself both as a Tunisian and as a Muslim. The letters he had sent to Algeria asking the people to lay down their arms and submit to the French had received wide publicity and discredited him. At home, opposition came to the fore and promoted a strong anti-French party in government circles. When Mustafa Bey came to the throne, the consuls reported that the anti-French faction was now in power. Though indeed French influence in the Regency suffered a momentary setback, the trends set on foot nonetheless continued to promote European infiltration and, in the wake of this, French imperialism came back on the scene.

> I first set foot in Barbary forty years ago and have acquired the conviction not only that no Maghribi, however weak, would ever obey a Christian, but that he would never accept to walk by a Christian's side or live with him on an equal footing. Europeans may conquer Maghribis or keep them for a time in subjection . . . they will never be able to force them to accept an administration, police, advanced laws or arts from a power which does not speak the language of the Quran or share with them the prayers, fasts, and ceremonies commanded by the Holy Book.
>
> Letter from Consul Mathieu de Lesseps to the French Commander-in-Chief in Algeria, General Clauzel, 18 November 1830.

Tripoli, in this period, is probably the most interesting of the three Regencies since a similar situation is here highlighted by such features as Tripoli's proximity to the strategic zone of international confrontation, Tripoli's active trade in this period, and political tensions in the Regency itself. Yusuf Qaramanli's independent stand during the Napoleonic wars, involving help to the French and a refusal to comply with Ottoman orders to the contrary, did not have support at home. This was demonstrated by such events as the following: in June 1801, the Pasha granted a French convoy which had succeeding in avoiding the blockade, permission to land stores at Derna. The people there, however, took to arms and opposed the landing which had to be called off. It is therefore by a look at the local scene that we shall begin since in fact the dashing Pasha, in spite of his strong personality and ruthless action, was faced with persistent opposition.

One of Yusuf Qaramanli's first tasks when he seized power in 1796 was to crush opposition in the Syrt Gulf in view of the fact that this cut off communications both with the east through Cyrenaica, and with the south through Fezzan. Initial political and military action was directed against the Awlad Sulayman, all-powerful in Syrtica. Their leader Sayf al-Nasir was – or so local tradition has it – murdered in 1800, and the Awlad Sulayman were beaten in battle in 1805. One of Sayf al-Nasir's sons, probably Ghayth, had died fighting Yusuf Qaramanli at Misurata, the other, Ahmad, died during the fighting in 1805. Of the tribal chief's two grandsons, one, 'Abd al-Jalil, was taken to court as a hostage, the other, also called Sayf al-Nasir, remained with the Awlad Sulayman who, in spite of their defeat, persisted in opposition. A further battle in 1811 scattered the 700 surviving warriors together with their leader into the desert parts of Cyrenaica. There again Yusuf Qaramanli sent troops to hunt them out and, after yet another defeat in 1816, the tribe more or less disappeared from the scene, nothing more being heard of it until 1830.

'Abd al-Jalil, an honoured guest but a virtual prisoner in Tripoli, came to be closely associated in a military capacity with Yusuf Qaramanli's Saharan policy. The loss of revenue from Mediterranean sources after European peace had been reestablished as well as the troubled situation on the Sudanic confines, led Yusuf Qaramanli to undertake direct action to secure control of the caravan trade. A military expedition was sent to Ghadames in 1810 and set up direct Qaramanli control over the Tuareg trade. A similar attempt was made with respect to Fezzan whose autonomous sultanate only brought in an annual tribute of 5 thousand thalers. In 1811, on the advice of an influential Tripoli merchant, al-Mukani, who knew the region well and had been Yusuf Qaramanli's ambassador to Bornu in 1807–8, a plot was hatched to eliminate the ruling family and establish al-Mukani in its stead, the latter promising to pay the Pasha three times as much in tribute besides organizing trade and slave-raiding on a more systematic and profitable footing. A military expedition was sent out to Fezzan and was able, a little treachery aiding, to kill off the former rulers. Al-Mukani was appointed Bey of Fezzan and ruled with an iron hand from 1811 to 1820. In 1820 he was replaced by another Qaramanli nominee, Mustafa al-Ahmar, though al-Mukani remained on the scene, his Saharan experience being invaluable. During his governorship, Al-Mukani crushed all local opposition, including that of the Awlad Sulayman who, in this period, increasingly tended to push out southwards. With Qaramanli help, he set on foot powerful predatory expeditions which, every year, brought in some 1000 to 1500 slaves from the regions of Kanem, Borku, and Bahr al-Ghazal.

This led to a redefinition of Tripoli's relations with the declining though still powerful southern state of Bornu. Bornu also wished for closer ties with Tripoli because in the troubled situation which prevailed locally around 1800, Yusuf Qaramanli was seen as a useful although dangerous ally. The royal adviser to the Bornu dynasty, Muhammad Al-Amin himself had a pro-Arab policy shown up by the welcome afforded to Arab nomads and refugees who were incorporated into Bornu's fighting force and helped withstand 'Uthman dan Fodio's encroachments and the attacks of principalities such as Bagirmi which had shaken off the shackles of Bornu control. The fact that Muhammad al-Amin belonged to the scholar class and had family connections in the Fezzan, may have contributed to this. Closer links between Bornu and Tripoli were negotiated by al-Mukani during his 1807–8 embassy.

From 1815 onwards, Tripoli's position as an independent Mediterranean state was increasingly undermined by the power of the new trading states of Europe and the pressures they exerted in the region. This made an expansive Saharan policy a necessary antidote. It involved stronger military action in Sudanic Africa and Qaramanli troops pushed ever deeper into the region.

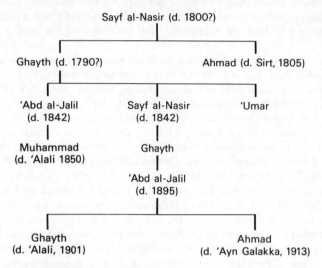

Fig. 6.1 *The genealogy of the Sayf al-Nasir*

From 1818 onwards, expeditions concentrated on the rich trading state of Kanem which by now had only tenuous connections with its former suzerain, Bornu. The neighbouring Sultanate of Wadday had moreover staked a claim on Kanem. Yusuf Qaramanli's army acted on Tripoli's account in the matter of raiding but as Bornu's ally in political terms. Plans were drawn up in Tripoli where it was estimated that the campaign would require some 6000 men and cost £25 000. The subject was broached with the British consul to see if a loan could be raised but this was refused in 1820. Yusuf Qaramanli was consequently forced to maintain the earlier working partnership with Kanem. In 1821, his army met up with Muhammad al-Amin's and, whilst upholding the latter's authority, raided on Tripoli's account. The campaign brought in some 6000 camels and as many slaves. Similar expeditions are recorded up to 1824.

The result, however, was no victory. Not only was Yusuf Qaramanli unable to establish control over the southern states or Bornu, but even the Fezzan proved untrustworthy as a necessary relay. Britain was moreover pressing for peace in the south. A still further problem and one which was later to weigh heavily in the balance, was the presence at the head of the Qaramanli army of 'Abd al-Jalil. Life at court had not made the grandson of Sayf al-Nasir a courtier and he had not forgotten that he was the leader of the Awlad Sulayman. He proved his fighting capacity in Kanem. In 1830, 'Abd al-Jalil came out openly against Yusuf Qaramanli and called his fellow tribesmen to arms. With his men he overran Fezzan and in 1831 captured the town of Murzuq where he set up as independent sultan, even having money minted in his name. His victory was, however, short-lived and the following year he was forced to evacuate the capital of Fezzan. He and the Awlad Sulayman nonetheless continued to roam in southern Libya besides pushing southwards to Bornu and Kanem on their own account. Yusuf Qaramanli in spite of a strong military policy had reached neither of his two goals: he had failed to re-establish communications in Libya since the Arabs of Syrtica continued to stand out, and he had not established full control over the Sudanic trading posts.

His failure on the Mediterranean front was even more obvious. It was demonstrated during a spectacular war at the beginning of the 19th century against an as yet minor Mediterranean trading partner: the USA. In the early part of the war which lasted from 1801 to 1805, American shipping had been captured and Yusuf Qaramanli refused to set their crews free. This led a New England captain, William Eaton, who had been sent as American consul to Tunis in 1797, to put forward a plan. With what we would today term a group of marines, he would depose Yusuf Qaramanli and place in his stead, Ahmad, the heir legally appointed by 'Ali Qaramanli. The plan was accepted by the American government and William Eaton sailed for Malta and from there went to Cairo to look for Ahmad Qaramanli who had joined the Egyptian army. In December 1804, the authorities in Cairo approved the plan and allowed Eaton to recruit some 60 Europeans of various nationalities, besides contacting Ahmad Qaramanli then serving in Upper Egypt. They met up and marched into Cyrenaica not without the two groups soon being at loggerheads. At the end of April 1805, they reached and captured Derna. The wild American scheme was now to fall through because Yusuf Qaramanli had deemed it wiser to accept American claims and come to a peaceful settlement. At Derna, Eaton received orders from a ship offshore to re-embark, taking with him only the Europeans and Ahmad Qaramanli. Yusuf Qaramanli was consequently allowed to rule over Libya in peace, his brother Ahmad being taken to Syracuse where he lived off an American allowance until his brother pardoned him in 1809. Peace between the two brothers was, however, to be of short duration and in 1811, Ahmad once again fled to Egypt where he eventually died. Peace with America did not mean peace of mind for the now ageing Pasha.

The new preponderance in the region of France and Britain together with their rivalry was also reflected in the growing influence of their respective consuls. Both consular representatives in Libya were very typical of the Mediterranean system of consular representation and forceful personalities in their own right. Colonel Hanmer Warrington who served in Tripoli from 1814 to 1846 and whose ten children were all born and brought up in the Regency, was closely involved in local trade and politics. His daughter Emma, and later her sister Jenny, were married to Thomas Wood, British vice-consul at Ben Ghazi. One of his sons, George, ran a regular steam ship service between Malta and North Africa from 1843 to 1845, whilst another, Henry, was killed in 1854 on a geographical expedition organized by Vogel to map out the route to Bornu; yet another son seems to have been acting vice-consul at Murzuq in 1855. The French consul, Baron Joseph Rousseau, *en poste* in Tripoli from 1825 to 1829, was an orientalist whose family, besides being related to the French philosopher Jean-Jacques Rousseau, served in the Middle East and North Africa from generation to generation. Nor was orientalism foreign to the milieu; Rousseau's Swedish colleague, Gräberg de Hamsö (1822–28), was a distinguished Arabic scholar. The personal feud between the French and British consuls provides an insight into how Saharan and Mediterranean factors could combine to create an explosive situation.

Relations between the two consuls had had a more auspicious beginning since Rousseau's son Alexandre Timoleon had courted one of Warrington's daughters before being turned down by the consul. The rejected suitor, if we are to believe his father, died of grief and a plaque commemorating his *'amour insensé'* (wild love) was put up at the consulate in Tripoli after his death in 1829. A better welcome was afforded to a British officer and explorer, Major Gordon Laing, who arrived in Tripoli in 1825 in order to map out the desert route to Timbuktu via In Salah. He married Emma Warrington. Though the explorer successfully reached In Salah in 1825 and Timbuktu in 1826, he was murdered on his way out of the latter town, probably on 22 September 1826. Laing's body and all his personal belongings disappeared.

When news of the sorry event reached Tripoli, Colonel Warrington raised an outcry. One of the questions he asked was: what had become of Laing's papers, including those sent off from Timbuktu prior to his death? By a strange coincidence, if indeed it was one, Consul Rousseau in July 1827 published an account of Timbuktu in a French journal and, in 1828, the French explorer, René Caillié successfully effected the journey and published an account of his travels in 1830. Warrington was now persuaded that the French consul, with the help of a well-connected Tripoli family, the Daghis, had laid hold of his son-in-law's papers and used them both for personal ends and to prevent the British reaching Timbuktu first. The quarrel was pushed to the extreme limit, the authorities in Tripoli themselves becoming involved because of accusations against the Daghis family. Both men put personal grievances before national interest and Rousseau, in a fit of anger, broke off diplomatic relations with Tripoli and sailed back to France. This personal decision taken without prior notice to the French government, created an embarassing situation which Paris was forced to countenance.

What if any truth there was in Warrington's accusation is difficult to say since the French commission of inquiry set up to investigate the matter gave an ambiguous ruling. Material proof seems to have been lacking especially in view of the fact that Rousseau's personal belongings, which included some 460 manuscripts, many of which were precious documents in Arabic which the unscrupulous orientalist had 'borrowed' from his Muslim friends, were irretriveably damaged on the return journey. The commission, though it cleared Rousseau, nonetheless deprived him of his post and he was retired from the consular service.

In Tripoli, the ageing Pasha had shown his incapacity to face up to the situation created by the feuding European consuls. His weakness was further indicated a few months later when the French attacked Algiers. The Dey asked for help but Yusuf Pasha only made a non-committal reply, expressing the vague hope that 'the French (may God exterminate them) would leave without having obtained any success'. In August 1830, a French squadron under the command of Admiral de Rosamel visited Tunis and Tripoli, forcing humiliating treaties upon the Bey of Tunis and the Qaramanli Pasha. Not only did Yusuf Qaramanli agree to put an end to the practice of tributes from European states, he also agreed to limit the size of the Regency's fleet, to meet the bills of French creditors, and to pay a war indemnity. He also publicly apologized for his behaviour to Consul Rousseau. This sparked off the irate Warrington who came up with similar demands, including the payment of 200 000 piastres due to British traders. Warrington energetically and even violently upheld these throughout 1831 and, on 30 May 1832, came up with an ultimatum threatening to break off diplomatic relations. In spite of the Pasha's efforts to meet these conditions by exceptional tax-levies, he was in no position to pay and Consul Warrington momentarily withdrew on board a British ship in August 1832.

The situation in Libya was by now out of control. The depressed tribesmen were up in arms and Tripoli was a hotbed of intrigue. 'Abd al Jalil Sayf al-Nasir who was now all-powerful, openly called for the abdication of Yusuf Qaramanli and won over the *kulughli*-s to his views. On 12 August 1832, Yusuf Qaramanli gave in. This did not however solve the problem as public opinion was divided over the succession: Tripoli, the ruling class, and the French (now represented by Consul Schwebel) favoured 'Ali Bey, one of Yusuf Qaramanli's sons, the *kulughli*-s and Warrington upheld Muhammad, the son of the former pretender Ahmad. The Sublime Porte hesitated. The abdication of Yusuf Pasha thus set the stage for the last act of the Qaramanli dynasty.

We may summarize the situation by saying that the North African states had met the onslaught of European power in a dispersed order and in a divided frame of mind. If popular opinion reacted directly, often with vigour and clear-sightedness, the ruling class was far too enmeshed in political and economic problems to do more than try and maintain its position, turning to its advantage, if it could, the difficulties its neighbours were faced with. The situation, already apparent in 1800, had, by 1830, isolated Muslim countries one from the other and created in the Regencies the situation which was to lead to more direct foreign involvement.

SELECTED READING LIST

Egypt
Ayalon, D., 'The historian al-Jabarti and his background', *Bulletin of the School of Oriental and African Studies*, xxiii, 2, 1960.
Bernoyer, F., *Avec Bonaparte en Egypte et en Syrie, 1798–1800. Dix-neuf lettres inédites retrouvées, transcrites et présentées par Christian Tortel*, (Abbeville, 1976).
Guemard, G., 'Les auxiliaires de l'armée de Bonaparte en Egypte', *Bulletin de l'Insitut d'Egypte*, 9, 1927.
Herold, J., *Bonaparte in Egypt*, (London, 1963).
Jabarti 'A. al-, *Ajaib al-Athar fi al-Tarajim wa al-akhbar*, (Bulaq, 1879).
Moreh, S., *Al-Jabarti's Chronicle of the first Seven Months of the French Occupation of Egypt*, (Leyden, 1975).
Savant, J., *Mamelouks de Napoléon*, (Paris, 1949).

Turc, N., *Chronique d'Egypte 1798–1804*, Arabic text and French translation by G. Wiet, (Cairo, 1950).
— *L'Egypte indépendante. Projet de 1801*, (Cairo, 1924).

Morocco
Brignon, J. et al., *Histoire du Maroc*, (Paris, 1967).
Drague, G., *Esquisse d'histoire religieuse du Maroc*, (Paris, 1952).
Laroui, A., *Les origines sociales et culturelles du nationalisme marocain (1830–1912)*, (Paris, 1977).
Michaux-Bellaire, E., 'Le Wahhabisme au Maroc', *Afrique Française. Renseignements coloniaux*, (1928).
Zayyani, A. al-, *Al-Turjuman al-Mu'arib 'an Duwal al-Mashriq wa al-Maghrib*, (Paris, 1886; Amsterdam, 1969).

The Regencies
Allen, G. W., *Our Navy and the Barbary Corsairs*, (Connecticut, 1965).
Barnby, H. G., *The Prisoners of Algiers. An Account of the forgotten American-Algerian War 1785–1797*, (London, 1966).
Charles-Roux, F., *Bonaparte et la Tripolitaine*, (Paris, 1929).
Irwin, R. W., *The Diplomatic Relations of the United States with the Barbary Powers, 1776–1816*, (North Carolina, 1931).
Lyon, G. F., *A Narrative of Travels in North Africa in the years 1818, 1819, and 1820*, (London, 1821).
Micacchi, R., *La Tripolitania sotto il dominio dei Caramanli*, (Rome, 1936).
Monod Th., *De Tripoli à Tombuctou. Le Dernier Voyage de Laing. 1825–1826*, (Paris, 1977).
Rennell, R., *General William Eaton*, (London, 1932).
Serres, J., *La Politique Turque en Afrique du Nord sous la monarchie de Juillet*, (Paris, 1925).
'Umar 'A., *Imhiyar al-usrat al-Qaramanliyyat fi Libiya*, (Tripoli, 1966).
Zawi, T. A. al-, *A'lam Libya*, (Tripoli, 1971).
Zeltner, J. C., *Pages d'histoire du Kanem*, (Paris, 1980).

CHAPTER 7

THE LIMITS AND POSSIBILITIES OF INDEPENDENCE: EGYPT UNDER MUHAMMAD 'ALI (1805–48)

Before pursuing our account of military aggressions, European or non-European, let us look again at Egypt where a new political regime was being set up with the country's modernization as its objective, a trend which was only to appear later in the century in other parts of North Africa. This gave Egypt a lead with respect to the Maghrib which was not without influence on economic, social and cultural patterns in those countries. It also marked Egypt's conversion to a new European-promoted world order dominated by the economic necessities of industrial states. In this chapter we shall be led to ask ourselves what this modernizing trend actually implied for Egypt and Egyptians. We shall also be led to pose a difficult problem: did these reforms consolidate Egyptian independence as they were intended to, or did they merely play into the hands of European capitalism, thus paving the way for imperialism?

EGYPT UNDER MUHAMMAD 'ALI

The coming to power of Muhammad 'Ali

Egypt's status during the first half of the 19th century, which corresponded to the long reign of the Viceroy Muhammad 'Ali from 1805 to 1848, was the direct result of international agreement. The Great Powers reluctantly agreed to leave Egypt alone in order that the balance of power in the Mediterranean might be maintained, the route to India being far too important to be in the hands of any single European state. It was consequently decided to restore Egyptian independence and even, for greater security, to encourage the setting up of a strong, cohesive state, whilst at the same time leaving room for European control through the Ottoman Sultan whose rights as suzerain were maintained. The European powers were thus agreed that Egypt should once again be administered by the local *mamluk bey*-s. But who, in 1803, among the *bey*-s was capable of exerting effective political authority? Murad Bey who had been one of the strong men of the former period and who had fought the French throughout the occupation from his base in Upper Egypt, died in 1802. Ibrahim Bey returned with the Turks, but he had lost ground. Two of Murad

Bey's *mamluk*-s had come to the fore, one of them being Muhammad Bey al-Alfi whom the British favoured. He had even been invited on an official visit to London in 1803–4. His immediate rival was 'Uthman Bey al-Bardisi who had local connections. There was also the Turkish-appointed viceroy, Khusraw Pasha. A number of other leading personalities could influence the situation by supporting one or other faction. Chief of these was 'Umar Makram who was the leader of the religious class with the rank of *naqib al-ashraf* and who was further respected because he had not been compromised by French rule and had chosen to live out the occupation in Jaffa.

The chaotic situation after the occupation, aggravated by local and international tensions, left little room however for the finesse of diplomacy as Muhammad Bey al-Alfi's failure to make good his claims showed. Energy, brute force, and military discipline were the keys to success and these were not to be found in the rival *mamluk* factions disorganized by the war, but in an Albanian contingent which had been levied as part of the Ottoman army of reoccupation when the combined Anglo-Turkish attack on the French had been launched. This Albanian contingent had as its second in command Muhammad 'Ali, born in 1769 in the Macedonian town of Kavalla where his father commanded a troop of irregulars. After landing in Egypt and showing its strength and discipline, the Albanian contingent had proved that it was an independent force to be reckoned with. In May 1803, it had mutinied in Cairo because of arrears of pay, and had forced the Turkish viceroy to flee for safety to Damietta. The Albanian commander was named *qaim maqam* (acting viceroy) but he was killed a few days later. His successor was Muhammad 'Ali.

In the short space of a year – early 1804 to May 1805 – Muhammad 'Ali was to combine forceful action and tactical skill to become the undisputed master of Egypt. He first made an alliance with 'Uthman Bey al-Bardisi to gain local support and to eliminate the rival *mamluk*, Muhammad Bey al-Alfi. He undertook to weaken the military warlords by driving most of them out of Cairo, and then undermined the position of the Turkish-appointed viceroy. To this end he won over the *'ulama* class by the intermediary of 'Umar Makram and on 12 May 1805, the religious establishment formally deposed the Viceroy, appointing Muhammad 'Ali on 14 May as *qaim maqam*. The Sultan accepted the situation and ratified Muhammad 'Ali's position by sending a *firman* appointing him Viceroy in July 1805. This still had to be built up into effective power both on the home front and on the international scene.

Muhammad 'Ali's early military reforms

That the international problem and European involvement in Egypt had not ceased with the withdrawal of foreign troops was evidenced by an attempted British landing at Alexandria in March 1807. Effective Egyptian resistance combined with international pressures led the British to evacuate the zone on 14 September 1807. This nonetheless demonstrated the importance of an efficient military force to guarantee national independence. Muhammad 'Ali who, like other Muslim rulers, had been impressed by Napoleon's army, set about reorganizing Egypt's armed forces on a similar model. This implied doing away with the *mamluk*-s. Muhammad 'Ali was all the more prone to this policy because he wished to undermine the *mamluk*-s' position of power. On 1 March 1811, Muhammad 'Ali's will was given practical effect in a bloody and treacherous incident. The leading *mamluk*-s were invited to a ceremonial reception at the citadel and were killed one after the other as they entered the palace. (It should nonetheless be pointed out that the officer corps continued to be recruited from former *janissary* and *mamluk* families who, throughout the 19th century, provided the army with top-ranking officers.) The implementing of the new military policy was among the first measures taken by Muhammad 'Ali, who recruited some 800 French soldiers who had stayed on in Egypt after the evacuation. After conversion to Islam these became instructors. This was followed up by offers to French and Italian officers after the Vienna settlement. Under Colonel Sèves, better known under his Muslim name of Sulayman Pasha, the Europeans officered regiments and trained local recruits. To obtain a sufficient number of soldiers, Muhammad 'Ali envisaged using slaves and it was with this end in view that he sent out two military expeditions in 1820 and 1821 to Sudan in order to establish control over slave-trading centres. Muhammad 'Ali more particularly wished to conquer Dar Fur but he failed in this and had to limit himself to annexing Kurdufan. In the next chapter we shall look in some detail at the invasion and its implications for Sudan, but we may at this stage note that Sudanese-imported slaves, who were at first used on an extensive scale in the Egyptian army, soon proved inadequate. In particular a high mortality rate made the experiment a failure, and in the latter part of Muhammad 'Ali's reign there was growing recourse instead to conscription, both of Sudanese and Egyptian peasants. Muhammad 'Ali's regime thus had a strong military bias as is shown up by expenditure in this field which in the late 1830s amounted to 200 million Egyptian piastres, over half the country's annual budget.

Independence on the Mediterranean stage also required a navy to turn a landlocked army into an international force. Muhammad 'Ali decided to have a fleet built and the first orders were placed at Leghorn, Trieste, and Marseilles. The fleet was, however, entirely destroyed in 1827, at Navarino Bay. Without wasting any time, Muhammad 'Ali set about rebuilding it and to this effect he had shipbuilding yards set up at Alexandria, together with new harbour facilites. Under the orders of a French engineer, De Cerisy, some 40 000 Egyptians were set to work and by 1839, Egypt had a navy of 33 ships of various sizes, besides 40 others intended for transport. Clot Bey puts the number of sailors on the payroll at the time at 15 463, and that of the dockyard workers at 4075.

Muhammad 'Ali's foreign policy

Egyptian rearmament obviously had international implications, especially as a powerful army rarely remains inactive. The Great Powers had actively encouraged the setting up of a military regime in Egypt in order to protect the northern end of the Red Sea. They were also led to approve of the invasion of the Sudan which would extend this protection southwards. On the other hand they were against Egyptian involvement in the Mediterranean itself. Involvement could however hardly be avoided in view of Egypt's connection with the Ottoman Empire whose suzerain rights had been confirmed by the Great Powers. Revolts in Turkey's Mediterranean provinces led to appeals for help to the vassal state. The Greek revolt in the 1820s was a case in point, and Muhammad 'Ali sent his fleet and a military contingent to the area in

A portrait of Muhammad 'Ali

When I first went to reside in Egypt in 1839, Mehemet Ali, though an old man, was still in his full intellectual vigour. He was a man of short stature, well-proportioned, and with a striking countenance. His face was of the Albanian type, with something of the Tartar. He had a large thick nose, high cheek-bones, small mouth, eyes small but bright as a hawk's and as keen, with a long white beard and shaggy white eye-brows. He dressed in turban and gombaz and always wore his curved Mameluke sword, having received permission from Stamboul to retain his ancient habiliment, in consequence of his old age. He was a man of restless vigour, inquisitive, shrewd, and talkative. In disposition he was cruel, subject to caprice, and violent, but with occasional generous instincts. He had the vices in fact and the virtues of the ancient Osmanlis, and had nothing in common with his Circassian descendants of our day. His Court was purely Turkish – that is to say, Turkish-speaking. He himself had learnt Arabic late in life in order better to manage the fellahin.

John Ninet, 'Origin of the National Party in Egypt', *The Nineteenth Century*, January 1883.

exchange for the promise of Morea as part of his dominion. The Egyptian expeditionary corps showed its fighting strength by crushing local nationalist resistance in 1824–5 but, as we saw earlier, the Great Powers intervened in Navarino Bay in 1827 and imposed Greek independence on Turkey by the 1828 Poros Agreement. The project of a *pashalik* of Morea for Muhammad 'Ali thus fell through, and Egypt's ruler was reminded that the Eastern Question was fundamentally a European problem.

The ambiguous status of Egypt as a state recognizing Turkish suzerainty involved a tension-fraught relationship with the Sublime Porte. Egypt's long tradition of Middle Eastern expansion could only be emphasized by the military strength of the regime which contrasted with Turkish weakness, particularly evident in the 1807–26 period following on the forced abdication of the Sultan, Salim III. On the other hand, traditional respect for the head of the Muslim Empire was important for the low-born Albanian who depended morally and psychologically on the Sultan for such legitimacy as he could claim. This led Muhammad 'Ali alternately to support and contest Ottoman authority. We thus find him as early as 1811 upholding the Sultan's claims as 'the Servant of the two Holy Sanctuaries' (Mecca and Medina). This led to Egyptian military action in Arabia where the Islamic fundamentalist Wahhabi movement had taken control in the 18th century. Egyptian troops fought in Arabia from 1811 to 1818. Over and beyond their religious significance, the operations highlighted by Muhammad 'Ali's pilgrimage in 1814 gave the Egyptian viceroy command over the other shore of the Red Sea. Invasion and military control over Arabia has always been a dangerous temptation for Egypt as the breakdown of its control over the Hijaz and coastal regions in 1840 showed.

Muhammad 'Ali also had ambitions in the Regencies which had been encouraged by the initial French plan of a joint attack on Algiers. Though this had been thwarted because of determined British opposition, Muhammad 'Ali was to make several further moves to this end. In 1830 he had asked the Sublime Porte to appoint him Governor of Algeria or, at least, of Constantine. This implied an eventual claim on the two other Regencies, Muhammad 'Ali being particularly interested in Tripoli since Sudanic caravans tended to go there to avoid paying high taxes in Egypt. In 1834, he broached the subject with the Sultan, promising to repress the insurrection in Tripoli, should his rights as governor be recognized by the Sublime Porte.

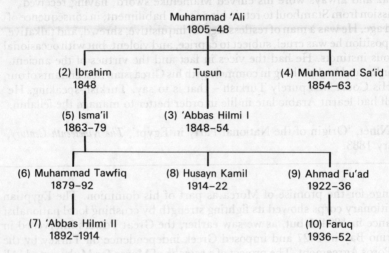

Fig. 7.1 *The dynasty of Muhammad 'Ali*

Egypt's relations with Turkey were, however, difficult, especially when Sultan Mahmud II (1808–39) launched an active policy of reform characterized by greater centralization. He viewed Muhammad 'Ali's growing strength and independence with disfavour. This led to a showdown when the viceroy undertook to re-establish Egypt's former frontiers with reference to the *Mamluk* Sultanate which had comprised Syria and Lebanon. Fighting ensued, and in 1839 the Sultan formally declared Muhammad 'Ali a traitor. Once again, however, the Great Powers intervened and worked out their own solution to the crisis on the basis of equilibrium in tension. The Convention of London was signed on 15 July 1840, by Great Britain, Russia, Austria, and Prussia. The French, on 10 July 1841, signified their approval. The Sultan was led to agree to granting Muhammad 'Ali hereditary rights over Egypt, thus satisfying an upstart's pride. On the other hand he demanded that the number of soldiers in the Egyptian army be brought down to 18 000. The Powers having agreed, pressure was brought to bear on Egypt by such means as a revolt stirred up by British and Turkish agents in Lebanon. The British fleet further made a show of strength off Alexandria. Muhammad 'Ali agreed to withdraw from Syria and Lebanon.

This account of Muhammad 'Ali's foreign policy ends with the 1841 *firman* granting him hereditary rights. It marks the full achievement of his ambitions and the end of his career since, from 1840 onwards, the old Albanian was becoming senile, his functions being carried out by his son Ibrahim who was formally invested in 1848. Ibrahim Pasha died that same year and 'Abbas Hilmi I succeeded (1848–54). Muhammad 'Ali himself lingered on another eight months, dying in Alexandria on 2 August 1849.

MUHAMMAD 'ALI'S ECONOMIC AND SOCIAL POLICIES

In the light of Muhammad 'Ali's career, one might be led to see him as a *condottière* following in the steps of the gubernatorial dynasties of early Muslim Egypt. This would be misleading since Muhammad 'Ali's personality is in fact far more complex: firstly because he was an extrovert who made Egypt his field of action; secondly because his apparent pragmatism also indicated an awareness on his part of deeper structural changes in the world at large, and his will to place Egypt on a par with other historically active nations. It is therefore in the light of this curious mixture of empiricism, modernization, and ultimate failure to make good Egypt's independence that we must examine the far-reaching changes which took place during his reign.

Agricultural reforms
A new social and economic policy was set on foot from the start, since the elimination of the *mamluk*-s and *janissaries* also did away with the traditional system of land tenure in terms of large estates conceded as *iltizam* (tax-farms). Extensive private property disappeared as confiscated lands passed under state control. This made it possible for Muhammad 'Ali to introduce a new state-planned agriculture for cash-crop production. Peasants became wage-earning labourers and even surviving private farms were placed under state control as agriculture was organized by agents and production was bought up or collected as tax payments. The system, however, met with considerable opposition, both at rural level and from the wealthier classes debarred from traditional investment in land. To these difficulties were added those connected with commercialization of cash-crops so that the system was progressively abandoned, and by the end of Muhammad 'Ali's reign private ownership reappeared on an extensive scale as large grants of land were made to state dignitaries and members of the viceroy's family. Moreover wealthy local notables were able to consolidate their land holdings by buying up those of peasants too poor to pay heavy taxes or preferring exile to conscription. Even the *iltizam* system reappeared in a modified form (*'uhda*) as rich persons took over control of villages by agreeing to pay the peasants' tax arrears and to meet future liabilities. This led to the development of a new land-owning class made up of absentee landlords and rural notables.

The changes introduced through state management of agriculture should not however be underestimated. The switch over to cash-crop production involved a new conception of agriculture no longer seen as the means through which local subsistence and self-sufficiency could be maintained, but in terms of commodities to meet requirements of the foreign market. This implied a changeover to new crops and techniques. We thus find Muhammad 'Ali

111

bringing in 1500 gardeners from Greece to set up or develop plantations of linen, opium, olives, or vegetables. Requirements were increasingly dictated by industrial needs, chief of which was the demand for raw materials for the textile industry. Efforts were therefore made to promote the production of silk; mulbery trees were planted and by 1839 the country was producing some 600 000 kg of silk. More important still was the conversion of national agriculture to a dominant crop: cotton. Initial efforts made at the start of Muhammad 'Ali's reign included imports of long-fibre cotton plants from America and recourse to foreign engineers to promote its growth in the Delta. Production in the early years was around 7000 tons a year and by 1813 the figure was four times higher. By 1839, it had reached 50 000 tons.

The significance of this conversion of local agriculture to cotton is to be seen not only in terms of a dominant European economy which determined the demand and set the price of the local commodity, nor even in terms of marketing which implied the growing presence of Europeans or their representatives in Egypt; it also implied deep structural changes in Egyptian society. The development of state farms led to an extension of irrigation on a Pharaonic scale. In the Delta area plans for the building of a dam were made and canals were cut on an extensive scale. It is estimated that some 2000 km of canal were dug during Muhammad 'Ali's reign. This was done at great human cost by means of corvée labour: contemporary sources claim, for example, that some 313 000 *fellah*-s conscripted in seven different provinces worked at one time or another on the Mahumudiyya Canal. In one single year, 12 000 men are said to have died of hunger or exhaustion while under forced labour. By these means perennial agriculture was extended and production increased.

This implied a considerable worsening of the peasants' lot, since the new permanent irrigation meant that people worked all the year round. Unhealthy conditions prevailed, since work was carried out knee-deep in water and the canals required constant clearance. New disease conditions developed with hepatitis, trachoma and bilharziasis becoming prevalent in rural areas. The prevalence of disease is illustrated by the fact that the population failed to increase despite a high birth rate, and by the fact that the peasant stock was permanently weakened so that recourse to immigration from the south, where healthier conditions prevailed, became a permanent feature.

Conditions were aggravated by the fact that production was largely dependent on human effort and that machines were rarely used. The scouring of canals, the planting of cotton and the treatment of plants (notably elimination of fungus disease by removing rotten leaves), besides picking and ginning, were largely manual tasks. Muhammad 'Ali's agricultural policy needed extra farm hands. To this end nomad tribes were forcibly sedentarized and efforts were made to recruit labourers from as far off as the Hijaz. Women were increasingly used for field work as were children, who were particularly suited to check plants for fungus growth. That peasants resisted the change is proved by the prevalence of revolts which were forcibly repressed by military means. We find mention of such peasant revolts in 1820–1, 1823–4, 1826, and 1846. In some cases the soldiers – who were themselves often conscripted peasants – refused to fire on the insurgents.

Urban change and industrialization

Changes were also under way in the towns. The traditional *madina* was no longer the centre of activity, but merely a poorer quarter on the outskirts of the modern town. Town growth on modern lines was indeed spectacular but it largely bypassed traditional quarters and even supplanted older inland towns such as Cairo since there was now an emphasis on harbour settlements where commerce with Europeans was active. The changes already apparent in Bonaparte's time became more marked and Alexandria, which by 1830 had a population of around 60 000, was now to all intents and purposes the country's unofficial capital. New modern suburbs developed. Dockyards were busy. Public and private works were under way and the viceroy's family itself spent most of its time in Alexandria where Muhammad 'Ali had a splendid palace built for himself at Ras al-Tyn.

Towns and boroughs also experienced industrial development as a key part of Muhammad 'Ali's far-reaching economic policy. This was intended to produce raw materials not only for the foreign market but also for local transformation. Between 1805 and 1839 he had some 500 factories set up. They included three sugar refineries and a number of silk-weaving factories (the largest of which was set up in Khoronfish in 1816). A paper-mill was opened in Cairo in 1834, besides other plants for the making of saltpetre, glass, dyes, and for the extraction of vegetable oil. The most important and most numerous factories were those connected with cotton-weaving. This system also included recourse to private looms. People received raw cotton from the government and home-made cloth had to be handed over. All cloth bore the government stamp and workers were not allowed to keep back any for private sale. The government, of course, fixed the price of cloth which was bought from the producer at about half the price for which it was later sold. Here, even more than in the field of agriculture, difficulties arose.

The causes of failure are self-evident. Egyptian industry proved uncompetitive because no adequate preparations were made for its adaptation to local conditions. It was moreover dependent on Europe. Egypt did not even have local sources of energy or materials for a national industry. Coke and iron had to be imported. Machinery came from Europe, often at considerable cost and with no adequate means of maintenance. With the machinery came European engineers to set it up and managers to run the factories. This proved generally costly and the Europeans were often ill-adapted to the local work force. The fact that workers were hostile to the industrialization project and had to be forcibly recruited for work in the factories further undermined efficiency. Products were thus uncompetitive, not only with respect to the foreign market but even at home where a free trade policy made European-produced goods cheaper. The factories proved a liability rather than an asset and by the turn of the century most of them had been closed down.

Their impact on Egyptian society and on workers recruited or forced into industry (who do not qualify as an actual working class) was nonetheless considerable. The factories were often large unsalubrious buildings. The spinning-mill at Shibin thus had 1250 workers, that of Qaliyub 600, and at al-Mahallat al-Kubra, 3000 out of a population of about 8000 were employed at the factory. Working conditions were scandalous. Not only were salaries low but workers had to pay for faulty pieces of work or for the repair of machines. Pay came late. Child labour was commonplace and women worked side by side with the men. They were particularly oppressed since they not only had to carry out traditional female occupations at home but had lower salaries than the men. Moreover, working conditions were harder for them; in the overheated factories men worked almost naked whilst the women were expected to remain heavily veiled. Here, as in Europe, popular opposition expressed itself in various ways, including arson. J. A. St. John, author of a book on Muhammad 'Ali published in 1834, noted that out of 23 spinning mills concerning which he had information, 'all had at some stage or other seen fires break out'. Workers, moreover, had no form of collective organization. Government control and a large potential labour force made it impossible for workers to defend their rights. Passive opposition, notably in the form of unproductive behaviour, was therefore their sole means of expression. The hard-working Egyptian was thus seen by his employers and by foreign observers as a lazy industrial worker. This, together with mismanagement explains why the policy of industrialization was gradually abandoned, turning Egypt into a mere producer of raw materials for industrial Europe.

The economy as a whole
The situation still has to be appreciated in the overall context of national economy. In Egypt production costs were kept low, but this should be seen as part of a precapitalist system on which new economic policies were inadequately grafted. Conscript labour characterized the changes forcibly undertaken. Where salaries were paid, these were atrociously low. Ordinary factory workers and soldiers had from 10 to 15 piastres a month, with a special advantage for the soldier, who at least had his upkeep in the barracks. Farm workers were paid even less. Conditions became more difficult as the years passed since salaries remained unchanged in a period of rising costs of living. A sure sign of underdevelopment was the growing dependence of workers on the artificial stimulus of tea, coffee, sugar, and opium. These had to be paid for with money and increased the workers' dependence.

Egypt's export-orientated economy certainly benefited in this period from European demand, although it was also hard-hit whenever an industrial crisis occurred, as in the 1840s. National revenue doubled in the reign of Muhammad 'Ali to reach 60 million French francs in 1845 (the standard rate of exchange being 25 francs for £1 sterling) but income distribution became increasingly unequal so that workers benefited but little from national wealth. On the other hand they were hard hit by rising prices. This inflation reflected

Fig. 7.2 Depreciation of Egyptian currency in Muhammad 'Ali's time

1805 – 1 French franc = 1 Egyptian piastre
1821 – 1 French franc = 1.4 Egyptian piastres
1825 – 1 French franc = 2 Egyptian piastres
1829 – 1 French franc = 2.55 Egyptian piastres
1833 – 1 French franc = 3.33 Egyptian piastres
1843 – 1 French franc = 4 Egyptian piastres

Egypt's fragile economy: through constant depreciation the local currency lost a quarter of its international value between 1805 and 1843.

The changes underway were not merely economic and the new conditions to which the Egyptian workers were subjected are only one aspect of a total disruption of traditional society and the inception of a new social and economic order.

MODERN EGYPT IN THE MAKING

Muhammad 'Ali's view of modern Egypt implied a different form of state-management based on centralization and greater control over the social order which had previously remained largely autonomous. The development of state authority was thus paralleled by the destruction of the traditional institutions which had up to then overseen social life. In the process new dominant social categories appeared, or old ones redefined their objectives and lifestyle.

The centralization of administration

The development of state-management cannot be separated from the means of coercion it used: the viceroy's role was defined by a more autocratic use of his traditional powers and the implementing of his policies by military means. It also involved the setting up of a complex centralized system of civil administration. The traditional tax-collecting department was reinforced and extended, and local administrations were set up in parallel to central government to uphold tax-collectors in the exercise of their functions. Egypt

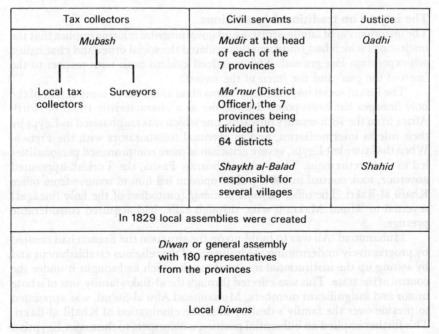

Tax collectors		Civil servants	Justice
Mubash		*Mudir* at the head of each of the 7 provinces	*Qadhi*
Local tax collectors	Surveyors	*Ma'mur* (District Officer), the 7 provinces being divided into 64 districts	
		Shaykh al-Balad responsible for several villages	*Shahid*
In 1829 local assemblies were created			
Diwan or general assembly with 180 representatives from the provinces			
Local *Diwans*			

Fig. 7.3 *Local administration in Egypt*

for this purpose was now divided into seven provinces (four for the Delta, one for Central Egypt, two for Upper Egypt), subdivided into 64 administrative districts, each under a *ma'mur* or district officer. Traditional community life was disrupted not only by the new economic order based on state-planned production, but by a parallel attempt to control local village communities which were now constituted into *nazir-liks* placed under the jurisdiction of village headmen (*shaykh al-balad*). The latter were increasingly influential rural notables and their self-awareness as a social group is an important aspect of social change in this period.

Two other measures contributed to the growth of the new all-important state institution as the means through which social changes were overseen. The first was the creation of administrative departments at governmental level. As defined by the 1837 decree which set them up, this change emphasized the new importance of technical ministries. The government thus comprised seven sections: the Interior, Finance, War, the Admiralty, Education, Public Works, Trade and Foreign Affairs. The second measure was the setting up of assemblies through which influential sectors of opinion could be informed of government decisions and policy. These assemblies (which can hardly qualify as parliamentary institutions) were set up in 1829. They included local assemblies of nominated members and a *diwan* or general assembly in which rural notables had a preponderant position, since they represented the majority of the 180 representatives chosen at provincial level. It is in their attitudes towards public service and parliamentary representation that the rising classes of Egyptian society came to express their personal and collective ambitions, thus promoting political self-expression.

The impact on traditional institutions

The introduction of administrative and governmental reforms implies that the institutions which had traditionally regulated the social order and channelled self-expression lost ground. This is indeed evident both with respect to the 'men of the pen' and the 'men of the sword'.

The loss of social impact of the *'ulama* class and even to some extent of the holy lineages has been pointed to earlier as a characteristic trend of North Africa from the 18th century onwards, one which was emphasized in Egypt by their role as intermediaries, and as eventual collaborators with the French. When the latter left Egypt, severe criticism of more compromised personalities led to their retirement. Thus when Khusraw Pasha, the Turkish-appointed governor, took control in 1801, public opinion led him to remove from office Khalil al-Bakri. The office of *naqib al-ashraf* (custodian of the holy lineages) reverted to 'Umar Makram who, through exile, had acquired considerable prestige.

Muhammad 'Ali was to build up on the situation the French had created by progressively undermining the influence of the religious establishment and by setting up the institutional means through which he brought it under the control of the state. This was effected through the al-Bakri family, one of whose minor and insignificant members, Muhammad Abu al-Su'ud, was appointed to preside over the family's destiny after the elimination of Khalil al-Bakri. This further implied an influential position with respect to the major Egyptian sufi orders which were traditionally led by the leader of the Bakri family and fraternity. It was through Muhammad Abu al-Su'ud and, after the latter's death in 1812 through his son, Muhammad Efendi (*circa* 1775–1855) and grandson, 'Ali (1804–80), that the viceroys extended the network of state control over the various fields where the social impact of the religious establishment was strongest: in the field of teaching, of fraternities, of holy shrines, and of religious fairs and festivals.

A first step was made in 1812 when Muhammad 'Ali, at the request of the dying Muhammad Abu al-Su'ud, appointed Muhammad Efendi not only leader of the Bakriyya, but of all the Egyptian fraternities, following this up in 1816 by another decree naming him *naqib al-ashraf*. Not only did this point to more direct state involvement in the working of the religious institutions, but it also meant the loss of control of al-Azhar university over fraternities since the latter had often provided fraternity *shaykh*-s and carried out part of its teaching in the *zawiya*-s which were now placed under al-Bakri's control. Al-Azhar's lack of pugnacity in the matter was further shown up by a long dispute between al-Bakri and the rector of the mosque-university as to who was to have the right of jurisdiction with respect to disputes arising in holy lineages or fraternities. It ended in a settlement in 1847 granting full rights to al-Bakri. The fact that the latter further controlled the benefits accruing to the religious establishment through *waqf* property, which Muhammad 'Ali placed in the hands of a state-appointed board presided over by al-Bakri, further increased his power. Another field of state intervention was with respect to the rights of fraternities to preach and establish lodges. These, in Egypt, had traditionally been assimilated to the *iltizam* system, and fraternity *shaykh*-s could obtain the right of *qadam*, or exclusivity in a particular district. Muhammad 'Ali built up this as other privileges whilst, at the same time, enforcing state control since the right of *qadam* was granted by al-Bakri and was further used to prevent the extension of newer or more active sufi orders.

Through the *naqib al-ashraf*, who in effect was a viceregal representative at the head of an increasingly complex department in charge of religious affairs, Muhammad 'Ali and his successors cut off traditional religious bodies from free social interplay and brought them progressively under state control. By the middle of the 19th century, the religious institutions had become state-dependent, not only because their rights and privileges were subordinated to al-Bakri's permission and to viceregal decree, but because their social activities were regulated by his department. Even the holding of *mawlid*-s or religious feasts at a shrine required government permission, the holy lineage having in any case a subordinate position as ceremonies were presided over by al-Bakri or his delegate.

In spite of this, as we shall see, tactical retreat was nonetheless the occasion for the building-up of more militant religious attitudes which later came to the fore, both in more official al-Azhari circles and in rural holy lineages.

The 'men of the sword' even more characteristically than the 'men of the pen' were brought under state control by Muhammad 'Ali. Here too it should be pointed out that the dominant position of the *mamluk*-s had in fact been undermined in the period preceding Muhammad 'Ali's rise to power, and though he did away with the two economic and social privileges which defined their power, namely private armed retainers and rural property, he maintained them as figureheads, the symbols of autocratic powers which in fact were concentrated in his hands. Thus Muhammad 'Ali, who was not unaware of the dangers of European penetration, never personally communicated with foreigners, but did so through government ministers, heads of departments, army officers, and court personnel – all of whom were recruited from former *mamluk* and *janissary* families.

This, however, was to some degree a mere veneer, as the effective power of the administration was increasingly vested in new categories of civil servants. Technical requirements no less than Muhammad 'Ali's tolerant attitude with respect to religious minorities led to a growing number of Europeans being recruited to high office. They staffed the ministries, where their reports largely dictated government decisions. At various intermediary and higher echelons were to be found Levantines from various parts of the eastern Mediterranean. The Copts who had traditionally provided the civil service with subordinate employees, staffed the Ministries of the Interior and of Finance, especially in rural postings. These were the men who now prepared and upheld viceregal policies and who were consequently part of the powerful state machine which was remodelling Egyptian society on new lines.

The growth of class stratification

The overall trend of social evolution in this period can be defined as leading to class stratification. This was evident in terms of disparity of revenue. Whereas the working class increasingly contributed to national wealth, it received little by way of benefit. On the other hand, relations with the Euopean market provided possibilities for wealth on an unprecedented scale. Between these two extremes, we find civil service salaries which themselves reflect uneven distribution. In the army, the ordinary soldier had 15 piastres a month, a lieutenant 350, a colonel 800, and a general 12 500. In a factory, the manager was paid about 500 piastres a month, but if he was a European, his salary was at least four times higher. The chief secretary or accountant was paid about 300 piastres, the doorkeeper 30, and the worker half as much.

Class stratification was further underlined by a changing way of life. Whereas the ordinary Egyptian continued to speak the local Arab dialect, to eat traditional food and dress in the Egyptian long tunic, trousers and cap, the ruling classes increasingly lived in European style. This involved homes in the modern quarters of towns, and the use of foreign languages (principally French) in a business but also in a social capacity. They gave up wearing oriental clothes (not Egyptian dress which they had never worn) and adopted the newly-fashionable Turkish version of the frock-coat known as *stambuli*. The turban disappeared in favour of the long-tasseled fez. Younger men trimmed their beards and some even went clean-shaven. The lead was taken by the Viceregal family. Muhammad 'Ali continued to wear oriental clothes but he was the last Egyptian sovereign to do so. His palace at Alexandria was a curious mixture of Ottoman luxury and Parisian elegance. French was not only spoken at court but later became the official language.

Between the poor and the ruling classes we find Egypt's middle classes; a new meritocracy, promoted by its functions in the new social order, but not assimilated by the ruling class which remained foreign and clung to its privileges. A close connection exists between the urban-based petty bourgeoisie and the wealthier rural families from which they generally came. Participation of native Egyptians in the new regime came through education and the latter was itself the result of civil service requirements. This implied a change in educational policy. Whereas in former times this had been an al-Azhar privilege used to promote a scholar class whose interests were essentially cultural and religious, new requirements were technological. Muhammad 'Ali saw education as a system to train civil servants: it was to be secular in its teaching and professional in its objectives. It is indeed typical that the first school opened under the new policy of state education should have been set up to train land surveyors (1817). It was followed up in 1827 by a medical school, and in 1836 by one specializing in the study of foreign languages. As a state concern, education was reorganized in 1837 and schools were placed under the supervision of the government department for education (*diwan al-madaris*).

The influence of modern education was further underscored, in some cases, by training abroad. Napoleon had already envisaged sending Egyptians to study in France but it was one of his scholarly entourage in Egypt, Edme-François Jomard, who later finalized the project and won over Muhammad 'Ali to it, even though Italy had come up with a counter-project. In 1826, Muhammad 'Ali sent a first batch of students to Paris. They were between 40 and 50 in number and their ages ranged from 15 to 37. A few came from the ruling elite, but others were sons of village notables. They were first taught French before following a general course for two years. They then specialized in one of 15 subjects including military administration, chemistry and agronomy. The school developed with the arrival of new batches of students in 1829, 1830, 1832. By then their number was 1500. The experiment was terminated by Muhammad 'Ali in 1835, but it was resumed on a different basis in 1844 with the setting up in Paris of a Military Academy for Egyptians. Class stratification was underlined as members of the viceroy's family were put in one section, sons of *bey*-s in another, and a few chosen elements from rural families in a third.

The modern-type education created an *esprit de corps* among the meritocracy of rural origin. In the Egyptian context, which debarred them from access to higher positions to which the *mamluk*-s clung as a class privilege, their group solidarity was intensified. The self-awareness of this rising group was promoted not only by a common involvement in the changes under way in Egypt and a common way of life, but also through the bond of literacy, which was encouraged by the development of a national press. Up to then the only papers known had been Turkish ones or publications undertaken by Bonaparte (in French or Arabic). Their impact had been almost nil. In 1822, Muhammad 'Ali imported a printing press which was set up at Bulaq (where Bonaparte's press had functioned). The first paper published was a weekly in Turkish which came out in 1828. Later to become bilingual (Turkish and Arabic) and finally Arabic, *Al-Waqai' al-Misriyya* was an official gazette. Various other journals and even an important literary review were published and by the turn of the century they had become commonplace although their influence was limited by government censorship. The fact that the official gazette had as its editor Rifa'a al-Tahtawi, one of the leading thinkers of the age, not only helped the spread of new ideas but intensified this as translations of major European works were published by him.

Education and foreign travel fostered a new political self-awareness in the rising meritocracy which expressed itself by demands for greater participation in governmental affairs through democratic rule, the latter being considered synonymous with parliamentary representation. Muhammad 'Ali had himself made a limited move in this direction by setting up local assemblies where rural notables had acquired political experience and consolidated their positions as representatives of rural society. The general assembly in which they were a majority brought this to national level, besides giving rural notables the possibility of identifying their views with those of their class who were part of Cairo's meritocracy. Interaction between the two led to a new common standpoint making parliamentary democracy the antidote against despotism and hereditary *mamluk* privileges. A struggle on these lines was to characterize political aspirations during the second half of the 19th century. It is therefore useful at this stage to consider the ideological context which was to characterize the new meritocracy, especially because it owed much to a remarkable man, Rifa'a al-Tahtawi (1801–73).

A new dissatisfied elite . . .

My interpreter and assistant, Mohammed Effendi, a young fellah who had been educated at the Ecole Normale at Paris, and a man of extensive knowledge, gave me my earliest political ideas about Egypt. His history is typical of the causes which have produced the nationalist movement. Mohammed was a native of Shibbrekit in Baheyra, son of a sheykh el Belled. At the age of sixteen he had been sent to Paris by the Viceroy with many others to receive a European education at the French mission, and afterwards, being a youth of promise, to the Ecole Normale, where he took his degree in letters and sciences and qualified to be a professor when he should return to Egypt. He returned with the character of being the best pupil of the mission, and expected to receive a correspondingly high appointment at Cairo. Instead, however, of being thus employed, he was, by the jealousy of the Circassian and Turkish influence at Court, and *because he was a fellah* and one whose talents they feared, left as a clerk in a low office at the salary of £3 a month, doing no more than the work of a common interpreter for several years, and it was considered a high advancement for him when he was transferred to work under me in a like mean capacity. I have no hestiation in saying that this young man was qualified by his knowledge and his talents for almost any intellectual charge that could have been found for him in Egypt. But the unlearned Turks stood between him and success . . .

John Ninet, *Origin of the National Party in Egypt*, 1883.

Rifa'a al-Tahtawi and Islamic reformism

One of the claims to fame of the Egyptian school in Paris was the presence there from 1826 to 1831 of Rifa'a al-Tahtawi, a young religious scholar sent as acting chaplain to the students. His observations of life in France led him to a new awareness of his own Islamic society and its place in history. Considering that Islamic civilization which had once dominated the world was now uncompetitive and static, al-Tahtawi was led to analyze the reasons for the Muslim world's decline. His appreciations seem to echo attitudes which European social philosophy of the time had made fashionable by means of such slogans as 'the struggle for existence', the 'survival of the fittest', 'progress', and 'self-help'. Al-Tahtawi was thus the first of a series of Muslim reformers who had a new dynamic and militant attitude, promoting intellectual and social efforts which were seen as each successive generation's responsibility with respect to God's message. Al-Tahtawi, who was to influence later Muslim reformers such as Muhammad 'Abduh and Jamal al-Din al-Afghani, reminded his contemporaries that mere ignorance of Europe was an attitude of defeat in a world characterized by the technical superiority of the infidel. Only by acquiring those very means by which Europe had become all-powerful could Muslims reassert their identity; nor, in his eyes, was this in itself sufficient. Only by developing literacy could awareness of the respective values of civilizations grow, and with it the feeling of urgency which would promote necessary reforms.

Thus al-Tahtawi was led to support Muhammad 'Ali's efforts in the field of education in which he himself was to play an important role. He even advocated – though timidly – schooling for girls. Significantly, however, opposition to this was widespread and it was only in 1873, the year of al-Tahtawi's death, that the first government primary school for girls was opened. Another positive trait al-Tahtawi noted in Europe was the growing demand for democracy in terms of parliamentary rule. The Muslim ideal was democratic but, in later empires, despotism had become increasingly marked. Al-Tahtawi pointed to this as one of the chief causes of Islamic decline.

Al-Tahtawi thus appears as the forerunner of later North African ideology, and yet his own conclusions were barely sketched out, although the basic elements of the reformist doctrine were there: to meet the challenge of history the Muslim world must open itself out to foreign experiences. It must reform itself from within and make the necessary efforts, both in material and intellectual fields, to reaffirm its destiny as a triumphant march towards a transcendent ideal. What this message signified in social practice depended largely on the degree of political self-awareness of the national community and its collective capacity to become historically efficient. In Muhammad 'Ali's time, the message was significant essentially for the new managerial class. Muhammad 'Ali publicly approved it by naming al-Tahtawi to various official posts including that of editor of the official gazette. Moreover, he had al-Tahtawi's account of his stay in France, *Takhlis al-Ibriz*, published in 1834.

Al-Tahtawi's teaching was, in an initial phase, seen as ideological justification of Muhammad 'Ali policies. The fact that these implied the disruption of Egyptian society and the appearance of class stratification on new lines, with increased hardships for the peasants and workers, was overlooked by the bureaucratic and managerial class which developed in the wake of the new policies. Literacy, technical training, participation in the economic development of the country and a claim to participation in political decisions were part of a new social attitude to which al-Tahtawi brought the backing of his powerful mind.

What this new class ideology failed to take into account was that the concept of progress which it was thus taking over from the *bourgeois conquérants* of Europe involved a scale of values commonly referred to as the 'ladder of progress' which used technological progress as a yard-stick by which to measure the relative position of different nations. Industrial Europe was thus seen as being on the highest rung of progress with other nations dragging behind. Future colonial invasions were thus justified by the belief that Europe would be bringing civilization to backward peoples. The rule of one social class over another was justified on the same principle since that sector of society involved in technological advances had a natural function of leader with respect to other classes and society as a whole. Egypt under Muhammad 'Ali was already demonstrating that the 'ladder of progress' meant domination for some and submission for many at home, whilst also opening out the country to foreign penetration and the growing influence of European capitalism.

SELECTED READING LIST

Abdel-Malek, A., *Idéologie et Renaissance Nationale: l'Egypte Moderne*, (Paris, 1969).
'Abduh, I., *Tarikh al-Waqai 'al-Misriyya*, (Cairo, 1942).
Abu-Lughod, I., *Arab Rediscovery of Europe, a Study in Cultural Encounters*, (Princeton, 1963).
Ahmad, J., *The Intellectual Origins of Egyptian Nationalism*, (London, 1960).
Baer, G., *A History of Landownership in Modern Egypt, 1800–1950*, (London, 1962).
Cattaui, R. & G., *Mohamed-Aly et l'Europe*, (Paris, 1950).
Combe, *et al.*, *Précis de l'Histoire d'Egypte par divers Historiens et Archéologues*, Vol. III, (Cairo, 1933).
De Jong, F., *Turuq and Turuq-Linked Institutions in Nineteenth Century Egypt*, (Leyden, 1978).
Dodwell, H., *The Founder of Modern Egypt. A Study of Muhammad Ali*, (Cambridge, 1931).
Douin, G., *Las Mission du Baron de Boislecomte. L'Egypte et la Syrie en 1833*, (Cairo, 1927).
Fahmy, M., *La Révolution de l'Industrie en Egypte et ses Conséquences Sociales au XIXe Siècle (1800–1850)*, (Leiden, 1954).
Ghorbal, Sh., *The Beginnings of the Egyptian Question and the Rise of Mehemet Ali*, (London, 1928).
Holt, P. M. ed., *Political and Social Change in Modern Egypt*, (London, 1968).
Issawi, Ch. ed., *The Economic History of the Middle East. 1800–1914, A Book of Readings*, (Chicago and London, 1966).
Louca, A., *Voyageurs et Ecrivains Egyptiens en France au XIXe Siècle*, (Paris, 1970).
Rivlin, H., *The Agricultural Policy of Muhammad 'Ali in Egypt*, (Cambridge, Mass., 1961).
Sabry, M., *L'Empire Égyptien sous Mohammed-Ali et la Question d'Orient (1811–1849)*, (Paris, 1930).
Shayyal, J. al-, *Tarikh al-tarjama wa al-thaqafiya fi 'asr Muhammad 'Ali*, (Cairo, 1951).
Souriau, Ch., *La Presse Maghrébine*, (Aix-en-Provence, 1969).
Tahtawi, R. al-, *Complete Works*, (Beryruth, 1972–5).

CHAPTER 8

WARS OF CONQUEST IN THE FIRST HALF OF THE 19th CENTURY: SUDAN, LIBYA, ALGERIA

The reader may by now have come to the conclusion that no clear-cut line separates the colonial from the precolonial period and it is indeed true that Bonaparte's invasion of Egypt was as much if not more 'colonial' than the 1830 attack on Algiers: moreover, efforts to build up a constructive response to the challenge of European-promoted changes could itself undermine independence. In this chapter, three military conquests will be examined, only one of which – that of Algeria by France – is generally termed colonial because it involves one of the Great Powers which built up an empire. We may nonetheless ask ourselves whether, in fact, it differs as radically as generally supposed from other conquests carried out by Muslims, whether that of Sudan by Egypt or of Libya by the Ottomans.

TURCO-EGYPTIAN RULE IN SUDAN

The country Muhammad 'Ali invaded in 1820 was not Sudan as we know it today but merely the Funj Sultanate, by then a decadent state with little effective authority over the surrounding populations and further weakened by dissensions within the reigning family. In spite of this we should not underestimate the collective capacity of the Sudanese to oppose foreign aggression. Here, as in other tribal lands, the prevailing pattern of interaction was largely organized and supervised by holy lineages of supposed sharifian origin who not only regulated the social and political order but expressed the self-identity of the Sudanese as Muslims. Here, as elsewhere, they also promoted Arabic scholarship. In the period preceding the Egyptian invasion they had partaken in the more general Islamic trend of sufi revival in terms of fraternities having an often extended following. The Sudanese *tariqa*-s (fraternities) were themselves often local offshoots of the major orders of the Muslim world, as for example the Majdhubiyya, a sub-order of the Qadiriyya, founded by Ahmad bin Muhammad in the middle of the 18th century, which had its religious centre at al-Damir where its influence reached far beyond the local Ja'ali population; so too the Tayyibiyya founded in the 18th century by Ahmad al-Tayyib (died 1824) as an offshoot of the Egyptian Sammaniyya which was itself part of the Khalwati revival in North Africa. A more recent order was the Khatmiyya, or Mirghaniyya as it is often called, which had been founded in Sudan by 'Uthman al-Mirghani (died 1851) who had come to

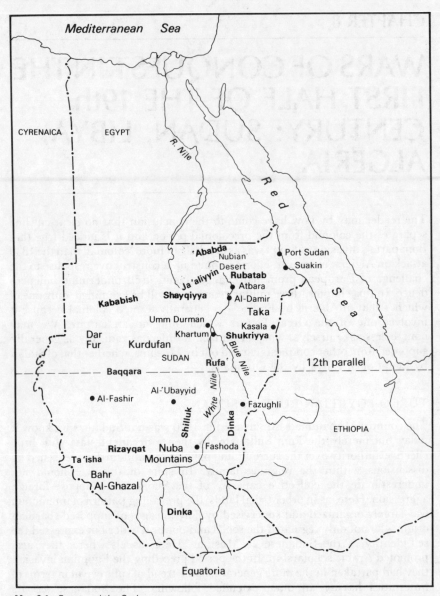

Map 8.1 *Egypt and the Sudan*

Sudan to reform religious practice, just prior to the Egyptian expedition, in 1817.

In Egypt, preparations for the military expedition included an official *casus belli*, namely the refuge found in the Funj sultanate by rebellious *mamluk*-s. As early as 1812, Muhammad 'Ali had officially requested their expulsion. The invasion also required religious justification since the projected conquest was that of one Muslim state by another. Muhammad 'Ali claimed he was acting on behalf of the Ottoman Sultan, legitimate heir to the leadership of the Muslim community as a whole. The Sudanese were to be integrated into the empire. *'Ulama* were consequently asked to go to Sudan with the army to explain this. The involvement of the Ottomans in what has been called Turco-Egyptian rule in Sudan was, in fact, limited to this moral patronage, later backed up by a *firman* granting Muhammad 'Ali government of the provinces of Nubia, Sennar, and subsequently Dar Fur and Kurdufan. Two armies were brought together: one under Isma'il Kamil Pasha, a son of Muhammad Ali, which went to Sudan in the summer of 1820, the second under Muhammad Bey Khusraw which left the following year with Dar Fur as its objective.

The weakness of the Funj political institution may have led Muhammad 'Ali to underestimate the difficulties in his way. Although the sedentary populations of the Nile – often collectively referred to as the Awlad al-Balad – generally submitted with little resistance and the Funj Sultanate capitulated in June 1821, the Shayqiyya tribe offered resistance in 1820 and, two years later, sparked off a widespread uprising. Moreover, there were strong well-organized nomad or semi-nomad confederacies including the Shukriyya camel owners between the Nile and River Atbara, the Kababish north of Kurdufan and the Baqqara of southern Kurdufan and Dar Fur whose fighting capacity was not negligible in spite of their outmoded armaments. Their reactions in the face of the invading power were, however, divided. The Shukriyya became staunch supporters of the Turkiyya (as the Egyptian regime was locally called) whereas the Kababish and Baqqara remained largely out of control, alternatively hostile or friendly as their interests dictated.

In important aspects of the undertaking, Muhammad 'Ali's venture was far from a success. It failed notably in one of its main objectives, namely the conquest of Dar Fur. Khusraw Bey failed to make his bid good and had to content himself with annexing the Dar Furi Sultan's eastern dependency, Kurdufan. Muhammad 'Ali moreover had sanguine hopes of obtaining gold from the south. This also proved a failure not only because he was unable to conquer Dar Fur, the gateway to central Africa, but because rumours of Sudanic wealth proved largely imaginary. The reported alluvial gold was never found and even the gold mines of Fazughli which the Egyptians conquered as early as 1822 were of limited value. The setting-up in 1821–2 of a fiscal organization based on heavy taxation of the Awlad al-Balad at the rate of 15 Maria Teresa thalers per slave, ten per cow and five per sheep or donkey, provoked widespread revolts in 1822, notably among the Ja'aliyyin leading to a cruel repression by Khusraw Bey and the destruction of the holy centre of al-Damir. The cost of the expeditionary corps and of a regime which was always to be strongly military was especially heavy, even if by 1827 the Egyptians were masters of the northern part of the country, and in the years which followed, reconnoitred and to some degree extended their influence southwards so that by 1841 they had penetrated up the Nile some 1000 km south of Khartum.

We may ask ourselves why Muhammad 'Ali should have undertaken this difficult and costly invasion. The answers to such a question have a characteristically colonial flavour. One can point to reasons connected with home politics including the check put on Egyptian expansion in the Mediterranean by Turkey and the Great Powers. Muhammad 'Ali had initially experienced difficulty in keeping his unruly army under control. Undisciplined elements such as the Albanians were consequently sent southwards to hunt out rebel *mamluk*-s. Subsequently Sudan became a province to which seditious officers or persons considered as political agitators were sent to keep them out of mischief. Moreover, Muhammad 'Ali had created an army on modern lines for which practical military training was necessary. Sudan provided this at no diplomatic cost.

Sudan was also to be a colony in the sense that it was expected to provide for the home country's needs. Muhammad 'Ali's first requirement was slaves who were conscripted for the new professional army (*al-nizam al-jadid*). The march on Dar Fur had as an objective the control of the Sudanic slave trade. As this failed, the Egyptians had recourse to recruiting the slaves who in Sudan traditionally carried out most of the agricultural work in the Nile Valley. Heavy taxation in a country short of cash was intended to provide these. Since even this could not meet Muhammad 'Ali's inordinate demands, slaves were forcibly seized throughout the region and raids were organized along the ever extending southern frontier. In 1821 training centres for these slaves were set up, notably in Aswan. By 1823, there were some 30 000 recruits and when 'Uthman Bey arrived in 1824 as commander-in-chief, he brought with him five newly constituted battalions of *jihadiyya* or Sudanese slaves. The experiment also proved unsatisfactory and had to be partially abandoned: as a result of harsh and unsatisfactory conditions to which the slaves did not adapt, mortality was too high. Muhammad 'Ali was instead to have recourse to conscription both of Egyptians and Sudanese.

Economic exploitation was carried out in Sudan with a ruthlessness at least equal to that of other colonial regimes. It was characterized in the first place by levies. Colonized people were expected to pay for the upkeep of the invaders and bring in profit on top. In Sudan this was aggravated by two factors: gross mismanagement and the general attitude of the men sent out, for whom Sudan was fair spoil.

Foreign rule was also characterized by the determination to make the Sudanese a dominated population. This was evident not only in personal relations, where Egyptians had every right to carry off a man's property or women with impunity, but also in the more general pattern of relations between the two social categories. A typical detail illustrates this: a Sudanese passing an Egyptian officer was expected to dismount.

How this affected social groups is important for the historian. Tribes were assessed in terms of their usefulness to the invaders. We thus find tribes such as the Shukkriyya (between Atbara and the Blue Nile) and the Shayqiyya (south of Dunqula) favoured because they provided the Turkiyya with a corps of irregulars who were particularly ferocious when it came to collecting taxes from the peasants. Other tribes were regularly overrun and tribal cohesion was broken down in the process.

To break the spirit of resistance, the Turkiyya undertook to neutralize or eliminate the holy lineages. The head of the Majdhubiyya fraternity, for example, was exiled after the destruction of al-Damir. More generally, we find them being reduced to lay status and made to pay taxes from which holy men

Fig. 8.1 Sudan during the reign of Muhammad 'Ali

Dates	Military Governors	Main events
1820	Isma'il Kamil Pasha	July 1820: army left Cairo for Sudan. Resistance of the Shayqiyya but submission of the Dunqula, the *mamluk*-s, and part of Ja'aliyyin. June 1821: the Funj Sultanate surrendered. Sennar occupied. April 1821: a second army left Cairo under command of Muhammad Bey Khusraw and conquered Kurdufan.
1822–4	Khusraw Pasha	Auriferous region of Fazughli conquered. Fiscal system organized. November 1822: widespread revolts.
1824–5	'Uthman Bey	Arrived with five battalions of Sudanese slave soldiers. Set up a military post at Khartum. Revolts cruelly repressed. Drought, famine, and epidemics of smallpox.
1825	Mahu Bey	Policy of conciliation. Sudanese consulted through local assemblies. Shaykh 'Abd al-Qadir came to the fore as adviser on tribal affairs.
1825–38	'Ali Khurshid Pasha	Policy of conciliation stepped up. Opponents invited to return. Local assemblies convened. 'Abd al-Qadir appointed *shaykh al-mashayikh*. The development of Khartum. 1827, 1830: unsuccessful military expeditions up the Nile, in Shilluk and Dinka country. 1831–2: unsuccessful campaigns against the Hadendowa of the Taka and frontier war with Ethiopia. Expansion towards the Red Sea marked by the setting up of a military post at Kassala. 1835: Khurshid Pasha appointed *Hukumdar* (Governor-General). 1836: Drought, epidemics of cholera.
1838–43	Abu Widan	Fiscal system reorganized. Occupation of the Taka. Winter 1838–9: Muhammad 'Ali visited Sudan. 1839, 1840, 1842, Salim Qabtan explored the White Nile up to Gondokoro.
1843–5	Ahmad Pasha Manikli	Expedition against Hadendowa.

were traditionally exempted.

As in Egypt in 1800, officially authorized intermediaries appeared on the scene to advise on tribal affairs. An obscure *shaykh* called 'Abd al-Qadir came to the fore and under Khurshid Pasha he became an influential person. Some religious personalities were similarly promoted. Thus, in order to undermine the influence of the Majdhubiyya, the Egyptians encouraged the Khatmiyya whose influence spread throughout Sudan, even extending over into Egypt. They were helped to establish control over former Majdhubi strongholds, including al-Damir, so that when Muhammad al-Majdhub returned from exile in 1830, he was forced to confine his activities to the Red Sea mountain area. The Mirghani family was to be conspicuous for its pro-Egyptian and later anti-Mahdi stand.

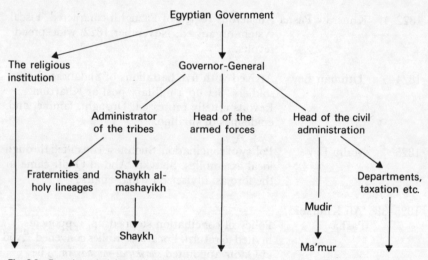

Fig. 8.2 *Egyptian administration in the Sudan*

These more or less pragmatic forms of colonial rule progressively evolved to a more consistent form of foreign administration. In 1835, the military commander was granted the title of *hukumdar* or governor-general having full military and civil authority. The country was divided for administrative purposes into districts and subdistricts with at their head respectively *mudir*-s and *m'amur*-s. Different departments were set up in Khartum which, under 'Ali Khurshid Pasha, became the colony's capital. Special emphasis was placed on those departments which were to bring in money, namely the tax-collecting office largely staffed by Copts, and the customs office which controlled trade routes and navigation on the Nile. An Egyptian-sponsored religious establishment appeared in the wake of the *'ulama* who had come to Egypt with the army and whose authority was gradually extended over the local population. Efforts were further made to set up in Sudan the same type of state control over more popular forms of religious practices as were instituted in Egypt by means of the prerogatives of the *naqib al-ashraf*. Such intermediaries between holy men and the administration were appointed in the major centres under Turkiyya control. These efforts, however, were not to be integrated into an overall system of control until 1849–50.

With respect to Sudanese tribes, the initial period of military repression progressively gave way to a policy of conciliation intended to promote collaboration. Under Mahu Bey and Khurshid Pasha this was formalized by the setting up of a special branch of the administration to deal with native affairs. Indirect rule was to some degree promoted by means of assemblies to which tribal chiefs and other notables were summoned, and it is in this context that shaykh 'Abd al-Qadir's position became official and he was appointed *shaykh al-mashayikh*, an appointment he retained until his death in 1857.

One can therefore consider Muhammad 'Ali's conquest of Sudan as being on similar lines to other 19th-century invasions, whether by European or non-European powers. They all reflect an imbalance of power and the use of the technological (notably military) superiority of one nation to oppress a weaker one. The aim is the same: exploitation of conquered territories.

THE SECOND OTTOMAN OCCUPATION OF LIBYA

The Turkish invasion – or re-invasion – of Libya took place in 1835. It was the result of convergent factors involving Qaramanli weakness, imperial ambitions, and Ottoman prestige.

Qaramanli weakness in a strife-ridden national and dynastic context was brought out by the abdication of Yusuf Qaramanli on 12 August 1832. This, as we shall now see, was no solution to Libya's problems. Yusuf Qaramanli appointed as his successor his son 'Ali who took over formally in Tripoli, and was recognized by the townspeople, the military and religious authorities of the city and the foreign community – the new French consul Frederic-Louis Schwebel being particularly active in his support. In the Menshiya, however, the *kulughli* community refused to pay allegiance and supported the rival claim of Muhammad, the old Pasha's nephew. This was stirring up an old quarrel which had divided public opinion when Ahmad and Yusuf had struggled for power. The *kulughli*-s were here actively supported by Consul Warrington who had returned to the Regency in August 1832 but had set up in his country residence in the Menshiya where the Maltese who carried out most of Britain's trade with the Regency found a ready welcome and a profitable trade. The consul, in spite of government orders to maintain a strict neutrality, continued to fight it out with his French rival with Qaramanli princes as pawns in the game. The Sublime Porte's hesitations were shown by the fact that it officially ignored Yusuf Qaramanli's abdication, thus avoiding having to send out a *firman* of investiture of his successor.

The tribes were generally divided, those of the Tripoli coast from Zawiya to Misurata being for Muhammad whilst Cyrenaica upheld 'Ali. The major tribal confederacies under their lordly leaders refused to side with one or other party. This was particularly the case of 'Abd al-Jalil Sayf al-Nasir in the east of the country, and of the Shaykh of Tarhuna and of another leader who came to the fore in this period, Ghuma al-Mahmudi, who commanded the western tribes. Early in 1833 the latter finally sided with 'Ali and this was followed up in the summer of that same year by an agreement between Ghuma and 'Abd al-Jalil. Though officially siding with Yusuf Qaramanli's nominee, the tribal chiefs in fact sought to preserve their independence.

A Turkish mission of inquiry arrived in the Regency on 18 August 1833 and from Tripoli the Ottoman envoy, Shakir Efendi, went on to Tunis. The Libyan problem was a source of concern in the region and the Bey of Tunis expressed his intention of sending out an army with Ottoman permission, either to uphold 'Ali Pasha or to set up his own brother, Mustafa. The Sublime Porte, fearing French reactions, was finally led to intervene more directly: in September 1834, 'Ali Pasha received a *firman* of investiture. The Sublime Porte appealed to the insurgents to lay down their arms and accept the new ruler. This proved unavailing and a naval and military force was brought together to go to Tripoli and restore peace. Shakir Efendi returned on 20 May 1835, followed on the 26th by a squadron of ten warships and ten troop transports under the command of Najib Pasha. Some doubts remain as to what Najib Pasha's actual instructions were: was he to try and enforce 'Ali Qaramanli's nomination or to depose him? Diplomatic documents suggest that he deliberately chose the second solution which the Sublime Porte had merely envisaged as a last resort, if after three months, peace had not been restored. The fact that Najib Pasha was replaced at the head of the expeditionary corps on 10 July 1835 by Ra'if Pasha, former Governor of the Dardanelles, would tend to suggest that the *coup de force* in Tripoli had not met with full approval. The decision, however, was also part of a context of growing involvement of the major powers in the Mediterranean. Both France and Britain, not to mention Egypt and Tunisia had designs on Tripoli and the Ottomans were led to check these by a countermove of their own.

On arriving off Tripoli, Najib Pasha sent a message to 'Ali Qaramanli requesting him to come on board. The pretext given was that Najib Pasha wished to go ashore accompanied by the local ruler. 'Ali Qaramanli complied, but, once on board, was not allowed to land again. Najib Pasha and his men went on their own to the castle and there announced the Sultan's orders: Tripoli no longer had the status of a province, and Najib Pasha was in full control until the Sultan appointed a governor-general. Thus Ottoman sovereignty over the Regency was affirmed in the face of the world. It was to last until the 1911 war between Turkey and Italy.

What this actually meant for Libya and for the Libyans is a somewhat different story. The very fact that a stratagem had to be used to depose the Qaramanli Pasha shows that it was expected that the move would meet with opposition, even if the Sultan's prestige remained high. Turkish rule in the first place meant military occupation and this, in the face of popular armed resistance, took the form of a long-protracted war of invasion. The Ottoman army from its base in Tripoli had to fight its way outwards. The western part of Tripolitania, the Jebel Nafusa, and the Fezzan stubbornly opposed Turkish penetration. It took the Ottomans some seven years to 'pacify' even the region of Tripoli, eight years to occupy the Fezzan and Ghadames, and 23 years before an end was put to resistance in the Nafusa mountain area. The fight against the tribal confederacies was particularly fierce. The Awlad Sulayman held out and in 1839 'Abd al-Jalil even envisaged an attack on Tripoli. Beaten in battle in 1839 he and his men withdrew to Fezzan. 'Abd al-Jalil fought his last battle in 1842. He was captured and executed by the Turks. His son Muhammad took command of the tribe and, with those of his followers who refused to submit, decided to move further southwards along the trans-Saharan route where they had formerly fought for Yusuf Pasha. Muhammad and about 1000 warriors went first to Borku and Kanem where they fought, first as allies of Muhammad al-Amin of Bornu and of his son and successor Bashir, and later on their own account. By 1870 they had become masters of Kanem. The Awlad Sulayman were from then on to decline and today the tribe survives merely as a minor group in Chad. Ghuma al-Mahmudi too continued in opposition and fought it out in Jebel Nafusa until his death in 1858. The period we are considering here is therefore one of military invasion and foreign rule with its sorry tale of acts of cruelty.

In many ways, therefore, in spite of the prestige of the Ottoman Sultan and of the common bond of Islam, the establishment of direct Turkish control had effects very similar to those of a colonial invasion. Libyans today find it somewhat difficult to assess the significance of this period. It was obviously not simply a colonial regime. It was also a stand against European encroachments which was positive both from Turkey's and Libya's points of view. In the early period, some very able governors were sent out to Tripoli, notably Tahir Pasha, ex-Minister of the Navy, already mentioned as the Sultan's mediator between the French and the Dey of Algiers. Others proved less capable, and even corrupt, while Libya, like so many colonies, suffered from a rapid turnover of governors who had no time to become acquainted with the local situation. Thus in the first two yeas of Ottoman rule, five *pasha*-s had come and gone: Najib Pasha, Ra'if Pasha, Tahir Pasha, Husayn Pasha, and Namik Pasha. Nonetheless the Turks were able to replace the weak and strife-ridden government of the last Qaramanli-s by a new administration. Libya was divided into two provinces, that of Tripoli which included the Fezzan, and that of Cyrenaica. Each province (*wilaya*) was further divided into four districts (*mutassarifat*-s). The provincial governor and heads of districts were assisted by an administrative council whose members were in part elected, in part nominated. Tripoli, whose population was around 10 000, was the provincial capital, that of Cyrenaica being Ben Ghazi. The administrative link between the two provinces was not, however, established until 1871. This reorganization with a marked tendency towards centralization, was to be the framework within which, in the second part of the century, efforts were undertaken to modernize the country.

THE FRENCH CONQUEST OF ALGERIA

Algeria is often seen as illustrating the essence of colonial rule. This view is to some extent based on a later reality, one which came into its own during the French Third Republic (1870–1940) whilst in the preceding period the significance of events is far less clear, not only because the conquest of the country took several years (from 1830 to 1847, and still longer if one takes revolts of the Saharan region into account) but because French policy itself was for a long time uncertain.

The nature of the conquest
Charles X and his prime minister Polignac, who had launched the attack on Algiers, were themselves undecided as to the course to follow, and a negotiated

settlement involving French evacuation was in fact in view when the July revolution put an end to chancery discussions. The new regime headed by King Louis-Philippe (1830–48) at first shelved the problem and it was its very liberalism which led to a more cooperative British attitude and to France's decision, in view of this, to stay in Algeria. The decision, however, was only taken in 1834 and, as often in colonial situations, responsibility was left to men on the spot whose initiatives sometimes had far-reaching consequences. This underscores the role of the three generals-in-chief who were in command in Algiers during this period and whose personalities and attitudes set the pattern of relations between invaders and invaded.

General Clauzel was appointed after the fall of Charles X, and arrived in Algiers on 2 September 1830. He found a disorganized army: men camped around the city indulging in looting and wanton destruction. Lack of hygiene was beginning to tell and epidemics spread; indeed the climate was to be the chief ally of Algerian opposition to French rule as medical records prove. Between 1830 and 1840 hospital care was provided in 88 381 cases. During the same period some 80 000 men died, generally from disease. Thus in 1843, of 4692 deaths recorded, only 84 were on the battlefield. Clauzel began by bringing the troops back into the city in order to restore discipline, the move being interpreted by the British consul, St John, and many other observers as the first step towards withdrawal.

For the Algerians, the city's fate grew harder. The army requisitioned private and religious buildings in violation of agreements that had been made. When General Clauzel agreed to send part of his troops home, Algerians were recruited in their stead. Plans for the use of native auxiliaries had been laid as early as 1830 and on 10 October of that year the *zouaves* (from the name of the Kabylie Zuwawa tribe) had been set up. Recruitment was irrespective of nationality, although Algerians were later regrouped and became the 8th Company of the Zouave regiment. This recruitment of local men was very much resented by the population and when the battalion was first assembled, only 257 men turned up (including the French officers) whilst 287 were missing, of whom 221 were officially classified as deserters. Those who stayed on became close collaborators of the French and often oppressors in their own right. Never was this truer than in the case of Yusuf, a former Tunisian *mamluk* of Christian or Jewish origin, who took an active part in all the campaigns and who according to Pellissier de Reynaud, a good contemporary witness, was a man of 'bloodshed and looting, a man to be abhorred by all honest people as he is by the Arabs who reflect on us the contempt and hate he arouses in them'. Cruelty was indeed increasingly becoming characteristic of fighting in Algeria as tribal chiefs – Bu Mezrag of Kabylie, Bin Zamun of the Flissa tribe – took to arms. The French retaliated by a number of limited military operations in the course of which such wanton acts of cruelty were committed that General Clauzel himself was horrified.

In Algiers, an administration had to be set up almost from scratch since the former Ottoman institutions and personnel had been done away with. This brought once again to the fore people whom the Algerians hated or despised, such as the Bacri-s. Jacob Bacri was appointed head of the Jewish community, a function generally held by worthier men. Other no less unscrupulous persons acted as French agents, both in a political and financial capacity, as the buying up of property in dubious circumstances got under way. The go-betweens were sometimes Muslim. Chief of them was one Ahmad Buderba who had been involved in a fraudulent bankruptcy and who, when the French conquered Algiers, had gone to Paris to offer his services. He was rewarded by being made custodian of property belonging to the Holy Shrines of Mecca and Medina, but was finally dismissed for dishonesty.

General Berthezène, Commander-in-Chief in Algeria, to Field-Marshal Soult, French Minister of War. Letter dated 29 October 1831.

When I came to these half-civilized shores, I considered it my duty to honour France by my personal conduct in order that the King's rule be respected and appreciated. Justice and constancy seemed to me the best means to this end. But although I have always borne this in mind, I must admit in all sincerity that I am convinced that never under the Turkish regime, were the inhabitants of this land open to so many vexations and acts of injustice. I cannot change the situation because many facts do not come to my attention, and because I do not find in any or almost any of my subordinates the will to do equity. How often have I not been ashamed to see the French character thus debased in the eyes of the civilized world which through its consuls observes us, and even before the Africans whom we despise but who have sharp minds. Here, as I have on several occasions pointed out to you, people have come only to loot public and private wealth. Some have the impudence to suggest that I should do and let do, set two standards, allow the inhabitants to be robbed because it is money which will go to France, and that I should force the people to flee the country in order to seize their goods and property. Indeed it is a simple system, and no great talent is required to apply it; but I make bold to say that this is not only infamous and unjust, but also a dangerous path to follow.

Translated from the French original in Ch.- A. Julien, *Histoire de l'Algérie contemporaine*, Paris, 1964, p. 87.

Clauzel, who had been disavowed by his government for personal political initiatives involving Tunisian support for the conquest, was replaced in February 1831 by General Berthezène, a straightforward man, averse to corruption and other malpractices which were by now rife in Algeria. Not only was he unable to check them, but it cost him his posting. The Duke of Rovigo, who followed, was a very different sort of man who during his stay in Algiers – from December 1831 to March 1833 – gave a sinister turn to French rule. Unlike his predecessor, he made efforts to promote French settlement, notably in farms around the capital. As an ex-chief of police who had long relied on informers, indirect pressures, and other forms of manipulation, he decided that a similar system should be introduced to deal with the native population. He set up the first Arab Bureaus whose task this was to be. He also attempted to extend French rule by limited military raids, not only in the province of Algiers but further afield. Military campaigns showed Rovigo to be a ruthless officer for whom elementary human rights, not to mention lives, meant nothing. An example will serve to illustrate the point: a report, which later turned out to be false, had attributed some misdoing to a small tribe called the Uffiya. The general ordered the tribe to be exterminated to the last man, woman, or child. Only a few individuals escaped by being taken under the protection of some more humane French officers. The soldiers returned from their expedition loaded with booty, carrying on their saddles the heads of their enemies. Rovigo ordered the shopkeepers in Algiers to light up the streets and remain open so that the soldiers could trade their loot. A contemporary Algerian observer, Hamdan ben 'Uthman Khudja, in his personal account, *Aperçu historique et statistique sur la Régence d'Alger*, published in Paris in 1833, states that bloody ear-rings and bracelets with remains of severed wrists were sold. Though the innocence of the Uffiya tribe had been proved, its chief was nonetheless formally executed. Many other such acts of cruelty and injustice are on record. They set the tone of French military rule in Algeria.

Rovigo can further be characterized by the contempt he showed for the Algerians, as individuals and as a people. This expressed itself in particular in his disrespect for Islamic traditions and values. Once, to build a road and an esplanade, he destroyed a local cemetery, much to people's indignation. The bones were thrown up on the roadside. It is even said that some of them were later collected and traded in Marseilles where they were used in the making of sugar. Incredible as the fact may seem, it is attested by medical authorities in Marseilles, and in Algiers by Clauzel's former secretary, Louis Adrien Berbrugger (1801–69). Another signal event, and one which was to remain a symbol of colonial oppression, was the decision taken by Rovigo, when the need for a Catholic church was felt, to take over and put to this use a Muslim mosque, the beautiful Ketshawa. When the Algerians pointed out that this was contrary to the conventions signed when Algiers capitulated, Rovigo declared he would cut off the heads of those who opposed his will and would, if necessary, storm the building. He further ordered that after the mosque had been occupied, a cross and the French flag were to be hoisted on top of the minaret and guns were to fire a salute. The army indeed had to force its way in as thousands of Algerians massed in and around the Ketshawa to try and preserve the holy building. The latter was solemnly opened as a Catholic church on Christmas Day 1832.

These policies and the spirit in which they were carried out did more than anything to bring home to people what French rule signified. As the British consul was to put it in a report to the Foreign Office on February 26, 1835:

> During the five years of the occupation the conduct of the different governors under which it has been placed has so completely indisposed the natives towards the French and shown their total ignorance for the means of colonising that I am convinced nothing but a system of extermination can give the French any chance of occupying any territory beyond their outposts.

Indeed people were now increasingly determined to oppose the French. This is true of all sections of society. Dignitaries such as the ex-Bey of Tittari or the Agha, the nominal head of the Arab tribes, had been humiliated and had turned against the French. Urban notables had fled the town, or had sought the protection of other Muslim states. Some had even gone to Paris where they constituted an active 'Moorish Committee', openly critical of the doings in Algeria. On the spot, the need to organize collective resistance was the main topic of discussion. Popular leaders or holy men came to the fore, attracting large audiences as they made impassioned pleas for the defence of Islam.

Initial resistance to the conquest: Hajj Ahmad Bey

Two major movements at this time embodied Algerian will to resist: that of Hajj Ahmad Bey in the east, and that of 'Abd al-Qadir in the west. In 1833, Constantine, the eastern province, had not as yet been conquered. Its local administration had been set up by the former Ottoman regime and had at its head a *bey*. The province was wealthy and up to the French invasion had furnished Algiers with cereals, and timber for shipbuilding. It was also well populated (two-fifths of the total population of the Regency). The province comprised three different regions: that of the Kabylie mountains to the north, the western agricultural zone, and in the south a desert area inhabited by nomad Arab tribes. It was economically and socially, if not politically, turned towards the east. There was constant interaction with neighbouring Tunisia and Libya, as also with the rest of the Mashriq by land or by sea. The Bey who ruled the province from 1826 onwards belonged to a local gubernatorial family. His father and grandfather before him had occupied posts in the local Turkish administration. Hajj Ahmad Bey was himself a *kulughli*, his Algerian mother being the daughter of one of the major hereditary tribal chiefs of the south, the Bin Gana. Hajj Ahmad was indeed the only *kulughli* to have risen to high position in the Algerian administration. Well aware that the French officers in 1830 were negotiating with the Tunisians with a view to conquering Constantine, Hajj Ahmad undertook to organize his province on a defensive basis, emphasizing his determination to remain independent.

He began by reorganizing his troops. This involved the disbanding of the *janissary* corps and the recruitment of 2000 regulars, generally men of tribal origin. Moreover, he could depend on civilian support for the fight against the French, and contemporaries estimated at 30 000 men the army he could turn out. Though generally considered a somewhat ruthless autocrat, we find Hajj Ahmed Bey setting up democratic institutions including a local assembly made up of tribal chiefs, city personalities, and *'ulama* to which decisions were submitted for approval. He further decided to suppress all non-Quranic dues which during the Ottoman period had weighed heavily on the people. Hajj Ahmad, like other resistance leaders, including 'Abd al-Qadir, made a point of returning to strict orthodoxy in this matter. The Treasury further benefited from favourable economic conditions then prevailing, due partly to an active trade with the south which had begun going to Constantine after the French occupation of Algiers. In this initial period, Hajj Ahmad also made a significant move in assuming the title of *pasha*. This implied leadership of Algeria as a whole and was upheld by expressions of his firm determination to fight the French. The title was, of course, a Turkish one and had to be confirmed by the Sultan. Hajj Ahmad therefore applied to the Sublime Porte but received no answer. To understand this we must bear in mind the embarrassment of the Sultan who, though he welcomed local initiatives reaffirming Turkish sovereignty, was not prepared to grant the title of Governor to the Bey of Constantine, this being tantamount to recognizing

French rule over the rest of Algeria. In Turkey, political circles seem moreover to have been divided as to the course of action to be followed, the result being that nothing, in fact, was done.

The first French attack on the Eastern Province was made when the harbour of Bone was taken briefly in 1830, and permanently in 1832, thus cutting off the province's communications with the outside world. Hajj Ahmad could no longer receive help by sea and this was all the more serious in view of French pressures on Tunisia to prevent him using the overland route. The situation in Bone itself was highly unpleasant as a result of the appointment as commanding officer of the ex-*mamluk* Yusuf whose cruel practices and overbearing ways revolted French and Algerians alike. General Monck d'Uzer declared himself at the time 'disgusted by the intrigues of Yusuf . . . who is devoured by ambition. He wants at all costs to become Bey of Constantine. It is indispensable that the Governor remove him from Bone and place him under the orders of Colonel Marey who will keep him in check.' Not only did such warnings go unheeded, but the governor was influenced by Yusuf who persuaded him that the people of Constantine would welcome the French in general and Yusuf in particular. This led to a first campaign in 1836 during which the French learnt to their cost that Yusuf's views in no way reflected the reality of the situation. The French army failed to storm the town and had to retreat in painful conditions.

Hajj Ahmad was aware that confrontation was inevitable and he made every attempt to strengthen his position. He armed the population and made alliances with influential families and tribal chiefs. He also kept a watchful eye on goings on in Algiers and in Paris where the Moorish Committee had appealed to public and parliamentary opinion. Hajj Ahmad's chief political agent was his father-in-law, Hamdan ben 'Uthman Khudja, whose reports throughout this period were unduly optimistic, leading some historians to question his sincerity. Hajj Ahmad also renewed appeals to the Sultan and sent Hamdan ben 'Uthman Khudja to Istanbul to ask the Sublime Porte to send out a relief force. Appeals also went to the Turkish Governor of Tripoli. Hajj Ahmad's letters were increasingly insistent: 'we have endured difficulties and sufferings too great to be imagined, all this to safeguard religion and we declare ourselves to be Ottoman subjects . . . we can only resist with your help. You are our only hope.' Even European public opinion was called upon and, in 1834, a petition signed by 2307 persons was sent to the British parliament which, as the signitaries put it, was 'well-known for its defence of human rights'. It pointed to acts of injustice being committed in Algeria and asked for help. Obviously in the international context of the 1830s, no help could come from outside.

Hajj Ahmad was probably realistic enough to know this as can be inferred from his efforts both to fortify the region and to enlist popular support. He consulted the *diwan* on every move and kept it informed of French attempts to negotiate. He would point out that he was for peace but could not accept French offers for religious and political reasons, especially in view of the bad faith of the French who had shown total disregard for Muslims and agreements made when Algiers had capitulated. The French were by now determined to avenge the affront of the 1836 defeat, but General Damrémont who was then in command, was not prepared to leave anything to chance. He therefore made prior arrangements for peace on his western flank by coming to terms with 'Abd al-Qadir. There was no love lost between Hajj Ahmad and 'Abd al-Qadir and the latter showed little inclination to support the pro-Ottoman Bey. In 1837, General Damrémont with 20 400 men and a strong force of artillery moved into the Eastern Province. Last efforts were made by the French to get Hajj Ahmad to negotiate, but these proved unavailing and the attack was launched. On 13 October 1837, the town of Constantine was taken with considerable loss of life on both sides. The town resisted street by street, and defeat was followed up by murder and looting.

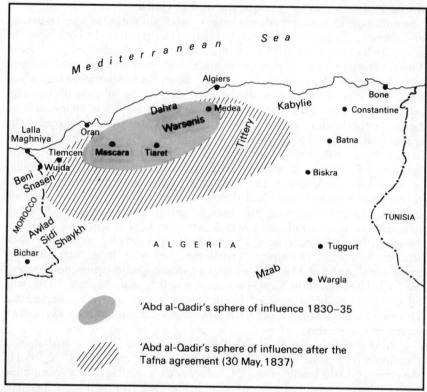

Map 8.2 *Algeria in 1850*

The resistance was over.

Hajj Ahmad had, however, escaped. He had adopted the technique which had been so successful during the previous attack, leaving his faithful second-in-command Bin 'Aisa in Constantine while he and his men stood by in order to attack the army as it withdrew. On this occasion, the plan fell through and Hajj Ahmad himself had to take to flight. With a small group of faithful followers he retired to the southern marches of Algeria where he fought on for another 11 years. By 1848, a year after 'Abd al-Qadir's surrender, Hajj Ahmad was an old and sick man, no longer even able to ride on horseback. Most of his men and all his private papers had fallen into French hands. For him, too, the end had come. He negotiated honourable conditions of surrender with the French commander of Batna. Hajj Ahmad was first taken to Constantine where he saw his empty and ruined palace, then to Algiers where he was given a house and allowed to end his days in peace. Modern writers have generally not given Hajj Ahmad the place he deserves in the history of Algerian resistance. His pro-Ottoman feelings so constantly proclaimed were not such as to please either the French colonial historians or later Algerian nationalists. Both, for different reasons, were inclined to favour his western rival, 'Abd al-Qadir.

Initial resistance to the conquest: 'Abd al-Qadir

The situation in western Algeria where 'Abd al-Qadir led the resistance movement is in many ways parallel to that of Constantine. In both cases the provinces had been isolated by the rapid fall of Algiers and of the province of Titteri. The danger of European encroachments had been brought home in both cases by the loss of a major harbour: Bone in Constantine, Oran in the west. The loss of Oran was all the more distressing in view of Tunisian collaboration with the French. In both cases ultimate defeat stemmed from lack of support from Muslim states: Tunisia and the Turkish empire in the case of Constantine, Morocco in that of western Algeria. The king of Morocco, Mulay 'Abd al-Rahman, had from the start shown his unwillingness to become involved in an international conflict, and had resisted popular pressure both in Morocco and Algeria to make him come out openly as sovereign of a region which had close ties with Morocco besides a common tribal and fraternity network. Pressures, moreover, were exerted by the French who sent out the Earl of Mornay to Morocco in 1832 to warn the sovereign against helping the Algerians. The resistance was thus left to organize itself without Moroccan patronage. Tribal meetings were held, with the holy lineage of a *zawiya* of Mascara, which had strong Qadiri connections, taking the lead. The chief of the lineage was an ageing holy man, Muhay al-Din, who felt that circumstances required that he pass over command to a younger man. He chose his son, 'Abd al-Qadir, who was accepted by delegates convened to a large tribal assembly.

'Abd al-Qadir, whom we shall see here essentially as a soldier, was therefore a traditional holy man. He was born in 1808 and, until 1822, lived in the precincts of the family *zawiya*. His education was no less typical, combining sound religious scholarship with intimate knowledge of the local tribes. His only contacts with the Turks had been during a short stay at Oran where he had been sent to further his education. He was revolted by the petty tyranny and irreligiousness of the Turks and was later to be consistently anti-Ottoman and pro-Algerian, in spite of efforts made in 1840 to enlist support for his movement from the Sublime Porte. In 1827, 'Abd al-Qadir performed the Holy Prilgrimage with his father and stayed two years in the East. In the course of his education, he had acquired a great love of books and learning, and this was to remain a dominant trait of his personality. More important still, though of a more intimate nature, was his involvement in sufism. Over and above the more mundane practices of the fraternities, including the family-sponsored Qadiriyya, a deeper mystical trend in accordance with the teaching of Ibn 'Arabi, the 13th-century Andalusian *shaykh al-akbar* (a title reserved for only the greatest mystics), prevailed in 'Abd al-Qadir's family and he himself was initiated to this by his father and later by Shaykh Khalid al-Naqshbandi whom he met in Damascus during his journey to the Holy Places. Many contemporary witnesses mention the fact that, in spite of politics and fighting, 'Abd al-Qadir maintained a private spiritual life involving mediation and mystical trances. This aspect of his personality was to sustain him during his long captivity and was to come to the fore during his last years of exile.

In view of this deeply religious outlook, 'Abd al-Qadir's fight against the French cannot be understood without reference to religious ideology. 'Abd al-Qadir came to the fore as a resister because the *jihad* is a Muslim's duty. In line with this we find 'Abd al-Qadir assuming the title not of *pasha* (which has merely political significance) but that of *amir al-muminin* or 'Commander of the Faithful'. He was also sometimes called 'Sultan of the Arabs' but this, it should be remembered, has little precise meaning. In fact 'Abd al-Qadir avoided any political inferences as to his role and, as his father had done before him, even on occasion accepted the title of *khalifa*, or representative of a free Muslim ruler, here the King of Morocco. The notion of *jihad* is itself complex. In the difficult context of the 19th century when the *dar al-Islam* or 'Land of Peace' became the *dar al-harb* or 'Land of War', the duty of a responsible leader was to safeguard the community. This implied a *hijra* or tactical withdrawal, either actual flight and exile, or a closing-in of the community upon itself, this, if necessary, involving 'under necessity' some sort of *modus vivendi* with the invaders.

The organization of 'Abd al-Qadir's resistance between 1833 and 1839 thus paradoxically came to involve a pact of coexistence with the French by means of which the Algerian leader obtained a free hand in regrouping his partisans whilst leaving the French in command of the coastal zone and allowing them free access to the area. The agreement was reached in 1834 by 'Abd al-Qadir and General Desmichels who was in command in the west of Algeria without however the French government having given its approval. On various occasions, fighting broke out: the French, for example, being defeated at Macta on 28 June 1835, but successfully conquering Mascara a little later. Both sides, however, wanted peace: the French because they were not strong enough to launch a full-scale attack, especially as more extensive occupation had still not been decided upon; moreover it was necessary, first, to eliminate resistance in the east of the country. The Algerians needed time to organize themselves on military lines. A more solemn agreement called the Treaty of Tafna, although it could only, in fact, be an agreement and a truce, was concluded on 30 May 1837. If left 'Abd al-Qadir in full command both over western and central Algeria, in fact some two thirds of the country. This has sometimes been seen as a betrayal of Hajj Ahmad and the latter saw it as such: 'They [the French and 'Abd al-Qadir] have both agreed to be against me,' he told the Ottomans, adding, 'with the blessing of France, he will try and eliminate all trace of your presence in the Province of Constantine'. This view was also held by the French General, Bugeaud.

'Abd al-Qadir was no mere opportunist, however, even if he felt little compunction to uphold Turkish authority in Constantine. As a traditional leader basing his rule on tribal consensus, he needed time to convince each group. Moreover he was to some degree dependent on the support of traditionally influential holy lineages who were not always prepared to back him. Indeed major fraternities were hostile: the Tijaniyya opposed him as did the Darqawiyya, the latter also recruiting 'Abd al-Qadir's brother in order to contest his pre-eminent position. Slowly, however, step by step, through personal prestige and skilful diplomacy, not to mention the help provided by the French in the way of weapons, 'Abd al-Qadir was able to bring the people under his banner as far out as the borders of Constantine. The organization he set up had resistance to the French as its objective and was organized on a traditional tribal and religious model. Indeed accounts of the time often recall former resistance movements, including that of Jugurtha against the Romans. We thus find him setting up citadels in tribal territory to afford protection to civilians and to serve as stores both for food and for military equipment. Similar descriptions are to be found in Sallust's account of the war against Jugurtha. Even the places where 'Abd al-Qadir built his granary-citadels (Tafraut, Sa'ida, Taza, Bughar, Tagdemt) have historical tradition behind them. At Tagdemt (just south of Tiaret, the famous Berber fortress of the Middle Ages), 'Abd al-Qadir set up his capital. It was a rocky stronghold overlooking a river, the Wad Mina. When there the Amir continued to live in a tent, but the town itself comprised many buildings including a number of workshops. Weapons were made at Tagdemt and money was minted. This organization took time to build up and it is a proof of 'Abd al-Qadir's dedication that he did not allow himself to be lured into a false sense of security.

The defence system involved a military reorganization of the population which recalls older historical traditions of North Africa no less than modern conditions of guerilla warfare. 'Abd al-Qadir recruited a regular army, estimated at 10 000 men, mostly infantry. They were divided into battalions and wore distinctive clothing. They were mobile forces, and though some remained with 'Abd al-Qadir's permanently roaming camp, others were concentrated in various posts (1000 at Medea, 1400 at Miliana, 1800 at Mascara, 2500 at Tlemcen, and 2000 in the east of the province) from where they could launch rapid raids. This army was also supported by non-regulars, namely tribal contingents whose number was variable. They were less dependable since political and economic factors determined the degree of their enthusiasm, but they made up the numbers which could turn the tide. The tribesmen generally provided the cavalry. Even at the height of his military career, 'Abd al-Qadir was probably never able to turn out more than 50 000 men. A hierarchized administration completed the system. The country was divided into zones for this purpose, each headed by a *khalifa*. The number of these increased as the influence of 'Abd al-Qadir spread, growing from two to eight (respectively those of Tlemcen, Mascara, Miliana, Medea, Hamza, Medjana, and two for the southern districts). Each of these districts was subdivided into areas under the command of an *agha*, and further subdivided into tribal groups under the leadership of a *qaid*. At the lowest echelon of the sub-tribe were *shaykh*-s. They all received their orders from the Amir, had salaries and the wherewithal to fight. The *khalifa*-s were recruited from among 'Abd al-Qadir's most faithful followers and were appointed in a permanent capacity. The *agha*-s were replaced every two years, and the *qaid*-s and *shaykh*-s every year, although, in practice, they were often reconfirmed in office. 'Abd al-Qadir's *khalifa*-s all came from dominant holy lineages with fraternity affiliations – the period has indeed sometimes been called 'the age of the Arab sharif-s'. Thus Tlemcen and the surrounding district was under the leadership of a Kabylie, Bu Hamidi, who was an important member of the Qadiriyya, Mascara was also under Qadiriyya patronage and its *khalifa* was 'Abd al-Qadir's cousin, Mustafa bin Thami, whilst the *khalifa* of Miliana came from a religious family of Golea.

'Abd al-Qadir's following must be appreciated in its proper context, and the context was war. The only point open to discussion was who would start hostilities and when. On 3 July 1839 a tribal assembly met at Taza, one of 'Abd al-Qadir's fortified posts situated south-east of Miliana. The decision to declare war was taken and officially announced on 20 November 1839.

The Algerian forces at first met with little French resistance but in February 1841 General Bugeaud returned to Algeria to take command. He had already in the earlier period leading up to the Tafna Treaty fought against 'Abd al-Qadir and had had time to consider the problems involved and the type of warfare which could bring results given the popularity of the movement. The war, he felt, could only be won by creating a climate of terror by the destruction of villages, the burning of fields, and wholesale slaughter. There was an implacable logic in Bugeaud's theory and a cruel determination in his officers to put it into practice. A French officer, Saint-Arnaud, informs us in his chatty letters that according to orders received: 'I shall burn everything ... kill everyone' – and that is precisely what he and his fellow officers and men did, as official reports testify. This inhumane policy, carried out for two years, 1841–2, had the required effect of bringing people to submission.

'Abd al-Qadir saw popular enthusiasm wane. Even his regular army dwindled. By constantly moving and launching daring raids, he tried to remain on the offensive and uphold a flagging popular morale. The French were often bewildered by his incredible audacity and apparent ubiquity, but this could not interrupt their slow, relentless progress. One after another, 'Abd al-Qadir's strongholds fell: Taza and Tagdemt on 25 May 1841; Tlemcen on 1 February 1842, al-Asnam (which the French renamed Orleansville in honour of the royal family) three months later. The mountainous region of Warsenis was also taken that year, and the tribes, one after another, made their submission. One may consider as typical the statement made by the *shaykh* of the Beni Urag: 'I will tell 'Abd al-Qadir: I have lost six sons for you in battle; the tribe has sacrificed everything for you, we can do no more since you cannot protect us'. By the spring of 1843, the Amir had lost his last fortified post, Teniet. The most crushing blow came in May 1843 when a small French detachment fell on the wandering population of faithful servants, officials, craftsmen, and tribes, besides 'Abd al-Qadir's family – some 30 000 persons – which constituted the Amir's nomad capital. The French attack was a complete surprise and in the panic that ensued, they overran the camp with little difficulty or loss of life. 'Abd al-Qadir's mother and wife escaped in the confusion, but most of the camp surrendered. Not only was 'Abd al-Qadir's prestige irretrievably lost but he was by now an almost solitary fugitive.

'Abd al-Qadir was well aware that isolation ultimately spelt defeat. Just as Hajj Ahmad had looked to the east for support, so 'Abd al-Qadir was to look to the west. As the local situation became increasingly difficult, Morocco became ever more important for him. It was less a question of political backing or even military help as the need to keep the frontier open so that the resisters could find refuge there or use Moroccan territory as a military base. 'Abd al-Qadir was also aware that he had the support of the border tribes. In November 1843, with the remnants of his army, he once again crossed over into Morocco. French reaction was not slow to follow. General Bugeaud marched westwards and occupied Lalla Maghniya, on the right bank of Wad Kis, a few miles beyond the frontier which, since the end of the 17th century, had been fixed at Wad Tafna (at the level of Tlemcen). This had the immediate effect of stirring up the Moroccan tribes. National indignation was such that Mulay 'Abd al-Rahman could do no less than send the army out under the command of Sidi Muhammad, his nephew. The royal camp was set up on the bank of Wad Isly, near the town of Wujda (Oujda). French diplomacy had decided on forceful action which, in August 1844, took the traditional form of a naval demonstration: a French squadron under the Prince of Joinville was sent to the shores of Morocco bearing a ultimatum. In the meantime, Bugeaud had been ordered to refrain from any act of aggression. It soon became evident that the Moroccan sultan would give way, but the Prince of Joinville nonetheless decided that a fine flourish was called for and on 6 August 1844 he shelled the harbour of Tangier, following this up by a similar attack on al-Sawira on 16 August. Bugeaud, not to be outdone and in spite of orders to the contrary, crossed Wad Isly on 13 August and attacked the Moroccan camp. By noon the battle was over, and the French had captured the camp and taken many prisoners. The French government decided to accept the benefit of the victory which won for the undisciplined Bugeaud the title of Duke of Isly. In terms of diplomatic and military pressure on a weak Moroccan government, the French move was wholly successful. A treaty was signed between France and Morocco on 10 September 1844. It left the frontier problem unsolved, thus paving the way for future French encroachments, whilst at the same time obtaining the portion of territory between Wad Tafna and Wad Kis which was annexed to Algeria. The Moroccan Sharif complied with French requests concerning 'Abd al-Qadir who was formally declared an outlaw on Moroccan soil. The Amir who had taken refuge among friendly tribes in the mountainous region of Wad Muluya, had to cross back into Algeria.

The last phase of the Amir's resistance (1844–47) followed as the Amir was forced to move about constantly to escape the French and their spies. French methods however had so aroused popular hostility that even as the Amir's forces waned, the banner of revolt was taken up by others. In 1845, armed opposition flared up throughout Algeria. In Dahra, a religious leader, Muhammad bin 'Abdallah, better known by his nickname Bu Ma'za, preached open revolt and people flocked to his side. His movement spread through the Chelif and the Warsenis, threatening the new French centre of Orleansville, and was to last until Bu Ma'za's capture on 13 April 1847. There were other such revolts, the most important of which were in the regions of Hodna and Titteri. The French army once again had recourse to the cruellest methods of repression, including the smoking to death of refugees who had taken shelter in caves. As local uprisings took place, the French forces had to be redeployed and this brought 'Abd al-Qadir a brief respite. A few signal victories, notably at Sidi Brahim in September 1845, revived flagging hopes. 'Abd al-Qadir renewed his efforts to bring the tribes to unified action, but he was largely unsuccessful although he found cooperation among the Kabylie tribes of the Djurjura and the Ulad Sidi Shaykh of the south-west.

The defeat of 'Abd al-Qadir was the result both of the waning force of resistance in Algeria and the now determined hostility of the Moroccan Sultan who felt personally threatened by the kind of popular enthusiasm the Amir could stir up. When, in July 1846, 'Abd al-Qadir and his men once again withdrew into Moroccan territory, they were attacked by the sharifian army. The Algerians won the day, but a number of Algerian refugees in and around Fas were massacred. Abd al-Qadir's faithful *khalifa*, Bu Hamidi, who was at court negotiating, died mysteriously, and he is generally considered to have been poisoned.

'Abd al-Qadir had to fight his way back into Algeria, there to meet with another enemy, the French. Moved by the plight of his followers, who included wounded and defenceless women and children, he decided to negotiate honourable conditions of surrender. On 23 December 1847, terms were agreed between 'Abd al-Qadir and the French general, Lamoricière. The Governor of Algeria, the Duke of Aumale, son of the King of France, pledged his word that 'Abd al-Qadir would not be made prisoner but would be allowed to go into exile in a Muslim land.

Thus with the surrender of 'Abd al-Qadir in 1847, the capture of Bu Ma'za the same year and the surrender of Hajj Ahmad Bey the following year, ended the initial phase of Algerian resistance. To appreciate this apparently successful French conquest, a number of facts must be taken into consideration. French victory had only been obtained at the expense of a long war and continuous military efforts. In 1846 France had 108 000 men in Algeria, a third of its total armed forces. The way in which the operations were carried out destroyed opposition, but created a new and permanent rancour. Even before the early resisters had surrendered, new opposition groups had appeared. In this initial period, the French made for themselves a reputation which was to persist, one of tyranny, injustice, and bad faith. The latter was all the more deeply resented because it involved religious betrayal as when mosques were converted into churches – or national betrayal as was shown up by the fate of 'Abd al-Qadir who was not allowed to leave for a Muslim land, but was imprisoned in France. In 1848, the French monarchy fell and was replaced by the Second Republic. Although General Lamoricière who had negotiated 'Abd al-Qadir's surrender was named Minister of War, the Amir continued to be detained in France, and he was only freed on 16 October 1852, by Louis-Napoleon Bonaparte, the future Napoleon III. But this is already part of a new political context, that of the second half of the 19th century.

SELECTED READING LIST

I – Sudan

Brett, M. (ed.), *Northern Africa. Islam and Modernization*, (London, 1973).
Hill, R. L., *Egypt in the Sudan. 1820–1881*, (London, 1959).
Holt, P. M., *Holy Families and Islam in the Sudan*, (Princeton, 1967).
Warburg, G., 'Sudan in the 18th and 19th centuries', in M. Milson (ed.,), *Society and Political Structure in the Arab World*, (New York, 1973).

II – Libya

Feraud, L. C., *Annales tripolitaines*, (Paris & Tunis, 1927).
Ibn Isma'il 'U., *Inhiyar hukm al-usrat al-Qaramanliya fi Libya, 1815–1835*, (Tripoli, 1966).
Kakia, A. J., *Libiya fi al-'ahd al-'uthmani al-thani, 1835–1911*. (Tripoli, 1947).
Misrati 'A. M. al-, *Al Silat bayna Libiya wa Turkiya al-Tarikhiya wa al-Ijtima'iya*, (Tripoli, 1968).
Rossi, E., *Storia di Tripoli e della Tripolitania della Conquista Araba al 1911*, (Rome, 1968).

III – Algeria

'Abd al-Qadir al-Jazairi, *Kitab al-Mawaqif*, (Damascus, 1966–7, second edition).
Ageron Ch.-R., ''Abd el-Kader et la première resistance algérienne' in *Les Africains*, Vol. I, (Paris, 1977).
Berthezène, P., *Dix-huit mois à Alger ou Récit des événements qui s'y sont passés depuis le 14 juin 1830 ... jusqu'à la fin de décembre 1831*, (Montpellier, 1934).
Blunt, W., *Desert Hawk. Abd al Kader and the French Conquest of Algeria*, (London, 1947).
Churchill, Ch. H., *The Life of Abd el-Kader, ex-Sultan of the Arabs of Algeria*, (London, 1867).
Cherif, M., 'Expansion européenne et difficultés tunisiennes de 1815 à 1830' *Annales*, 25, 1970.
Chodkiewicz, M. (trans.), *Emir Abd el-Kader. Ecrits Spirituels*, (Paris, 1982).
Christelow, A., 'Saintly descent and wordly affairs in mid-nineteenth century Mascara, Algeria'. *International Journal of Middle East Studies*, 12, 1980.
Danziger, R., *Abdel Qadir and the Algerians' Resistance to the French and Internal Consolidation*, (New York, 1977).
Emerit, M., 'Les Mémoires d'Ahmed dernier bey de Constantine', in *Revue Africaine*, 93, 1949.
Emerit, M., 'Le Mystère Yusuf' in *Revue africaine*, 96, 1952.
Jouhaud, E., *Yousouf, esclave, mamelouk et général de l'Armée d'Afrique*, (Paris, 1980).
Julien, Ch. -A., *Histoire de l'Algérie Contemporaine*, (Paris, 1964).
Khudja, H., *Aperçu Historique et Statistique de la Régence d'Alger, Intitulé en Arabe 'Le Miroir'*, (Paris, 1833).
Mercier, E., *Les Deux Sièges de Constantine* (1836–1837), (Constantine, 1896).
Mzali, M. S., 'La Cession de Constantine et d'Oran à des Princes tunisiens' in *Revue Tunisienne*, 1948.
Pellissier de Reynaud, *Annales Algériennes*, (Paris & Algiers, 1854).
Temimi, 'A., *Le Beylik de Constantine et Hadj Ahmad Bey (1830–1837)*, (Tunis, 1978).
Yacono, X., 'La Régence d'Alger en 1830 d'après les commissions de 1833–4' in *Revue de l'Occident Musulman et de la Méditerranée*, 1 and 2, 1966.

PART III
THE IMPERIAL THEME 1848–82

INTRODUCTION

An account of the period 1848–82 points to imperial expansion as the major trend. Why, we may ask ourselves, did this become so important around 1850? Not only does this warrant a brief look at the chief characteristics of an industrial and capitalist society which launched into an outgoing policy, but also at the term *imperialism* – 'A many-sensed word that makes music to long ears' as a verse in *Punch* put it in 1878 – which, before coming to have its present Marxist-defined meaning, embodied the contradictory aspirations of the second half of the 19th century. As a word in the making, it ideologically parallels the changing pattern of the society it sought to define.

It may surprise some readers to learn that in Europe the word was first used in a generally derogatory sense to qualify the *coup d'état* by which the President of the Second French Republic, who also happened to be the nephew of Napoleon I, seized power and had himself proclaimed Emperor on 2 December 1852. Autocratic and socialist (in the Saint-Simonian usage of the term), Napoleon III was seen by many as seeking a demagogical alliance of the people and of bourgeois entrepreneurs over the head of parliament, and it was to this that the term *imperial* was applied, as also to the military irredentism which went with Caesarism and was further to be expected of a descendant of Napoleon I. Liberal governments in Europe generally viewed this change in French politics with considerable distrust when not with actual hostility. Napoleon III was himself to justify this view by military involvements which led to his downfall in 1870 and yet, paradoxically, the word *imperialism* had by then evolved: it reappeared when Disraeli provided the Tories with a new image of Britain as a mother-country ruling over far-flung colonies and dominions. In 1876, 'Greater Britain', at Disraeli's suggestion, was given a new symbol: Queen Victoria became Empress of India. Not that the term was not hotly debated. Many Imperialists and most Liberals upheld 'the natural influence which a great power, though confining itself to its own territories, always exercises in the world', as Goldwin Smith put it in *The Empire*; but at the same time they opposed what they considered a vainglorious and dangerous 'pride of the empire'; indeed the electorate rejected Disraeli in 1880.

Various negative aspects of imperialism had indeed been brought out. They involved the problems of an extended, loose-knit empire ('a motley mass of British colonies') which could only be unified through constant military expansion, not only in terms of new colonies but also of control of strategic routes and naval bases. Disraeli's whole policy with respect to the Eastern Question which directly concerned Turkey and its provinces, showed this up. Defence of the passage to India implied indirect control of Egypt and it was obvious that at the first sign of trouble in the region, Britain would step in. The same policy emphasized the need for naval bases and led to specific military and diplomatic moves by Britain in the Mediterranean where the occupation of Gibraltar was followed up by that of Malta during the Napoleonic Wars, and that of Cyprus obtained from Turkey in exchange for support in the Russo-Ottoman war of 1876. The balance of power policy – i.e. an equipoise of the great states, France, Britain, and Russia – implied the provisional preservation of the Turkish Empire and led Britain to support the latter in difficult situations in which the risk of armed confrontation was great – and indeed the painful Crimean War of 1853–6 brought this home to France and Britain. Moreover the need for rapid actions in the military, diplomatic, or economic fields was a dangerous risk to parliamentary government, one which Disraeli took on several occasions. He bought the Suez Canal shares without the prior consent of parliament, he brought Indian troops to the Mediterranean on his own initiative during the Russo-Turkish war of 1876 with a view to eventually occupying Egypt, and he acquired Cyprus before asking parliament to ratify the *fait accompli*. The rise of rival ambitions among the various European states further emphasized the dangers of the imperial conception of world strategy.

On the other hand imperialism had much wider economic relevance and to this business circles and liberal opinion were not hostile: 'Imperialism, if it merely means the protection of the best interests of the English, every Englishman is an Imperialist'. The fact that economic developments in Europe, notably those of industry, depended increasingly on foreign imports of essential raw materials, related poorer nations to technologically advanced ones. The former also acquired new significance as the home market became saturated. By 1880, the economic prosperity of a country such as Britain was 'geared to the ability to sell to the outside world the output of one worker in every five' (R. S. Seyers). This amply justified the project of Imperial expansion since, as Lord Salisbury put it just after the Congress of Berlin (1878):

> The commerce of a great commercial country like this will only flourish – history attests it again and again – under the shadow of empire, and those who give up empire in order to make commerce prosper will end by losing both.

Capitalism and industrialization, which had brought about class stratification, also created a new class order of nations as workers, no less than factory-owners or bankers felt the common need of having dependent nations to uphold their own economic growth. Imperialism was in this sense an economic venture which had military features and ultimately led to political takeover.

What were the main aspects of the economic changes underway in industrial Europe which were reflected in the imperial venture? The first, of course, was financial. A new trend had been set on foot by the massive inflow of gold (the American Gold Rush of 1849 and the discovery of mines in Australia a year later) which increased the world's stock of monetary gold by an average 4 per cent a year between 1850 and 1873, thus explaining economic buoyancy and confidence in advanced projects. These had been channelled through a fast developing banking sector. The older class of merchant bankers such as the Barings and Rothschilds promoted new farflung relations; but new banks were being created in great numbers, including business banks to meet the needs of industry. We thus find the French Pereire brothers closely connected with Napoleon III's projects and setting up the Comptoir d'Escompte in 1848 and the Société Générale in 1852. Powerful joint stock banks had appeared and these played a key role attracting private savings to industry. The oldest of these was the Société Générale pour favoriser l'Industrie Nationale, founded in Belgium in 1822. By the 1880s, Britain, for example, had 117 joint-stock banks and 250 private ones, the joint-stock banks further extending their activities by means of local branches. Banking practice and adapted legislation was evolved. Central banks – the Bank of England founded in 1694, the Banque de France (1800), the National Bank of Belgium (1822) – had their functions defined by law in this period, including the privilege of issuing paper money. Various other acts of parliament and notably those concerning limited liability were passed; companies were legally defined: for example in Britain the 1865 Private Companies Ltd. Act which was paralleled in an 1867 French law. The Stock Exchange developed and financial centres extended their activities to other countries. As foreign bills became commonplace in the second half of the 19th century, London became a short-term lender to the world, and a clearing house for international payments. Credit control was effected through the bank rate and open market operations.

The development of a new world order changed the very aspect of industrial states and also increasingly of peripheral zones including North Africa. As the demographic trend slowly began to rise, town growth became the characteristic feature of industrial society. The population of London rose from 2.3 million in 1850 to 3.8 million in 1880, that of Paris in the same period from 1 million to 2.3 million, and that of Berlin from 420 000 to 1 million. A similar trend was underway in Cairo, Alexandria and other North African ports. But even more characteristically new industrial concentrations appeared – Le Creusot in Northern France, which had been a mere borough of 8000 inhabitants, had become a town of 24 000 by 1865. These new towns were sometimes centred around a single firm such as the Krupps factory at Essen, or the Cockerill works at Seraing in Belgium.

Industrial development was based on the iron and steel industry. Between 1851 and 1871, the combined iron output of Britain, France, and Germany rose from about 2.75 million tons to 8.5 million, with Britain largely in the lead (6 million tons). It upheld technological innovation, a continuous process since James Watt had invented the steam engine in 1769 and Cartwright the power loom in 1785.

The development of the iron and steel industry led to improved means of communications, and notably to the setting up of a complete railway network, first in Britain (1848–78), then in France, before extending out through Europe to the Middle East and North Africa (to Egypt in 1851, to Tunisia in 1856, to Algeria in 1860). Railways in their turn contributed to industrial development by making transport easier, faster, and considerably cheaper. By 1870 transport by rail cost a fifth of road transport. Railways also helped to promote the export trade and maintain economic prosperity. In Britain, commodity exports between 1850 and 1860 rose by about two-thirds, between 1850 and 1860 by 90 per cent and by a further 60 per cent between 1860 and 1870. This was further integrated into a world pattern of communications as shipping developed. Steamships replaced packet ships, cutting travel time by half. New shipping companies were set up, beginning with the Royal Mail Steam Packet Company founded by Cunard in 1839, and new lines were opened throughout the world. Thus North African harbours became regular ports of call for weekly or monthly services from Britain or France, besides more frequent ones from Gibraltar, Algeria, or Malta. Egypt and Algeria became winter resorts for European tourists and even Morocco was included in the famous *Joanne Guide Books* in 1874. The growth in passenger and trade shipping is illustrated by the constant increase of registered tonnage which passed from 186 000 tons in 1850 to 1.5 million tons in 1870. This led to the organization of shipping at international level. Brokerage, chartering, and insurance laws were passed and Lloyds, which had been the main international insurance market since the 17th century, established new adapted regulations which in the form of the Act of Incorporation of 1871 still apply today. Further regulations made in this period include the 'British rules for the prevention of collision at sea' (1862) which were made internationally binding at Washington in 1889.

The world pattern was not only promoted by industries but it helped uphold the new economic order based on imports of raw materials for European industry (including cotton and wool) and exports of manufactured goods including Manchester ware which now swamped North African markets. It also created possibilities of foreign loans and investments for European capitalism through banks.

Nonetheless the industrial process was a fragile one which the new ruling class of bourgeois entrepreneurs, financiers, and politicians only imperfectly mastered. A sense of ever possible disaster overrode the whole scene, however rosy, as even the most powerful sectors could collapse, sending industrial or banking dynasts to bankruptcy, leaving their workers and shareholders in the lurch. A series of minor or major crashes underlies the whole history of industrial development. De Lesseps of Suez Canal fame came to disaster over the Panama Canal project in 1889; the Cockerill works collapsed, the Pereire Brothers were forced to sell out in 1866–7; Krupps of Essen, the well-established private bankers Baring & Baring, as so many other firms at some stage faced bankruptcy. Their fate depended on the banks who could save them. A deep-rooted fear underlies the hymns in praise of technology and industry which expressed themselves in the public ceremonial of international functions such as the 1851 Crystal Palace Exhibition, or the opening of the Suez Canal in 1869. The 'hungry forties' were a living memory which periodical crises (1848–9, 1857, 1867) brought back to mind, until the 1873 crisis, which was deeper-rooted and had more lasting effects, brought people's worst fears back into the limelight. Older or ill-adapted manufactories disappeared, and, as the home markets afforded ever fewer possibilities, an all out effort was made to turn underdeveloped countries into new fields of expansion through which industrial growth could be pursued. To develop the market, the region had to be reorganized economically and managed on different lines, which implied new and direct forms of European control. This background underlines and explains the imperial venture.

CHAPTER 9

ALGERIA IN AN IMPERIAL DESIGN

The imperial design was more particularly focused in this period on Algeria, left by the French government to the care of the army which, at the turn of the century, came into the limelight. It liked to identify itself with its imperial conquest, and officers often affected to wear Muslim dress in their leisure hours and to ape the Arab style. Parisian painters were in great demand and helped to spread the fashion of orientalism in art. And yet it was also in the same period that the status which was to be that of Algerians, that of a subject people, was defined. The curious mixture of admiring fascination and contemptuous oppression also coexisted in the make-up of the president-prince who, with the help of financiers and industrialists, came to power as Napoleon III. He faced the difficult task of defining a policy with respect to Algeria, which the 1848 constitution had officially defined as French territory. A symbolic gesture had at the outset marked his attitude towards the Algerian problem. On 16 October 1852, shortly before he became Emperor, Louis-Bonaparte, in a spectacular imitation of Arab chivalry, went to the castle of Amboise where 'Abd al-Qadir was still prisoner, to inform the Amir that he was now a free man . . . not however so free as to be allowed to return to Algeria. After a short stay in Paris where he was treated as an honoured guest and granted a pension of 100 000 francs, 'Abd al-Qadir left for the East.

NAPOLEON III's POLICY IN ALGERIA

The emperor who until the 1860s had little real experience of Algeria, took measures which realized both the legal fiction that Algeria was French and his own Saint-Simonian beliefs that progress in the Muslim world would come from industrialization. Saint-Simonian socialism was then represented by Prosper Enfantin (1796–1864) who had lived in Egypt with his disciples between 1832 and 1837 and who had tried there to promote the union of East and West. He had visited Algiers in 1839 and was now in Paris trying to bring industrial firms and banks to take an interest in the colony. That the emperor was himself in favour of such views is proved by the imperial decree of 8 April 1857, which provided for a network of railways in Algeria. Enfantin had also convinced the Talabot brothers, financiers of the Société Générale engaged in industrial investment, of the soundness of his views. They had undertaken to develop iron ore extraction in the region of Bone and would have followed this up with the building of an industrial plant locally, had not French industrialists successfully opposed the project.

Napoleon's personal views on Algeria came from an official visit he and the empress paid there in 1860. He was pleased with the reception from the army which he saw as promoting imperial grandeur. His reaction to the European civilian element which had voted against his accession, was less enthusiastic. He admired the work carried out with respect to urban infrastructure, but on the other hand he disapproved of the egotistical attitudes of the civilians who wanted greater political rights and ever more land for settlement. Particularly striking in a context characterized by the contempt of Europeans for Algerians, was the attitude of the emperor and

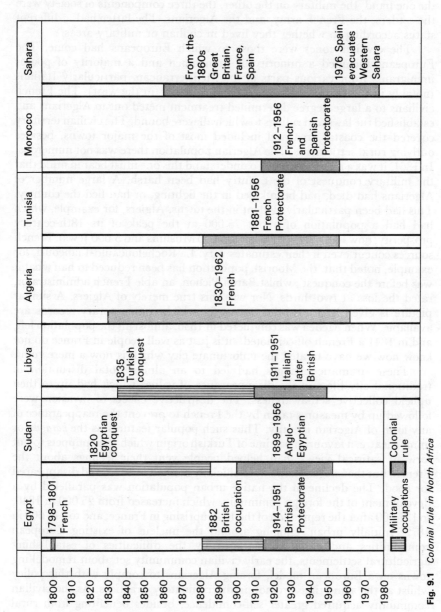

Fig. 9.1 Colonial rule in North Africa

151

empress to their native subjects whom they treated on an equal footing with the French. There could be no doubt that a new policy was in the offing. However, to understand its implications it is necessary to describe in more detail the social groups present in Algeria and the way they had evolved in the years since the defeat of 'Abd al-Qadir in 1847. A fairly clear distinction, upheld by administrative practice had divided the country into two regions and three component groups: the two types of district were the civilian zone on the one hand, the military on the other, the three components of society were the settlers, the French army, and the Algerians. The latter had a different status according to whether they lived in civilian or military areas.

The civilian zones were those to which Europeans had come. The Europeans included a minority of Frenchmen and a majority of poorer immigrants from various parts of the Mediterranean, particularly Italians (notably in the east of the country) and Spanish (in the west). The French civilians to a large degree determined treatment meted out to Algerians and established the laws and rulings to which all were bound. The civilian territory covered the coastal area and included most of the major towns, besides outlying rural settlements. The Algerian population there was not numerous. In 1861, it was a mere 358 760. To understand this one must bear in mind that the military conquest of the country had been harsh. A large number of Algerians had died, had been killed in the fighting, or had fled the country. This had been particularly evident in the towns. Algiers, for example, which had had a population of about 75 000 at the peak of its 18th-century prosperity, now had only 30 000 left (25 000 Muslims and 5 000 Jews). French sources concur even if their estimates vary. La Rochefoucauld-Liancourt, for example, noted that 'the Moorish population has been reduced to half what it was before the conquest', whilst Baron Pichon, an able French administrator, rated the loss at two-thirds. Nor was this true merely of Algiers. A similar picture is given by most other towns for which contemporary records are available. When Medea was conquered in 1836, almost all the population left, and in 1841 a French officer noted: 'it is just as well people in France do not know how we have treated the unfortunate city which is now a mere ruin'.

These dramatic changes had led to an almost total disruption of traditional city life and the disappearance of values which had up to then upheld collective self-awareness. The destructive effects of invasion were followed up by measures taken by the French to prevent the reappearance of any form of Algerian identity. Thus such popular features as the *karaguz* or mime theatre, a favourite pastime of Turkish origin which used puppets to put forward satirical views, had helped people vent their feelings about the French, but the *karaguz* shows were officially banned in 1843, and disappeared for good. The decline in the native urban population was paralleled by a development of the foreign community which increased from 25 000 in 1840, to 131 000 after the repression of the 1848 uprising in France, and to 244 600 in 1872. Initially urban, clinging around the nucleus of existing European communities and easily discouraged by the difficulties of establishing agricultural settlements, the early civilian community set about remodelling towns on a European model, forcing Algerians to comply with this policy whilst at the same time promoting discriminatory practices. As the civilian community acquired greater self-confidence, besides benefiting from rural immigration from Italy and Spain, Europeans, encouraged by the authorities, turned to agriculture. A new and permanent feature was the European demand for grants of land. These could only be acquired by taking them from the Algerians, a measure not favoured by the army which, in some cases, attempted to protect the natives, and more generally feared the disruption of peasant life and the revolts which might ensue were Algerians to be deprived of their means of subsistence. The trend to colonist settlement was, nonetheless, irreversible.

Government-sponsored efforts to encourage rural settlement had indeed been made from the start but in many cases had failed, and early colonists had moved into town. Greater success was achieved when farmers with money ('capitalist colonization') had appeared in 1834, and by 1839 25 000 Europeans had settled in the countryside, although their numbers later fell because massacres perpetuated by the troops of 'Abd al-Qadir had discouraged colonists. A more systematic policy of settlement was undertaken by General Bugeaud, who had lands granted to retired soldiers (*imperium*, in his view, being based on the sword and the plough) and encouraged capitalist colonization. Among signal examples were the founding of the Union Agricole around Saint-Denis du Sig in 1845, large concessions of land in the province of Oran in 1847 and in that of Constantine in 1847. The problem now was shortage of available land which could only be obtained by confiscation, Algerians being very loath to sell. Such a policy was undertaken. A measure adopted on 24 May 1843 confiscated *habus* property; another provided for the recuperation of inadequately farmed lands, refusing to take into consideration the fact that Algerian economy was a mixed one, largely relying on pastoralism. Thus 200 000 hectares were converted into European settlements, of which 168 000 were in the region of Algiers. This left the Algerians of the province with only 32 000 hectares, so forcing many of them to flee southwards or, no longer having the pastures to feed their flocks, to become labourers on European farms. The arrival of immigrants in 1848 led the government to make further confiscations and by the end of 1851 there were 4773 concessions without the demand for land being satisfied – indeed Europeans were increasingly clamorous for what they called their 'rights'.

The greater part of Algeria, where European civilians were as yet few in number, was considered military territory. Europeans had to ask for permission to travel there and the local people were under the control of the army by means of its specialized section: the Arab bureaus. There was of course much tyranny and arbitrary rule by officers who were responsible to none but themselves, but officers who for personal motives chose to work in the Arab bureaus, were often also keenly interested in the society they were expected to administer. The first major European studies on Algeria in the modern period were carried out at the time by such men who were sympathetic to those whom they considered their protégés, and were also often overtly hostile to civilians whom they saw as ignorant and hard-fisted. They also knew that the granting of lands to Europeans could only mean starvation and revolts in the tribes. Their self-confidence in the 1850s was upheld by the pro-military regime of Napoleon III.

Algerian native society, which had been hard-hit in the towns, was better preserved in the rural areas. It was nonetheless being subtly modified by the foreign regime. The army considered that its function was to oversee local society without intervening in its working except to obtain acceptance of and respect for French rule. This implied recourse, if necessary, to coercive measures: military repressions and military courts (which, in 1858, became disciplinary commissions). As far as possible, however, the officers tried to bring the people to accept this of their own free will. They were therefore led to try and win over influential families and bring them to collaborate with the French. Two different categories of influential families existed. The first were the religious arbiters whose anti-Christian sentiments the army feared, so that

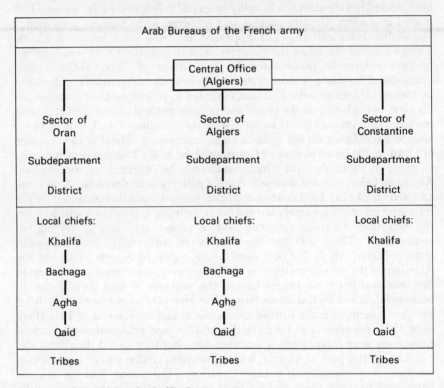

Fig. 9.2 *Native administration in Algeria*

it generally tried to undermine their positions; the others were lay families, notably tribal chiefs who had acquired influence under the Turks. Agreement with these was generally easier to reach since the notables had been used to collaborating with a foreign administration (albeit a Muslim one) on whose favours they depended to achieve a position of superiority in a democratic tribal context generally hostile to such power-stands. Moreover, they represented a military force which could be turned to good account. We thus find the Arab bureaus promoting actual feudal lords from traditionally dominant lineages. They also maintained for these chiefs the titles in use under the former Ottoman administration. We thus find on the tribal scene in the 1840s and 1850s such men as 'Ali bin Ahmad, *khalifa* of the province of

Constantine, Hamza, *khalifa* of the Awlad Sidi Shaykh, Muhammad bin 'Abd Allah bin Wali, *khalifa* of Mina and Muhammad al-Muqrani, *khalifa* of the Medjana.

These leaders and their tribal contingents played an important part in bringing Algeria under French rule since they were expected to provide military assistance whenever required. An ambiguous status of interaction between resistance and repression was maintained since the new chiefs appointed by the French had often been at the head of the resistance movement in former times and, later, out of moral conviction or to avenge some slight from the authorities, they might be led to revolt again. Thus the Sharif of Wargla who fought the French from 1849 to his capture in 1853, had begun his career under Bugeaud who after beating him in 1841, had appointed him *khalifa* of western Algeria. An even more striking example is that of the Awald Sidi Shaykh, a border-tribe of south-west Algeria which extended over the Moroccan frontier, and was very often in opposition to constituted authority, both for economic and religious reasons. The tribe which claimed religious (i.e. holy lineage) origins and had its own fraternity, the Shaykhiyya, was often involved in fighting the French (in the 1850s, 1864–9, and in the 1880s) and it was to keep the Awlad Sidi Shaykh under control that the French had bestowed favours on its tribal leader, Sidi Hamza. He was appointed *khalifa* and showed himself a staunch supporter of the French, notably by fighting on their side at Laghwat in 1852 and against the Sharif of Wargla in 1853. Feudal abuse of privileges was to arouse not only tribal discontent but French concern, so that when Sidi Hamza died somewhat mysteriously in Algiers in 1861, his sons, Abu Bakr and Sliman were reduced to the inferior rank of *bashaga (bash-agha)*. Sidi Sliman turned against the French and in 1864 joined a movement of radical religious opposition led by Sidi Lalla, thus sparking off a long period of resistance. The dangers of the policy promoted by the French are here exemplified: the new native lords were sometimes responsible for increased oppression which, should the French attempt to curb it, could further lead the privileged tribal chiefs to side with the opposition.

Another result of French military rule was the following up of the policy of recruiting Algerians into the army. Former *janissaries* had been recruited in Oran and Mostaganem. They became the 3rd batallion of the Zouaves. In 1841 the Spahi-s (native cavalry) and three battalions of riflemen made up essentially of *kulughli*-s were established. In 1855 Napoleon III envisaged making military service obligatory but in the face of opposition, gave up the idea. By 1848, there were 6600 Algerian volunteers serving in the French forces in North Africa out of 87 000 men. Their first use on foreign battlefields was during the Crimean War. The idea was of course popular with the emperor and projects were even aired to have most of the military work in Algeria done by native recruits – all ranks above that of captain being, of course, given only to Frenchmen. Local officers and the governor-general, Field-Marshal MacMahon later opposed this on the grounds that the loyalty of local troops could not be depended upon.

This was the type of society Napoleon III met with in Algiers during his 1860 visit and which gave him the impression not only that Muslims were in no way hostile to him personally, but that they further expected of him that he protect them from civilian claims on their lands and other forms of oppression.

The army on the spot was itself divided, a pro-Arab minority siding with royalists in favour of the emperor whilst the rest remained hesitant or openly sided with the generally republican colonists.

Back in France, Napoleon III put his new policy into effect. Algerian tribal chiefs continued to be favoured and several of them were invited to court. The emperor inaugurated an official policy of blandishments which included generous distributions of the *légion d'honneur* decoration. At the same time he made praiseworthy efforts to become knowledgeable on the subject of Algeria and experts were called in for consultation. This brought to the fore as the emperor's chief adviser on Algerian affairs a man called Isma'il Urbain (1812–48), a Saint-Simonian who had lived in Egypt in Muhammad 'Ali's time and had there converted to Islam. He had gone to Algeria in 1837, hoping to promote peaceful coexistence between the warring parties but had had little success with the French officers who despised him for his pro-Muslim attitude and even more for being of West Indian stock. Now Isma'il Urbain was able to bring Napoleon III to share his views and adopt a policy which, extending beyond Algeria, was intended to uphold imperial prestige throughout the Mediterranean.

Two important measures were taken in this period, namely the two laws which defined the status of Algerians in the imperial context. The two laws voted by the Senate on 22 April 1863, and on 14 July 1865, are known as the *Senatus-Consult*. The first, which was intended to protect Algerians from European claims on their lands, defined the tribes as land-owning communities. Their property was to be registered as such and land-deeds made out. The capacity of the settler community and of the administration on the spot to thwart such measures was soon revealed, as measures were interpreted in a way which directly benefited the colonists. Thus land-deeds established considerably reduced the holdings of the tribes. Two examples may serve to illustrate this: when the Awlad Kusayr received their deed on 11 April 1862, they found that their lands had been reduced by a third, and in November of that same year, the Beni Tur lost 1300 hectares out of a total of 4000, the 740 families of the tribe being thus left with under 0.5 hectare per head. In more or less every case, the result was the loss of about one-third of tribal property. The second *Senatus-Consult* was no less a half-way measure which the European community turned to its advantage. It defined Algerians as French subjects, but not citizens with full rights. Thus they were deprived of advantages such as the right to vote, but were expected to share obligations with the French in such matters as paying taxes.

Napoleon's second visit to Algeria in May 1865 was preceded by a statement of policy in an imperial speech on 12 January 1863. Two contradictory objectives were defined: 'to try and win the hearts of the Arab people and to protect the colonizers'. The necessary balance was to be worked out by the Arab bureaus which 'together with the tribal chiefs have the difficult task of administering the country'. Needless to say colonists were furious, not only because the emperor left the army in charge in Algeria but because he recognized the existence of the Algerians as a specific community. The term 'Arab people' must further be seen in the light of imperial policy which not only upheld the traditional French view that Algeria and the other Regencies were not under Ottoman sovereignty, but further pointed to new irredentist ambitions, involving the eastern end of the Mediterranean and notably Lebanon. This was to lead the emperor further to magnify his role as protector of the Arabs in a letter dated 6 February 1863, which did not hesitate to term Algeria an 'Arab Kingdom'. This was obviously to further arouse the furore of the colonists and their supporters. The emperor had stated: 'Algeria is not strictly speaking a colony, but an Arab Kingdom. The natives and the colonists have an equal right to my protection and I am no less the Emperor of the Arabs than the emperor of the French'. That this was an ambiguous statement and one which Napoleon III could in no way back up was illustrated during his visit which though it lasted eight days instead of the two originally planned, merely led to contradictory points of view being expressed to a silent Emperor.

In spite of the army's role as a third force and the emperor's own assumption that he was the arbiter of Algeria's destiny, it was obvious that a breakthrough would be made in favour of the settler community which further had the backing of social and economic forces at home. It indeed came with the Third Republic which took over in France after the downfall of Napoleon III in 1870 and was carried out on the spot by the settler community in the wake of the repression of the Algerian 1870 uprising.

THE 1870 UPRISING AND ITS CONSEQUENCES

1870 was to mark the last major attempt by Algerians to reconquer their independence until the 1954 War of Liberation. It had various and obvious causes, including the mutiny of Spahi regiments which refused to go to France to take part in the war against Germany. There was also a conflict of long standing between the colonial authorities and one of the tribal chiefs, Ahmad al-Muqrani. The latter had considered himself personally insulted when the French had demoted him to the rank of *bashaga* after the death of his father, the *khalifa* Muhammad in 1853. The French had not been slow to see that Ahmad al-Muqrani had not come out strongly in their favour during the Awlad Sidi Shaykh uprising of 1864–5, and they even suspected him of supporting the latter. The new regime of the French Third Republic was seen by the *bashaga* as a personal insult since he was not prepared to take from a civilian the orders which he had formerly received from army officers. There were also deeper and more general causes of discontent in the country. People had suffered greatly from the military campaigns. Many men had been killed, the tribes had been broken up and ruined. The army rarely hesitated to burn villages and crops, or to confiscate cattle. A few random examples may be quoted to illustrate this: in the Kabylies, in 1865, 500 head of cattle, 4000 sheep, 9200 goats, and 300 horses had been confiscated when the Rishiya tribe surrendered. The army also took several hundred prisoners, including women and children. A few days later the tribesmen still fighting were exterminated to a man. Official recommendations to spare human lives and protect property went unheard. In the region of the Flittas, 15 000 head of cattle were taken, a village burnt, 100 tribesmen killed, and 4000 hostages placed under army control, many of them dying because of ill-treatment. In the west, the story is the same and the governor-general writing to Napoleon III in 1865, mentions the fact that half the livestock of Oran had been lost. The French moreover had an accepted practice, that of making the rebels pay for the cost of the operations. Thus the Minister of War, General Randon, writing to his commanding officer on the spot in 1864, stated:

> You have given me to understand that you will be able to recover the greater part of the cost of war by levies on the tribes who have taken part in the uprising; this is most desirable so as not to give further argument to the opposition to cry out against Algeria, its military commanders, the Arab bureaus and other clichés it indulges in.

Consequently Oran was taxed over 3 million francs for its part in the uprising. The fact that only just over 2.5 million actually reached the Treasury is also part of the nature of military rule in Algeria, something which the Minister could do little more about than add three question marks to his query in February 1865: 'What has become of 3,000 camels, 30,000 sheep, etc. taken by Generals Yusuf, Ducrot, Legrand, and others???' By these and other means the army was breaking the spirit of rebellion. However it also left a ruined society open to every encroachment of the colonists when the downfall of Napoleon III, and the army's loss of prestige and authority, gave civilian rule a free hand in Algeria.

New laws granting lands to immigrants, and notably to refugees from Alsace and Lorraine, caused considerable concern and were one of the main factors which sparked off the 1870 uprising. Another was the intense misery of the peasantry, hard-hit by several years of famine and actual starvation. The French authorities had done little to help and the Bashaga al-Muqrani who had himself spent not only all his available money but had borrowed 350 000 francs to provide relief, was particularly angry when creditors became pressing and the governor-general refused to help him out. Al-Muqrani's reasons for taking part in the revolt were largely personal. The Rahmaniyya fraternity's reasons for organizing armed opposition were of a more popular and religious nature. Its leader, the aged Shaykh Haddad decided to take the lead of the movement and on 8 April 1870, he formally declared Holy War. He and his sons set about organizing the 150 000 men who came forward at the call.

In a matter of weeks, the insurgents were in control of all eastern Algeria, European farmers had been killed on their farms – the figures are put at about 100 – and the uprising had spread to more or less every part of the country. The French army knew it had to react quickly and energetically and it moved in to the Kabylie mountains which were the stronghold of the Rahmaniyya and the region from which many of the combatants came. Al-Muqrani was killed in battle on 5 May 1871. The French pushed forward and, after heavy fighting, took Fort National in the heart of the Kabylies. On 13 July the Rahmaniyya *shaykh* surrendered together with his sons. The last battles in the region were fought in October. Elsewhere opposition petered out, except in Tuggurt and Wargla which held out until early 1872.

The Muqrani revolt, as it is often called, had been as fierce as it had been brief. There had been 340 armed encounters. At least 200 000 Algerians had taken part in the fighting and some 800 000 persons were involved. They had been defeated by a better organized and better equipped army of 85 000 men.

The French had lost 2686 men – though more than half died from disease and not actual fighting. The number of Algerian casualties is not known – it rarely is, because even when available such facts were not thought worthy of mention. The aftermath of the 1870 uprising showed up the repressive nature of French rule whose main objective now was to implement a policy of colonization. The uprising was put to good account. The punishment meted out was more cruel than the campaign. The rebels, either as individuals or collectively as tribes, had fines and confiscation of land inflicted on them. A war indemnity of 36.5 million francs was imposed on 298 peasant communities and their lands were confiscated. It was estimated that it would take them at least eight years to pay. In fact the last instalments were only paid in 1890 and, as an administrator of the time put it, 'all the work of the natives goes to paying the treasury and interest rates'. The confiscation of land served colonist views ('it will allow us to take over immediately the lands we need') and though it had been stipulated that, with government permission, peasants could buy back their property, this was, in practice, only allowed for poorer lands in which settlers were not interested. The resilience of Algerian society was, however, a surprise and, in spite of dire straits, peasants made every effort to recover their lands then, or later when some colonist farms proved failures. The amount of land taken over officially after the uprising amounted to 2 639 600 hectares which was the collective property of 313 communities. To this were added individual fines and confiscations. Thus 1778 persons lost 54 461 hectares of farm land, and real estate to the value of 643 509 francs. The fines and money raised by these means amounted all told to nearly 11 million francs. Half the amount was spent to buy land elsewhere, notably in the province of Oran, to settle European immigrants. As the French historian, Charles-André Julien, pointed out, the Algerians had been sentenced in various capacities: as belligerents, they were made to pay a war indemnity; as natives they had their lands confiscated; and as French citizens a great number of them, chosen more or less at random, were taken to court and condemned on often the flimsiest evidence to deportation.

The cost of the last wholesale attempt to shake off French rule had been heavy. The tribes had lost their best lands in the process and an estimated 70 per cent of their resources. In spite of the great vitality of peasant society in North Africa, and notably in the Kabylies, they were not to recover for many years from the blow. The 1870 uprising thus marks the end of mass resistance to the conquest and the beginning of what an Algerian nationalist, Ferhat Abbas, called 'the colonial night'.

THE CROSS VERSUS THE CRESCENT

To end this chapter, a word must be said about the ideology of imperialism, or rather one particular aspect of it used in Algeria to combat the cohesion of Algerians, and beyond them that of North African Muslims in general, and also to uphold and justify European expansion. Outdated though religious fanaticism and the crusading spirit may seem in the late 19th century, they were nonetheless used as an imperial tool, the paradox being that this policy, though apparent from the start, became actively militant not under the army regime, nor under the Second Empire, however much it had recourse to religious argument, but during the Third Republic which was otherwise characterized by its strongly secular and indeed anti-clerical attitude which, in France itself, resulted in the breakdown of relations between church and state. That a different policy could be pursued in the colonies was cynically pointed out by the French politician Gambetta, who told Archbishop Lavigerie: 'anticlericalism, Monsignore, is for France. It is not a commodity for export'.

Official attacks on Islam

From the start, Algeria had suffered from religious persecutions. The conquest opens on the scene of the French army storming the Ketshawa mosque to turn it into a Roman Catholic church. The same fate was to befall several other mosques including the 'Ali Bitshin mosque which became Our Lady of Victory (with the ambiguity as to what sort of victory was being referred to) and the Qasba Berrari mosque which became the Church of the Holy Cross. More insidious practices were set on foot including a ban on the Holy Pilgrimage, justified by the authorities on sanitary grounds but, in fact, with the objective of preventing Algerians from spreading the sorry tale of their sufferings or seizing on the occasion to leave the country for good. The policy of local authorities, particularly in the civilian districts, was to undermine Islamic institutions. This was particularly apparent with respect to the *shari'a* or Muslim courts of law whose activities were restricted. Even in this field, French law overrode local jurisdictions since the Algerians, if they so wished, could appeal to a French court. Though the 1865 *Senatus-Consult* was intended by the well-meaning emperor to uphold Algerians' rights – they could, for example, acquire French citizenship – it was interpreted in the hostile atmosphere of Algeria as an attempt to deprive people of their religious status and therefore of their identity. Significantly, we find few requests for French nationality either from the Muslim or Jewish sectors of the population. Between 1865 and 1 November 1867, only 56 Muslims and 115 Jews made applications.

In the matter of schools, the invasion of Algeria and the setting up of the French regime was marked by a dramatic decline in literacy. In the rural areas, schools disappeared during the fighting and the French officers were generally loath to see them reopen because they were expected to foster the spirit of resistance. This was part of a more general distrust involving the whole complex institution of the *zawiya* which, in rural areas, acted as a meeting place, a centre of guidance under the leadership of a religious lineage, a school and the seat of a sufi fraternity. When the French officers had succeeded in winning over a number of rural notables who had traditionally mediated between the Turks and the peasantry, they found that these were not as closely imbedded in the social fabric as they had imagined and that religious lineages and the *zawiya*-s were, in fact, more closely involved in social interaction. This led the Arab bureaus to be very wary of such institutions and their multifarious activities. They went to considerable trouble to list and describe the religious establishments – hence major compendiums such as Depont and Coppolani's *Les Confréries Religieuses Musulmanes* (Algiers, 1897) which are still today standard reference books. The Arab bureaus made systematic efforts to curtail the activities of the *zawiya*-s especially those involving contacts with pupils (schools) or disciples (sufi fraternities).

Further, they attempted to infiltrate the religious establishments with their own agents and to manipulate holy lineages, some of whom thereby became discredited agents of colonialism. Those who made an active stand against the French were often involved in revolts which led to their being imprisoned, deported or exiled. After creating a vacuum, the Arab bureaus were asked by the Saint-Simonian emperor to set up schools in their districts. Obviously army officers were not necessarily good pedagogues, and what the Algerians wished for – namely proficiency in Arabic and a Muslim self-awareness – were not to be found in the new schools to which they systematically refused to send their children. In the 1860s, the Arab bureaus which had encouraged the experiment, were forced to conclude that 'all has failed because of the insuperable objections of the masses'. Indeed, as one report puts it, 'the natives consider that sending their children to school is the worst form of corvée we can force upon them'.

The situation was no better in the civilian zone where Napoleon III's well-meaning efforts once again had different results to those he had hoped for. Thus 'mixed schools' and an 'Imperial College' were set up. Their aim was the 'assimilation' of natives, a key notion in French colonial policy in its more generous aspects, but one which failed both because the European settler community refused such infringement on what it considered its privileges, and because the Algerians also collectively signified their hostility to it. Even the Imperial College, which recruited its pupils from leading families which were already actively collaborating with the French, had disappointing results: 99 Algerian pupils in 1865, 81 in 1866. One of the causes of failure is brought out unwittingly by an official report which proudly notes that the pupils were speaking French all the time. What the Algerians collectively knew was that their cultural and religious identity was intimately connected with proficiency in Arabic which has both a lay and religious status. French interference in this field was deeply resented; all the more so in view of the fact that the overt or sometimes unconscious aim of such schools was to privilege 'modern' European studies to the detriment of Muslim culture. Thus urban schools – generally called *madrasa*-s – which had traditionally trained candidates for public functions saw their role decline when the French took them over. In Algiers, Tlemcen, and Constantine, there were all told only 130 pupils in 1865 and 152 in 1866 and these no longer came from respectable families which had generally furnished candidates for official posts. A French administrative report sadly noted that the pupils came from 'the lower strata of society, a class which cannot give us respectable magistrates'. This progressive decline in educational standards is part of the general atmosphere: a kind of cultural withering. The fact that people clung fiercely to narrow basic religious tenets hardly compensates for the impression of cultural sterility which pervades in late 19th-century Algeria.

The reader may sometimes have had the impression that the opposition in Algeria resulted partially from misunderstanding: French ethnocentrism adding blunder to blunder and thus giving rise to a cohesive Muslim reaction of negativism. That this is not exactly the case and that French colonial policy involved a direct onslaught on the Muslim religion as such is exemplified by the case of a zealous prelate, Archbishop Lavigerie (1825–92), who brought out the latent crusading spirit inherent in imperialism.

Lavigerie and the crusade against Islam

Lavigerie, who arrived in Algiers as the city's new archbishop in 1867, was imbued with a great hatred of Islam and the firm conviction that his mission was the conversion of Muslims to Christianity. He was determined to go ahead whatever objections he met with and these were soon apparent. The army was against this sort of trouble-stirring and Napoleon III himself sternly advised:

> Archbishop, you have a great task before you: that of making 200 000 Catholics live moral lives. As for the Arabs, leave them to the Governor-General whose duty it is to keep them in order and bring them to accept our dominion.

Lavigerie, however, had the *ultima ratio* of conviction: the self-will which pays no heed to arguments or political necessity. He began by winning to his side the settler community whose objectives he publicly upheld. He then turned to what he considered his mission. In the last few years before the downfall of the Second Empire, he had laid the foundations of a militant church by creating two religious orders – the White Fathers and the Missionary Sisters of Africa – and he had sent them out into the field to found religious establishments, including orphanages and dispensaries.

These establishments were set up notably in the Kabylie region where a divide and rule policy was at work, upheld by theories which opposed Arabs to Berbers. Lavigerie who took seriously his responsibility as successor of Saint Augustine, North African bishop of the 4th century, claimed that Berbers had been Christians in antiquity and that this had, he believed, left its mark. His mission, he stated, was to bring them back to the fold. All his available clergy were put to the task and the archbishop went ahead with his plans in spite of local resistance, both from the Algerians and from French army officers. The situation prevalent in Algeria at the time facilitated his task. Between 1866 and 1869, a severe drought had reduced harvests to record low figures. The situation was worsened by other natural factors including a plague of locusts, an earthquake at Blida, and an epidemic of cholera. Sheep and cereals had almost disappeared from the markets and cattle had died or had had to be killed because of lack of fodder. It is estimated that half of the country's livestock thus disappeared. For the poorer Algerians, the situation became dramatic. Starving people wandered about the country and the death toll was terrible. Official figures, generally considered to be underestimates, mention 300 000 deaths. The French official attitude was both irresponsible – little or nothing was done – and callous – efforts went essentially to covering up the situation. Lavigerie, who already had experience in Lebanon of collecting and distributing relief funds, went actively to work, and it is to his credit that he was able to raise large sums of money and distribute funds which, in 1868, amounted to 800 000 francs.

Once this has been said, it must also be admitted that the famine was in fact a godsend for his evangelical mission. Orphaned children roamed the country and the tribes who had not the wherewithal to feed them were prepared to take them to the religious orphanages where they could be saved from starvation. The priests and nuns of the mission thus came to have 1753 children of whom about half, after disease had taken its toll, lived on in the orphanages. However, the children were also baptized and special care was taken to instruct them in the Catholic religion. When the worst of the famine was over, relations came to claim the children. The priests strenuously opposed this. Lavigerie who believed he was saving their souls, showed that he personally was prepared to go to almost any length to keep them. He faced up to public protest and even attacks on the orphanages. He quarrelled with the military authorities who, being aware of the political repercussions, tried to bring him to a more conciliatory attitude. He was even to break openly with the Governor-General MacMahon whose recommendations he systematically ignored. Lavigerie also bought a rural estate at Maison Carré, just outside Algiers, where his protégés were brought up. Several later became novices and priests. The others were married to other Algerian Catholics and settled in special villages set up for them in the Chelif valley. Thus Saint-Cyprien in the Attafs became a Christian community with an establishment belonging to the White Sisters, some 20 Algerian couples and, in 1874, a hospital for the natives.

The actual impact of Lavigerie's action should not be overestimated even if he did create a small community of Christians, victims of a political project in which they had no share, Algerians who were aliens in their own land and community. Lavigerie's attempts indeed failed in view of the hostility and general opposition of the Muslim community which protected its members, including defenceless children, and proved its capacity to die or to leave Algeria rather than give up its faith. Even in periods of acute distress because of famine, the nuns and priests were only able to adopt a few abandoned children. Moreover the political theory which had upheld the project: the belief in a fundamental difference between Berbers and Arabs which made the former pro-European by temperament and pro-Christian by heredity, had proved a fallacy. Though the 'Kabylie myth' persisted in French colonial traditions, it was given up as official policy. The 1870 revolt in which Berbers and Arabs fought side by side, no less than common opposition to imperialism in all its manifestations, including evangelization, led to a more adequate colonial appreciation: 'The Kabylie, like the Arab, belongs to the race of the jackal which only appears resigned and can never be tamed' (Louis Vignon, *La France en Algérie*, 1893).

Nonetheless the efforts of Lavigerie and of the White Fathers to introduce Christianity in a Muslim society played an important role in clarifying the ultimate significance of imperialism. The archbishop had a fanatical zeal when it came to childish souls whom he considered as the Church's property. Far from trying to placate Muslim feeling, the archbishop added insult to injury by publicizing his activities. Thus Algerian orphans were taken to Rome to be solemnly baptized. Humane feelings of pity for starving children had given way to religious fanaticism, and the latter itself was increasingly seen as an all-out offensive against the Muslim religion as Lavigerie in his pastoral letters and public preaching poured out his hatred of Islam and his will to see the Cross everywhere replace the Quran. Muslim reactions could be just as fanatical, but they could also express themselves in reasonable terms which did not exclude absolute dedication. We find such an attitude in the letter a religious leader, Bin 'Ali Sharif, wrote to the Vice-Governor:

I have read the Archbishop's letter of the 6th April last in which he states that he wishes to replace the Quran by the Bible to regenerate the Arabs. This letter has considerably distressed the Muslims. I am a man of religion and all Muslims of my generation share my feelings. We would rather see our children die than become Christians. No compromise is possible on that score. You solemnly promised us freedom of conscience. Should you break your word, we would not be held to ours.

That the struggle against imperialism would ultimately be played out not in the material field, but in terms of cultural and religious values is brought to the fore.

Lavigerie's wider ambitions

The kind of irredentism which characterizes imperialism also characterizes Lavigerie's crusade. In the years which followed the French change of régime in 1870 up until Lavigerie's death in 1892, the prelate developed his action in two directions with the active support of the Vatican. He attempted to establish the Catholic Church on an official North African wide basis, and he made his own explorations and encroachments in the Saharan regions.

With respect to a North African see, Lavigerie was to take as his model the historical precedent of the early Christian Church which had existed on the continent in the last years of the Roman Empire with Carthage as a bishopric. The Tunisian town had further significance for the French because Saint Louis had died there, and, as we saw earlier, they had obtained from the Bey of Tunis permission to build a chapel commemorating the event. In 1876, Lavigerie obtained permission from Pope Pius IX to make this church a cathedral, besides setting up a hospital and a school. Leo XIII, who became Pope in 1878, concretized this by officially making Carthage a see, appointing Lavigerie head of the Church of Africa with, in 1882, the rank and dignity of Cardinal, thus highlighting what a recent biographer of his called 'the interplay of Imperialism and Missionary'.

Lavigerie also shared with imperialists of his time the lure of the Sahara which, as the years passed, increasingly came to be seen as the last empty space open to colonial greed. In August 1868, Lavigerie had gone to Rome and pleaded with Pope Pius IX to allow him to open missions in the south. He had described the extensive Saharan regions which spread from Sudan to the Atlantic as open to missionary zeal. Soon after, Lavigerie was appointed apostolic delegate for the Sahara and Sudan. He immediately undertook to send out exploratory missions. His close collaborator, Father Charmetant, was sent out to the tribes around the Mzab and he came back with a favourable and optimistic report which led Lavigerie to set up an establishment in Laghwat in 1873. The order he had founded, the White Fathers, were to have evangelization of the Sahara as their privileged task. The fact that their number had increased from three or four in 1868 to over 100 in 1874 further increased the archbishop's optimism. However, it soon became apparent that any move further south into the Sahara would meet with stiff resistance and that the Algerians were prepared to go to the length of murdering exploring priests. Lavigerie's missionaries soon learnt this to their cost: three priests sent out in December 1875 to explore their way to Timbuktu were murdered by the

Tuareg in April 1876 in the region of In Salah. The same fate awaited three other missionaries sent out to Timbuktu in 1881. Lavigerie followed this up by showing interest in other parts of Sudanic Africa and in the region of the Great Lakes where he hoped to set up an active Catholic mission which would have promoted French influence in East Africa. He did indeed succeed in setting up his mission but, here too, accidents were frequent. Several priests in Tanganyika were murdered in 1881. The hostility he met with led Lavigerie to set up a new order, one of warring monks whom he named the Armed Brethren of the Sahara. It turned out to be a short-lived effort to promote the faith at gun-point.

In the overall pattern of imperial expansion, cultural and religious factors thus played their role, but before considering the counterattack of Islam, further aspects of imperialism must be gone into, and notably economic encroachments apparent throughout the continent, but nowhere more evidently so than in Egypt and Tunisia.

SELECTED READING LIST

Ageron, Ch.-R., *"L'Algérie algérienne" de Napoléon III à de Gaulle*, (Paris, 1980).

Burzet abbé, *Histoire des désastres de l'Algérie (1866–1868). Sauterelles, tremblement de terre, choléra, famine*, (Algiers, 1869).

Emerit, M., 'Le Problème de la conversion des musulmans d'Algérie sous le Second Empire. Le conflit entre Mac-Mahon et Lavigerie', *Revue historique*, 223, 1960.

Julien, Ch.-A., *Historire de l'Algérie contemporaine*, (Paris, 1964).

Lavigerie, Ch. M. A., *Recueil de lettres publiées par Mgr. l'Archevêque d'Alger sur les oeuvres et missions africaines*, (Paris, 1869).

Napoleon III, *Lettre sur la politique de la France en Algérie, adréssée par l'empereur au maréchal de MacMahon, duc de Magenta, gouverneur général de l'Algérie (20 juin 1865)*, (Paris, 1865).

O'Donnell, J. D., *Lavigerie in Tunisia. The Interplay of Imperialist and Missionary*, (Athens (USA), 1979).

Rey-Goldzeiguer, A., *Le Royaume arabe*, (Algiers, 1977).

Trumelet, C., *Histoire de l'insurrection des Ouled Sidi Cheikh (sud algérien), de 1864 à 1880*, (Paris, 1884).

Zurcher, M., *La Pacification et l'organisation de la Kabylie orientale de 1838 à 1878*, (Paris, 1949).

CHAPTER 10

EGYPT: A VICTIM OF IMPERIALISM

If, as it is sometimes said, Muhammad 'Ali on his deathbed whispered: 'My grandchildren will reap what I have sown', this ambiguous phrase may well serve as a caption to this chapter which deals with the various trends set on foot in the earlier part of the century, but seen here in their ultimate consequences in an imperial context. There is consequently a remarkable continuity in events but a changing pattern of meaning which stems not so much from the trends set on foot in Egypt but from their significance in the world order. This chapter will deal essentially with those changes which were part of the modernizing trend and their progressive takeover by imperialist forces.

MUHAMMAD 'ALI'S SUCCESSORS: THE SEQUENCE OF EVENTS

'Abbas Hilmi I (1848–54)

'Abbas Hilmi I who was viceroy from 1848 to 1854 can best be described as a man who was not hostile to modernity but who wished to do away with the European commitments it involved – a contradiction, as he was to learn. Thus, both in Egypt and Sudan, he pursued Muhammad 'Ali's policies. In the colony, local administration was developed, courts of law were set up in Khartum, and the first government schools were opened. In Egypt similar policies were followed as national revenue continued to rise and cotton production increased. At the same time it was quite obvious that Europeans or their agents (often Christian Arabs) had been attracted to the country in growing numbers, encouraged by Muhammad 'Ali's *laissez-faire* attitude. This gave greater importance to the consuls who ruled over sometimes large communities made up of their own nationals and 'protégés' from other countries. They had the right to hear cases involving their nationals, even if one of the parties was Egyptian. This was part of the Capitulations, a diplomatic agreement come to with Turkey at the time of Sulayman the Magnificent and which had been extended to the autonomous provinces, and even to independent states such as Morocco. The influence and involvement of the consular corps in local politics and business were further upheld by the traditional practice of long-term appointments, with a number of families specializing in Mediterranean posts which were passed on from one generation to the next. A case in point is the De Lesseps family and notably Mathieu de Lesseps (1774–1832) who had been *en poste* in Sale (1791), Tripoli (1797), Tangier (1799), and Cairo (1800) before being appointed consul-general in the Egyptian capital in 1804. He ended his career as consul-general in Tunis (1827–1832). Of his three sons, Ferdinand, Theodore, and Jules, Theodore was at the Ministry of Foreign Affairs in Paris, Jules was

Fig. 10.1 Egypt: main events under the Viceroys 'Abbas Hilmi and Muhammad Sa'id	
1848	'Abbas Hilmi became viceroy.
1853	Crimean War. Egyptian troops sent to Turkey's help.
1854	Muhammad Sa'id became viceroy. Suez Canal concession deed signed. Foreigners set up a company for navigation on the Nile.
1856	End of the Crimean War. Military service became obligatory in Egypt.
1857 (Jan. 1)	Railway between Alexandria and Cairo opened. A museum of antiquities opened at Bulaq.
1859 (Aug. 5)	Reform of the land-holding system. Private property re-established and state monopolies abolished. Foreign investors set up the Medjidiyé, a shipping line.
1859	Cairo-Suez railway opened. Cutting of the Suez Canal began.
1861	Cotton boom.
1862	Muhammad Sa'id sent a contingent of 1200 Sudanese to take part in the French campaign in Mexico.

vice-consul in the Middle East before becoming a business man with interests in Tunis, and the Bey's consular representative in Paris, whilst Ferdinand was to acquire world fame as the engineer who cut the Suez Canal. Ferdinand de Lesseps (1805–94) had himself begun his career in the consular corps, notably at Tunis (1828) and Alexandria (1831) before retiring from public service in 1849 after political disagreement with his government. However he kept up relations with his Egyptian friends.

'Abbas Hilmi, like Muhammad 'Ali, had other tense relations with the Ottoman Empire. 'Abbas Hilmi wished for closer ties with the Sultan and hoped the latter would help him not only resist foreign encroachments but expel the French from his country and protect him from their North African irredentism. Turkey, itself in a difficult position, was promoting reforms which involved greater centralization, notably in the matter of provincial administration. 'Abbas Hilmi was not prepared to give up his own independence. To mediate Egypt's relations with Turkey, he had recourse to Britain which was considered to be an ally of the Arab states against France and Russia. Britain did indeed agree to uphold the respective independence of both parties, but the price to be paid was one that was ultimately dangerous: the building of a railway between Alexandria and Cairo. Both the Ottoman and Egyptian governments considered it wiser to give way and official permission for the building of the railway was given in October 1851. 'All roads lead to Rome' imperialists used to say in antiquity and, now, even efforts to build up independence furthered European penetration.

Muhammad Sa'id (1854–63)
Muhammad Sa'id (1854–63) – a complete contrast to his dour nephew who had been the preceding viceroy – had in common with his father, Muhammad

'Ali, an outgoing temperament and easily became enthusiastic over ambitious projects. Having travelled in Europe, he was interested in changes taking place there and their possible adaptation to Egypt. He lacked, however, his father's keener political intelligence.

The start of his reign was marked by the Crimean War (1853–6) in which Russian irredentism was opposed by Turkey with the help of France, Britain, Sardinia, and contingents from loyal provinces including Egypt. A tense international situation did not prevent the viceroy from living out his reign in jovial style. This involved an open welcome to former friends, including such men as Ferdinand de Lesseps whose communicative enthusiasm charmed the Viceroy. One of de Lesseps' ambitious projects was the cutting of a canal to connect the Red Sea and the Mediterranean. Not, of course, that de Lesseps was himself the inventor of the project which had often been aired in the past. Bonaparte had had preliminary surveys made and the founder of French socialism, Saint-Simon (1760–1825), considered it one of the ways by which progress might be encouraged. Saint-Simonian adepts had attempted to win Muhammad 'Ali over to the idea but he had persistently refused the plan, knowing it would curtail Egypt's independence. His son was less far-sighted, but it is also only fair to point out that times had changed and that technology was now seen as the touchstone of history. Muhammad Sa'id easily let himself be persuaded and the formal deed of concession for the Suez Canal was made out in on 15 November 1851.

In 1856, Muhammad Sa'id paid an official visit to his Sudanese colony. Though in two minds as to whether the occupation should be maintained, he finally decided to keep the colony and reform its administration, notably the tax-collecting department. Efforts were indeed undertaken and more efficient governors appointed, but army mismanagement of public funds was too well established a practice to be done away with by mere viceregal will.

Muhammad Sa'id's optimism was in no way crushed, especially since it was upheld by an economically favourable situation. Egypt had achieved an enviable position on the world market, chiefly because of its exports of cotton which though inferior in quantity to Indian cotton (India produced six times more) was infinitely superior in quality and indeed the best long-staple cotton in the world. The value of cotton exported in 1865 amounted to £5 million.

There was, however, another side to the problem. The economic boom was bringing an ever greater number of Europeans to Egypt. Some were tourists come to spend the winter months in Egypt, others were travellers on their way to India or the Far East, but many were on the lookout for business. Between 1857 and 1861, an average 30 000 entries a year were recorded at Alexandria. Travelling around in Egypt was now commonplace and easy, the journey from Alexandria to Cairo and eventually Suez being by train. In fast-changing Cairo, Europeans could feel at home. They had places to stay in modern quarters, besides a world-famous meeting place: Shepheard's Hotel founded in 1841. As A. M. Broadley was to put it in *How we defended Arabi*, published in 1884:

> The verandah of Shepheard's Hotel is something more than an ordinary lounge or pleasant site of Oriental dolce far niente, – it is an Egyptian institution. When we hear in London that 'European opinion in Cairo

is deeply moved', that 'European interests are threatened to their foundations', that 'European public opinion approves', or that 'Anglo-Egyptian sensitiveness is outraged', we should know that the inmates of the balcony at Shepheard's have spoken.

European bankers were moreover beginning to show a considerable interest in Egypt. Some 64 per cent of Egypt's foreign trade was done with Britain and involved dealing with British banks. When, in 1862, Muhammad Sa'id raised one of the first of Egypt's international loans, it was placed by a reputable European firm, Fruhling & Goschen. Private bankers would also visit Egypt as, in 1854, did Emile Erlanger, then a newcomer to finance. He met De Lesseps and showed interest in the Suez Canal project. Other financiers were on the spot and were to benefit by having both European banking relations and social intimacy with the Egyptian ruling class. The most famous of these was Herman Oppenheim who belonged to the Cologne and London banking family. He had set up in Alexandria and negotiated Muhammad Sa'id's international loan. As the Khedive's chief intermediary, he had considerable responsibility in Egypt's indebtment to foreign bankers, besides contributing to a similar situation in Tunisia.

Muhammad Sa'id was also faced with the problem his predecessors already had with Capitulatory privileges. These had developed inordinately as the foreign community grew and many unscrupulous characters appeared who would find any pretext to claim damages from Egyptians. These were invariably upheld by their consuls. Muhammad Sa'id tentatively had the problem broached with the consuls to whom it was pointed out that the existence of some 17 different consular courts, each having its own code of law was at best confusing. He suggested that a common system be worked out. The consuls, adamant that their privileges be in no way impinged upon, turned a deaf ear.

It may be said that it was in Muhammad Sa'id's time that imperialism as a national cancer showed its first symptoms. At the end of his reign the once carefree Muhammad Sa'id worried helplessly as the Canal project got under way. Digging began on 25 April 1859, with the viceroy refusing to attend the ceremony. The Sublime Porte refused to sanction the project and the British were openly critical of the viceroy's weakness with respect to De Lesseps and his Compagnie Universelle du Canal de Suez. The situation was aggravated by the state of the Treasury: Muhammad Sa'id died leaving debts of £7 million of which £3 million were owing on the first major European loan.

Isma'il Pasha 1863–79

Isma'il Pasha (1863–79) – once a pupil of the Egyptian Military Academy in Paris – was less naively optimistic than his uncle Muhammad Sa'id, but more ambitious and, in any case, increasingly enmeshed in the imperial process. From his predecessor he inherited two major international political problems: the Capitulations and the Suez Canal. With respect to the consular courts, the viceroy asked his Prime Minister, Nubar Pasha – an astute Armenian determined to uphold Egyptian rights – to prepare a memorandum to be submitted to the foreign powers. The memorandum, whilst not attempting to do away with the capitulatory system as such (indeed it was to be maintained

Fig. 10.2   Egypt: main events during the reign of the Khedive Isma'il (1863–79)

1863 (April)	Sultan 'Abd al-'Aziz visits Egypt.
1864	Napoleon III arbitrates in favour of the Compagnie Universelle du Canal de Suez. International loan (placed by Oppenheim), £5 704 000.
1865	Peasant revolt crushed near Asyut. International loan, £3 387 000.
1866 (May)	International loan. Isma'il Pasha visits Turkey. Egyptian troops sent to Crete. *Majlis al-nuwwab* (Egyptian parliament) convened.
1867	International loan, £2 080 000. Isma'il Pasha granted title of Khedive.
1869	Prince and Princess of Wales visit Egypt. Khedival tour of European capitals. Opening of the Suez canal.
1870 (February)	Sir Samuel Baker leaves for Equatoria. International loan, £7 143 000.
1873 (June 8)	*Firman* grants Egypt greater autonomy. Oppenheim loan, £32 000 000.
1874	International loan, £5 000 000.
1875 (June 28)	Mixed courts sets up.
(Nov. 25)	Khedive's Suez Canal shares bought by Britain.
(Dec.)	Cave mission of inquiry. Egyptian expedition defeated in Abyssinia.
1876 (March)	Further Egyptian defeat in Abyssinia.
(March 23)	Cave report submitted.
(April 8)	Khedive suspends payment of Treasury Bills.
(May 2)	Setting up of the *'Caisse de la Dette Publique'*. Egypt supports Turkey, at war (Balkans 1875–8).
1877	Anti-slavery convention signed by Egypt and Great Britain.
1878	Fall in sales and price of cotton.
1879 (Jan.)	New powers granted to the International Control Commission. Rothschild loan.
(Feb.)	Parliament criticizes loss of sovereignty and army mutinies. Growing opposition to Europe.
(June, 25)	Sultan, at the request of the Great Powers, deposes the Khedive.

until 1937), recommended that the various consular courts should be done away with and replaced by a common 'mixed court', which would include both Egyptian and foreign judges, the latter being formally appointed by the viceroy. The code of law which the new courts were to apply was to be devised by an international commission on the basis of the French legal system. The consuls agreed to discuss the project which had obvious advantages from a European point of view and agreement was finally come to in 1873. France, always slow to accept any change of established practice, only gave its consent in 1874. The new code of law was drawn up, and the mixed courts were set up in 1875.

Although aiming at a restriction of foreign privileges on Egyptian soil and the re-establishment of Egyptian sovereignty in judicial matters involving Europeans and Egyptians, mixed courts, in fact, marked an increase in imperial pressure. The courts were staffed almost entirely by Europeans and ruled according to a legal system quite foreign to the native Egyptian. Not only did many judges have the prejudiced mentalitites of their time, but the proceedings were in a foreign language of which the less educated Egyptian had no knowledge. Recourse to lawyers was necessary and this was detrimental to the poorer classes. The new code of law had been evolved to deal essentially with commerical or financial affairs involving, as they increasingly did, foreigners or 'protégés' whose interests were thus upheld. The peasantry itself was hard hit as heavy taxation led to borrowing money on mortgage. A new class of usurers – often Greeks or Syrians – were active in the countryside in the wake of tax-collectors. Muslim law is traditionally against usury but the mixed courts conveniently had a mortgage law which provided for recovery in a summary fashion. How the courts functioned in this respect is best described by a contemporary witness of events, Van Bemmelen, who was himself a judge of the mixed courts:

> It will hardly be credited in Europe that an Arab debtor sued in the International Courts of Egypt can be foreclosed upon within three days of the falling due of his debt in a court presided over by foreign judges, on evidence given in a foreign language, and according to a foreign procedure, and that his only methods of defence is to employ a foreign lawyer to argue for him in a tongue he does not understand.

A praiseworthy effort at reducing the exorbitant privileges which the Capitulatory system entailed thus led to an important sector of the judiciary passing into foreign hands. The fact that this applied more particularly to the sector through which European penetration was effected – namely the commercial field – further led to Egypt's economic system being increasingly brought into line with capitalist requirements.

Isma'il Pasha also made a praiseworthy attempt to obtain a revision of the Suez Canal concession. Though he put over a political message 'the Canal was to belong to Egypt and not Egypt to the Canal', capitalism and the structures of industrial society got the better of him. Foreign governments upheld the imperial venture, the French backing the Compagnie Universelle du Canal de Suez, the Sultan with British consent granting a *firman* accepting the project on 19 March 1866, and the British ultimately, in 1875, buying up Isma'il Pasha's shares. The Canal was opened on 17 November 1869, and, in its first years, proved a liability.

The Suez Canal was only one, albeit the most spectacular, of the projects carried out during Isma'il Pasha's reign. The viceroy modernized the country's infrastructure in nearly every field. Railways were extended and a project for a railway connecting Egypt and Sudan was on record. Telegraph wires had been put up. Alexandria harbour had been modernized and lighthouses built; moreover perennial agriculture had been extended to Upper Egypt. Social reforms had also been undertaken, though on a more limited scale. A state postal service was set up in 1865; a limited parliamentary reform was undertaken in 1866; Arabic became the official language of the country in 1870 (though French remained the language at court), a national library was opened in 1870, state education was developed (1868) and the first government school for girls was opened in 1873. The Khedival Geographical Society was founded in 1875. The economic situation of the country, which had at first benefited by the world shortage of cotton, suddenly declined. American cotton reappeared in the late 1860s, and in the 1870s the industrial crisis set in on Europe, badly hitting the textile industry. Isma'il Pasha was in ever greater financial straights and had to have recourse to long-term loans from such bankers as Oppenheim and Rothschild, besides short-term ones (notably from the Crédit Foncier). Banks and bankers had never been as much in evidence in Egypt. Men like the Frenchman Bavray (an agent of the Rothschilds), private Paris bankers such as Marcuard and Dervieu, not to mention Herman Oppenheim, were advisers of the Pasha, procuring ready cash at great expense. European banks such as the Crédit Lyonnais, the Banque Impériale Ottomane, the Société Générale, the Comptoir d'Escompte de Paris, the Anglo-Egyptian Bank, the Bank of Egypt, were all represented in Egypt by the 1870s.

The country's difficulties were aggravated by the high investment costs of projects undertaken, often characterized by overpriced European technology and know-how. Difficulties were also aggravated by persistent mismanagement of Sudan, leading to local revolts and the necessity to repress them by military action. There was moreover a fruitless war in Abyssinia where the Egyptian army was twice defeated in 1875 and 1876, although part of Somalia was successfully occupied. There was also generally prodigal expediture and financial mismanagement in which Europeans had their share of responsibility. Isma'il Pasha had thus largely rebuilt both Alexandria and Cairo. By 1872, Cairo had a population of 350 000, and by 1882, 374 000, of whom 19 000 were foreigners. The two main cities now had gas lighting (1866 in Alexandria, 1868 in Cairo) and other improvements, but also less necessary embellishments such as Cairo's Opera House, opened in 1869. The Uzbekkiyya Gardens, the rendezvous of cosmopolitan society, had been expensively redesigned by a French gardener. Also in line with prodigal expenditure was the financing of costly geographical expeditions, notably that of Sir Samuel Baker who, in 1870, was sent out to Equatoria to claim the territory in the Pasha's name. It also involved courting the Sultan as Muhammad 'Ali already had. In 1866, Isma'il Pasha paid an official visit to Istanbul and, by means of lavish presents, he obtained a decision that hereditary succession in his family should pass from father to eldest son (and not to the eldest male of the family in accordance with Muslim tradition). In exchange, the viceroy agreed to the doubling of Egypt's annual tribute to the Sultan. In July 1866, he sent an Egyptian contingent to suppress a revolt in Crete (Crete was under Turkish sovereignty until 1897). On 8 June 1867, he further obtained for himself and his successors the title of *khedive* (from the

Persian *khediv* or king) which placed him above the Ottoman governors of provinces who had the title of *wali*. On 8 June 1873 he obtained a *firman* granting Egypt almost full autonomy. He was no less extravagant in his relations with Europeans who were invited to Egypt and entertained on a lavish scale as when the Prince and Princess of Wales visited the country in February 1869. He himself made a costly European tour in 1869.

A long series of international loans bear witness to the fact that the Khedive was living above his means. The loans amounting nominally to £68 497 000 were negotiated by major banking firms: Oppenheim, Fruhling and Goschen, the Anglo-Egyptian, and Bischoffsheim. They were raised successively in 1862, 1864, 1865, 1866, 1867, 1868, 1870 and 1873. It was in this context of financial expediency that the Khedive was led to sell his Suez Canal shares to Great Britain in 1875. News of the Khedive's willingness to sell had been communicated to Disraeli, then Prime Minister, by a journalist, possibly acting at Oppenheim's suggestion. The Prime Minister made a quick decision and, without waiting for parliament's consent, asked Lionel Rothschild to put up the necessary £4 million.

By 1876, Egypt was on the brink of insolvency, just like its suzerain, the Ottoman Empire, which had gone bankrupt in 1875. On 8 April the payment of Treasury bills was suspended. This led the Great Powers to move in by means of indirect financial control. Between 1876 and 1879, the situation, though confused, evolved rapidly as bondholders had commissions of inquiry set up. Various sources of revenue were put aside for the payment of the debt. The bondholders were represented by the Caisse de la Dette Publique (May 1876) and a dual system of control over revenue and expenditure was set up under joint British and French control.

No real results could be achieved, however, without control of government policy, and in 1878, the Great Powers set about establishing this by having two European ministers in the cabinet and reorganizing its working procedure. There was opposition from the Khedive whose sovereignty was being curtailed, and from public opinion. The army took the lead in voicing criticism and it staged several demonstrations. The Great Powers thus came to the conclusion that more direct action had to be taken and that in the first place the reigning Khedive had to be got rid of. Pressures on the Sublime Porte led to the sending of a telegram to Khedive Isma'il on 25 June 1879, informing him that he was deposed and replaced by his son Tawfiq. On 30 June 1879, the ex-Khedive left for exile, first to Italy (1879–88) and then to Turkey where he died in semi-confinement in 1895.

Khedive Tawfiq, though the legitimate heir, came to power under unfavourable auspices. Not only were his possibilites of action extremely limited because of European political and economic control, but he was regarded by his subjects as a mere puppet. Part of the army rose up against what it considered the corrupt ruling class of Egypt, and various currents of opposition increasingly identified themselves with its stand, leading both to a wholesale uprising and to British intervention. In September 1882, the British expeditionary corps conquered Cairo and, although it re-established Khedive Tawfiq on the throne, it made Egypt, *de facto* if not *de jure*, a protectorate.

THE SUEZ CANAL: A FEAT AND A LIABILITY

When considering the implications for North Africa of the changes underway in industrial centres of Europe, one of the first things which comes to mind is the Suez Canal. This probably reflects its almost symbolic significance which warrants a more detailed examination and an assessment in terms of the imperial process which progressively undermined Egypt in the second half of the 19th century.

When the Suez Canal concession deed was offically granted by Muhammad Sa'id on 30 November 1854, de Lesseps returned to Paris to float the Compagnie Universelle du Canal de Suez. He won over to his project the empress and a number of political backers who in the process were given founder shares and 10 per cent of profits. Who these politicians and influential persons were remained a well-kept Suez Company secret. De Lesseps was also able to override opposition in Turkey and Great Britain, not without rumours of bribery circulating. By his over-assertive personality, de Lesseps was able to get matters underway. A subscription was opened in 1858 and the company's capital fixed at 200 million French francs divided into 400 000 shares. The Egyptian contribution was considerable. The viceroy had subscribed at the outset for 182 023 shares and put up 45 per cent of the capital. Further, he had made extensive land grants, some of which had nothing to do with the Canal project itself. Unlimited labour was to be provided by corvée. Muhammad Sa'id was later induced to buy up a further 85 506 shares in circumstances which led to temporary estrangement with De Lesseps. Digging began on 25 April 1859.

Muhammad Sa'id lived long enough to regret having launched an operation fraught with financial and political difficulties, and which was intended to enrich shareholders rather than Egypt; but it was left to his successor Isma'il Pasha to face up to the situation when he became viceroy in 1863. Though not unfavourable to the Canal project, he was shocked by the terms agreed to by his predecessor, including corvée labour which he declared he would abolish. There were at the time some 12 000 men working under compulsion. Indeed these 12 000 should, in fact, be multiplied by three since as one contingent was at work, another was wending its way back, whilst a third was being conscripted. This was all the more scandalous in view of the fact that modern technology could have done away with much of the painful work as was later shown when trough dredgers were introduced, making it possible to dispense with about three-quarters of the labour force. The Khedive also decided to do away with other liabilities. Egyptian shares were to be paid for in bonds, and he annulled scandalous grants of outlying arable land which would have created a European sector of agriculture. He also less widely requested a revision of original plans by a commission of engineers with a view to reducing the width of the Canal.

Political, industrial, and banking circles cried out in indignation. They were particularly adamant that corvée labour should continue. The Khedive took the company to court – in Paris, since it was French. The latter's ruling proved inoperative. Napoleon III then proposed his arbitration. Ingenuously Isma'il Pasha accepted. Napoleon's ruling in July 1864 not only upheld the Company in every respect including right to unlimited *corvée* labour, but condemned the viceroy to pay damages assessed at £1 520 000. The findings were at the time considered 'a judicial curiosity'. It would be truer to say they were a cynical support of national enterprise and imperial oppression.

The opening of the Canal on 17 November 1869, offered the occasion for an apparent reconciliation in a common hymn of praise to technology and progress. Cynical though one can consider the attitude of European imperialists to have been, it was also in some ways naively sincere. De Lesseps, unscrupulous as he often was, had his own share of entrepreneurial faith when he wrote of the cutting of the Canal: 'there was not a camel driver among us who did consider himself an agent of civilization. That is why we succeeded'. The fact that the opening ceremony was essentially a European gathering did not bother the 6000 guests to whom the Khedive lavishly extended the nation's hospitality. No expense had been considered too great to place the ceremony on a par with great industrial gatherings such as the International Exhibitions of London or Paris. Even an opera – Verdi's *Aïda* – had been commissioned, though in fact it was *Rigoletto* which was staged. The French Empress performed the opening ceremony. Today the whole scene appears gawdy and unedifying. One cannot forget the untold suffering and loss of life the Canal entailed for the Egyptian peasantry who provided the labour force. Moreover it meant a wealth in which Egypt was to have little share. Politically it was the fetters which retained Egypt captive until Gamel Abdel Nasser's spectacular gesture in 1956.

The Canal was not only a long-term political liability. It was also a financial one in the short term. The cost of construction had been more than double the original estimate of 200 million French francs. In spite of technical feats – the Canal was 92 miles long, varied in depth from 26 to 72 feet, had sidings to allow ships to cross, besides numerous other facilities – the use of the waterway proved difficult. It was narrow, and groundings were frequent. Moreover shipping was slow to take advantage of possibilities offered, especially in view of the fact that technical alterations had to be made to equipment. Older routes, including the overland railway from Suez to Alexandria, continued in use and the switchover was only made gradually. Thus British mail continued to cross overland until 1888. For these and other reasons, traffic in the Canal developed only slowly: a mere 436 000 tons in 1870. The Company owed a lot of money, running costs were high and revenue small. In 1869, outstanding debts were over 7 million French francs and in 1870 the company was unable to pay dividends. Shares fell to 208 French francs, less than half their nominal value. De Lesseps himself was led to consider disposing of the waterway, eventually to the Turkish government, but nothing came of these efforts. The Khedive who besides his preferential issue shares, held common stock and a right to 15 per cent of the profits as representative of the Egyptian government, saw his investment as of doubtful value.

This may explain how, in 1875, Disraeli was able to make Britain the largest single shareholder by acquiring the Khedive's 176 000 shares. This did not however mean that the British government acquired voting rights in proportion since the Khedive had been deprived of these, a fact probably, at the time, overlooked by Disraeli. On the other hand, the investment was a sound one since the shares, by the beginning of the 20th century, were worth eight times their purchase price and were bringing in over a million pounds a year in dividends. And yet, quite obviously, the problem was not so much an economic as a political one, since Egypt no longer had any say in the Canal which became an international enclave. Why should the Khedive, and therefore Egypt, have deprived themselves of their share in the major international concern on national soil, thus consolidating the power of the Company as a state within the state, and of foreign nations as shareholders?

THE IMPACT OF PUBLIC DEVELOPMENT SCHEMES

The Khedive at the time was in far too desperate financial straits to take this loss of sovereignty into consideration. It was part of an overall process of dependence which was largely underway. National economy was defined by the world market for raw materials such as sugar, gum, etc. but it was also and chiefly dependent on its sale of cotton. An optimistic attitude had been created at the turn of the century by the cotton boom. Production had risen from 87 000 bales in 1850 to five times that figure in 1865, and was to rise ninefold by 1890. The rise in price had been even more marked: $7\frac{1}{2}$d. per lb in 1861 to $21\frac{1}{2}$d. in 1862 and after the recession of the 1870s, to $29\frac{3}{4}$ d. in 1883.

This had encouraged the Khedive to launch into public and private expenditure involving not only prodigal spending but also long term costly investment projects. In the field of education, efforts to promote literacy had led to the opening of 4600 schools where some 60 000 pupils received schooling. To extend perennial agriculture to Upper Egypt, 112 canals totalling over 10 000 km had been put into service. The Ibrahimiyya Canal – 268 km long and 14 m wide – had been cut. The railway network increased from 490 km to 1881 km and 6000 km of cable were laid for the telegraph service.

That the projects were open to criticism is true: thus the Egyptian peasant paid the most and gained the least in the process. Not only were his civil rights limited (one might quote as an illustration of this the fact that Egyptians were not allowed to go from one district to another without having a special permit) but his material condition worsened even if the high price of cotton in the 1860s did improve standards of living. He now worked harder and paid more taxation. The tax system, it should be remembered, was based essentially on rural property. Agricultural revenue was estimated at the time of the British invasion at £15 million a year, of which over £4 million were paid in taxation. It should further be remembered that though there were a few feudal landowners and a small class of wealthier rural notables, the majority of the Egyptian peasants only had a few feddans of land – a feddan is 0.42 hectares – and an estimated three-quarters of the population had under 5 feddans (owned or rented). Moreover, through the iniquitous system of corvée labour, the peasants provided the workforce by which these works were carried out. In 1882, 173 000 men were thus conscripted for 151 days; in 1884, 60 000 men were used for 161 days in the Delta region alone, and in 1886 some 109 000 days of labour were provided. The fact that these figures also refer to the period of British occupation indicates that European control brought little improvement in this field. On the other hand, Egypt generally paid highly or well over the odds for the installation of European machinery and engineering

Fig. 10.3 Public works undertaken in Egypt 1863–79

Works	Cost in £ sterling	Comments
Suez Canal	£6 700.000	After sale of shares
Canals	£12 000.000	8400 miles
Bridges	£2 150.000	430 bridges
Sugar factories	£6 100.000	64 factories set up
The Alexandria harbour	£2 542.000	(Greenfield and Elliot contractors)
Work at Suez	£1 400.000	(Dussaud Brothers contractors)
Waterworks at Alexandria	£300.000	
Railways	£13 361.000	910 miles
Telegraphs	£853.000	5200 miles
Lighthouses	£180.000	15 built
	£46 264.000	

Statistics given by A. Sammarco.

works. The fact is pointed out by contemporary observers. Thus E. Dicey stated in the *Nineteenth Century* (December 1877) that the railways built in Egypt had cost four times what they should normally have done, and according to Sir Rivers Wilson (later a minister in the Egyptian cabinet) the contract price for harbour facilities at Alexandria was twice what it should have been. One may therefore take the same balanced view as Stephen Cave who 1876 was to draw up the report of the International Commission of Inquiry:

> Egypt may be said to be in a transition state, and she suffers from the defects of the system out of which she is passing, as well as from those of the system into which she is attempting to enter. She suffers from the ignorance, dishonesty, waste, and extravagance of the East, such as have brought her suzerain to the verge of ruin, and at the same time from the vast expense caused by hasty and inconsiderate endeavours to adopt the civilization of the West.

Long term investments and prodigal spending had led the Khedive to growing dependence on foreign loans and therefore on bankers and intermediaries who helped him raise them, men such as Herman Oppenheim, Emile Erlanger or Nissim de Camondo. Lord Cromer was certainly accurately describing the situation when he stated that 'Ismail Pasha added, on an average, about £7 000 000 a year for thirteen years to the debt of Egypt'. Conditions moreover were increasingly detrimental as the Khedive's credit waned. Of the £68 497 000 borrowed, much went to pay banking fees and commissions and only £48 787 000 in fact reached the Treasury. As the

---

*A CONTEMPORARY OBSERVER APPRECIATES THE SITUATION IN
EGYPT IN 1876*

With Ismaïl, however, all the evils of the foreign immigration made
themselves immediately felt. In 1864 the price of cotton suddenly fell, and
innumerable hands were thrown out of employment; and taxes being
simultaneously raised, the working population became distressed and
uneasy. . . . The Greeks and Syrians are moneylenders born; and in every large
village they opened credits with the distressed peasantry, going, moreover,
round the districts for the special enlargement of their trade. The fellah, called
upon to pay more than he had and threatened with the kurbash, fell in spite of
himself a victim at 30, and 40, and 100 per cent. I have myself known instances
of as much as 200 per cent having thus been taken per annum; and it is in great
measure on the gains of usury during this period that the modern cities of
Alexandria and Cairo, representing so many millions sterling, have been built.
Till the year 1876, however, though usury was rampant in the country, it was
still in a certain measure checked by the difficulties thrown by Moslem law in
the way of recovery of debts made on mortgage. The fellah was practically
unable to mortgage his land; and his liabilities were, therefore, limited to the
personal property he might possess. But in 1876 Nubar Pasha introduced his
famous "Réforme judiciaire", for which he has gained in Europe the name of a
great statesman. It was the *coup de grâce* of the peasant. Loans upon mortgage
were by its operations made easy and secure, and the international courts
made recovery of debts, real or pretended, against the Arab fellahin a matter of
certainty for the foreign money-lender.

John Ninet, *Origin of the National Party in Egypt*, 1883.

---

situation worsened, Egyptian bonds lost much of their value and by 1875
short-term treasury bonds bearing 20 per cent interest were being sold for a
quarter of their nominal value. No less typical of inroads made on national
economy was the 1878 Rothschild loan of £8 500 000 for which the bank took
over as guarantee some 252 000 hectares of Khedival land.

In a context characterized by indebtedness, economic recession and
creditors' pressures, the Khedive was forced to suspend payment of Treasury
Bills on 8 April 1876 and to agree that the Great Powers, acting on behalf of
bondholders, should step in.

FROM FINANCIAL DEPENDENCE TO POLITICAL CONTROL

The sale of the Khedive's Canal shares to the British government in 1875 can
thus be seen as the culmination of a process of escalation as financial pressure
led to economic and, soon, political control. The suspension of payment of
Treasury Bills led to the setting up of a foreign Commission of Inquiry to
report on the state of the country's finances and to suggest necessary remedies
meeting bondholders' claims. In the report submitted in early 1876, a not
unfavourable view was taken of Egypt's economic, and the Khedive's own
personal capacities:

These statistics show that the country has made great progress in every way under its present ruler; but notwithstanding that progress, its present financial position is, for the reasons that have already been stated, very critical.

The reasons stated make overt criticism of international banking practices:

... the expenditure, though heavy, would not of itself have produced the present crisis which may be attributed almost entirely to the ruinous conditions of loans raised for pressing requirements, due in some cases to causes over which the Khedive had little control.

The interests of bondholders and banks were nonetheless upheld by their respective governments.

The administration of the Public Debt

Control of the debt having been established by means of a *Caisse de la Dette Publique* forced upon the Khedive on 2 May 1876, measures were taken placing control of public expenditure and revenue in the hands of a British and a French commissioner. The actual management of the debt was then organized. Special revenues were put aside for this purpose. They included taxes from four provinces and revenues from shipping and railways, and commodities such as tobacco and salt. The Egyptian government was to manage as best it could with what remained.

The officials of the Caisse collected their dues irrespective of the hardship this caused in a country hard hit by recession and in which the 1878 harvests were particularly inadequate. Farman, the American consul of the time, described the pitiful plight of the Egyptian peasantry:

The facts are that the monies had to be raised by the most cruel pressure upon the people and by the then growing crops of wheat in Upper Egypt. One of the consequences of the forced exportation of this wheat was the late famine in Upper Egypt, of which pitiable accounts are given by many travellers, though its real extent has been concealed as much as possible. One American told me that at one place he saw three bodies of those who had died of starvation and a hundred persons who were mere skeletons, many of whom when given bread had not the strength to raise it to their mouths.

A further proof of the conditions which then prevailed was the spread of cholera in 1882–3. Cromer himself later admitted that the International Commission had gone about its work in an inhumane fashion, but he blamed this on French rapacity. The authorities became concerned, not perhaps so much because of the hardship Egyptians endured, but because it was killing the goose that laid the golden eggs. As the British consul, Lord Vivian, put it to Lord Salisbury, the Foreign Secretary:

I fear the European administration may be unconsciously sanctioning the utter ruin of the peasantry – creators of the wealth of this country, for which, as the English element is predominant in the administration, I hold that Englishmen are incurring a serious responsibility.

This led to various measures being taken, including the setting up of a new Commission of Inquiry on 27 January 1878 which recommended such measures as the confiscation of khedival property. The Khedive and his family according to Lord Cromer owned at the time some 916 000 acres.

The Egyptian tax-collectors, of course, were as inhumane as Egypt's creditors or even more so, but even the most barbarous measures such as flogging or taking hostages, could not bring in more money from the over-taxed and desperate peasants who increasingly fled their lands or mortgaged them to usurers who were active in the countryside.

In spite of the efficiency of Lord Cromer who had been appointed Commissioner of the Debt on 2 March 1877, and who was considered by his admirers as 'a financial wizard and a man of incorruptible honesty', it was obvious that no headway could be made unless the general policy of the government could be brought into harmony with the Debt's requirements and the general interests of the Great Powers. This progressively led to a political takeover. In 1878, a new ministry was set up under Nubar Pasha in which the ministers were to be collectively responsible and two portfolios – Finances and Public Works – were reserved to Europeans. Public opinion was particularly indignant at this form of foreign encroachment and expressed itself in the overt opposition of many junior officers. On 18 February 1879, the army, with 'Arabi at its head, staged its first public demonstration. The consuls sanguinely believed the main cause of complaint to be arrears of pay. Financiers' backing of imperialism was once again illustrated as Rothschilds 'advanced a loan of £400,000 . . . and the officers were paid' (Lord Cromer, *Modern Egypt*).

Army protest was also seen by European observers and notably by Lord Cromer as part of a political plot by Khedive Isma'il to get rid of his Prime Minister who resigned on 19 February 1882. This sealed the Khedive's fate, although a last attempt was made by the Great Powers to control Egypt indirectly by means of a cabinet imposed on the Khedive by Waddington, the French Minister of Foreign Affairs, and Lord Salisbury, the British Foreign Secretary. The new Prime Minister was to be the Khedive's eldest son, Tawfiq, and the Khedive himself was no longer to attend cabinet meetings. The two Europeans of the former ministry, Rivers-Wilson and de Blignières, were reappointed with exorbitant powers. Not only did they have an absolute right to veto but were to be consulted on the choice of ministers. The Khedive counter-attacked on 7 April 1879 by dismissing the cabinet – a move described by Lord Cromer rather singularly as a 'coup d'état' – and asking Sharif Pasha to form a new ministry from which Europeans were to be excluded and which was to be composed of 'éléments véritablement Egyptiens' as the Khedive put it, in French of course, since this was by now the language of the ruling classes.

The Great Powers took prompt action. Sir Frank Lascelles, British Agent and consul-general, acting on Lord Salisbury's instructions, wrote the following communication to the Khedive on 19 June:

EGYPT: A VICTIM OF IMPERIALISM

The French and English Governments are agreed to advise your Highness officially to abdicate and to leave Egypt. . . . We must not conceal from Your Highness that if you refuse to abdicate, and if you compel the Cabinets of London and Paris to address themselves directly to the Sultan, you will not be able to count either upon obtaining the Civil List or upon the maintenance of the succession in favour of Prince Tewfiq. (Quoted by Lord Cromer in *Modern Egypt*.)

Diplomatic pressure was brought to bear on Turkey, not only by France and Britain but also by their ally on this occasion, Bismark. The Sultan agreed to depose the Khedive and name in his stead the candidate of the Great Powers, the Khedive Tawfiq. By the summer of 1879, Egyptian independence was hardly more than a facade.

The modernizing policy undertaken by Muhammad 'Ali and his descendants had failed since it had not built Egypt up into a powerful independent nation, but had paved the way to dependence, to foreign control, and ultimately, under Khedive Tawfiq who was forced upon Egypt by the Great Powers, to political subservience. This does not mean that popular opposition was not growing and taking shape. In this period it expressed itself essentially through resistance from the army. 'Arabi Pasha had come to the fore as a political and popular leader. What the 'Arabi Pasha movement embodied for Egypt; its sociological and cultural origins, and its contribution to future nationalist movements will be studied in a subsequent chapter.

SELECTED READING LIST

Bell, M., *Khedives and Pashas*, (London, 1884).
Boudet, J. et al., *Le Monde des affaires en France de 1830 à nos jours*, (Paris, 1952).
Bouvier, J., *Les Rothschild*, (Paris, 1967).
Crabitès, P., *The Spoliation of Suez*, (London, 1940).
Cromer Earl of, *Modern Egypt*, (London, 1908).
De Leon, E., *The Khedive's Egypt*, (New York, 1877).
Douin, G., *Histoire du règne du Khédive Ismail*, Vol. I and II, (Rome, 1933–4), and Vol. III, (1936–1941).
Farman, E. E., *Egypt and its Betrayal*, (New York, 1908).
Hallberg, Ch. W., *The Suez Canal*, (New York, 1931–6).
Hull-Nack, J., *Egypt as a Field for British Enterprise*, (London, 1882).
Landes, D. S., *Bankers and Pashas*, (London, 1958).
Lesseps, F. M., de, *Lettres, Journal et Documents pour servir l'histoire du Canal de Suez*, (Paris, 1887).
Lesseps, F. M. de, *Souvenirs de 40 ans*, (Paris, 1887; English translation 1887).
Linant de Bellefonds, *Mémoires sur les principaux travaux d'utilité publique exécutés en Egypte*, (Paris, 1972–3).
Nelson, N., *Shepheard's Hotel*, (London, 1960).
Ninet, J., *Lettres d'Egypte 1879–1882*, (Paris, 1979).
Rifaat, M., *The Awakening of Modern Egypt*, (London, 1947).
Sabri, M., 'Nubar Pasha' in *Encyclopedia of Islam* (1st edition, Vol. III).
Sabri, M., *L'Epoque d'Ismail*, (Paris, 1932).
Sammarco, A., *Les Règnes de 'Abbas, de Sa'id et d'Isma'il*, Vol. IV, (Rome, 1935).
Schonfield, H. J., *The Suez Canal in World Affairs*, (London, 1952).
Wilson, Sir, A., *The Suez Canal. Its Past, Present and Future*, (London, 1939).

CHAPTER 11

TUNISIA: A SIMILAR CASE

Fig. 11.1 Main events in Tunisia 1837–81

1837–1855	*Ahmad Bey.*
1840	Opening of the Bardo Military Academy.
1846	Slavery abolished.
1855–1859	*Muhammad Bey.*
1857	The Fundamental Pact.
1858	Town council of Tunis set up on August 30th.
1859–1882	*Muhammad al-Sadiq Bey.*
1860	The *Raid al-Tunisi* published.
1861	Tunisian Constitution promulgated. The Supreme Council set up.
1862	Khayr al-Din resigned as President of the Supreme Council.
1863	First Erlanger loan.
1864	Peasant revolt led by 'Ali bin Ghadahem. The Constitution suspended. In August, repression of the revolt by General Ahmad Zarruq.
1865	Second Erlanger loan.
1866	'Ali bin Ghadahem thrown into prison where he died on 11 October 1867.
1869	International Financial Commission set up in July.
1874	Khayr al-Din became Prime Minister.
1875	Treaty of commerce signed with Great Britain.
1877	Khayr al-Din resigned as Prime Minister.
1878	Congress of Berlin (13 June–13 July). Mustafa bin Isma'il appointed Prime Minister on 23 August.
1881	The French army marched into Tunisia (24 April) and the Treaty of Bardo signed on 12 May.

The story of Tunisia parallels that of Egypt during much the same period. Similar processes find their expression in the same events, and the same political attitudes. Of course imperialism was exerting a common pressure on North Africa, but imperialism also adapted to different contexts. Morocco and Libya thus present a somewhat different picture, as does the progress of explorers, traders, and soldiers in the *bilad al-Sudan*. The analogy therefore points to a deeper structural interrelationship. There is a real sense of Muslim unity in North Africa which tends to highlight Egypt as the gateway to the Holy Places, a flourishing centre of trade, a reputed seat of learning, and in

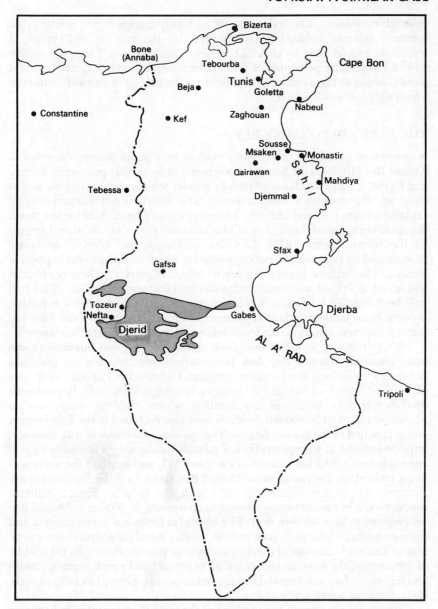

Map 11.1 *Tunisia*

more recent times, as a country having taken the lead on the path to modernity. The latter was particularly reflected in the personality and policies of Muhammad 'Ali with whom such political leaders as the Tunisian Bey Ahmad tended to identify themselves. Ambiguously in both cases, the identification led to a common admiration for Napoleon. The lead taken by Tunisia in the wake of Egypt further points to a similar social, political, and cultural evolution. The existence of a highly-cultured bourgeoisie, the constant Islamic rethinking underscored by the role of al-Zaytuna, a university second only to al-Azhar, besides recourse to a Turco-Circassian *mamluk* class as the personnel of state management, largely explain common trends, whilst at the same time highlighting the specific historical context in which they were actualized.

THE EARLY REFORMIST BEY-S

A modernizing trend is particularly evident in Tunisia during the reign of Ahmad Bey (1837–55). Though largely inspired by similar policies in Turkey and Egypt, it was also characterized by greater self-awareness and the will to build up the country's independence. The international context largely explains a more national outlook. The conquest of Algeria had broken down the up-to-then underlying feeling of Maghribi unity, as also traditional respect for the Sultan. In the 1830s the Ottoman Empire had both a vacillatory attitude and an expansionist policy, neither of which could have the support of Tunisia. The Sublime Porte had given no help to Algeria. On the other hand it had invaded Tripoli and envisaged a similar conquest of Tunisia. This had only been avoided by France's determined attitude. The danger was further brought home by the continuous presence of French warships off the Tunisian coast. Awareness of national independence and its fragility were thus fostered.

After an initial period of hesitation marked by frequent missions to and from Istanbul, Ahmad Bey had progressively severed most of the links between Tunisia and the Ottoman Empire. To build up Tunisia's defensive capacity he undertook to bring the army up to modern standards. Recruitment was increasingly from military families whose children were sent to Muhammadiyya to be trained. Soldiers were also recruited in the Sahel region and garrisoned in the town of Sousse. Top-ranking officers were still, however, imported *mamluk*-s. European offers of military assistance – a favourite form of encroachment – had been made as early as 1827, and by 1833 the army was being trained on European lines. Ahmad Bey also set up the Bardo Military Academy for junior officers in 1840 with the help of French military instructors. The modern army ultimately comprised 26 000 men. Ahmad Bey also wanted to have his own fleet. The arsenal at Goletta was reorganized and during an official visit to France in 1846 the Bey asked for a naval officer to be sent to Tunisia to command the fleet and instruct naval officers. By the middle of the century, the navy had six ships, all of which had French captains. Ships and regiments had a national flag – the red crescent – devised in 1833 to make clear Tunisian sovereignty at sea.

Structural changes in the working of the state were tentatively begun as education was partially reorganized, notably at the Zaytuna, a monetary reform undertaken, and a national bank founded which was to have the privilege of paper issues. Growing state expenditure was evident not only in these fields but also in more extravagant ways, including palace building to which Ahmad Bey was addicted. To meet requirements in the matter of administrative personnel, Ahmad Bey stepped up the traditional system of acquiring *mamluk*-s in the Middle East. It was in the early part of the century that the men who were later to dominate the political scene arrived in Tunisia.

Among earlier acquisitions we find Mustafa Khaznadar, born in 1817 in the island of Chio, but bought in Constantinople. In Tunis, he became the boon companion of the future Ahmad Bey who, on accession, appointed him head of the treasury: *khaznadar* is in fact the Turkish term for this function. He also became the Bey's brother-in-law when he married Kalthum, Ahmad Bey's sister. Mustafa Khaznadar became Prime Minister in 1837, a position he maintained under three successive *bey*-s, more or less continuously until 1873. In 1839, arrived in Tunisia Khayr al-Din, a Circassian who was then about 16 years old. A few years later he became the recognized leader of the movement which promoted the modernizing trend in Tunisia. Some Europeans having close links with the Regency were also integrated into the system, the chief example being the Raffo family and notably Giuseppe Raffo (1795-1862), born in Tunis where his father was a captive, who, under Ahmad Bey, was the country's Minister of Foreign Affairs. His son Felice (1822-78) was to continue the family tradition.

With respect to the economy, Ahmad Bey failed to take into account the importance of agriculture except as the traditional source of revenue through taxation. No efforts were made to improve methods of farming or production and yet, because of economic changes in which Tunisia necessarily found itself involved, exports of agricultural products continued to rise, playing an important role in the government's overall balance of payments. The fact that imports paid a mere 3 per cent customs tax further made Tunisia an attractive market from a European point of view. The major commodity sent out to Tunis, notably from France and Britain, was cloth, but industrial exports were already being stepped up. These were paid for notably by Tunisian foreign sales of cereals and olive oil. Some efforts were however made to promote a semi-industrial sector including a textile plant, a foundry and a gunpowder factory, but these were no more a success than Muhammad 'Ali's similar ventures, and for much the same reasons: they were dependent on European technology and management, and were uncompetitive.

Ahmad Bey was also faced with the problem of a fast-growing European community. He himself was a tolerant man who, even more characteristically than Muhammad 'Ali, had an open-door policy. We have mentioned the fact that he accepted Europeans in various governmental departments. He also took the lead in the Muslim world with respect to the abolition of slavery, decreed in 1846. His own attitude probably led him to underestimate an already evident problem since the European community which was a mere thousand or two in 1800, increased to 8000 in 1834, and 12 000 in 1856. Of these, the majority were very poor immigrants from outlying districts of the Mediterranean, and notably from Malta. They constituted a kind of lumpenproletariat to whom the Capuchin monks (settled in the Regency since 1624) ministered. Consuls used this immigrant mass as a pressure group. British claims to being the protector of the Maltese were particularly strongly stated by the Consul General Sir Thoms Reade (*en poste* from 1825 to his death in 1849) when his troublesome clientele created incidents. More important still was the arrival of the imperial vanguard: businessmen out for contracts, industrial concerns after new opportunities, and bankers ready to finance them.

The predominance of these and related factors over nationally orientated reforms became evident at the turn of the century and increasingly dominated the trend of events. Before considering this, we must turn to the brief reign of Muhammad Bey (1855–59) during which the reform programme was brought to a political conclusion by a constitutional law (*'ahd al-aman*). This was embodied in a Fundamental Pact (*qanun asasi*) promulgated by royal decree on 10 September 1857. Modelled on similar Turkish charters of 1839 and 1856, it defined the rights of Tunisians. The fact that Jews then lost their inferior *dhimmi* status and became full citizens should be noted, as also the fact Europeans were allowed to own property and act in professional capacity. In the wake of the Pact a number of significant reforms were undertaken which the Beys accepted with ever greater reluctance. A town council was set up in Tunis (30 August 1858), various decrees reorganized governmental and administrative practice (1860) and an official gazette, the *Raid al-Tunisi*, the first Tunisian newspaper, appeared (July 1860). The reforms culminated under Muhammad al-Sadiq Bey (1859–82) with the 1861 Constitution which separated judicial, legislative, and executive powers. It limited the Bey's prerogatives, created new courts of law and a supreme council acting both as a parliament and a supreme court. Khayr al-Din was the first president of the supreme council and attempted to make it play to the full its constitutional role. He met with considerable resistance and obstruction from the Bey and his Prime Minister, Mustafa Khaznadar. At the end of 1862, Khayr al-Din handed in his resignation and retired from public life.

THE FUNDAMENTAL PACT AND SOCIAL REACTIONS

The Bey's hesitant move towards constitutionalism met with mixed reactions which emphasized new social and ideological differences in Tunisia's traditionally well-knit society.

A part of the ruling class, which included more intellectually-minded *mamluk*-s such as Khayr al-Din and the friends they had in the bourgeois and scholar class, were in favour of reform and considered this ought to have political consequences including a more democratic working of the state and a constitutional monarchy. The men who, like Khayr al-Din, formed part of the reform committee of 1857–61, had travelled to Europe or Turkey and were particularly anxious to do away with oriental despotism. As Khayr al-Din put it to his colleagues: 'Our prince will have those powers which are still held by the Sultan, by the Emperor of France, by the Queen of England, and other constitutional monarchs'. This was however also seen as a return to the democratic practice of the Prophet and the early Muslim community.

The constitution and the reforms that went with it aroused considerable opposition in various sectors of opinion. The Bey, increasingly hostile to what he saw as a curtailment of his powers, seized the first occasion (1864) to suspend the constitution. The more traditional bourgeois and *'ulama* were against innovations contrary to standard Muslim practice. The consuls and European circles in general, who had welcomed the Fundamental Pact which had provided them with openings, became increasingly hostile as they saw in the reformists and their measures a barrier between them and profitable business deals by means of more complaisant courtiers. The chief opposition, however, and the one which brought about a general uprising in 1864, was in rural Tunisia. People there were opposed to such measures as the creation of modern courts of law which made justice slow and costly. They were opposed to new taxation since this was being used by the government to increase fiscal pressure. A new form of taxation, the *mejba*, had been instituted and in December 1863 the rate had been doubled by the government. Popular opposition also had political implications, including a reaction against European encroachments, a levelling tendency, and a strong Islamic self-assertiveness.

The uprising broke out in spring 1864 as the army undertook one of its regular twice yearly tax-collecting campaigns. It brought to the fore a popular leader, 'Ali bin Ghadahem, and in a matter of weeks the movement had spread to most of the rural areas of west and central Tunisia. Towns such as Qairawan – still prestigious as the country's first Muslim capital – sided with the peasants. The political objectives of the movement were recorded in a legal document dated July 1864. Taxes other than those sanctioned by the Quran were to be done away with, the constitution was to be abrogated because it was not in conformity with the Quran, and the new courts of law were to be abandoned because they impinged on *shari'a* rulings. The movement also showed its sensitivity to European encroachments and it is significant that one of its first actions should have been to cut down the telegraph which had been set up in 1859–60 to connect Tunis and Algiers. The movement showed strong self-discipline and little looting or personal vengeance is recorded, although some more oppressive *qaid*-s (governors) were brought to account. The levelling tendencies were brought to the fore and 'Ali bin Ghadahem said of himself: 'I am not a leader. I am one of the people'. The title he took further had religious connotations: *bey al-umma*.

A coalition against the peasants was formed but the occasion was first of all seized on as a pretext for the suspension of the Constitution and the elimination of the reformists. The Bey received the support of the Great Powers, who from the start of the conflict had sent their fleets to the region, and from a Turkish envoy, who though received with enthusiasm by the population – 'Muslims congratulate themselves in the streets', noted a contemporary – avoided committing himself and later had funds sent to support the Bey. The Europeans also provided money and military equipment.

The causes of the rapid breakdown of the insurrection are several. In the first place unity of aim did not prove sufficient to rule out traditional tribal rivalries which Prime Minister Khaznadar successfully played up. 'Ali bin Ghadahem himself did not prove equal to the task and his wavering attitude (perhaps encouraged by the leaders of the sufi fraternity with which he was connected, the Tijaniyya) led him early on to envisage negotiations and compromise. No less important was divergence of political appreciation within the movement once it had got underway. When the following ceased to be merely rural and found support in the towns and in the coastal regions, the urban middle class proved conservative, as opposed to the more radical peasant element. The military campaign undertaken in August 1864 by the *mamluk* general Ahmad Zarruq ruthlessly crushed the insurrection. Its leader 'Ali bin Ghadahem for the time being fled to Algeria, but when he returned in 1866 under the safe-conduct of a Tidjani *shaykh*, he was thrown into prison where he died on 11 October 1867.

FINANCIAL MISMANAGEMENT AND ECONOMIC DIFFICULTIES (1865–1869)

By the middle of the 1860s, social cohesion had to some extent broken down under the stress of change. The depressed condition of the rural population was emphasized after the brutal repression of the 1864 uprising by epidemics (cholera in 1867, typhus in 1868) following on bad harvests and heavy taxation. Not only had the reformists been forced into retirement by the suspension of the constitution, but upholders of traditional values were themselves pushed into the background as parvenus – men of Khaznadar's making – came out in favour of interaction with European business circles which were themselves now more assertive.

The growth of European influence

European consular influence was increasingly evident, often because of the personalities of the men sent out to Tunisia. Léon Roches arrived in Tunisia as French consul-general in 1855 with a favourable reputation since at an earlier period of his career he had converted to Islam and joined the ranks of 'Abd al-Qadir's followers. The British representative, Richard Wood (1806–1900), whilst not being able to rival Léon Roches in the matter of Quranic citations, was nonetheless more authentically oriental and had a keener insight into Tunisian politics. He had been brought up at the embassy in Istanbul and may indeed have been of Jewish Armenian stock. A long tenure of office (he remained in Tunisia from 1855 to 1879) helped him play a significant part in shaping British policy and upholding this on the spot. Consular efforts were seconded by able employees who, though Tunisians, were protected by capitulatory privileges and ultimately acquired foreign nationality. Moses Santillana worked in the British consular offices for over 50 years, from 1820 to 1870, and was accused by the French of such 'crimes' as upholding Hajj Ahmad Bey's resistance in Constantine by providing him with contraband stores. The French consuls employed as interpreter and agent Gabriel Valensi, also a Tunisian Jew, whose family was actively engaged in international trade. The granting of foreign protection was, as we can see, being used to further European interests and indeed to undermine national sovereignty, all the more so in view of the fact that the system developed inordinately in the period here under consideration. A census made in 1881 puts the number of 'protégés' at 11 770.

The European community itself acquired a more cohesive structure as churches and schools opened. The Italian community, numerically the most important, and more dynamic after Italian unity was established in 1861, had important Catholic establishments often set up by the Capuchins. An Italian school had been opened in 1831, followed by the Collegio Italiano in 1866 and a technical college in 1870. The French, though not numerous, made every effort not to be outdone. They too had set up a religious establishment in the wake of Ahmad Bey's grant of a site for a chapel. A hospital was opened in 1843 and one of the leading teaching establishments, the Collège Bourgade (1841–63), was also French. Equally active in the Regency were the European Jewish philanthropic associations: in 1866 an Italo-Jewish school had been opened. In 1877, the French Alliance Israelite appeared on the scene. In July

1878, it opened its first school which was run with Anglo-Jewish association funds. Religious tolerance, notably in the higher strata of Tunisian society, helped promote such efforts. We thus find Muhammad al-Sadiq giving land in 1878 for the building of a synagogue.

Living and working conditions for Europeans were also improved in the coastal towns with the arrival in the Regency of doctors and other men who provided services essentially to a growing European clientele. The increase in the European population had been made possible by the Fundamental Pact and, though the constitution was suspended, European development was in no way curtailed. European preponderance in the 1860s can best be illustrated by sea traffic. Not only did shipping lines set up regular services with Tunisia, but freight ships became more numerous. Thus Goletta which was Tunisia's major harbour, had about 600 ships calling every year, representing a tonnage of 80 000. Growing imbalance is further indicated by the fact that, during the same period, Tunisian tonnage amounted to a mere 20 000 with about 60 small boats.

Fig. 11.2   Shipping lines operating regular services to Tunisia in the 1860s

---

Touache Company: weekly service from Marseilles to Tunis via Stora and
            Bone (1860)
Two British Shipping Companies calling more or less regularly at Goletta.
Rubattino Company: twice monthly service between Genoa, Cagliari, and
            Tunis.
Italian Line: Twice monthly service between Palermo and Tunisia (1863).

Financial corruption in the ruling class

Even more important than the national debt itself was the situation it created as Tunisians lost confidence in a government where mismanagement and corruption were rife. European bankers and businessmen with few scruples found willing abettors in the ruling class now back in power with Mustafa Khaznadar. This was not, of course, new, but it developed inordinately in the years now under consideration. Mustafa Khaznadar's long term of office which lasted well-nigh half a century, built up embezzlement of public funds into a national institution. He had set up a powerful patron-client network, placing men of his own at the head of key sectors of administration and politics. Thus he considered he had made the fortune of Khayr al-Din by giving him his daughter in marriage and was always to consider any criticism from the latter as the basest form of ingratitude. Most of the Khaznadar's protégés were far less reputable persons. Thus, for example, Mahmud Bin 'Ayyad (c. 1810–80), the son of an important dignitary of Ahmad Bey's time, had begun in business by opening a bank with the Khaznadar's help. Always with the prime minister's support he rose to the rank of minister and spent most of his time building up an immense fortune of which the Khaznadar had his share. Typical of malpractices of the time is the fact that he sent his illegal gains abroad. This made him a wealthy property owner in Paris. His close connection with France was revealed when he secretly applied for French nationality in 1850. This was granted him in 1851, by which time he had sought safety in Paris where, for many years, theTunisian government sued him for restitution of illegal gains, without the French courts proving particularly cooperative. Khayr al-Din had had time to mediate on those aspects of prevalent corruption and their consequences, including capital haemorrhage, during his stay in Paris in 1853–6 to represent the Tunisian government's view in the court case against Ben 'Ayyad. Such examples of scandalous fortunes made to the country's detriment could be multiplied. We shall limit ourselves to one other significant case chosen from the Tunisian Jewish community where several individuals owed their careers and fortunes to the Khaznadar. Nasim Samama (1805–73) who had been a servant of Ben 'Ayyad and the Khaznadar was, with the latter's help, appointed head of the Jewish community. In 1860, he became head of the Department of Finance. He too fled the country in 1864 taking with him his ill-acquired fortune. Once again we see such practices condoned by public opinion in Europe since Samama was able to settle in Paris and later in Leghorn where he died in 1881, leaving a fortune of nearly 30 million French francs, besides an aristocratic title granted by the King of Sardinia in 1866.

From 1850 onwards, and even more particularly after the suspension of the constitution had given them a free hand, Khaznadar and corrupt palace circles launched into a policy of extravagant public spending which did not have for itself the long-term justification of many of the Khedive's investments at the same period. Moreover business contracts were often a mere pretext for draining money to private purses, both foreign and Tunisian. The cynical remark made by a French consul, De Lagau, aptly summarizes the situation from an imperial point of view: 'we have in this part of Africa almost all the advantages of possession without its inconveniences'.

Financial difficulties: taxation, loans and bankruptcy

To meet expenses, the government had recourse to taxation which became even more oppressive and unjust as the *mejba* was doubled and trebled in the 1860s. Oppression was intensified by the collection method used: agricultural produce was bought up by tax-farmers at arbitrarily fixed prices, the loss incurred being further increased by the practice of selling it in advance to foreign creditors. The most arbitrary measures were forced upon the hard-up peasantry such as fictitious arrears of taxation or special levies for 'war purposes'. Not only did the ruling class cut itself off from the population which was increasingly hostile to the government, but the latter's needs could no longer be met from national resources.

The government was thus faced with a growing deficit and had recourse to payment by means of bills which it was unable to pay on time. Here too scandalous practices were rife with men such as Samama claiming the Treasury was empty and buying them back from creditors at less than half face value whilst charging full costs in government accounts. The Bey who in 1860 owed 19 million piastres or 12 million French francs, by 1862 owed already 28 million francs. The fact that the local piastre was to be constantly devalued and that the loans to which Khaznadar had recourse were, for the most part, raised in France will lead us here to quote sums in French currency.

Money at the time was readily available in Europe and interest rates generally under 5 per cent. Such loans were being currently raised to finance projects in Europe and further afield. From 1860 onwards these foreign loans were registered at the Paris or London Stock Exchange. Bankers' agents, on the look-out for new opportunities, offered their services to governments in financial straits. Khaznadar was now ready to accept such offers. His recourse to unscrupulous intermediaries having the same end in view as himself, namely personal profit, was to lead to even more catastrophic results than in Egypt where similar loans had at least been kept within the bounds of legality.

The first of Tunisia's state loans was made in 1863, prior to the peasant uprising. Khaznadar had forced the as yet hostile *diwan* to countenance his project of a French loan of 25 million francs. Khaznadar and his agents waved aside more reputable bankers such as the Rothschilds who offered to lend at 8 per cent with no amortization and negotiated with a newcomer in international finance, Emile Erlanger, who though having connexions with the banking family of the same name and the Pereire Brothers of Crédit Mobilier fame, was as yet on the fringes of the Banking establishment. The Tunisian loans provided him with the opportunity which was to make him a millionaire. He began by a lavish distribution of gifts to win over Tunisian political circles and eliminate rivals. Sir Richard Wood claimed Erlanger had offered him 500 000 French francs to dissuade British banks which had made offers. Erlanger also enlisted the support of members of the French government. On 10 May 1863 the agreement was signed and registered on the French Stock Exchange. Financial circles were surprised, and that is a mild term, by Erlanger's audacity, especially in view of the fact that he had no money to put up. Erlanger had recourse to financial backers including Oppenheim of Alexandria who negotiated Khedival loans, and Rudolph Sulzback, representative of the Saxe-Meiningen firm of Frankfurt. The money was to be provided in 6 instalments between Summer 1863 and May 1865.

Details of the complex deal show up scandalous practices. Thus the loan was of 35 million francs (costs included) but the 78 692 shares having a nominal value of 500 francs each came to 39 340 000 francs, though they were sold under par at 480 francs. The sum over and above 35 million simply disappeared in the process. The commission charged was 14.5 per cent which seems to have been partly shared out between Khaznadar and other intermediaries. The money was paid into a special account where more disappeared, including 3 million francs withdrawn by Samana. The money had been raised to settle Tunisian debts but did not in fact serve this purpose since the stock had not attracted investors and was in fact bought up by Erlanger or Khaznadar with money from the loan. The Tunisian government, which had given the *mejba* as a guarantee, further agreed to amortization and interest rates at the rate of 4 200 000 francs a year. Repayment was spread out over 15 years and the cost all told was 63 million francs. The net result was that no debts had been paid and that national indebtedness which had been of about 30 million francs was doubled. Khaznadar was already on the look-out for a fresh loan.

In 1864 he borrowed 5 million francs for 18 months from an Austrian banker, Morpugo, who had set up in Alexandria and was in partnership with Oppenheim. Only half a million was actually paid into the Treasury.

In 1865 a new international loan was floated by means of such banks as the Comptoir d'Escompte. The banks, whilst themselves taking no risks, encouraged their clients to buy stock by such significant assurances as 'that the Bey of Tunis is now under the moral protection of France'. Their profits were, however, considerable and included commission costs of 18 per cent. Moreover, various complicated forms of embezzlement were practised. Once again the number of bonds sold (73 568 at a nominal value of 500 francs, but sold by the banks at 380 francs) exceeded the 25 millions franc loan officially registered. Nearly 3 million francs thus simply disappeared as did other sums in various curious ways. This was all the more scandalous in view of the fact that the French government had given its official backing, besides encouraging the public to invest without pointing out the risks incurred with respect to a penniless country.

The bankers and their agents were now all-powerful in Tunisia where in partnership with Khaznadar and his clique numerous business contracts were signed, some of which involved sheer dishonesty. We thus find two ships being sold in 1865 by Morpugo and a French businessman named Audibert to the Bey for 250 000 francs. As their price indicated, they were supposed to be brand new, but on arrival they were found to be disabled ships incapable of going to sea. That same year a frigate estimated at 2.5 million francs was bought for the Tunisian navy. It turned out to be a mere corvette worth a million francs. Erlanger provided 100 cannons, the most modern available he claimed, though they were in fact out of date and secondhand. They had been bought for a mere 200 000 francs but were sold to the Tunisian government for 1 million. When the man who had originally sold them was questioned, he replied: 'The Prime Minister wants to make 500,000 francs on the deal. I cannot stop him and I have no say in the Tunisian government's affairs'. No less scandalous were the concessions being granted to Europeans by means of Erlanger, as for example Ahmad Bey's clothmaking factory which had closed down many years previously and which was now, for a small rent, let to a European, the Bey further agreeing to repair the workshops and buy up the production which was to consist of uniforms and blankets for the army.

Not only was the country under the shock of the brutal repression of the peasant revolt of 1864 but its national self confidence was undermined by governmental immorality. Such was the state of Tunisia when it was faced with bankruptcy in 1869, Khaznadar and his bankers having failed in their attempt to raise a fresh loan of 100 million francs. The national debt was thus about 122 million francs, besides interest overdue amounting to 15 million francs. In July the Bey was forced to accept an international commission which was to run the finances of the country and manage the debt. Tunisia was in the same situation as that in which Egypt was to find itself in 1876.

IMPERIAL PROGRESS AND TUNISIA'S LAST STAND (1869–1881)

Khayr al-Din's reforms

As in Egypt the setting up of an international commission marked the first stage in the process of political take-over which took place almost simultaneously in the two countries – 1881 in Tunisia, 1882 in Egypt – Britain invading Egypt, and France, Tunisia. A further parallel is that in both cases a last desperate stand was made by men who should be considered as early nationalist heroes. The parallel should not, however, be pursued too far: 'Arabi Pasha was a native Egyptian of rural stock who was first and foremost an army officer, even if he briefly took part in governmental activity. In Tunisia, the last stand was made by a foreign-born *mamluk*, Khayr al-Din, who was a statesman rather than a soldier.

Three stages mark an intensification of the process of colonial take-over: the first was the creation of the international commission which had less power than its counterpart in Egypt, chiefly because Richard Wood had made every effort to avoid the French being too powerful. There were six representatives of the creditors (two Frenchmen, two British, and two Italians) whilst the executive committee was composed of two Tunisians and a Frenchman. The fact that Khayr al-Din was called back to office to preside over the commission gave the national element greater weight because Khayr al-Din could not be a stooge. His honesty and efficiency were, moreover, known to all, including Villet the appointed foreign representative on the executive committee. He was a French civil servant from the treasury and was to prove a useful ally of Khayr al-Din's because of his experience in financial matters. Khayr al-Din was faced with a complex task involving unification of the debt, conversion of all claims into new bonds, the setting aside of specific revenues, new management of revenue and taxation and the drawing up of a balanced budget. These objectives required the prior settlement of a political problem: the elimination of Khaznadar and his corrupt clique. Here again, for a time, colonial and nationalist views converged.

A palace plot were therefore prepared in which Khayr al-Din undertook to undermine his father-in-law's authority by means of the Bey's favourite, Mustafa bin Isma'il, a low-born Tunisian with nothing but his master's favour to recommend him. With the Europeans as attentive bystanders, the struggle was played out in oriental fashion. Khayr al-Din and his friends obtained their first open victory when Khaznadar's ally, General Ahmad Zarruq, was tried and condemned for his repression of the 1864 uprising. Numerous political and financial scandals were brought to light: embezzlement with respect to the 1863 loan, protection afforded to a British banker, Ranking, to set up a bank of issue to be called the London Bank of Tunis, and so on. The Bey procrastinated in the face of the scandal and would not have disavowed his prime minister had not Khayr al-Din come up with a trump card: a very complete substantiated account of Khaznadar's corrupt practices. The report had been drawn up by Villet and showed that Khaznadar had embezzled some 21 million francs since 1863. On 20 October 1973, the Bey asked his prime minister to resign and a few months later a Commission of Inquiry declared him liable to the Tunisian Treasury for 25 million francs. As he too had sent his fortune out of the country, his property was confiscated and later made *habus* to pay for the upkeep of Sadiqi College.

Khayr al-Din, supported by the reformist intelligentsia which had stood by him during the difficult years 1864–9, was appointed prime minister and immediately undertook to modernize Tunisian institutions and government. His achievements were remarkable and he promoted a wide variety of reforms which have marked Tunisia up to the present. The administration was entirely restructured, with the setting up of civil departments under the Grand Wazir or prime minister, a ministry of war, and of the Navy. Not only were the functions and prerogatives of each department defined down to the smallest detail but new forms of control were established. Khayr al-Din in this showed a Napoleonic mania for detailed regulations. Moreover, in contrast to the previous period in which Europeans had in ever greater numbers been recruited into government service, Khayr al-Din reversed the trend and dismissed them, especially when they were known to have had links with the Khaznadar. Among those eliminated was Elias Mussali, a Greek Catholic born in Cairo in 1829, who between 1847 and 1872 had occupied an important function in the Ministry of Foreign Affairs. He was even better known for having a beautiful wife, Luiga, through whom interaction between court circles and European consuls or businessmen was effected. Also replaced by a Tunisian was Mansur Carletti, a Muslim convert from Cyprus, who was in charge of the *Raid al-Tunisi*. Another person who disappeared from the political arena was Felice Raffo.

Among the first measures taken by the new ministry were those tending towards retrenchment and better management. These soon brought Khayr al-Din into conflict with the international commission as he attempted to regain control of conceded revenue. Through strict control, corruption largely disappeared. The support this nationally-orientated policy obtained is indicated by civil servants' acceptance of a cut of their salaries by a third. All facile solutions, including the devaluation of the Tunisian piastre, were rejected. Between 1873 and 1877, in spite of economic difficulties, the Tunisian budget remained balanced. Khayr al-Din's management has gone down in history as a rare example of efficiency and economy.

Even more important were the structural reforms undertaken in almost every field. *Habus* property, though remaining a private rather than a state concern, was placed under the control of a board in April 1874. Accounts had to be regularly presented and though profits continued to serve those charitable ends which donors had stipulated, efforts were made to promote upkeep and repair, especially with respect to urban property. In the field of education, modern teaching was promoted and Sadiqi College – which until Tunisia regained independence in the middle of the 20th century was to be the chief training centre for modern elites – was founded. More classical establishments, including the Zaytuna university-mosque, were reorganized. Efforts were made in several other cultural sectors, special attention being paid to public libraries and to the development of publishing. The reorganization of provincial administration met with opposition from hereditary gubernatorial families but was nonetheless carried out by means of decrees (1870, 1872, 1877) which defined the attributions and sources of revenue to which *qaid*-s had a right. Direct control was set up to eliminate petty tyranny and illegal profits. Here again Khayr al-Din's measures proved successful and led to the Prime Minister's having great popularity in rural areas. The reform of the judicial system was examined by a special commission comprising *mufti*-s of the two rites represented in Tunisia (the local Maliki *madhhab* and the Turkish-imported Hanafi school). Both rites were maintained, a plaintiff having the recourse to one or the other. In October 1876, a new supreme court was set up in Tunis, and ordinary courts were established in 15 main towns. In smaller centres *qadhi*-s officiated. In 1872, further legislation was enacted to protect the Jewish courts of law. More delicate was the problem of consular privileges in view of the outcry consuls raised whenever the subject was broached. The French agent Roustan did not hestitate to claim that he did not 'recognize the right of any Tunisian authority to arrest or interrogate a French subject for any reason whatsoever' (letter to Khayr al-Din, 21 July 1876). This attitude was, however, undermined by the fact that discussions concerning mixed courts were underway in Egypt and would create a precedent. The prime minister was consequently able to go ahead with his plans and new mixed courts were in fact set up on similar lines to those of Egypt.

In Tunisia as elsewhere in North Africa, the protection afforded to natives by virtue of the consuls' capitulatory privileges was a growing source of concern. Here again, Khayr al-Din attempted to check the extension of the practice by recognizing protections given prior to 1864 but dealing more strictly with recent cases. The consuls, however, refused to apply the new regulations which, in effect, would have stopped one of their most useful means of penetration and a practice which was the source of much profit. A particular aspect of this problem which was of concern to the government was the presence in Tunisia of some 200 000 Algerian refugees, many of whom had preferred exile to French rule. The French made every effort to stop emigration and to prevent political agitators from finding refuge in Tunisia. Muslim law however makes it incumbent to welcome refugees and integrate them into the community. A compromise was ultimately worked out and a Franco-Tunisian agreement was signed in March 1876 specifying that there were to be two categories of Algerians: those who had definitely left their native land and were to be considered as Tunisians and those who came on a temporary basis, for personal or business reasons, and who were to be under French consular jurisdiction.

Khayr al-Din's reforms outfaced by imperial expansion

Khayr al-Din's measures, important though they were in themselves and as expressions of national sovereignty, were not sufficient to restore the nation's effective independence. This was not only due to the heavy debt with which Tunisia was saddled and which only allowed the government to dispose of a third of its revenue, but also to the fact that beyond the facade of boundless activity, Khayr al-Din in fact had no real economic policy. In many ways he shared the views of a mercantile age of free enterprise which, in the Tunisian context, was to emphasize imbalance. Khayr al-Din, in the first place, did not take into account the fact that Tunisia was basically an agricultural country and that its revenue was essentially from this source. Though some reforms were undertaken: attempts to settle nomads, to promote irrigation, and redefine peasant status (notably that of the *khamas* who rented land by sharing the crop with the owner on a 1:4 basis), no real attempt was made to change peasant society or agricultural techniques. These consequently remained archaic with the added liability that large tracts of land which were *habus* remained unproductive. Consequently rural taxation which was the chief source of revenue was subject to the hazards of climatic factors and a subsistence economy constituted a permanent threat to stability.

In the towns, traditional crafts and their guilds were also to come under the influence of Khayr al-Din's mania for regulations and the high standards he set; but this was merely ignoring the fact that imported goods were not only making national products uncompetitive but even ruining local workshops and craftsmen. This was particularly clear in the *shashiya* industry whose excellence was recognized throughout the East. *Shashiya* exports fell off dramatically as inferior, cheaper goods appeared on the market, produced in Austria, Turkey, or France. Whereas some 3 million francs' worth had been sold annually in 1861–3, figures fell by half in 1864. Five years later *shashiya*-s brought in a mere 850 000 francs and by 1875, no more than 250 000.

Laissez-faire also implied an open door policy which underscored the inroads made by European capitalism on the national economy. The fact that these further reflected the political strategy of imperial nations, not to mention their rival claims, disrupted government planning and increased dependence. Such infrastructural changes as can be pointed to were invariably the results of concessions granted to foreigners. First on the scene under the able guidance of Richard Wood, who had obtained for Britain a very favourable commercial treaty in 1875, were the English with such concerns as the Ranking Bank, the Tunis Railways which operated a line between Tunis and Goletta, and the New Gas Company. These generally proved economic failures: the Ranking Bank closed its offices in 1876 and the Foreign and Colonial Gas Company which preceded the New Gas Company went bankrupt in 1875; moreover they did not have the capacity to promote development. The Italians who stepped up their pressure in this period and appointed a particularly assertive consul, Licurgo Maccio who was consul-general in Tunis from 1866 to 1883, had such commercial interests as a tobacco factory, a printing press, and shipping lines. The French, after a period of stagnation following on the unification of the debt which had been detrimental to French bondholders, were again active on the scene with the help of Theodore Roustan, appointed consul in 1874. He too promoted French interests in the Regency. He began by offering to set up modern port facilities at Carthage and when Khayr al-Din refused this, obtained in compensation the right to build a railway between Beja and Dakhla Jendouba, 40 km from the Algerian frontier. The contractors were the Société des Batignolles through a subsidiary, the Compagnie des Chemins de Fer de Bone à Guelma, which sought and obtained French government backing after Roustan and Villet had pointed out the strategic value of such a railway. One of the more recently founded banks which was to play an important role in the constitution of a French colonial empire, the Banque de Paris et des Pays Bas, agreed to finance the project. Needless to say the French strongly urged that the railway be extended as far as the Algerian frontier, but this was categorically refused by the Tunisian government. A number of other such projects were under discussion but by then Khayr al-Din, who never lost sight of the fact that Tunisian independence must come first, had become an obstacle to foreign penetration. The European states interested were consequently on the lookout for a suitable occasion to bring about his downfall.

This occurred in 1877. The economic situation that year turned against Khayr al-Din. On the one hand the country went through one of its cyclical periods of bad harvests, on the other hand, the international market was bad and prices of raw materials fell drastically. Thus Khayr al-Din's narrow margin of budgetary balance was imperilled as national revenue decreased by a third (11.5 million Tunisian piastres in 1877). At the same time expenditure reached record high figures – nearly 15.5 million Tunisian piastres – because of rising imports and bondholders' dues. Further difficulties were created because of Turkey, which was once again at war with Russia and asked the Regency for help. Tunisia, which had sent out contingents on former occasions including one for the Crimean War, could hardly refuse to do so now, especially since it had reaffirmed its loyalty to the Ottoman Sultan in 1871. Khayr al-Din consequently decided to open a subscription. The French, whose policy it was to claim that no links existed between the Ottoman Empire and the Regencies, were outraged and Consul Roustan accused Khayr al-Din of fanaticism; nor was the Prime Minister to find comfort or encouragement at the palace where the Bey, who had always felt that the appointment of Khayr al-Din had been forced upon him by the International Commission, was under pressure from the Prime Minister's enemies. They included partisans of the former Prime Minister and those of the personally ambitious favourite Mustafa ben Isma'il, besides Europeans who through their friends or by means of the press spread rumours accusing Khayr al-Din of working for the Sultan against the Husayni dynasty. Relations between the Bey and his Prime Minister were increasingly tense and on 19 July 1877, after a particularly unpleasant discussion, Khayr al-Din tendered his resignation, which was accepted. The reformist era was over and Tunisian independence with it.

The prelude to the French invasion

As Khayr al-Din and many of his friends left for exile, Khaznadar returned briefly to power before being replaced as Prime Minister on 23 August 1878, by the incompetent favourite, Mustafa bin Isma'il. European penetration through government contracts, industrial concessions, and the buying up of rural property reached an unprecedented scale. Scandals were rife, not so much because of Tunisian dishonesty but because of the attempts of rival French, Italian, and British concessionaires to get in first at any cost. Full support was given by consuls not only to *bona fide* businessmen, but to the scum of industrial society in order to make headway for a particular nation. Theodore Roustan upheld such unjustified claims as those of Ferdinand Sancy who took over a 12 000 hectare farm, Sidi Tabet, without carrying out the clauses of the contract and who demanded damages on top. The British and French consuls fought it out over Enfida, a large farm which Khayr al-Din had put up for sale, the British consul upholding the more than dubious claims of a Tunisian, Levy, who happened to have British citizenship. Even religion was turned to colonial ends as Archbishop Lavigerie moved in from Algeria in 1877. His White Fathers fought and ultimately won their holy war against the Italian Capuchins, even the British becoming involved as they stood up for the rights of their 7000-strong Maltese community. Lavigerie, moreover, never lost sight of the fact that Islam and Muslim independence were his chief enemies and his priests were given orders to collect as much information as they could. This was communicated to Roustan, rendering 'more services than an army corps' as an Italian newspaper put it. Characteristic details, they illustrate the sorry tale of Tunisia under the onslaught of converging imperial

The fortune of Mustafa bin Isma'il according to A. M. Broadley, *Tunis Past and Present*, 1882

A glance, therefore, at a list of Mustapha's more notorious gains during the past ten years will be useful as a warning to those who have rendered themselves responsible before the world for the destinies of the Tunisian Regency, and to the ordinary reader it may perchance be interesting as showing the profits of a lucky favourite at even a petty Oriental court.

NAMES OF ESTATES	LOCALITIES	NOTES
Ain Sciala	Beja	
Sidi Soltan	Beja	
Elzrelli	Beja	Sold to General Hamida
Arbir	Beja	Ben Ayad for
Sciauatt	Tebourba	500 000 francs.
Nahba	Mater	
Elzriba	Mater	
Ermil	Mater	
Elmebtuh	Bizerta road	
Buarada	Elfahs	Sold to Signor Rivol-
Borj Elamri	Tunis	tella and a syn-
Elazib	Bizerta	dicate for 975 000
Ghiran	Bizerta	francs
Fritisa and Asciafir	Bizerta	Sold as in the last
Beny Ata	Bizerta	case for 200 000
Beny Meslem	Bizerta	francs
Sidi Hassan	Bizerta	
Gafur	Tebouraak	Not sold but worth 600 000 francs
NAMES OF ESTATES	LOCALITIES	NOTES
Elmornaghia	Manouba	Not sold, but worth 200 000 francs
Seltan	Hamman-el-Lif	Not sold, but worth 300 000 francs
Village of Grambalia	Hamman-el-Lif	Not sold but worth 1 500 000 francs
Mkada	Bizerta	
Udai	Bizerta	Not sold, but worth
Elzaina	Bizerta	300 000 francs

In addition to all these splendid properties:–
100 000 olive-trees at Menzel.
Two caravanserais in the city of Tunis.
Twenty shops.
Jewels of the value of 3 000 000 francs belonging to Sy Mustapha Khaznadar, the disgraced favourite, and Sy Ismael Sunni and Sy Rescid, the strangled ministers.
Furniture worth about 1 500 000 francs, belonging to the same persons.

attacks. The centre of decision-making was not, however, in North Africa itself, but in Europe.

Tunisia's fate was sealed at the Congress of Berlin in 1878. Italian and French rivalry had reached a high pitch, Italy considering it had a major claim on Tunisia because of its large national community settled in the Regency; France, on the other hand, held the view that possession of Algeria gave her prior rights. The French were all the more aggressive in view of the major defeat they had suffered at German hands in 1870. Britain was now less adamant in its opposition to France: not only would a further weakening of the latter endanger the balance of power policy to which Salisbury and Disraeli clung after recent Russian encroachments on Turkish sovereignty, but Britain needed international acquiescence in its presence in Cyprus. At the Congress, Britain made a tentative suggestion that France be given a free hand in Tunisia. This was upheld by Bismark who thus hoped to assuage France's wounded pride and turn its attention from its lost provinces of Alsace and Lorraine. Moreover, as Bismark foresaw, this would be driving the wedge into French and Italian solidarity, and indeed, as his astute statesmanship had foreseen, Italy joined the Triple Alliance (Germany, Austria, Italy) in 1882. The change of attitude was signified locally and indirectly by the forced retirement in 1879 of Sir Richard Wood on the flimsy pretext of administrative reorganization involving a necessary 'general massacre of aged official innocents' as a Foreign Office official put it. The French were not deceived, and extended wholehearted thanks for being rid of the staunchest supporter of British and Turkish interests in Tunisia. In spite of Italian objections and a strong anti-colonial feeling in France, the imperial power prepared to move in.

The last and quite minor problem which remained was for France to devise some sort of *casus belli*. In a most opportune fashion it was now found that a border tribe, the Khrumir, was guilty of some misdemeanours and the French Parliament voted credits for 'border operations'. The Bey's offer to deal with the problem himself was refused, and two French columns crossed the Algero-Tunisian frontier on 24 April 1881, whilst a third landed at Bizerta. Roustan pointed out to the Bey that he had to choose between abdication or signing a treaty establishing a French Protectorate. Under duress the Bey signed the Treaty of Bardo on 12 May 1881.

The Signing of the Bardo Treaty

Muhammad al-Saddiq Bey granted General Bréart an audience at the request of the French consul.

The General and his staff crossed the gardens, dismounted in front of the palace and went up to the reception hall where Mr. Roustan was waiting for them. After being introduced to the Bey, the officers were given seats. General Bréart took a paper from his pocket and read out the following statement:

The government of the French Republic wishes to put an end to present difficulties by an amicable arrangement which will fully safeguard Your Highness's dignity and it has done me the honour of choosing me for this mission.

'The Government of the French Republic wishes to maintain your Highness on the throne and to uphold your dynasty. It is not in France's interest to reduce in any way the Regency's territorial integrity. It merely demands those guarantees it considers necessary for continued friendly relations between the two governments.'

The Bey listened to the reading of the ten articles of the treaty with resignation and requested a delay to think the matter over. The General calmly replied: I will wait for your answer until 8 o'clock this evening. The Bey stated that he must consult his Council and that the delay was insufficient. The General answered: we want an answer today. Mr. Roustan pointed out that all the articles of the treaty had already been discussed with Prime Minister Mustapha who was present at the audience, that they had been debated at length in Council and that the Government must by now have made up its mind. Muhammad al-Saddiq made further objections. General Bréart repeated that he must have an answer that very day and could not agree to delays without infringing the very precise instructions he had received from the Government of the Republic. All that he could was to extend the delay by an hour, until 9 o'clock that evening.

Two hours later the treaty was signed ...

Translated from Joseph Reinach's account in *Revue politique et littéraire* 21 May 1881.

SELECTED READING LIST

Broadley, A. M., *Tunis, Past and Present. The Last Punic War*, (London, 1882).

Brown, L. C., *The Tunisia of Ahmad Bey, 1837–1855*, (Princeton, 1974).

Ganiage, J., *Les Origines du Protectorat Français en Tunisie (1861–1881)*, (Paris, 1959, reprinted Tunis, 1969).

Gifford, P. & Louis, W. R. (eds), *France and Britain in Africa. Imperial Rivalry and Colonial Rule*, (New Haven and London, 1972).

Julien, Ch.-A., *L'Affaire Tunisienne 1878–1881*, (Tunis, 1981).

Khayr al-Din, *Aqwam al-Masalik fi ma'rifat ahwal al-Mamalik*, Tunis, 1867; translated into English by L. C. Brown, *The Surest Path*, (Harvard, 1967).

Kraiem, M., *La Tunisie précoloniale*, (Tunis, 1973).

Marsden, A., *British Diplomacy and Tunis 1875–1902*, (Edinburgh and London, 1971).

Mzali, M. & Pignon, J., 'Documents sur Khereddine', *Revue Tunisienne*, 18–44, 1934, 1935, 1936, 1937, 1938, 1940.

O'Donnell, J. D., *Lavigerie in Tunisia. The Interplay of Imperialist and Missionary*, (Athens, U.S.A., 1979).

Raymond, A., 'Salisbury and the Tunisian Question (1878–1880)', *St. Anthony's Papers*, No. 4, 1961.

Slama, B., *L'Insurrection de 1864 en Tunisie*, (Tunis, 1967).

Smida, M., *Khereddine ministre réformateur*, (Tunis, 1970).

Temimi, A., *Recherches et Documents d'histoire maghrébine. L'Algérie, la Tunisie et la Tripolitaine (1816–1871)*, (Tunis, 1970, reprinted 1980).

Tlili, B., 'Kheredine réformateur et homme d'Etat, tunisien et ottoman' *Les Africains*, vol. VIII, (Paris, 1977).

Ziadeh, A. N., *Origins of Nationalism in Tunisia*, (Beyruth, 1962).

CHAPTER 12

IMPERIALISM CLOSES IN

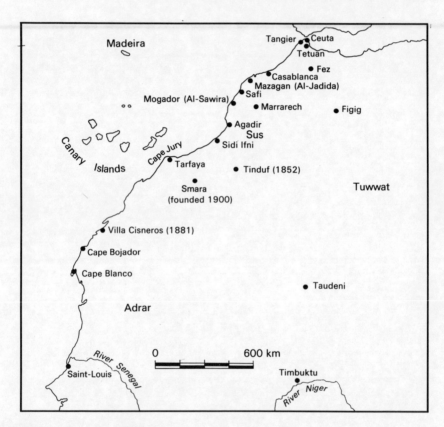

Map 12.1 *The western approach*

After 1850 we can see imperialism closing in on the northern part of Africa in a pincer movement: in the west along the Atlantic coast and in the east up the Nile valley. Throughout the *bilad al-Sudan* explorers and military missions were pushing deeper into the heart of the continent. The Bahr al-Ghazal, Lake Chad, or Timbuktu were now objectives both for explorers and military missions.

THE WESTERN APPROACH

The western approach involved imperialist progress along the strategic and commercial routes of the Atlantic, underscoring the importance of Morocco which the French conquest of Algeria had to some extent isolated from its Maghribi context. It attracted attention because it was situated at the crossroads of the Mediterranean and Atlantic trade and was a purveyor to the world market of both Saharan and Moroccan commodities. Morocco consequently came to focus rival European ambitions, including those of Spain, which considered it had a historical claim in the region.

After Morocco's defeat at Wad Isly, on the Algerian border, Britain had come to the fore and posed as the champion of Moroccan independence. Once again we find a remarkably well-informed consul able to forge British policy in the region during his long tenure of office, from 1845 to 1886: Sir Drummond-Hay. The fact that he had spent part of his youth in Tangier where his father had been consul before him, spoke Arabic and knew almost everybody, made him an accepted member of Moroccan society and a man whose opinion was heeded. He did his best to serve both Moroccan and British interests, admiring as he did more traditional aspects of Muslim society whilst, at the same time, believing in the need to promote a European type of progress in the country. This he saw as the only possible safeguard of Moroccan independence in the imperial context of the 19th century. Among his signal contributions to the promotion of British interests in Morocco was the 1856 treaty which gave Britain a privileged nation status and opened the way for British trade and investments. He largely contributed to a situation in which Britain was the preponderant European nation in the sharifian kingdom.

Although imperial pressures on Morocco were clear, one should nonetheless bear in mind that in spite of its weakness, Morocco showed a stubborn will to uphold national integrity, and the three successive sovereigns of the period – Mulay 'Abd al-Rahman, 1822–59, Sidi Muhammad, 1859–73, Mulay Hasan, 1873–94 – all ably defended the nation and the state. This was particularly true of Mulay Hasan, a warrior-*sharif* in the best 'Alawi tradition, who made praiseworthy efforts to prevent the disintegration of Morocco by keeping tribal conflicts under control and avoiding frontier incidents with the French. He attempted to keep Europeans at bay and upheld the authority of the state, making energetic efforts to extend this, notably in the Saharan districts. He also made a limited number of reforms to adapt the country to a new economic world order. In spite of this, imperial progress could not be stayed.

European influence in Morocco

The development of trade on new imperial lines was upheld by infrastructural changes along the Atlantic trade routes. Shipping companies extended their activities to Morocco with three lines acquiring dominant positions in the 1870s: the French Compagnie Paquet, the British Mersey Steamship Company, and London Lisboa and North Africa line of steamers. Competition led to the Mersey Steamship fixing very low rates of freight and its rivals followed suit, thus cutting rates by about a third between 1870 and 1880. A growing number of ships called at Moroccan ports: they were about 700 a year between 1850 and 1855, about 900 in 1860, and over a thousand 10 years later. More than half of them were British. Passenger transport developed in parallel. In the 1860s there was a twice-weekly service between Gibraltar and Tangier (Longland and Cowell Company), a twice monthly service between Marseilles and various Moroccan harbours, a monthly service between Oran, Tangier, and Cadiz, besides the London-Morocco-Canaries service of the London Lisboa and North Africa. The Moroccan ports involved – Tangier, Larach (al-'Araysh), Rabat, al-Jadida (Mazagan), al-Sawira (Mogador), Safi – developed into international centres, whilst a newcomer, Casablanca (al-Dar al-Bayda) appeared. Up to the 1840s, Casablanca had had under 1000 inhabitants and only about 5 per cent of Morocco's exports left from there (mostly wool and cereals). By the 1850s, it dealt with about half the country's exports and by 1890 it was the country's chief trading centre.

Europeans, who were not allowed to settle inland or own property, concentrated in the ports where their presence was tolerated. Their numbers after a slow start grew fast with the number of residents passing from 389 in 1850 to 1360 in 1864 and 10 000 by the end of the century. Temporary residents or visitors were even more numerous: in Tangier, for example, nearly 7000 entries were recorded in 1887. These figures do not, of course, take into account 'protégés' who, in Morocco particularly, were not only numerous but a constant source of trouble for the *makhzen*. In the coastal towns European influence was increasingly visible not only at the level of social interaction with the local population but through the organization of a community life having its own social services including medical care, Christian churches and cemeteries, and the necessary infrastructure to uphold its activities. Thus European merchants had set up a private postal service between the major trading towns of the country. Gregory Abrines set up a private printing house in Tangier in 1880 and this led to the appearance of local European papers: the Spanish *Al-Moghreb al-Aksa* (1883) and the British *Times of Morocco* (1893). Banks appeared, including Morocco's first private business bank, Pariente's, which a Moroccan Jew opened in Tangier in 1844. The Pariente Bank, besides offering service to local firms, acted as agent for the Compagnie Algérienne, for Manchester's Bowker Bank and also had relations with Germany. A rival establishment set up a little later, Nahon's, acted for the Manchester and Liverpool District Bank, the Crédit Lyonnais, and the Banque de Paris et des Pays Bas. Much of Morocco's international banking business was carried out through Gibraltar, but by the 1880s foreign banks had also set up branch offices in Morocco, generally at Tangier.

What was the nature of the trade carried on with Morocco? Exports exceeded imports without this necessarily resulting in a favourable balance of payments since currency was leaving the country, nor did increases in quantity of goods necessarily mean a similar increase in value, as the price of raw materials fell from the late 1870s onwards. Morocco's exports were chiefly of raw materials, and notably cereals, for which there was a constant demand in Europe, which the Sultans found it increasingly difficult to refuse to meet. Wool was also required, although subject to crises in the European textile industry. This led to European traders' investing in Moroccan sheep farming. Since legislation did not allow them to own land, Europeans had recourse to local partners or stooge men whom they protected by means of the

Capitulations, even extending this collectively to farm labourers and herdsmen. Cases such as that of six Frenchmen who owned 16 000 animals in the Awlad Hariz region of Casablanca and whose 81 Moroccan employees were French protégés are by no means exceptional. The exact number of such protégés is unknown but estimates range from 2000–3000 in the 1870s. Not only were no official lists established, but some consuls would, on consideration, uphold unjustified claims to such protection. Protégés were a source of considerable trouble to the Moroccan government since they paid no taxation and would claim damages on the flimsiest pretext, always upheld by their consuls. The Moroccan sovereign was helpless to deal with the problem because consuls refused any discussion of the Capitulations, and even an international conference held in Madrid in May 1880 to deal with the problem in no way solved it but rather confirmed existing privileges.

Among export commodities ostrich feathers also figured; these were traded at al-Sawira after having been brought across the Sahara. The years 1865–1875 were highly prosperous, with record prices being paid; al-Sawira exported an average 3289 kg a year for a value of 507 800 French francs. Dependence on the European market was here shown up dramatically when South Africa appeared on the scene in 1880 as a producer, ruining the al-Sawira traders. Morocco's dependent status is also indicated by the fact that whereas it exported raw materials such as wool and cotton for the textile industry, it imported cloth from Britain, notably cheap cottons (22.5 million yards in 1877).

Peasant communities which had up to then been largely self-sufficient were now buying many things which had formerly been home-made and were consequently turning to cash-crop production to pay for these. Many ordinary objects of clay or copper were being replaced by European manufactured products. Manchester-ware was to be seen everywhere. It included tea-pots, sugar caddies, trays, etc. The adaptability of British industrialists must here be stressed, as special efforts were made to adapt production to local tastes. More important Moroccan trading families from Fez or al-Sawira were frequent visitors to European industrial centres, thus encouraging the process. By 1870, Germans were also beginning to compete in the fields where France and Britain had taken the lead. Metalware from Berg and Solingen was being sold as far out as the Sahara, and linen and cottons, known in Morocco as *amburgese*, were acquiring solid reputations.

New commodities were not only becoming commonplace but were soon to be considered indispensable. Such was at this time the case of the modest candle which made inroads on the peasant economy. Imports of candles trebled between 1870 and 1874 and trebled again between 1885 and 1890, by which time about 1.5 million kg were being imported annually. The most far-reaching of the social changes of the period was sweet mint tea which became a national beverage. Tea drinking had appeared in higher class society in the early 18th century but did not become general until a century later. In the period here under consideration, tea-drinking had become a national habit: 'everybody takes it', wrote the French consul at al-Sawira in 1874, 'rich and poor alike, at least three or four times a day'. Between 1870 and 1877 consumption nearly doubled, encouraged by falling world prices. If tea was a British trading concern, the sugar that went with it generally came from

Marseilles in the form of long pointed loaves weighing about 2.5 kg. During the 1870s, imports of sugar rose by about 75 per cent (1 895 144 kg registered in 1871, 3 273 702 in 1877) – and yet Morocco in the past had not only produced but exported sugar!

The influence of European industry and trade was thus apparent in even the humblest fields, spurred on by European competition between rival states and the common need to develop foreign markets which led to growing political pressure on Morocco to open itself to 'progress'. Early and typical forms of political pressure were offers of technical assistance, notably in the military field. The French in 1877 induced Mulay Hasan to accept a French military mission, ably led by Captain Erckman. The British, however, once again took the stage by sending out an officer from Gibraltar, MacLean, who during a long stay in Morocco acquired considerable authority. He was moreover chiefly responsible for the reorganization of the army on modern lines. Efforts were made by the Italians and Germans to follow up on this. An Italian arms factory was established at Fez (the *makina*) whilst Fritz Krupp obtained for the family firm contracts to build fortifications along the coast (1888).

'Cooperation' was not only military, and there were forms of 'peaceful penetration', as a contemporary termed it, which were no less important in promoting European influence in Morocco. Nowhere was this truer than in the sanitary and medical fields. The practice of sending out doctors at a sultan's request was not a new one but when the French permanent military mission arrived with a surgeon, Dr. Linares, on its staff, this was to have a more lasting influence. Indeed Dr. Linares, who was a permanent attendant at court and lived in Morocco from 1877 to 1902, was, as a French diplomat in Tangier put it, 'the best unofficial intermediary one could hope to have'. In the wake of medical assistance, an ever growing number of humanitarian missions were sent out to Morocco and extended their inquiries to such fields as slavery, prison conditions and the public beating of women for criminal offences. Permanent missions were set up, many being connected with evangelical organizations. Catholic priests – namely the Spanish Franciscans – had for centuries had official permission to minister to the Christian community in Morocco, and they had used their influence to further Spanish influence. Protestant missions on the other hand only appeared on the scene in the last quarter of the 19th century and their efforts were circumspect to avoid antagonizing Muslims. Proselytism was first undertaken among the Jews in 1875 by J. B. Crighton Ginsberg, but with little success. His efforts were upheld by the London Society for promoting Christianity among Jews. In 1882, under the guise of medical care, efforts were undertaken to establish relations with Muslims. A missionary called Mackintosh decided to settle in Tangier and enlisted the help of the British and Foreign Bible Society. In 1884, the North Africa Mission in its turn opened a centre in Tangier, later extending its activities to Arsila (1886), Fez (1888), Tetuan (1889) and Casablanca (1891). By 1894, it had 25 missionaries in the field. A Southern Morocco Mission was also founded and sent out into the field in 1888.

The nature and extent of imperial encroachment through philanthropy is even more apparent in the much publicized efforts of Jewish associations to help their coreligionists in Morocco. From 1860 onwards a new active concern for the latter was shown by such bodies as the Board of Deputies of British Jews, the Comité de Bienfaisance du Consistoire Israelite Universel, or the Board of Delegates of American Israelites. They interfered in local affairs by raising an outcry when suspected of proved acts of antisemitism took place, when discriminatory measures were taken, as in 1875, or in trials involving Jews, as in 1863, when two men were executed for murder. Much commented upon, both in Europe and Morocco, was the visit Solomon Rothschild paid to Tetuan in 1858, and that of Sir Moses Montefiore in January 1864. Montefiore (1784–1885) had defended Jews throughout the world and notably in the Middle East. In the 1830s he had obtained from Muhammad 'Ali better treatment for Egyptian Jews and in the 1860s the Turkish Sultan had made similar concessions. In 1864, it was the Moroccan Sultan's turn to give way to moral pressures. However much one may admire Montefiore's struggle against injustice, it should also be pointed out that he came to Morocco with a British naval escort to back him up.

The involvement of European powers in Morocco through Jewish philanthropical associations went much further. The Anglo-Jewish Association was particularly active in Tangier and al-Sawira where it opened a hospital and several schools. The French, not to be outdone had, by means of the Alliance Israelite Universelle (founded in Paris in 1860), launched into a programme of education which led to the setting up of a number of schools in Morocco, first in Tetuan (1862), then in Tangier (1864), al-Sawira (1863 and 1868) and Safi (1867). By 1868, it had 108 teachers in the field and its schools were attended by 1400 pupils. This had far-reaching consequences for the Jewish community in the country and for Morocco itself, as Jews increasingly went to settle in coastal towns where upgrading was possible. A new minority characterized by its close connection with Europe came to the fore and a rift within the national community was created, this being true not only of Morocco but of North Africa as a whole.

This may be seen as the by now familiar pattern of foreign encroachments. There were however signs that imperial pressure was being stepped up. The first was a direct aggression on Moroccan territory by Spain in 1860. Spain, which had always considered it had a prior claim on Morocco because of its *presidios*, wanted to remind the Great Powers of what it regarded as its historic rights. In 1848, it had forestalled the French by occupying the Zaffarine Islands. The Spanish then began to air a new project: the occupation of Tangier which would not only re-establish Spain's position as a colonial power, but counterbalance Britain's strategic command of the region from Gibraltar. British opposition to the project led to a more roundabout approach: the Spaniards decided to attack the Mediterranean harbour of Tetuan, just off the Straits. General O'Donnell who in 1860 led a right wing government in Spain, further hoped that military glory abroad would disarm opposition at home, and the official press and propaganda services were recruited to recall the 15th-century glory of Spain under its *Reconquista* sovereigns, Isabel and Ferdinand. No European objections were made, so an expeditionary corps of nearly 50 000 was brought together, and, on the slight ptretext that Spaniards building an outlying fort at Ceuta had been attacked, left for that town with General O'Donnell himself in command. The Moroccan army – both the royal forces and tribal contingents – surrounded the *presidio* and fiercely repulsed the Spaniards who, however, soon rallied and broke through the Moroccan lines. The invaders marched to Tetuan, fighting it out all along the 44 km of the way. The town fell on 5 February 1860.

The Powers, and more particularly Britain, were not in favour of Spanish expansion in Morocco. Efforts were made to obtain a negotiated settlement and the Moroccan Sultan was advised to adopt a conciliatory attitude. First Moroccan overtures in February were rejected by O'Donnell who had already declared Tetuan and its hinterland a Crown Duchy. Fighting and sickness taking a toll, the Spanish proved less bellicose when, a month later, new proposals were made. O'Donnell no longer demanded a right of permanent occupation but, instead, a war indemnity of 100 million pesetas (21 million Moroccan *riyal*-s) to be paid in nine months. This was an exorbitant demand if one considers that taxes from Morocco's richest province, Dukkala, amounted to 70 thousand *riyal*-s a year and that revenue from customs duties averaged a million *riyal*-s a year. The Spanish further demanded trading privileges, new rights for their citizens in Morocco and a territorial concession in the south, at an ill-defined place facing the Canary Islands. Morocco was faced with a proposal which to all appearances meant that the country would pass under foreign financial control or that, through non-payment, it would have to accept Spain's permanent presence with the future encroachments this might imply. Morocco nonetheless decided to face up to the financial burden.

In view of the then prevalent North African habit of relying on foreign loans, it is surprising that Sidi Muhammad should have chosen to appeal to the nation to help pay the indemnity. In contradiction to a commonly held view of Morocco as an anarchist society of conflicting tribes, people generously responded to the sovereign's appeal conveyed to them by the intermediary of influential holy lineages. The first instalment (25 million pesetas) having been met out of the Treasury, the second was paid partly by the tribes (15 million pesetas) and partly by a British loan (10 million pesetas). The Sultan was thus able to negotiate a new agreement with the occupiers. On 30 October 1861, the Spanish agreed to evacuate Tetuan once half the war indemnity had been paid. On 10 March 1862, they left.

Morocco: economic difficulties and attempts at reform

The Spanish imperial project had fallen through. It had nonetheless created the conditions of permanent economic and social weakness which, in spite of Mulay Hasan's effort to build up a powerful nation, paved the way to a similar situation to that which prevailed in other North African countries.

The process by which independence was undermined was first and foremost economic, since the 50 million pesetas still owing as part of the war indemnity was guaranteed by revenue from foreign trade. This led in 1862 to the Spaniards taking over customs houses in the harbours. Half the revenue from this source was to be kept by them, a quarter was to go to paying British creditors who had put up 10 million pesetas. Morocco was thus left with a mere quarter of customs revenue, and though ridiculously low tariffs could and indeed should have been increased, such an increase was adamantly opposed by the Powers. The *makhzen* was therefore forced to increase taxation – a highly unpopular measure. This led to changes in the traditional system which had formerly been paid in kind, and on a one tenth basis. A fixed annual estimation was now made with a further switchover to payment in cash. This allowed for an increase in taxation. The rich wheat-growing district of Dukkala for example, which had paid 70 000 *riyal*-s in 1861, was charged 90 000 in 1862 and 100 000 in 1863. Discontent was further increased by the necessity for the government to create new forms of taxation which did not have Quranic sanction. Toll houses were put up at city gates and duty levied on goods taken in and out.

Not only did Moroccans have to pay dearly to be rid of the invaders but an economic situation was created which, in years of poor harvests, could lead to great hardship. In the late 19th century, the sorry sight of hungry families trekking through the countryside reappeared, and indeed population migration took place on a scale comparable to that following from major epidemics, although it now involved small groups, or individuals, rather than tribes. State authority was moreover undermined by European pressures now openly exerted on Morocco. This was brought home by the Spanish officials in the harbours acting as customs officials. It was also apparent on the eastern frontier where French encroachments on border regions were being stepped up and were indeed, in the last years of the 19th century, to lead to actual occupation.

Mulay Hasan reacted by promoting military, political, and economic reforms. Reform in the administrative and educational fields was undertaken, special efforts being made to create a modern civil service. This implied a new type of education which Mulay Hasan did not promote at home. Rather, he sent students to study abroad. Some Moroccans were sent to Istanbul, others to Egypt, or to France. Modern technology appeared in Morocco where a printing press was set up and run by a Turk. In the agricultural field, efforts were made to improve production, besides modernizing the trading networks. These efforts were, in fact, limited and generally ill-adapted. Education could not be promoted on the basis of foreign grants to students, nor could the economy be modernized by mere technological aids. Though a hard-surface coastal road was built between Casablanca and Safi, it was soon out of use. Mechanization was also unavailing as when a steam-engine was set up in Tangier in 1862 or a sugar refinery set up in Marrakech. Those using new technology were given no training. Some more successful examples of help provided by technologically advanced nations can be pointed to, chief of which was the building of a lighthouse off Cape Spartell in the Straits as a result of an agreement come to in 1861, which provided that the building of the lighthouse was to be effected by its users (i.e. European states) and that its upkeep was to be Morocco's responsibility. In a similar way, we find harbour facilities improved. Nonetheless even those generally marked a step-up in European pressures: in 1863, Morocco obtained from Britain ginning machinery but, in exchange, was forced to lift the ban on the export of cereals.

To face up to a situation characterized both by tribal unrest at home and sporadic fighting between the French troops and border tribes, Mulay Hasan was led to increase the power of the armed forces and to reform the army to bring it up to modern standards. This was not only costly, but involved recourse to foreign assistance. Mulay Hasan first sought to obtain this from Turkey, but was ultimately forced to accept foreign advisers. A British officer, Qaid MacLean, thus became responsible for the reorganization of the

Moroccan armed forces.

With the help of the army, Mulay Hasan was able to tour the country permanently, not only with a view to bringing the tribes under subjection and making them pay their taxes, but also to bringing home a strong sense of national unity. These unifying policies further allowed the sovereign to appoint *makhzen* representatives in the districts, thus building up a more centralized administration which could effectively spread the royal word. This was particularly important in the border areas where *makhzen* control was generally limited but which now, because of French military encroachments, had to be reinforced. We thus find a sharifian official being appointed at Figuig in 1881 with jurisdiction extending as far as In Salah. The king further upheld this system by more traditional patterns of alliance with tribal chiefs who were given government status (*qaid*-s) such as al-Hajj al-Mahdi in In Salah or Qaid al-Dlimi in Tuwwat (1891), and with holy men and *zawiya*-s. Among efforts made in this period to promote sharifian authority in the south-east was the granting of new privileges to the holy lineage of Wazzan, which not only had a strong fraternity following in the region, but a measure of political control which was now, with royal help, stepped up.

In spite of these measures, structural economic weakness was not only apparent, but was to undermine Mulay Hasan's efforts to promote national independence. Morocco, like other countries, was now dependent on world market sales, and industrial crises directly affected peripheral economies. The situation which prevailed in European industry in the late 1870s thus had repercussions on Morocco, whose sale of wool declined. It is nonetheless a proof of Morocco's economic stability that the slump should have been staved off until 1877. In fact the years 1871–6, saw record high export figures, but when the reversal of the trend set in, it was made all the more dramatic by a series of bad harvests. In 1877, great hardship set in and cereals which had largely been sold in order to pay taxes and ultimately foreign debts, were almost non-existent and too expensive for poorer people, who fell victim to cholera and smallpox. The situation was sufficiently serious to move international opinion and in 1878 a Morocco Famine Relief Fund was set up. Morocco's international trade continued to decrease in volume and value until 1885. It is generally estimated that the value of exports between 1875 and 1885 declined by nearly half. The trend was only slowly reversed, further handicapped by the fact that currency left the country at the rate of over a million *riyal*-s a year. The economic imbalance was a symptom of a serious underlying monetary problem.

The currency problem which prevailed throughout North Africa can be illustrated by the case of Morocco. Traditional Moroccan currency involved gold, silver, and copper. The monetary crisis apparent from 1844 onwards is characterized by inflation. Al-Nasiri, a Moroccan historian of the time, pointed out that between 1844 and 1873, national currency had lost as much as 90 per cent of its value. It was also marked by a switchover to foreign coins. In the first place gold disappeared almost totally from the market and Morocco was left with a twin metallic currency: silver and copper. Copper was increasingly devalued. This was a world-wide trend, underscored in Morocco by the fact that the copper mines of the Sus had given rise to an active illegal minting industry. The copper ounce which in 1766 had been rated at 2.9 grains of silver, was worth only 0.72 a century later. The depreciation was particularly spectacular in the ten-year period between 1852 and 1862, with the rate of the *uqiya* (ounce) against the *riyal* (French five-franc coin) declining from 19 to 32.5. This had the usual result: people hoarded their silver; but as trade continued to require the latter, foreign coins became commonplace. Among them we find the thaler, the Spanish piastre (the peseta being a mere unit of count established in 1868), and the French Napoleon, locally called *al-luiza*; but it was the French silver five franc coin which increasingly prevailed until, under the name of *riyal*, it became standard money and reference for most transactions. This was true of international trade and agreements – thus the Spaniards in 1860 had demanded that the war indemnity be paid in *riyal*-s – but also of local trade. National accounts were now kept in *riyal*-s.

Various monetary reforms were undertaken by the Sultans and notably, in 1868, by Sidi Muhammad who tried to re-establish the *riyal* at its 1852 value of 19 ounces. This merely resulted in the appearance of two rates of exchange, both figuring side by side even on official documents. In 1881, a more complete reform was carried out by Mulay Hasan. This involved minting new coins in Paris, at La Monnaie, the French Mint. In view of the deficit in the balance of payments and growing dependence of local money on foreign standard rates of exchange, this too only served to emphasize Morocco's dependence.

IMPERIAL INROADS ON THE SAHARA

During the same period a continuous European advance was evident further south, in the Saharan regions. One can point to three converging but nonetheless distinct inroads: exploration of the Sahara, commercial and political encroachments along the western coast and, from 1870 onwards, more direct involvement of Morocco and imperial powers in the western Sahara.

European exploration

European penetration in Saharan and Sudanic Africa was upheld by a general public interest in as yet unmapped regions of Africa. This was largely monitored by the numerous learned societies and geographical associations of the time. The most important of these provided the connecting link between the public (members of the societies, patrons, scholars) and imperial circles (military and business pressure groups and governments). The learned societies largely determined the areas to be mapped, recruited the explorers and put up the funds. They had financial aid from such sources as chambers of commerce and the government, and also had the political support of the latter. This involved the active help of consuls in Africa. The men chosen for such journeys were, moreover, often army officers. The explorations became increasingly political as the chanceries upheld the *territorium nullius* theory according to which African territories had no legal existence as states unless this had been sanctioned in former times by international treaties, and could therefore be claimed by the nations whose enterprising explorers were first on the spot. The latter were often given treaties to be completed on arrival if local chiefs were willing to sign such agreements which put forward the foreign

211

Fig. 12.1   Major explorations in the Sahara carried out by Europeans in the second half of the 19th century

1850	Heinrich Barth went from Tripoli to Kano via Murzuq. In 1851 he visited Bornu and in 1852–3 pushed westwards as far as Timbuktu.
1852–5	Eduard Vogel explored Eastern Sahara and was killed in Wadday (1856).
1865	Gerard Rohlfs went to In Salah and to Murzuk. In 1866, he went from Fezzan to Bornu and from there to the Niger.
1868	Alexandrine Tinné, a Dutch woman explorer, travelled through Southern Algeria and visited the Mzab.
1869	Gustav Nachtigal went from Tripoli to Tibesti and from there to Bornu (1871).
1869	Alexandrine Tinné left Tripoli for Murzuq. From there she set off for Bornu but was killed crossing Tuareg territory.
1876	A German, Erwin Von Barry left Tripoli for the Niger but died in Tasili.
1880	An Italian expedition led by Matteucci went from Khartum to Kurdufan and Dar Fur.
1880	Henri-Oscar Lenz, financed by the *Afrikanische Gesellschaft* reached Timbuktu.
1880, 1881	2 French military missions under Colonel Flatters were sent to map out the trans-Saharan railway. The mission was massacred by the Tuareg in February 1881.
1884–1895	Fernand Foureau for France carried out 9 journeys exploring the Sahara.
1890–2	Parfait Louis Monteil went from Saint-Louis to the Niger Bend and from there to Fezzan and Tripoli.

power as the 'protector' giving 'assistance' to local rulers. The system was formalized in Europe by the International African Congress held at Berlin in 1884 which sanctioned the principle that occupation implied possession.

Exploration of the trans-Saharan routes, kept in the public mind by the legendary reputation of wealth and mystery which surrounded Timbuktu, had begun in the 1820s. Most such attempts, in spite of the cooperation of North African governments, often obtained under duress, ended in tragic failure. Mention has already been made of Major Laing's death near Timbuktu in 1826. Laing's father-in-law, Consul Warrington of Tripoli, further lost one of his own sons, Henry, who was killed on the way to Bornu with Vogel. This points not so much to Saharan and notably Tuareg fanaticism, as to awareness of the implications of such journeys. Information travels fast in the Sahara. The nomads, though not openly defying government orders, would, when the occasion arose, do away with the unpleasant foreigners whose progress in North Africa was no secret. By the late 1850s the imperialist significance of such explorations was clear. France had already staked a territorial claim by undertaking from 1852 onwards a systematic occupation of northern Sahara, various attempts being further made to encroach on neighbouring states and

Fig. 12.2 Geographical societies which promoted the exploration of North and Central Africa	
1821	*Société de Geographie de Paris* founded.
1828	*Gesellschaft für Erdkunde* (Berlin).
1830	The *Royal Geographical Society* in London took over from the *Society for the Promotion of the Discovery of the Interior Parts of Africa*. It received a Royal Charter in 1859.
1868	The *Institut Colonial* founded in France.
1873	*Société de Géographie Commerciale de Paris.*
1875	The *Khedival Geographical Society* (Egypt).
1876	*Société de Géographie de Marseille.*
1879	*Comité d'Etudes du Haut Congo* founded by King Leopold II in Belgium.
1882	Leopold II founded the *Association Internationale du Congo.*
1888	The *Comité de l'Afrique Française* set up.

to establish control over the trans-Saharan trade which was now no longer going to Algiers. In 1862, a French mission was sent to Ghadames to sign an agreement with the Tuareg who were to protect caravans on their way to Algeria. The British, however, countered this move by bringing pressure on the Turkish authorities in Tripoli who were persuaded to send troops and a new *mudir* to Ghadames. To the west, the same policy was defined in theory but impeded in practice by permanently difficult relations with the Awlad Sidi Shaykh.

In Europe itself, the imperial theme was now being orchestrated by new societies who subordinated geographical to political interests. This was the case with Leopold II's Association Internationale du Congo (1882) or the French Comité de l'Afrique Française (1888). One project evolved in these circles which caught the public eye was a trans-Saharan railway. The idea was first proposed by a French engineer, Duponchel, in 1875, who suggested that the railway extend from southern Algeria to Timbuktu via Tuareg territory. The project was taken seriously by the government which sponsored the commission which examined it in 1879 and decided that a military mission should be sent out to make a survey. The need to lose no time was brought home to the government by a counterproposal made by the German Rohlfs to build the railway from Tripoli to the Sudan. Whilst negotiations with the Moroccan government got under way – since the railway was to be partly on territory over which the 'Alawi-s exercized sovereign rights – Colonel Flatters and a military mission set out in 1880. They undertook a second journey in 1881, in the course of which the French forces were massacred by the Tuareg. The outcry in imperialist circles was considerable, not only because of the humiliation involved but because the setback was a serious one and, indeed, as keener observers guessed, implied a definite shelving of the project.

Western Saharan trade and attempts at European infiltration
Difficulties with the Tuareg focused imperial attention on the strategic and commercial importance of more westerly lying trans-Saharan routes. These

avoided the difficult Tuareg territory and their penetration could further benefit from a powerful base of operations, namely the Senegal where Faidherbe as governor (1854–65) had reorganized the colony, created a powerful tool of colonial expansion, the Senegalese Riflemen, and established control over both banks of the River Senegal where the Arab nomads came to trade. European observers further noted the intense trade carried out along these western routes. It involved a working partnership between tribally influential lineages of southern Morocco, notably the lay Awlad Bayruk of Gulimin and the religious Ait Sidi Ahmad u Musa of Tazerwalt, with the Fasi merchants. The *makhzen* both upheld this trade and benefited from it through taxes and an active commerce at home and abroad. The traders had rebuilt the Northern Saharan outpost of Tinduf in 1852 to serve as an entrepôt to divert some of the trade from the older centre of Tuwwat. The caravans, though privately organized, were also supervised by government officials, especially the regular annual caravan of some 1000 to 1500 camels which set out from Tinduf at the end of September and returned from Timbuktu in April. The journey took 50–60 days. In the 1870s the cost of transport was estimated at between 250 and 350 francs per camel-load (i.e. about 160 kg). Goods exported south have already been mentioned. They included cloth, tea, sugar, candles, cowrie shells, and metalware. Imports consisted of slaves (between 500 and 1000 every year between 1875 and 1885, although these are not full figures since they apply merely to Tinduf, whilst Tuwwat remained important in this respect), ostrich feathers and gum (both for the European market), besides other Sudanic commodities in smaller quantities, including limited supplies of gold. Buying and selling was carried out by factotums or intermediaries, the latter often being Jewish traders settled throughout the oases, and the former family partners of the Fasi concern. There were thus permanently some 12 to 20 Fasi-s settled in Timbuktu.

Government policy and European demand led in the 19th century to trade being increasingly diverted from the Muslim market (Fez or the trans-Maghribi route) to international centres, notably al-Sawira which became the new terminus of the trans-Saharan commerce. This was of considerable importance to the *makhzen*, not only because of 10 per cent taxes collected at al-Sawira, but because Saharan exports were an important factor in the overall balance of payments. Between 1860 and 1865, they represented some 20 per cent of Moroccan sales abroad; an average annual sum of 1 500 000 francs. In the following ten-year period, 1865–75, this trade decreased to about 900 000 francs, but still played a considerable role.

This highly profitable trade in which European merchants only intervened at the terminus of the journey – namely at al-Sawira – led them from the 1870s onwards to try and infiltrate the commercial circuits. There were, of course, here as elsewhere precedents, and the treacherous coast of north-western Africa had not only seen ships sail by in growing numbers but had been visited by Europeans. These were often shipwrecked mariners whose liberation was generally obtained with the help of the King of Morocco. Merchants had also come, generally prudently staying on board ship, but in at least one instance – Port Hillsborough set up in 1764–5 – making an attempt to set up a permanent post in the region of Argin. In the last quarter of the 19th century a somewhat similar attempt was made, one which in view of a changing world context was far more meaningful. In 1880, Mackenzie set up a small trading fort near Cape Juby. Mackenzie had the financial backing of Manchester businessmen who for the purpose set up the North West African Company (1874). He was a man of high-flown projects, and part of his plan was opening a waterway into the desert, but he also reflected the spirit of the age in wishing to combine 'Christianity, trade, and civilization'. Moreover he was practical enough to limit himself for the time being to trade. He and his partners made frequent visits to Mackenzie Fort where a permanent community had been established consisting of eight Englishmen (including a doctor who was often consulted by the Saharans), several workers from the Canary Islands, and a Syrian interpreter. Trade was not, however, up to expectations and Arabs were reluctant to deal with the Europeans in spite of the cooperation of the Awlad Bayruk.

One of the results of the building of Fort Mackenzie was to remind the Spanish that they had obtained a portion of territory in the region as part of the settlement of the 1860 war with Morocco. The problem was that the concession which was to be on the spot of a 15th century Spanish outpost called Santa Cruz, was ill-defined. This led to much international discussion with Spain claiming another ex-Santa Cruz, namely Agadir much further north. In 1884, the Spanish set up an outpost at Villa Cisneros.

The idea of trading directly with the desert tribes was based on the idea that this would be considerably more profitable than buying the same goods at al-Sawira. Local intermediaries would be done away with, as also would be the 10 per cent tax paid to the Moroccan government. Merchants who already had trading interests in southern Morocco were the first to be involved in the project. At al-Sawira a company was set up to make preliminary investigations. Such well-known names as those of Nicholas Paquet, W. S. Shuttleworth & Co of London and David de Leon Cohen of Marseilles were involved in the project. This was followed up by the appearance on the scene of several other companies including the Atlas Co, the North African and Soos Co, the Compañia de Pesquerias Canario-Africana, the Compañia Mercantil Hispano-Africana. The North African and Soos Co, founded by British traders in 1881, further hoped to obtain a mining concession near Sidi Ifni. The companies tried to win over to their projects the leading local families, including Muhammad wuld Bayruk and Husayn bin Hashem then head of the Tazerwalt holy lineage. Europeans now affected to consider the latter as an almost independent ruler. Wuld Bayruk had already made overtures to the Europeans and shown his willingness to share profits accruing from trade with them, whilst Husayn bin Hashem was contacted by various agents who, in 1881, invited him to sign a convention with the French Republic guaranteeing peaceful trade relations, the French for their part agreeing to build and defend a harbour in the Sus. The holy man though at first interested, was soon made aware of local and national opposition to the project, and he backed down.

The Moroccan government was, of course, extremely concerned by these encroachments. The consequences would indeed be serious were trade and government dues to pass into foreign hands, all the more so in view of the role played by north-south relations in national history. The *makhzen* under Mulay Hasan's energetic leadership decided on all-out resistance. This took several forms. Firstly, rival imperial ambitions could be played off one against the other. Sir John Drummond-Hay, who was known to be personally hostile to the Mackenzie trading post, was appealed to, and he upheld Moroccan views at the British Foreign Office. Secondly, Mulay Hasan sent out to the region a strong military force (1882 and 1886). Husayn bin Hashem was rapidly neutralized by traditional holy men manoeuvring whilst Muhammad wuld Bayruk saw his territory overrun by the army. A typical piece of *makhzen* manipulation led to the latter being appointed government representative in the region with strict orders to keep out all foreigners, a task which he carried out most efficiently from then on. In the course of the campaigns, the whole region was organized on a defensive basis with a new military town at Tiznit and garrisons at various points along the coast. At the end of the second campaign Fort Mackenzie was destroyed (1888).

These measures were effective because they had popular backing. This support was stimulated and upheld by the traditional network of holy men in close relationship with the Moroccan sovereign, none being more active than Ma al-'Aynayn who, in the last quarter of the 19th century, organized Saharan resistance to the French advance north from Senegal. Ma al-'Aynayn (1831–1910) who has already been described as a Saharan holy man and as an ally of the 'Alawi dynasty, settled as 'resident saint' in the Saqiyat al-Hamra in the late 1860s. He was very much aware of the danger of foreign invasion which had already led him to move north and, with the help of the Moroccan government, he set up a strong military organization throughout the Sahara. The efficiency of the system, unavailing though it turned out to be in spite of the dedication of its leaders, was demonstrated in the 1900s when a direct onslaught on Morocco was made by French imperialism.

THE EASTERN APPROACH

Imperialism was progressing no less evidently in the east of the continent than in the west and this was exemplified, in the first place, by Sudan where the characteristics of colonial rule were increasingly evident. This was to make the country into an operational base for expansion, both locally, as peripheral regions were brought within the scope of the Turkiyya and its expansive trading and military policy, and internationally with Sudan as an advanced post on the imperial road 'from Alexandria to the Cape'. Changes under way in Sudan should therefore be examined in this light. We should also ask ourselves what they meant for the Sudanese themselves.

Various factors can be seen as indicators of the nature of the Turkiyya. We thus find the rapid turnover of higher-ranking personnel, including the *hukumdar*-s or governor-generals, leading to minor officials on the spot, on whom the inexperienced officers largely depended, having considerable power. The inevitable habit of considering colonial privileges as natural and of treating Sudanese as inferior subject people to be oppressed at will was encouraged by the administration's turning a blind eye on individual failings. The Sudanese could find no redress for wrongs and a sense of injustice and humiliation prevailed of which we find an echo in contemporary documents including the proclamations of the Mahdi who reminded his people that:

'the Turks used to put your men in prison, bound with chains, used to

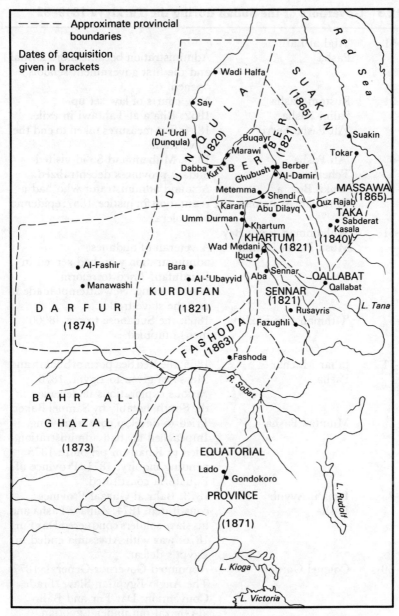

Map 12.2 *The Egyptian Sudan in the period immediately preceding the Mahdiyya*
(source: P.M. Holt, The History of the Sudan)

capture your women and children, and kill people, which is against the law of God. They had neither pity on your little children, nor respect for your old people. . . . They oppressed you greatly, and yet you obeyed their orders.'

217

Fig. 12.3 Governors of the Sudan during the Turkiyya 1849–82

1849–51	'Abd al-Latif Pasha	Administration became more formal and the first government schools opened.
1850–51	Rustam Pasha	New courts of law set up.
1851–3	Salim Pasha	1852: Rifa'a al-Tahtawi in exile.
1853–4	'Ali Pasha Serri	1854: first measures taken to end the slave trade.
1854–6	'Ali Pasha Tcherkess	1856: Muhammad Sa'id visited Sudan; provinces decentralized.
1856–8	Arakil Bey, a Christian Armenian	A sound administrator who had a reputation for justice. 1857: epidemic of cholera.
1858–61	Muhammad Rajik Bey	
1862–4	Musa Pasha Hamdi	A veteran of Sudanese administration who had served in Kurdufan. Tried to reform tax-collecting. New attempt made to end the slave-trade.
1864–5	'Uthman Bey Fakhry	1865: the Sudanese troops (8000 men) mutinied.
1865–71	Ja'far Mazhar Pasha	1865: the Red Sea ports of Suakin and Massawa given to Egypt. 1870: various explorations undertaken in the South, notably by Samuel Baker.
1871	Mumtaz Pasha	Tried to develop cotton growing. Impeached for bad administration. Died in Khartum prison in 1875 pending inquiry. 1871: Province of Equatoria constituted.
1873–7	Isma'il Ayyub Pasha	1873: Bahr al Ghazal Province constituted. 1874: Zubayr Pasha and his slave soldiers conquered Dar Fur. 1876: war with Abyssinia ended in Egypt's defeat.
1877–80	Colonel Gordon	Appointed Governor-General. 1877: The Anglo-Egyptian Slave-Trade Convention. Dar Fur and Bahr al-Ghazal put under Egyptian administration.
1880–2	Ra'uf Pasha	1881: the Mahdi began to preach.
1882	'Abd al-Qadir Pasha	Development of the Mahdiyya.
1884–5	Gordon Pasha	Killed by the Mahdiyya on 26 January 1885. Mahdist state set up.

Individual acts of tyranny were thus part of an overall system of oppression as officers indulged in slave-raiding on their own account or made illegal levies. Corruption and embezzlement were rife and this explains why the army, in spite of the fact that a civilian Department of Finance had been set up, continued to consider such functions as tax-collecting an army privilege. It is consequently impossible to assess the exact cost of the Turkiyya from the Sudanese point of view. Even figures at the Egyptian end which put annual revenue at £400 000 are unreliable. Some years later, Lord Cromer, attempting to draw an accurate picture of the situation, was forced to conclude: 'There is little use in endeavouring to ascertain what the real revenue of Soudan was at this time. No trustworthy accounts were kept'. The Egyptian government was aware of conditions prevailing locally and many efforts were made to reform the tax-collecting system, always more or less in vain in view of the fact that it was one of the main sources of illegal profit-making. In 1856, Muhammad Sa'id, the Egyptian viceroy, paid a visit to Sudan and was so horrified by what he saw that he was in two minds about maintaining the occupation. The decision to remain was accompanied by a series of measures all of which were intended to try and keep the army out of the financial administration. Muhammad Sa'id forbade the collecting of taxes by soldiers and ordered that they be withdrawn from the districts. The villages were in future to pay taxes through their *shaykh*-s or headmen. Taxes on irrigated land were to be reduced to encourage agriculture, and were only to be collected after the harvests. An assembly of notables was to be convened every year to register complaints. No more came of this than of a future reform by Musa Pasha Hamdi (Governor-General from 1862 to 1864) aimed at limiting illegal levies by supplying the Sudanese with stamped papers indicating taxes due. Also as a reaction against gross mismanagement we find Muhammad Sa'id's visit followed up by the appointment of men who had a reputation for justice and sound administration such as Arakil Pasha, a Christian Armenian, Governor-General between 1856 and 1858. The Turkiyya can thus be considered a combination of injustice and mismanagement. The fact that this was a view strongly put over – not without ulterior motives – by the British partner of the Anglo-Egyptian Condominium should not lead us to forget that it was also held by contemporary Sudanese, expressed notably by the Mahdi and the widespread acceptance of his movement.

Oppression expressed itself also in the socio-economic field where the Turkiyya had long-term undermining effects. As we saw in a former chapter, the Egyptians had set up an ambiguous dual administration: direct rule through army or civilian functionaries and indirect rule through tribal chiefs. Manipulation of notables, some of whom were deposed, some promoted, together with such typical practices as the taking of hostages to Khartum or ever more direct intervention from the administration, led to a breakdown of tribal solidarity based on the traditional influence of holy men and leading families. Tribes became powerful if they collaborated with the Egyptians. The Shayqiyya and the 'Ababda who took part in punitive expeditions were favoured and the 'Ababda tribal leader, Husayn Bey Khalifa, rose to the rank of Governor of Berbera. Along the Blue Nile the Shukriyya became prominent and their leader, Ahmad Abu Sinn (circa 1890–1870) also rose to high rank and became Governor of the district of Khartum. In contrast to this, a great number of cohesive communities were broken down into small administrative units. The overall result was a modified tribal layout with a marked tendency towards fragmentation.

Effects on individuals were no less negative, highlighted more particularly by Egyptian policy with respect to recruitment for military purposes. This was initially instituted in the form of Muhammad 'Ali's project for a slave army which deprived the *awlad al-balad* of their traditional labour force. In the second half of the century, a new policy was progressively implemented to reduce domestic slavery and put an end to the slave trade. This aggravated the marked decline in output, all the more so in view of the fact that Egypt did little to improve or even protect agriculture. Even measures taken in the 1870s to introduce cash-crop production, notably cotton, had negative results since by the time Sudanese cotton appeared on the market, the recession had set in and, as US exports grew, prices fell.

The switch over from slave recruitment to local conscription also had strong colonial implications. No attempt was made to take economic requirements into account and conscription thus further reduced the Sudanese labour force. Moreover conditions for new recruits were unsatisfactory, overcrowded barracks, insufficient stores, and pay-arrears being the rule. That this was largely due to mismanagement is made clear by Khartum's efforts to hide the facts from the Egyptian government. Thus, in 1865, some 8000 men mutinied because of long overdue pay. This was reported to Cairo with no mention of the cause of complaint and led to a brutal military repression. The soldiers were not only used to uphold the Turkiyya but increasingly came to be the rank and file of the army in Egypt itself. Their number were estimated at around 100 000. Ultimately they came to be used on foreign battlefields to uphold the prestige of an imperial power. The first instance of this is Sudanese participation in fighting in Mexico in 1864 where they upheld a French attempt to place Maximilian, Archduke of Austria, on the throne. The vainglorious Napoleon III had obtained from the no less vainglorious Viceroy of Egypt support for this ill-starred and indeed somewhat farcical Mexican venture in which mercenaries, including the Sudanese troops, showed much useless bravery.

The imperial onslaught of the Turkiyya on Sudanese society was also apparent in the religious field. Not only had Egyptian policy been geared towards reducing the role of *sharif*-s as regulators and upholders of the social order, but by creating government schools and new courts of law, it also deprived them of their more official and influential positions. Egyptian *qadhi*-s were appointed and local scholars were treated with open contempt. This was further emphasized by the fact that the Turkiyya introduced the Hanafi system in a milieu which, here as elsewhere in North Africa, was traditionally Maliki. The reaction of local scholars seems to have been similar to that which is to be found elsewhere in colonial situations: namely a conservative attitude dictated by the will to preserve fundamental values in the face of aggression. This was not conducive to self-searching or intellectual effort as Rifa'a al-Tahtawi sadly noted during his exile in Khartum in 1852. A further and more pernicious threat to the cohesion of Sudanese society came in the 1860s when the Egyptian administration set about choosing promising youths in the holy men circles in order to send them to Cairo to be educated. At al-Azhar a special quarter – *al-riwaq al-Sinnariyya* – was set aside for them. When these young men returned to Sudan with their oriental scholarship and their fine cultured Egyptian accents, they were seen as challenging the authority of their elders. They represented a new era characterized by the necessary acceptance of Egyptian superiority, and were themselves agents of an ultimate phase of colonial rule based on a counter-society of converted members of the elite. In the last years of the Turkiyya, Egypt depended to some degree for its authority on the collaboration of a few chosen Sudanese who were given posts in the learned institution and in the administration, where Sudanese officers received appointments. The process culminated in 1872 when a Sudanese, Adam Pasha, became acting Governor-General.

What, in the balance, can one consider as the positive achievements of the Turkiyya? In the first place territorial unity and extension. In the second, a central government together with a largely decentralized provincial administration. The provinces of Sudan by the end of the Turkiyya included: Dunqula, Bethe Compairbera, Khartum, Sennar, and Kurdufan, to which had been added Taka (1840), Suakin (1865), Equatoria (1871), Bahr al-Ghazal (1873) and Dar Fur (1874). It also, as we have seen, promoted a limited number of Sudanese as agents of the new administration. Sudan to some degree benefited from the modernizing trend set on foot in Egypt and more particularly from Khedive Isma'il's progressive though over-ambitious projects. Particular attention, for example, was paid to the organization of trading networks, even if these were essentially in Egypt's favour and heavily taxed. The fact that Sudanese exports had been seen initially as a government monopoly and were later conceded to Egyptian trading firms such as the Compagnie du Soudan constituted a barrier to European penetration. Moreover, Khedive Isma'il developed the necessary infrastructure for more active trade by means of a government fleet of steamers on the Nile and plans for a railway. Work on the latter began in 1873 in the frontier region of Wadi Halfa but had to be given up because of lack of money. It was later resumed by Lord Kitchener as part of the reinvasion of Sudan in the post-Mahdi period. The electric telegraph system in 1874 connected Khartum to Upper Egypt and in 1875 was extended to the Red Sea by way of Berbera. Moreover, access to the Red Sea was obtained by the Sultan's concession of Massawa and Suakin, first on a temporary basis to Muhammad 'Ali, and definitely in 1870. Suakin (now Port Sudan) commanded commercial relations via the Red Sea and was thus an important factor in promoting Sudan's position as a trading partner in its own right. Limited and largely selfish though these efforts were, they nonetheless provided the conditions for the later creation of a modern independent state.

THE SLAVE TRADE AND ITS ABOLITION

Arguments for or against the Turkiyya were to be propounded in the 20th century when they were recast on nationalist lines ('the unity of the Nile Valley' as opposed to 'Sudan for the Sudanese'); but in the 19th century they were largely coloured by people's views on slavery and the slave trade. This is true of Egypt which had conquered Sudan to use it as a base to obtain slaves, of the Muslim East which imported servants and concubines whether legally or after a clandestine fashion, and of Europe where a strong abolitionist movement developed, finding support in public opinion where somewhat ambiguous feelings prevailed since we find both righteous zeal and a morbid fascination with the subject. The Victorians themselves apparently saw no contradiction in decorating their homes with paintings illustrating the fashionable slave theme whilst at the same time expounding on 'oriental depravity'. Once this has been said, it must also be remembered that Sudan was indeed largely organized as a merchant state upholding the worst form of exploitation and this, moreover, goes largely to explain the Turkiyya's policy of territorial aggrandizement. Sudan which under Muhammad 'Ali had been limited to the present North Province and the regions of Khartum, the Blue Nile, Kurdufan, and part of the Upper Nile, came, in the 1850s to involve an ever-extending peripheral zone as northerners (Egyptian, Sudanese, and some Europeans) pushed westwards towards Dar Fur, south-westwards towards the Bahr al-Ghazal (the marshy river zone around the White Nile before it turns East near Fashoda) and southwards up the river towards the Great Lakes. In a third phase, in the 1870s, these territories were formally taken over by Egypt as part of the Sudan. The new southern provinces, in contrast to the Arabic-speaking Muslim north, were not only non-Arab but also non-Muslim.

The story of slave-raiding in 19th century Sudan thus highlights and defines the country's general evolution. The three phases of aggrandizement pointed to above also take the form of three different policies in the matter. Whereas under Muhammad 'Ali slave raiding had been a government policy largely carried out by army recruiters for military purposes and slave trading was itself seen as a state monopoly (established in 1828), the period of the 1850s marked a switch over to private capitalist enterprise. The viceroys not only gave up state involvement in the trade but made attempts to put an end to it. At the time, however, the opening up of the country to traders and Egyptian protection given to companies specializing in Sudanic commodities favoured the development of mercantile attitudes and undertakings. In the 1850s a motley crew of traders, often having their headquarters in Khartum, made Sudan a base from which raids were launched into the Bahr al-Ghazal and up the Nile. The 1850s also marked the heyday of European involvement in Sudan trade, bringing to the fore such men as George Thibaut, doyen of the foreign community since he had come out in Muhammad 'Ali's time. There was also a Savoyard called Antoine Brun-Rollet and an eccentric Welshman, John Petherick. More numerous and powerful were the Muslim merchants. Some were Syrians, others Egyptians, as, for example, Muhammad Ahmad al-Aqqad (died in 1870) who, possibly with viceregal backing, set up Aqqad & Co in which his brother, Musa Bey, and his son-in-law, Mhammad Bey Abu al-Su'ud were partners. Others still were Sudanese, such as Zubayr Rahma Mansur (1830–1930), a Ja'ali who was then a trader in the Bahr al-Ghazal. In this period, slave-raiding was to some extent a by-product of the ivory trade. As ivory became more difficult to obtain by peaceful means, force was used. This led traders to set up large armed bands, and they used for this both Sudanese (notably from the western nomad tribes) and slaves. By the 1860s, for example, Zubayr had actual slave-armies scouring the Bahr al-Ghazal. The taking of hostages soon became a common way of forcing people to hand over the required goods, and the hostages could themselves be disposed of on the slave market. As local conditions became more difficult, traders increasingly took advantage of local conflicts and encouraged internecine fighting which brought in slaves and cattle, thus compensating for decreasing revenue from ivory. In the space of a few years, slaves became the chief product of the trade.

At the same time, European traders who had contributed to this situation became fewer and more dependent on their Sudanese or Egyptian partners who controlled commercial circuits and had access to political circles, notably at the northern end of the routes. Growing public reprobation of such activities may also have played a role. Only the more unscrupulous continued to defy public morality. Chief of these was a Maltese, Andrea de Bono who, together with his nephew, Amabile Mussu, was in partnership with Aqqad. Muslim traders themselves had to take changing circumstances into account and justify themselves legally by using a khedival decree authorizing the personnel of Khartum to have slave retinues; 'a loophole which made possible the transport and sale of thousands of slaves annually' (P. M. Holt).

The trade was in fact protected by the complicity of all since most strata of Egyptian and Sudanese society derived profit from these lucrative activities, this being true both of the wealthy northerners who masterminded them and the poorer Sudanese who carried them out.

A more precise assessment of the Sudan slave trade in the quarter of a century preceding the Mahdiyya involves finer spatio-temporal distinctions with respect to three different inroads being made into central Africa. There was the south-west trade in the Bahr al-Ghazal and Dar Fur; the southern trade up the Nile, and the eastern trade on the borders of Abyssinia.

The first was largely dominated by the fact that the Dar Fur Sultanate had repulsed the Egyptian attack and that state involvement was here replaced by the individual actions of ruthless men who, if they succeeded, became merchant princes ruling over large territories by means of their armies. This was more particularly the case of Zubayr Rahma Mansur whose power grew between 1860 and 1870 until, in 1873, he was able to overrun one of the more powerful of the western tribes, the Rizayqat, who were under Dar Furi suzerainty. He followed this up by attacking the Sultanate itself and in July 1874, Ibrahim, the Dar Fur ruler, was killed. Egypt countenanced this independent move and the *hukumdar* received instructions to meet Zubayr at al-Fashir and establish him as governor with the title of Pasha. The Turkiyya was thus established in the sultanate which Egypt had failed to conquer half a century earlier, Zubayr himself was left in full command, and the Egyptian government was thus to sanction a capitalist and military undertaking which it was affecting to condemn. Nonetheless, as abolition became a major theme of international discussion, Zubayr Pasha was seen by the Khedive as a somewhat compromising ally and when the latter came to Cairo on an official visit in 1876, he was retained as a virtual prisoner. In Dar Fur and Bahr al-Ghazal, his slave-trading principality nonetheless survived under the leadership of Zubayr's son, Sulayman, who even extended the range of his activities westwards and opened new *zariba*-s or slave markets. In the meantime, however, the Egyptians prepared an expedition to reduce the independent province and Sulayman was declared a rebel. Illustrative of changing times is the fact that the military forces sent out were placed under the command of a European in Khedival service, the Italian, Gessi. In 1879, Sulayman and most of his lieutenants negotiated conditions of surrender. In spite of guarantees obtained, Sulayman and 11 of his companions were shot with Gordon's approval: 'Thus does God make gaps in His enemies' was his comment. That this did not mark the end of the merchant princes of the west is shown up by the subsequent history of Rabih, a man born in the province of Khartum who had served in Muhammad 'Ali's army before linking his destiny to that of Zubayr. Not trusting Egyptian promises, he refused to surrender with Sulayman and fled to the Lake Chad area where he set up an independent principality. Not only did he overrun the region and in 1893–4 destroy what remained of Bornu sovereignty, but he launched a religious movement on the Mahdi model and attempted to stave off French intrusions in the Chad area. He was ultimately killed by the French in battle in 1901.

The southern trade up the Nile valley does not have the same feudal characteristics but was carried out on more strictly capitalist lines, involving a great number of traders out for mere profit. The last trading outpost which could be reached by shipping was Gondokoro which by the 1850s had become a lawless but active centre. Though beyond Gondokoro navigation was impossible and the marshy overland route difficult, this did not deter the slave-raiders who from the late 1840s had sent out military parties which raided the region as far south as the Great Lakes. The majority of the slaves came from this region and it is there that the lowest value was set on human life. In the 1870s of the 10 000 or so slaves sent out to Egypt, possibly as many as 75 per cent came up the Nile. Conditions of transport and sale were particularly atrocious. As supply increased and demand decreased, the price set on human lives fell proportionately, a slave selling at a mere £2. Human beings were treated as mere chattels, herded on the boats which had come from Khartum to Gondokoro when northern winds blew. Death rates were as high as 50 per cent. Slavery combined with capitalist exploitation deprived the unhappy victims of every shred of human dignity.

I visited the establishments of the various slave merchants; these were arranged under large tents of matting, and contained many young girls of extreme beauty, ranging from nine to seventeen years of age. These lovely captives, of a rich brown tint, with delicately formed features, and eyes like those of the gazelle, were natives of the Galla, on the borders of Abyssinia, from which country they were brought by Abyssinian traders to be sold for the Turkish harems. Although beautiful, these girls were useless for hard labour; they quickly fade away and die unless kindly treated.

Samuel Baker, description of a slave market on the Abyssinian border

In the east a still different picture applied because of specific political and commercial factors. Egyptian expansion there was largely checked by the resistance of Ethiopia and the fighting capacity of border populations. Ethiopia under Theodorus II (1855–68) and later under King John (1872–8), was not only to withstand pressures but to inflict severe defeats on the

Egyptian army in 1875 and 1876. In spite of this, a highly lucrative trade was carried out on the border because of the high value set on Abyssinian goods consisting of such precious commodities as rhinoceros horns, an expensive aphrodisiac, and girl slaves who had the reputation of being 'black Venuses' and were a luxury in wealthy households, notably in Arabia. The use of the Red Sea ports further encouraged the trade although by the 1860s prices were falling, a slave bringing in about £20, an ugly woman fetching as little as £5 – 'the price of a donkey' as Samuel Baker, the British traveller, noted.

This brief outline points to the fact that over and above the ideological confrontation of East and West – the latter criticizing Islam on the grounds that it accepted slavery while hypocritically ignoring the condition of workers in industrial countries, the former pointing to what was, in general practice, the mild treatment of slaves in Muslim households and the widespread custom of granting them their freedom – the slave-trade partook of the cruelty of a capitalist era.

Links between European abolitionism and imperial expansion

The unbridled capitalism of the 1860s can also be seen as the forerunner of colonial penetration even if this was largely to justify itself on the moral grounds of abolition.

The transformation is apparent in the trading circles themselves; the Europeans in Khartum whose connection with the early trade has been pointed out, themselves adopted airs of Victorian respectability in the 1860s. Their conversion to abolitionist views won for them official favours. We thus find George Thibaut, after 40 years' trading, being recommended for the post of French consul in Khartum by the consul-general in Cairo who, in 1860, described him as a 'man of honour and experience'. His British colleague was to be John Petherick who had already acted as honorary vice-consul before being upgraded to full consular status. They were the vanguard of imperial interest and were soon joined by other European colleagues. By the time the Mahdist revolution broke out, there were Italian, American, Belgian, Austrian, and Greek consuls in Khartum.

European claims that the 'white man's burden' involved bringing civilization and Christianity to backward peoples, thus freeing them both from their native savagery and oriental oppression, was further illustrated by the Christian missions set up in Africa, Sudan being no exception. The Roman Catholic Mission was first on the spot and in 1853 it set up a permanent post at Gondokoro. Most of these undertakings were short-lived, including an attempt by Franciscans to open a mission on the Upper Nile in 1862. Efforts in Khartum were more successful and the Roman Catholic Mission ran a hospital there. It was also able to send nuns and priests out into the west and a Catholic centre functioned notably at al-'Ubayyid in Kurdufan. Over and beyond their humanitarian activities, these establishments also had more or less clearly perceived political overtones. Samuel Baker, who visited an Austrian missionary at St Croix on the Upper Nile in 1863, reported that the man had, over a bottle of wine, volunteered the information that the mission was really a pretext for spying out the country in order to pave the way for a Habsburg colony.

One may also view with mixed feelings the exploration of Sudan and its outlying districts during the 1860s. The 'discovery' of Africa by sponsored European travellers is also part of the progressive takeover of Africa by imperial powers, even if scientific aims are apparent to all, whilst the endurance and capacity of observation of some travellers is still a source of admiration today. The scientific quest which in some cases went hand-in-hand with missionary zeal is the necessary ideological complement to a political undertaking to which it contributed not only a rational justification but a Romantic aura. In this period the mysterious sources of the Nile are the eastern counterpart of legendary Timbuktu and both were put over as symbolic goals of human effort. In 1858, the Royal Geographical Society, supported by the British government, sent out Sir Richard Burton (perhaps better known for his translation of the *Thousand and One Nights*) with John Hanning Speke to Lake Tanganyika. Speke pushed on to Lake Victoria which he rightly identified as one of the sources of the Nile. On a subsequent journey with a fellow officer, John Grant, he returned to Lake Victoria and from there went to Gondokoro via the African kingdom of Buganda-Bunyoro. Whilst in Gondokoro (1863) he met a famous couple, the British traveller Samuel Baker and his companion Florence. The Great Lakes were also visited by David Livingstone. Moreover the desert axis Tripoli-Murzuq-Chad was now explored in terms of relations with the eastern or western trans-Saharan routes and Gustav Nachtigal who in 1868 went on a mission from Tripoli to Bornu, made the return journey by way of Wadday and Kurdufan, ultimately reaching Cairo in 1874. The record of his travels, *Sahara und Sudan* (published in 1879–81 and recently translated into English) was the major contribution to European knowledge of the area between the Nile Valley and the eastern part of the Sahara. That such missions were also part of the European scamble is demonstrated by the fact that Nachtigal's journey had been financed by the King of Prussia who wished to establish relations with the ruler of Bornu. Nachtigal's later mission to Cameroun (1884) which set up a German protectorate there, further brings the point home.

Egypt itself used similar methods and showed its willingness to subsidize explorations with a view to making territorial claims. These as we shall now see were successful with respect to Equatoria but failed further south in the region of the Great Lakes, the imperial alliance of Britain and Egypt being further revealed. As heroes of this adventure we once again find Florence (circa 1841–1916) and Samuel Baker (1821–93). Samuel Baker, after his first successful exploration of the eastern tributaries of the Nile (1862) and Lake Mwitanzige, renamed by him Lake Albert (1864), had returned to London where he became a boon companion of the Prince of Wales. When the latter paid an official visit to Egypt in 1869, he not only took Sir Samuel along with him, but made a suggestion to the Khedive: why should Baker not be sent out to annex the region south of Gondokoro to Egyptian Sudan? Further prospects were envisaged, both the high moral duty of suppressing the slave trade and the more material one of trade by means of a protected road set up between Sudan and the Great Lakes. This the British, of course, integrated into their larger strategy of a zone of influence extending from Alexandria to the Cape. The Khedive was led to approve of the plan and he made generous allowances for the expedition. Baker was to be in command, with the rank of Pasha and a £10 000 a year salary. He was to have 1400 men and a number of boats, besides a 13-ton steamer. The expedition itself cost the Egyptian Treasury £800 000 and was a partial failure.

The Bakers reached Gondokoro in April 1871 and made slow progress as they dallied on the way to uphold Khedival glory (Gondokoro was thus renamed Isma'iliyya) and condemn the slave trade. The latter, as they noted, had spread as 'a running sore' since their former passage. Several consignments of slaves were freed on the way, including some at Gondokoro where the governor himself was involved in the trade. As they pushed on, the Bakers themselves were forced to have recourse to the slave-traders for protection and, indeed, to imitate their ways, as the fate meted out to the Bari tribe showed, the latter being 'punished' both for its insolence in refusing Egyptian sovereignty and in order to obtain stores. In Bunyoro, they found the country largely depopulated and hostile. A meeting was nonetheless arranged with King Kabarega at Lake Kyogo (April 1872) and the Bakers seized on the occasion to solemnly hoist the Turkish flag and proclaim a Khedival Protectorate (May 1872). The Bakers nonetheless sensed growing hostility and hastily organized a retreat which was made difficult by the marshy ground and constant attacks by Africans armed with spears who were secretly encouraged, it would seem, by the slave-traders. A last stand was made at Fatiko, now in Equatoria, where a fort was built. The remnants of the expedition only reached Gondokoro in Spring 1873. Baker in April over-confidently asserted: 'The slave trade is at an end – and Egypt extends to the Equator'. The claim could hardly be substantiated. It nonetheless led to the setting up of Egyptian control over the northern part of the area, namely the present Sudanese province of Equatoria.

The integration of the southern provinces was marked by an expansion of European involvement in the region, although this was carried out officially in the Khedive's name and under the guise of the Turkiyya. This was more particularly demonstrated by the appointment of Europeans to most of the key posts in the colony. In Equatoria, Baker's departure was followed up by the appointment of Gordon as governor (February 1874). His instructions were to set up an Egyptian administration and 'to bring the populations into the way of civilization'. The fact that Abu al-Su'ud, the famous slave-dealer, was put on Gordon's staff gives a curious twist to this. In 1871, Khedive Isma'il had appointed a Swiss, Munzinger, as Governor of Massawa and the Red Sea coastal district. In the Bahr al-Ghazal, the Italian Gessi was appointed governor in 1878 after the defeat of Sulayman, Zubayr Pasha's son. Lupton, a British merchant navy officer, succeeded him in 1881 after having served for a time under Gordon in Equatoria. In the latter province Emin Bey took over from Gordon in 1878. Emin Bey, whose real name was Edward Schnitzler, also commanded a military expedition to Bunyoro in 1877 which however failed to capitalize on Baker's earlier efforts. In Dar Fur, an Austrian, Rudolf Karl von Slatin, became governor after having occupied a similar function in Dara from 1879 to 1881. Gordon himself was Governor-General of Sudan from 1877 to 1880.

Under Gordon's strong moral urge ('I go up alone with an Infinite Almighty God to direct and guide me') an all-out fight against slave-traders was undertaken. Gordon chased them out of Equatoria and destroyed their zariba-s, similar efforts being undertaken in the south-west by Gessi and Slatin.

This had economic consequences which directly contributed to the rise of the Mahdiyya. The local economy, as already indicated, was largely dependent on slavery. In the absence of structural change, the suppression of the trade and a decline in domestic slavery led to considerable hardship in Sudan where both agriculturalists of the Nile Valley and nomad tribes were hard hit. The fact that these changes were promoted under European influence and carried out by Europeans in khedival service led to further condemnation of the Turkiyya. The Mahdist message was a collective Sudanese response to this situation.

SELECTED READING LIST

I – The Western approach
Aubin, E., *Le Maroc d'aujourd'hui*, (Paris, 1904).
Ayache, G., 'Aspects de la crise financière au Maroc après l'expédition espagnole de 1860', *Revue Historique*, 220, 1958.
Barlett, C. J., 'Great Britain and the Spanish change of policy towards Morocco in June 1878', *Bulletin of the Institute of Historical Research*, 30, 1957.
Burke, E., *Prelude to Protectorate in Morocco*, (Chicago and London, 1976).
Cruickshank, E. F., *Morocco at the Parting of the Ways. The Story of native protection to 1885*, (Philadelphia, 1935).
Flournoy, F. R., *British Policy towards Morocco in the Age of Palmerston (1830–1912)*, (Baltimore, 1935).
Laroui, A., *Les Origines Sociales et Culturelles du Nationalisme Marocain (1830–1912)*, (Paris, 1977).
Lecuyer, M. C. and Serrano, C., *La Guerre d'Afrique et ses répercussions en Espagne. 1859–1904*, (Paris, 1976).
Miège, J. L., *Le Maroc et l'Europe*, (Paris, 1961–4).

II – Inroads on the Sahara
Barth, H., *Travels and Discoveries in North and Central Africa*, (London, 1857–8).
Barrows, L. C., 'The Merchants and General Faidherbe: Aspects of European Expansion in the 1850s', *Revue francçaise d'histoire d'Outre-Mer*, 61, 1974.
Boahen, A. A., *Britain, the Sahara, and the Western Sudan 1788–1861*, (Oxford, 1964).
Chamberlain, M. E., *The Scramble for Africa*, (London, 1974).
Ikime, O. (ed.), *Leadership in 19th-century Africa*, (London, 1974).
Martin, B. G., *Muslim Brotherhoods in 19th-century Africa*, (Cambridge, 1976).
Mercer, J., *Spanish Sahara*, (London, 1976).
Parsons, F. V., 'The North-West African Company and the British Government, 1875–1895', *Historical Journal*, 1, 1958.
Pascon, P., 'Du Sacerdoce au négoce: la maison d'Ilîgh', *Annales*, 35, 1980.
Vilar, J.-B., 'Ayuda española a Marruecos en la crisis de las protecciones consulares (1878–1879)', 381, *Africa*, 1973.
Zaytoun, F. S., 'Cape Juby', *The Scottish Geographical Magazine*, 13, 1897.

III – The Eastern approach
Adeleye, R. A., 'Râbih Fad'lallâh, 1879–1893: exploits and impact on political relations in Central Sudan', *Journal of the Historical Society of Nigeria*, 5, 1970
Brett, M. (ed.), *Northern Africa. Islam and Modernization*, (London, 1973).
Gessi, R., *Sette anni nel Sudan Egiziano*, (Milan, 1891).
Hassan, Y. F., *The Arabs and the Sudan*, (Edinburgh, 1967).
Hill, R. L., *Egypt in the Sudan, 1820–1881*, (London, 1959).
Hill, R. L., *Slatin Pacha*, (London, 1965).
Holt, P. M., 'Holy Families and Islam in the Sudan', *Princeton Near-East Papers*, 4, 1967.
Holt, P. M. and Daly, M. W., *The History of the Sudan*, (London, new edition, 1979).
O'Fahey, R. S., 'Slavery and the Slave Trade in Dar Fur', *Journal of African History*, 113, 1973.
Petherick, J., *Egypt, the Soudan and Central Africa*, (Edinburgh and London, 1861).
Shukri, M., *The Khedive Ismail and Slavery in the Sudan (1863–1879)*, (Cairo, 1937).

Stuhlmann, F. (ed.), *Die Tagebücher von Dr. Emin Pascha*, (Hamburg, 1919).
Warburg, G., 'Sudan in the 18th and 19th centuries', Milson, M. (ed.), *Society and Political Structure in the Arab World*, 1973.

IV – Imperial progress in the wake of the slave-trade

Baker, S., *Ismailia. A Narrative of the Expedition to Central Africa*, (London, 1874).
Casada, J. A., 'British Exploration in East Africa. A bibliography with Commentary', 5, *Africana Journal*, 1974.
Crabitès, P., *Gordon. The Sudan and Slavery*, (London, 1933).
Dunbar, A. R., *A History of Bunyoro-Kitara*, (Nairobi, 1965).
Gray, R. A., *A History of the Southern Sudan. 1839–1889*, (Oxford, 1961).
Hall, R., *Lovers on the Nile. An Idyll of African Exploration*, (London, 1980).
Nachtigal, G. H., *Sahara und Sudan*, (Berlin, 1879–81; translated into English by A. G. B. and H. J. Fisher, London, 1974).
Shaw, A. G. L., *Great Britain and the Colonies*, 1815–1865, (London, 1970).

Stiansen, E. (Ed.) ... Basel ... Dr. Abir Hagan Hamdan: Pr
Warburg, G. 'Sudan under Wingate: Administration in ... Milton ...
... Ibn Khaldun, O ...

El - Imperial power ...
Bates, C. Imperial ... Account of the Expedition ... Central Africa (1894)
Gandhi, J. A. British Expansion in East Africa ... Intelligence papers ... commercial ...
... Journal, 1977
Chailley, J. Dernier ... The Arab ... and State (1910) London (1970)
Dunlop, A. B. A History of Slavery, Anjuan (Uganda 1967)
Gray, R. A. A History of the southern Sudan ... 1839-1889 (1961)
Hill, R. Ancient ... Sudan An Aid to ... biograph ... Sudanese ... 1821 ... 1951
Santandrea, G. H. A History of ... Tribes ... B ...
(1964) London (1971)
Shaw, R. O. ... 'The Central Organisation of ... 1821 ...

PART IV
RESISTANCE IN THE 1880s

INTRODUCTION

Pressures increasingly exerted on North Africa by imperialism show the countries involved as being on the defensive, seeking after and failing to find self-preservation through a wide range of attitudes including imitation of European methods and a reliance on tradition. Such a view is itself largely imperialist and reflects a European-centred perspective which defines countries in terms of those factors of change which were seen as characterizing 19th-century history and which, according to standards set by dominant ideology, were classified either positively as 'modern' or negatively as 'traditional'. Such appreciations inadequately express the way North Africans themselves saw the process in which they were engaged. Indeed a North African point of view would not only tend to reverse this perspective but point to an overall capacity of Islam to face up to the challenge of aggression.

Two aspects of this response should be underlined. The first is that heightened awareness of a changing world and its potential or effective dangers, was built up over time through accumulated experience. The elaborate political responses of the 1880s which will be studied in this section are a far cry from the Alexandrians' panic when Bonaparte's army landed. The second is that this is part of a collective process which, though it involved human actors (Algerians in 1830 were obviously more aware of what European rule meant than the inhabitants of the Sahara at that time, and the experience differed from that, let us say, of the Sudanese during the Turkiyya), individual awareness was melted into an overall self-consciousness and sense of urgency. Men such as Sulayman al-Halabi or 'Abd al-Qadir played their part in creating a sense of public involvement by the public interest and emotion their fates aroused.

This points to the underlying unity of the Muslim world and the socio-religious structure which upheld it, bringing the common bond of religion to the fore. It not only provided a shared world-view but the means through which this was actualized on transnational lines. Particular emphasis must here be placed on the Holy Places as the centre of gravity of the Muslim world, one where, through the yearly pilgrimage, world-wide interaction was fostered. This was not only expressed by the subjective reactions of thousands of pilgrims but also by such institutionalized means as the teaching of reputed *'ulama*, the rulings of *mufti*-s, the spread of information and the building-up of attitudes through fraternities. The latter were indeed increasingly influential as spreaders of political messages on transnational and even transcontinental lines. A closer look at this Islamic infrastructure points to the role of men who, though not in the front of the political stage, made major contributions to this heightened self-awareness. Among such major figures whom historians rarely take into account, are men such as Ahmad bin Idris al-Fasi (1760–1837), a Moroccan as his name indicates, who had settled in the Hijaz in 1818 and become one of the most eminent teachers of the Holy City before conflicts with staider *'ulama* led him to settle at 'Asir, further south along the Red Sea coast, where the Wahhabi-s protected him. Ahmad bin Idris, by his personal influence among pilgrims from all parts of the Muslim world, contributed significantly to a neo-sufi revival which combined both the more rigorist principles of the Wahhabi-s and the mystical practices (*tasawuf*) of the *tariqa*-s. His more famous disciples included Muhammad bin 'Ali al-Sanusi and Muhammad al-'Uthman al-Mirghani. The former will be studied in this section since he set up a militant order in Libya – the Sanusiyya – which effectively resisted European encroachments both in Cyrenaica and the Sahara, whilst the latter has already been mentioned as the founder of the Mirghaniyya which, in Sudan, opposed the Mahdi's claim to being the 'Guided One'. Descendants of Ahmad bin Idris also set up a local dynasty at 'Asir whilst the Ahmadiyya-Idrisiyya which derives both from Ahmad bin Idris and Ahmad al-Tijani was active elsewhere in the Middle East, Asia, and the Malay Peninsula (where it was introduced in 1895). In a similar way one might point to the influence at the other end of the social scale – since Ahmad bin Idris's impact was more characteristically in lower strata of pilgrim groups – of higher sufi initiation, notably through *shaykh*-s of the great (*akbar*) tradition going back to the mystics of the past such as Ibn 'Arabi. This has already been mentioned as a family tradition into which the Amir 'Abd al-Qadir was initiated by his father. Here mention will be made of 'Abd al-Qadir's pilgrimage to Mecca in 1863–5 in the course of which he showed his deep interest in esoteric doctrines by seeking initiation from Muhammad al-Fasi. Muhammad al-Fasi was yet another Moroccan who had gone to the Holy Places and who resided there until his death in 1872. He was one of the last great spiritual guides in the Akbariyya line of transmission. The Amir's prestigious position as the victim of imperialism living out his last days in exile in Damascus owes perhaps as much to the secret web of the mystic tradition as to the legendary heroism of the early Algerian resistance, or perhaps it would be truer to say that both are closely intertwined in the overall pattern of Muslim self-awareness.

This brings out the capacity of Islamic social structures and cultural values to uphold identity, acting as General Lyautey – the first French Resident-General in Morocco in 1912 – once put it, 'as a sounding-board'. European-promoted changes themselves played a part in this whether by providing better, far-flung means of transport and communication, or by imperial policies which brought home a sense of danger, especially when, as was often the case in the latter part of the 19th century, this resulted in free or forcible exile of leading Muslim personalities. At Damascus, for example, not only Algerians and Tunisians, but also Indians, Egyptians, and Indonesians, brought with them and shared their respective experiences of colonialism.

In this section more typical and important movements of national resistance will be studied in historical context, the impact these movements had being largely determined by their adaptation to local conditions. One should nonetheless bear in mind the underlying pattern which has been sketched out and which brought to the fore the *jihad* as the conceptual framework through which Muslims elaborated on their attitudes in the face of the threat imperialism constituted not only in a material sense but also in a cultural and religious sense – as an attack on Islamic values and self-confidence. The *jihad* in its dual meaning – the fight against the enemy within the community, i.e. evil, and the enemy without, i.e. the foreign aggressor – underscores the connection between two types of reactions, arbitrarily and indeed wrongly dissociated by most European observers: reform implying a rigorist attitude which does not exclude facing up to and integrating changes, including those characterizing European superiority in various fields of activity, and an introspective critical attitude more concerned with pointing out decline since the pristine purity of the early Muslim community led by Muhammad and his four immediate successors. Both integrate dialectically past and future, belief in an early Golden Age and the will to move through a dark era of corruption and defeat to an ultimate phase of Muslim reassertion. Expectation of the Mahdi, 'the Guided One', who according to Muslim eschatology was to help reverse the trend of decline, is therefore part of the spirit of the age, further heightened by a millenarian outlook on the 14th century of the Hijra calendar which began in 1882. Reformism and fundamentalism are thus the twin poles of the Muslim effort to integrate their experiences with those of the political movements of the time, in an attempt to reaffirm their world-view and stake an optimistic historical claim.

CHAPTER 13

THE 'ARABI PHASE UPRISING: FROM MUTINY TO NATIONALISM

The outstanding position a man such as 'Arabi Pasha had, both in his own time and in the later nationalist pantheon, in spite of what was a short-lived venture to resist khedival corruption and weakness, demonstrates the keener and more critical self-view among North Africans which was in the making in the latter part of the 19th century.

THE 'ARABI PASHA MOVEMENT: FACTS AND EVENTS

The 'Arabi Pasha movement developed among a limited circle of Egyptian army officers in the 1870s. They set up a more or less secret association where junior officers who were for the most part from rural Egyptian society had occasion to criticize government policy and more specifically the higher military hierarchy. The latter at the time was still largely dominated by court families of foreign ('Turco-Circassian') origins. Criticism was, in fact, on professional rather than political lines, the officers complaining of the fact that higher ranks in the army were not open to them. They also criticized army management and more particularly the incompetence which had led to the disastrous defeat of two Egyptian armies sent out to Abyssinia in 1875 and 1876. In the course of the campaign 10 000 Egyptians had died.

The movement came out into the open when a demonstration was staged in front of 'Abdin Palace on 18 February 1879. This marks a turning point, since, although the leaders of what came near to being a mutiny stressed essentially professional causes of discontent and, moreover, by their submission, showed their respect for established authority, a new political stand was taken. Thus the prime minister, Nubar, and his two European colleagues in the cabinet were ill-treated and insulted. More significant still was 'Arabi Pasha's claim that 'the army had come there on behalf of the Egyptian people'.

The situation which prevailed in Egypt in 1879 gave heightened significance to army protest. The political atmosphere was strained in view of the fact that Khedive Isma'il had recently been deposed by the Sultan and that the new ruler, Muhammad Tawfiq, was seen as a puppet in European hands. The economic situation was no less explosive, particularly in the rural areas, because of the oppressive way in which the international debt was managed. The officers became the spokesmen of the nation and, as Sir Auckland Colvin then British controller-general in Egypt noted, 'Arabi Pasha was 'the real ruler of the country. He had the army at his back'.

The movement's objectives in this period were essentially better state management which alone could save Egypt from European encroachments.

This, it was believed, could only be achieved by giving the Egyptian elite a greater say in the running of affairs. In 1881, therefore, the movement demanded that the cabinet should resign; that a parliament should be convened; and that the armed forces should be increased. This in no way implied an attack on the khedival system as such, and it was within the framework of existing institutions that the officers hope to promote reforms.

In this they had the support of the new petty bourgeoisie, notably the civil servants who were largely recruited from upgraded rural families, and also that of the *shaykh al-balad* class which was preponderant in the Assembly of Delegates. The army officers' secret association had itself opened up its ranks to civilians and evolved into a political party, the *Hizb al-Watani* or Patriotic Party. In the Assembly, delegates were calling for a parliament having more effective powers. A strife-ridden situation persisted throughout 1880 and 1881, coming to a head in January 1882 when khedival prestige was seen as being definitely undermined. Two factors more particularly contributed to this: the fact that the Khedive had to give way to popular pressure and nominate a cabinet in which the opposition was largely represented ('Arabi Pasha himself became Minister of War) on the one hand and, on the other, a joint Anglo-French note on 8 January 1882, which pledged support to the Khedive, further incensing Egyptians who saw their ruler as a mere stooge. The Khedive, it was known, was about to ask the Sultan to help him re-establish his authority in Egypt; moreover in May a joint Anglo-French fleet arrived off Alexandria. Popular feeling rose to unprecedented heights, expressing itself in anti-European and anti-Christian riots in the course of which several people were killed. A Turkish mission arrived, but to no effect except to increase tension. The Khedive fled and ultimately found refuge aboard a British ship.

In Cairo the opposition took over, appointing a government of emergency. Some *'ulama* signed a *fetwa* declaring khedival rule illegal. People rallied to the movement and a new slogan 'Egypt for the Egyptians' came to the fore. Fraternity *shaykh*-s (notably those of the Khalwatiyya) were active in spreading news in Upper Egypt and Sudan, and calling upon people to support 'Arabi Pasha. Events in Egypt focused public opinion far and wide. Consuls reported agitation in various Muslim capitals and in Europe anti-imperialists came out in favour of 'Arabi Pasha, notably Wilfred Scawen Blunt (1840–1922), leader of a pro-Arab tendency in Britain. Political leaders nonetheless remained wary, not only the Sultan whose prestige was challenged, but also men such as the Great Sanusi in Cyrenaica who rightly foresaw that 'Arabi Pasha's uprising would play into foreign hands and lead to British intervention. This was not understood by many of his countrymen and Libyans on their own initiative formed a military corps which went to Alexandria to uphold the movement and defend the town in the event of a landing of foreign troops.

The British intervention

In the light of the widespread popular following 'Arabi Pasha could command and the way in which people spontaneously identified themselves with him, the course of action that he followed will no doubt appear disappointing. Events show him up as a poor tactician and as less of a revolutionary than a professional soldier not prepared to accept civilian involvement in the situation he had created. Indeed, as we shall now see, he had little faith in the ordinary Egyptian whom he had extolled.

Whilst the French and the Ottomans were discussing the possibilities of common action and the extent of each nation's participation, the British purely and simply landed in Egypt. On 13–14 July 1882, an expeditionary corps of Indian troops under Sir Garnet Wolseley was landed and occupied Alexandria. Once again we find Alexandria abandoned to its fate, little effort being made to organize resistance in an urban setting. The army had set up its headquarters at al-Kafr al-Dawar where, in official style, 'Arabi Pasha declared that 'irreconcilable war existed between the Egyptians and the English'. In spite of this, go-betweens were numerous, trying to negotiate a settlement acceptable to 'Arabi Pasha, to the Khedive, and to the British. The tendency was towards compromise rather than all-out resistance.

The situation favoured the British in their march forward. The Egyptian army was attacked at al-Tal al-Kabir on 13 September, and severely defeated. Once again 'Arabi Pasha had the possibility of withdrawing to Cairo and, with civilian help, organizing an effective resistance in the capital where the invaders, in spite of superior equipment and discipline, would have been hard-pressed. Once again the professional reflex and the soldier's traditional distrust of civilians were uppermost. Declaring that he wished to spare Cairo and its population, 'Arabi Pasha and his army surrendered. The road to the capital was open and the British walked in. With them they brought a much-discredited Khedive.

A contemporary witness notes Tunisian reactions at the fall of 'Arabi Pasha . . .

When the Tunisian Arabs learned that the man of whom they hoped so much was defeated and a prisoner, they felt almost as keenly as their Egyptian brethren the bitterness of despair. There is no doubt whatever that our victory in Egypt saved France a third expedition to Tunis, and crushed in the bud an Arab rising which would have extended from Cairo to Algiers.

A. M. Broadley, *How we defended Arabi* (London, 1894)

'Arabi Pasha, his chief supporters, and some 3000 men were handed over to khedival authority and thrown into prison (19 September) where the Turco-Circassian soldiery severely ill-treated them. 'Ali Fahmi Pasha, though wounded, was left without medical care. Many others, including the famous reformist thinker, Muhammad 'Abduh, were beaten up and tortured, either mentally or physically. One wonders what their fate might have been had not international pressure been brought to bear to ensure a regular trial. The British, who wished to avoid an outcry in the Muslim world and to establish their control over Egypt with the least possible trouble, were particularly adamant that no executions take place.

On 3 December 1882 began the trial of the Egyptian nationalists. Popular feeling went out to the accused and expressions of sympathy came from all sections of society, from the man in the street to khedival circles themselves, the princesses secretly sending gifts and offers of help. 'Arabi Pasha and his companions were – and this was something new and not to be forgotten –

> *Letter from Ahmad Rifat Bey to his English lawyer, A. M. Broadley.*
>
> In a few days you will return to Tunis and we shall go into exile. People will doubtless ask you much about Egypt, for any decision as to her ultimate destiny is as far off as ever. Our National aspirations are for the moment crushed, but do not believe they are dead. Our enemies are for the moment triumphant, and their voice has all the strength and loudness of success. They say Egyptian Nationalism (which I describe as the banding together of the oppressed in search of justice) has never existed at all; even if they admit there was such a spirit abroad they deny that Ahmed Arabi was its legitimate exponent, and they maintain, moreover, that Egyptian aspirations are aimless, because the people of Egypt are incapable of self-government, and must consequently be condemned to perpetual leading-strings (*tutelle*). Others go even further than this, and say Arabi frightened all Egypt into patriotism.
>
> from A. M. Broadley, *How we defended Arabi*, (London, 1884).

national heroes. 'Ahmad 'Arabi, the Egyptian' as he used to sign himself, could claim that he had been 'elected by the tacit and unanimous vote of five millions of his fellow-countrymen'. He was nonetheless condemned to death, the sentence being commuted to perpetual exile from Egypt and its dependencies. The same verdict was passed on Muhmud Sami, 'Ali Fahmi, 'Abd al'Al, Tulbas Pasha, Muhmud Fahmi, and Ya'qub Sami. Together with their families and a few servants, they were sent off to Colombo where 'Arabi Pasha remained until 1901. That year he was allowed to return to his native land where he died in 1911.

The ideology of 'Arabi Pasha's movement

'Arabi Pasha's political views and projects can be seen with similarly mixed feelings: they are powerfully-stated demands for greater democracy and justice in the face of khedival despotism and oppression, but are, in fact, limited in scope and in no way imply any radical structural change in Egyptian society. One should, of course, beware of inferring actual policy from manifestos, particularly so when dealing with movements which would inevitably have evolved in action, this being particularly the case with early ill-fated expressions of nationalism which did not find an adequate context in which to actualize. Nonetheless it is clear that 'Arabi Pasha was for a reformist rule which would have promoted the higher strata of native Egyptians as opposed to the peasants on the one hand and the 'Turco-Circassian' ruling class on the other.

'Arabi Pasha, in this, was merely reflecting the changes which had taken place in Egypt since Muhammad 'Ali's time and which the viceroy and his successors had insufficiently taken into account. He was also building on those ideas which were in the making in the progressive fringe of the Muslim intelligentisia. 'Arabi Pasha thus saw himself as the spokesman of the Egyptian nation (*watan*). This view tended to recentre the national image on the peasantry whose secular toil in the mud of the Nile flood was seen as the key to national identity, the heritage of 'true-born Egyptians' whom 'Arabi Pasha further defined as Arab and Muslim, thus underplaying the Copt minority, a view later rejected by 20th-century Egyptian nationalists who, notably in the Wafd Party, worked for the unity of the two communities. For 'Arabi Pasha, as for later Egyptian leaders, the claim to a *fellah* origin was not so much rational as emotional, and their proclaimed identification with peasants was to some degree artificial and belied by their way of life and outlook. It nonetheless played a key role in their view of themselves and of Egypt and helped to redefine the abstract overall view of the Muslim *umma* in the context of late 19th-century nation states.

It was in the name of the oppressed peasantry that 'Arabi Pasha criticized the khedival system. The latter was defined first and foremost in terms of a foreign ruling class. 'Arabi Pasha considered it was made up of 'non-Egyptian Muslims'. Their relationship to Egyptians was one of exploitation and oppression: they controlled decision-making, occupied all the higher posts, considered Egyptians as inferiors and mere taxpayers, further depriving them of education and civil rights, and keeping them 'in the lowest state of degradation and ignorance'. Over and above this, the Khedive's dependence on the Sublime Porte came under criticism. Not only was Ottoman suzerainty a source of expenditure because of the yearly tribute paid by Egypt and because of Ottoman appeals to Egypt whenever wars took place (the most recent being the 1876–8 war with Russia), but it was from there, as 'Arabi Pasha noted, that, in recent years, a host of parasites had come who now acted in various private or administrative capacities. Among them were the moneylenders who toured the country areas, helping peasants pay their heavy taxes before depriving them of their lands and therefore of their means of subsistence. The moneylenders 'have sucked the very blood of the peasant, and ill-treat the natives whom they despoil'. The presence of Europeans in Egypt and the pressures the Great Powers were able to exert were themselves seen as the result of Ottoman complaisance.

What remedies did 'Arabi Pasha envisage? We find these set out in a memorandum criticizing the conclusions of an official report made by Lord Dufferin in 1882 at the British government's request. Nationalist objectives were the following:

    a) the severing of links between Egypt and Turkey;

    b) the choice of an Egyptian to rule Egypt. 'Arabi Pasha did not exclude the possibility that such a person might be found within the khedival family itself;

    c) the government of Egypt should be on constitutional lines. There was to be a parliament of two chambers, an elected Lower House and a modified form of the Assembly of Delegates to act as an Upper House.

    d) Reforms should be undertaken in various administrative and social fields, special insistence being placed on state education and on courts of law which should be 'in accordance with the customs and nature of the inhabitants'.

    e) All citizens were to be equal before the law and the tax-collector.

    f) Particular importance was attached in this and other documents to agriculture and the peasant's condition. The peasant was to be protected against usury, and corvée labour was to be abolished.

g) With respect to foreigners, 'Arabi Pasha expressed very moderate views, simply suggesting that such posts as could be filled by Egyptians should be, but that foreign employees should be maintained when there was a real need for them. Equal opportunities should be given to all and where foreigners were recruited, their salaries should not be immeasurably higher than those of Egyptians.

The reader will no doubt feel that if the nationalist ideal comes over forcefully, the political means to implement it are curiously vague and limited. 'Arabi Pasha gives specific instances of abuses such as corvée labour or the great number of highly paid foreigners, but it is difficult to interpret these criticisms as a far-reaching policy. The memorandum, like other contemporary documents he signed, often gives the impression of expressing limited reformist views characterized by insistence on detail and persons rather than showing deep insight into the structural changes which were necessary to make nationalist views meaningful. 'Arabi Pasha probably does not rank high as a politician or ideologue; and yet a persistent aura surrounds him, reflecting something far deeper: an almost symbolic embodiment of the imperial predicament. That this also results from 'Arabi's position in Egyptian society was evident to contemporaries and is relevant to historians today.

THE 'ARABI PASHA MOVEMENT IN ITS SOCIAL CONTEXT

Simple though it is, the signature 'Ahmad 'Arabi, the Egyptian' has behind it the backing of a changing social context in which a new image of the modern Egyptian was being put across. The social category to which 'Arabi Pasha belonged was itself at the forefront of change and made a signal contribution to the new self-image.

The reader may well ask why it should have been an army officer who should thus have established a privileged connection with the nation's cause and embodied its protest. The role played by military coups in more recent history indeed points to such a question and, in modern views, 'coup-hegemony' as the Pakistani, 'Ali Bhutto called it, is often seen as characteristic of Third World states. This is probably, however, an inadequate assessment of the political role of the army in Muslim states, which is backed up by a tradition of long-standing. In an early chapter of this book, it was pointed out that the two institutions through which a trans-tribal national view was made operative were the religious establishment, 'the men of the pen' and the military-cum-administrative body involving a professional army recruited on non-tribal lines, and often made up of foreigners. Although 'the men of the sword' share power with 'the men of the pen' and are indeed subordinate to them in a Muslim theocracy, holy men and scholars being posed in a transcendental relationship, it is in fact the 'men of the sword' who tend more specifically to embody state legitimacy especially when this is reduced to the narrow framework of the nation (*watan*) as opposed to the larger conceptual framework of the Muslim community (*umma*).

In Egypt itself the state institution had been built up by means of a military personnel, whether that of the *mamluk* sultanate or in its more modern form through Muhammad 'Ali's centralized government which continued to pose as non-local or 'Turco-Circassian'. At the same time the building-up of national power and the diminishing foreign recruitment had led to growing recourse in Egypt to local conscription. In the modern-type army (al-nizam al-jadid) higher ranking officers continued to come from the foreign ruling class, but junior officers were now often Egyptians. They came from a particular social category, that of rural notables (shaykh al-balad) who, as we shall now see, were the dynamic force in a changing pattern.

The role of the shaykh al-balad

As a social category on the rise, the shaykh al-balad or umda-s had come to the fore through Muhammad 'Ali's administrative and agricultural policy. As Lord Cromer noted, 'The Oumdehs and Sheikhs are the corner-stone on which the edifice of provincial society rests'. They were the village headmen whose social and economic status had been improved as they developed into privileged intermediaries between the state and the peasantry. When government farms were progressively given up in favour of a return to private ownership and tax-farming, the village headmen increased their holdings at the expense both of former state-managed farms and the villagers whose taxes they helped to pay. Rise in economic power led to social ambitions. One of the ways in which upgrading was sought was through the possibilities afforded by modern education, and children from the shaykh al-balad class were increasingly trained to fill administrative posts. The latter were still largely in the hands of the army and here too shaykh al-balad recruitment was underscored by the loss of a traditional privilege suspended by Muhammad 'Ali, namely exemption from military service. Moreover, military academies which were the central feature of early state education, had from the start accepted a limited number of young men from rural families. The civil service itself, as it developed, demanded new educational standards which were increasingly met by the more promising elements of the shaykh al-balad class. As educated Egyptians of rural origin came more and more to staff government departments, a new petty bourgeoisie appeared on the scene, notably in towns such as Cairo and Alexandria where they were characterized by the emphasis they placed on literacy, by a westernized way of life, by new forms of social intercourse including cafés and associations, and by the role such media as the press played in their lives. The possibilities of upgrading were, however, curtailed on the one hand by state policy privileging recruitment of non-Egyptians and even Europeans for higher posts, and, on the other, by economic difficulties with low civil service salaries being affected by the constant depreciation of local currency. Class identity developed not so much in contradistinction to a rural background, but in relation to it, as the home village continued to play an important part in the civil servants' lives, through frequent visits, marriages, and property, the common background further upholding ties between civilians and soldiers. The country-based shaykh al-balad category was itself conscious of wider national implications which were expressed in such partially democratic institutions as the early Assembly of Delegates in which village headmen had majority representation. A collective claim was thus made to a share in power, if not to an actual replacement of what was increasingly seen as the oriental despotism of khedival rule.

'Arabi Pasha should therefore be seen against the background of other leading figures having generally similar social views. 'Ali Pasha Mubarak (1824–93), for example, was also the son of a village headman. In fact his family had provided scholars and judges for many generations before becoming landowners on a tax-farming basis. When 'Ali Mubarak's father found himself unable to pay government dues, the family was forced to leave the village. 'Ali Mubarak, after early schooling, was sent to work for a tax-collector but, when the occasion arose, he was sent to one of Muhammad 'Ali's modern educational establishments and later sent for further education to the Egyptian Military Academy in Paris. Among the 34 students sent out in 1844 we also find Isma'il, the future Khedive. 'Ali Mubarak on his return worked in various capacities in military schools and in technical departments of ministries. Typical of changing times and of the upgrading of young educated Egyptians is the fact that 'Abbas Hilmi should have appointed him a member of his Privy Council, together with two other representatives of rural meritocracy. Between 1850 and 1854, 'Ali Mubarak was in charge of the country's educational policy and he increased the number of state schools. He was himself in this period promoted to the rank of colonel. Though not in favour under Sa'id Pasha, he was later re-established in office and occupied the post of under-secretary of state for education, for public works, and for *waqf* property. His chiefs efforts were in the field of education (1868).

'Ali Pasha Mubarak characteristically conceived reforms on technical rather than political lines, belief in efficiency not being pushed to the point where existing institutions were contested. 'Arabi Pasha had a similar outlook. 'Ali Mubarak's career illustrates the limits of their common political project. Not only did he collaborate with the Khedive Isma'il on whose account he went to Paris to negotiate one of the country's ruinous loans, but he was also a minister in the hated 1878 cabinet, derisively called 'the European Ministry'. He was also, however, a supporter of 'Arabi Pasha and shared his views. He thus became a member of the *Majlis al-'Urfi* or government of emergency set up in July 1882. When opposition between 'Arabi Pasha, the Khedive, and the British led to confrontation, 'Ali Pasha was on the committee which attempted to work out a compromise. Under the British, 'Ali Pasha Mubarak resumed his functions at the head of the department of education. He was to show little sympathy for the more radical opposition of later nationalists, nor was he a staunch advocate of European-promoted changes. In fact he remains a man of khedival times and a witness of the changes underway in Egypt in the second half of the 19th century which he described in the 20-volume long *Al-Khitat al Tawfiqiyya al-Jadida li-Misr al-Qahira wa Muduniha wa Biladiha al-Qadima wa al-Shahira*. Men such as 'Arabi Pasha or 'Ali Pasha Mubarak were, in fact, at the crossroads of interaction between state and society. Though critical of state management, they are nonetheless respectful of the institutions they served, and though claiming to speak for the depressed categories of Egyptian society, they also expressed the ambitions of a class society in the making.

Religion and the 'Arabi Pasha movement

Had the 'Arabi Pasha uprising been merely the expression of a struggle in terms of class stratification, its import would have been limited. It owes its

THE 'ARABI PASHA UPRISING: FROM MUTINY TO NATIONALISM

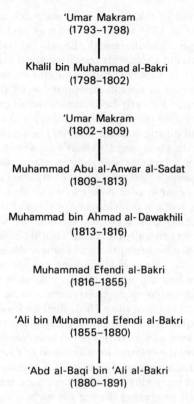

'Umar Makram
(1793–1798)

Khalil bin Muhammad al-Bakri
(1798–1802)

'Umar Makram
(1802–1809)

Muhammad Abu al-Anwar al-Sadat
(1809–1813)

Muhammad bin Ahmad al- Dawakhili
(1813–1816)

Muhammad Efendi al-Bakri
(1816–1855)

'Ali bin Muhammad Efendi al-Bakri
(1855–1880)

'Abd al-Baqi bin 'Ali al-Bakri
(1880–1891)

Fig. 13.1 *Holders of the post of* naquib al-ashraf *1793–1895* (from F. de Jong, *Turuq and Turuq-linked Institutions in nineteenth-century Egypt.*)

impact to a large degree to parallel changes in the religious establishment and these, in turn, upheld the movement and opened it up to heightened awareness of collective identity, setting on foot new trends of affirmation which Arabs were a little later to refer to as the *nahda* or renaissance.

Muhammad 'Ali's efforts to promote a centralized, state-dominated society had necessarily involved an indirect onslaught on the religious establishment in order to reduce its social influence. A wedge had been driven into the up to then well-knit corps of scholars and holy men by means of a viceregally appointed *shaykh* of the main sharifian families who undertook to consolidate state control over the religious institutions' multifarious activities including processions, seasonal fairs, devotions at holy shrines, and fraternity preaching. The fact that the viceregally chosen *shaykh* also controlled the main source of benefits on which the religious establishment was dependent, namely the above-mentioned activities and the *waqf*, gave him considerable if not full powers. The situation of imbalance thus created was upheld by the personal efforts of the al-Bakri *shaykh*-s who held the function throughout the 19th century. The traditional heads of the religious establishment – the al-Azhar *'ulama* – on the other hand, showed a persistent lack of pugnacity, therefore,

241

continually lost ground in the face of state encroachments. After the early battle fought and lost in 1847 when the rector of al-Azhar, after months of disagreement, accepted Muhammad Efendi al-Bakri's pretension to exclusivity in the matter of appointments with respect to fraternities and other connected institutions, including the more famous shrines, al-Azhar scholars withdrew from a number of socially orientated activities, including part of their teaching which had formerly been carried out in *zawiya*-s. This, in turn, limited the university-mosques' intellectual scope. As their influence over *tariqa*-s waned, we find mystic doctrine (*tawasuf*) being progressively excluded from the syllabus. At the same time al-Azhar's capacity to provide jobs in state administration to its scholars was brought almost to a standstill as the number of state schools increased, extending to university level when the *Dar al-'ulum* opened in 1872. The capacity of al-Azhar to stimulate effort whether in terms of study or social upgrading was no longer apparent as the few posts for which al-Azhar students could qualify were reserved for well-connected urban families. Rural students generally had disappointing experiences at Cairo and, after their studies, often returned to their home villages.

In the 1880s, as the 'Arabi Pasha movement spread, the chief religious institutions no longer had any major impact on public opinion and this was further emphasized by a step-up in government control. In October 1880 'Ali al-Bakri who had been in office since 1855, died and was replaced by his son 'Abd al-Baqi, an inexperienced young man who did not even have a reputation as a scholar. He was seen as a mere puppet in government hands and this was further emphasized by the reforms he was asked to carry out in order to still further curtail religious activities. The new 1881 regulations banned not only more spectacular and heterodox fraternity practices, but even more common and typical ones such as singing during the *hadra*-s or fraternity meetings. Public processions and *tariqa* involvement in them were controlled and curtailed, whilst religious feasts could only be celebrated if they were traditional and of long-standing. All new undertakings in this field were forbidden. This increased the secularizing trend which characterized the khedival government's conception of modernity.

That this did not correspond to the national spirit is revealed by the 'Arabi Pasha uprising, and this, in turn, shows that, progressively, and outside the scope of government control, a religious reaction had been built up. This was apparent in every religious field. Thus, in spite of the efforts of the al-Bakri-s to insulate *tariqa* influence by upholding the monopoly rights of the major orders in given districts (*qadam*), they had not been able to prevent the breaking-down of these fraternities where secessionist branches had developed. Moreover, foreign orders such as the Moroccan Tijaniyya and Darqawiyya acquired an important following in northern Egypt whilst Sudanic orders such as the Mirghaniyya extended north to Upper Egypt. One can further point to an actual fraternity revival which brought a large popular clientele to such orders as the Khalwatiyya which had originally been active in Turkish circles in Egypt but which, by the 19th century, had become influential in rural areas, and notably in Upper Egypt where it supported rural unrest resulting from the difficult situation created by the foreign debt. The Khalwatiyya groups were to be overtly pro-'Arabist.

No less important in building up a new rurally-based national identity were the holy lineages. The presence in rural areas of high-minded, cultured and influential scholars, often traditional in outlook but sometimes both independent and critical, was in many ways the result of al-Azhar's incapacity to provide promising students possibilities for upgrading. As social mobility declined, disappointed students returned to their native villages where they continued to carry out traditional holy men activities and to act as scholars and as custodians of shrines. Among the many examples of this provided by 'Ali Mubarak in *al-Khitat*, we might quote that of 'Abd al-Latif al-Qayati (1765–1842) and his descendants. Born as his name indicates at al-Qayat, then a small village of 1500 persons, 'Abd al-Latif was a sharif, had studied at al-Azhar, and was a Khalwati shaykh. He had considerable influence in his village where he spent most of his life. His son 'Abd al-Jawad (1812–70) and two grandsons, Muhammad (1838–1902) and Ahmad, followed in his footsteps and their prestige grew as veneration for their ancestor gave rise to an important *mawlid* or religious feast (first recorded in 1870). 'Ali Mubarak mentions the fact that it attracted pilgrims from all over Egypt. As the influence of Muhammad as head of the holy lineage grew, so did the degree of his political involvement. In 1881, the two brothers came out in support of 'Arabi Pasha and their names figure along with those of other rural notables on petitions demanding parliamentary democracy for Egypt. When matters came to a head, their position was clear. They justified their nationalist views on the grounds that there was a close connection between religion and government (*din wa dawla*) and that they had a moral and historical duty with respect to their country. As they were later to put it in an account of contemporary events, *Rihlat al-Shams*:

> That is what every nation does when it is attacked by another: it knows that it is better to defend itself. More than that, this is an obligation binding upon every person especially when the aggressor and the aggressed differ in their religion, their language, their beliefs, and their customs.

The Qayati-s contributed to the resistance by organizing public prayers for the victory of 'Arabi Pasha. When the tide turned, they, together with many other rural personalities, were thrown into prison and later banished from Egypt.

Nor was opposition to khedival rule a purely rural phenomenon. Its capacity to affect urban social groups and al-Azhar itself should also be stressed. In autumn 1881, we find *'ulama* and students of the university mosque coming out openly in favour of 'Arabi Pasha and demanding the resignation of the rector, Muhammad al-'Abbasi al-Mahdi who was known to be pro-khedival. The fact that the 10 000-odd al-Azhari-s were still a pressure group of some influence was shown by the fact that the government gave in and appointed a moderate, Muhammad al-Inbabi, as rector. It however refused the nationalists' candidate, Muhammad 'Ilish (1802–82), head of the Maliki rite who, though in many ways a traditionalist, nonetheless actively supported 'Arabi Pasha and later the government of emergency. After the defeat, he too went to prison and died there. His son 'Abd al-Rahman 'Ilish who was also a teacher at al-Azhar was condemned and banished from Egypt. Even more prestigious was the presence at al-Tall al-Kabir of Hasan al-'Idwi (1806–86), one of the more brilliant 'ulama who had won public recognition in the capital in spite of his rural background. After the defeat, he too was put on trial where he stuck to his position and criticized the Khedive. The court, however, dared not face up to the scandal of sentencing him and he was sent back to his native village.

Probably more important still is the fact that a new spirit was in the air and that it also defined itself in the al-Azhar context. The most illustrious representative of *shaykh al-balad* scholarship and one who had considerable impact on urban circles, was Muhammad 'Abduh (1849–1905). He too was involved in the 'Arabi Pasha uprising and his contribution in ideological terms far surpasses that of 'Arabi Pasha. 'Muhammad 'Abduh in many ways summarizes the main aspects of social evolution pointed to earlier. He was born in rural Egypt, near the great shrine of Tanta. Like 'Ali Pasha Mubarak, his early years were marked by family problems since his father too had been ruined by Muhammad 'Ali's rural policy and tax-system, the family being forced to leave their home village. At the age of 13, Muhammad 'Abduh went to study at the Sayyid Ahmad mosque of Tanta where the withering process of education by rote depressed him deeply. His keenness for religious learning and mystical concentration returned after a stay with his great-uncle Darwish Khidr in 1865 or thereabouts. Darwish Khidr was yet another example of those high-minded and dedicated men to be found in rural Egypt. He had formerly been a trader in Tripoli and had there been initiated to the Madani *tariqa* by Shaykh Muhammad al-Madani of Misurata, a disciple of Ahmad bin Idris al-Fasi. On his return to Egypt, Darwish Khidr settled in the village of Kanisat Urayn in the Gharbiyya province and spent the rest of his life overseeing his lands and ministering to people's spiritual needs. Of his great-uncle, Muhammad 'Abduh later said:

> He was the key to my happiness, if I have had any happiness in my life. He gave me back that part of myself which I had lost, and revealed to me what lay concealed in my own nature.

Muhammad 'Abduh later went up to al-Azhar where after graduating he stayed on as a teacher and had such famous students as Sa'ad Zaghlul, the future nationalist leader. He was at the same time interested in and involved in modern intellectual activities, including education and he himself became Head of the new *Dar al-'Ulum*. He was also particularly interested in new means of communication, especially the press. He had contacts with such men as Ya'qub Sanu' (1838–1912), a virulent satirist who was forced to leave Egypt in 1878 and go to Paris where he published a famous anti-khedival magazine called *Abu Nazzara Zarqa* ('The Man with Blue Eyeglasses). Muhammad 'Abduh himself became a journalist and wrote in such papers as *al-Ahram* which had recently been established in Cairo by two brothers from Lebanon. But the major influence in Muhammad 'Abduh's life in this period was his meeting with Jamal al-Din al-Afghani, an Iranian though he pretended to be an Afghan, who had travelled far and wide, and notably in India where Muslim opposition to British rule was active. Muhammad 'Abduh who had first met Afghani during an earlier visit to Cairo, had close contacts with him during the years 1871–9 when he became the latter's devoted disciple and publicized al-Afghani's message of political resistance to corrupt Muslim governments and the imperial policies they helped to promote. It was through al-Afghani that 'Abduh was led to expand his scholastic horizon. He read more extensively in the fields of history and philosophy and at the Dar al'Ulum lectured on such works as Guizot's *History of Civilization* and Ibn Khaldun's *Muqaddima* which had been published in Cairo thanks to al-Tahtawi's efforts. As tension mounted in Egypt in the wake of the 'Abdin Palace demonstration, both al-Afghani and 'Abduh came to be seen as dangerous revolutionaries by the Khedive. The former was expelled from Egypt in August 1879, and 'Abduh banished to his native village.

Recalled to Cairo in 1880, 'Abduh was appointed the editor of the official gazette, the *Waqayi al-Misriyya* although he was by now in open opposition to the regime and helped to mobilize support for 'Arabi Pasha. He was nonetheless critical of 'Arabi Pasha as an individual and even more as an army man in politics. Among public stands made by Muhammad 'Abduh in this period we find a statement of nationalist views which was sent to Gladstone and published in *The Times*. After the defeat, Muhammad 'Abduh was also thrown into prison and sentenced to banishment.

'Arabi Pasha can thus be seen as the man chosen by history to focus and embody the multifarious aspects of change in terms of more dynamic and frustrated sectors of rural society: the *shaykh al-balad* class and the progressive type scholars who provided the material and ideological incentive which made of an army mutiny the symbol of a new national image. Through a confrontation with the British army and khedival power, a point of no return was reached which led to new assessments. The older leaders, men such as 'Arabi Pasha or 'Ali Pasha Mubarak dropped out of the limelight as they clung to their times, whether in exile or at home, whilst other, younger, more dynamic men – often because of a court sentence condemning them to banishment – met the challenge of new times in the wider context of a Muslim world attacked on all sides by imperialism.

SELECTED READING LIST

Abdel-Malek, A., *Idéologie et Renaissance Nationale*, (Paris, 1969).
Ahmad, J. M., *The Intellectual Origins of Egyptian Nationalism*, (London, 1960).
'Arabi Pasha, *Mudhakkirat 'Arabi*, (Cairo, 1953).
Baer, G., *A History of Landownership in Modern Egypt, 1800–1950*, (London, 1968).
Baer, G., *Studies in the Social History of Modern Egypt*, (Chicago and London, 1969).
Bannerth, E., 'La Khalwatiyya en Egypte', *Mélanges de l'Institut Dominicain des Études Orientales*, 1964–6.
Blunt, W. S., *Secret History of the English Occupation of Egypt*, (London, 1907).
Broadley, A. M., *How we defended Arabi and his friends. A Story of Egypt and the Egyptians*, (London, 1884).
De Jong, F., *Turuq and Turuq-Linked Institutions in Nineteenth Century Egypt*, (Leiden, 1978).
Delanoue, G., *Moralistes et Politiques Musulmans dans l'Egypte du XIXème siècle (1798–1882)*, (Damascus, 1981).
Gendzier, I., 'James Sanua and Egyptian Nationalism', *Middle East Journal*, 15, 1961.
Heyworth-Dunne, J., *An Introduction to the History of Education in Modern Egypt*, (London, 1938).
Hourani, A., *Arabic Thought in the Liberal Age. 1798–1939*, (London, 1962).
Keddie, N. (ed.), *Scholars, Saints, and Sufis. Muslim Religious Institutions since 1500*, (Berkeley, Los Angeles, and London, 1972).

Kenny, L. M., ' 'Ali Mubarak, nineteenth century Egyptian educator and administrator', *Middle East Journal*, 21, 1967.

Mubarak 'A., *Al-Khitat al-Tawfiqiyya al-Jadida li-Misr al-Qahira wa Muduniha wa Biladiha al-Qadima wa al-Shahira*, (Bulaq, 1886–1888).

Ninet, J., *Arabi Pacha*, (Berne, 1884).

Rafi'i, 'A. al-., *Al-Thawra al-'Arabiyya wa al-Ihtilal al-Inglizi*, (Cairo, 1937).

Ridha, M. R., *Tarikh al-Ustadh al-Imam al-Shaykh Muhammad 'Abduh*, (Cairo, 1931).

Rowlatt, M., *Founders of Modern Egypt*, (London, 1962).

Schölch, A., *Agypten den Ägyptern! Die politische und gesellschafliche Krise der Jahre 1879–1882 in Agypten*, (Zurich and Freiburg, 1973).

CHAPTER 14

THE MAHDI"S MISSION IN THE SUDAN

The Mahdi described . . .

His outward appearance was strangely fascinating; he was a man of strong constitution, very dark complexion, and his face always wore a pleasant smile, to which he had by long practice accustomed himself. Under this smile gleamed a set of singularly white teeth, and between the two upper middle ones was a V-shaped space, which in the Sudan is considered a sign that the owner will be lucky. His mode of conversation too had by training become exceptionally pleasant and sweet. As a messenger of God, he pretended to be in direct communication with the Deity. All orders which he gave were supposed to have come to him by inspiration, and it became therefore a sin to refuse to obey them; disobedience to the Mahdi's orders was tantamount to resistance to the will of God, and was therefore punishable by death.

He called himself Mahdi Khalifat er Rasul (i.e. the successor of the Prophet) while his adherents called him "Sayid" (i.e. Master); Sayidna el Mahdi (i.e. our Master the Mahdi), or Sayidna el Imam (i.e. our Master who is in front). The Mahdi in his every action endeavoured to imitate and follow in the exact footsteps of the Prophet.

. . . by Father Joseph Ohrwalder, who was held captive by the Mahdi from 1882 to 1892. The account he gave of his experience was translated into English under the title Ten Years' Captivity in the Mahdi's Camp 1882–1892, from the Original Manuscripts of Father Joseph Ohrwalder, by Major F. R. Wingate, R. A., (London, 1895).

In 1883, the Mahdiyya, a political and religious movement of opposition to Egyptian rule, spread through the Sudan. In a matter of months, the foreign administration toppled and garrisons surrendered. The southern provinces were left stranded and divided in allegiance, whilst the rest of the country passed under Mahdist control. For the next 15 years, Sudan was to be an independent theocratic state. The event caused considerable stir in the imperial camp: the movement emperilled British progression southwards. It was marked by a humiliating defeat: the death of General Gordon at Khartum on 26 January 1885; but, even more, it forced upon all an awareness of an unexpected Muslim offensive spirit. Nonetheless the significance of the Mahdiyya remained mysterious to most imperial observers who saw merely xenophobia and fanaticism in the 'wild hordes of dervishes'.

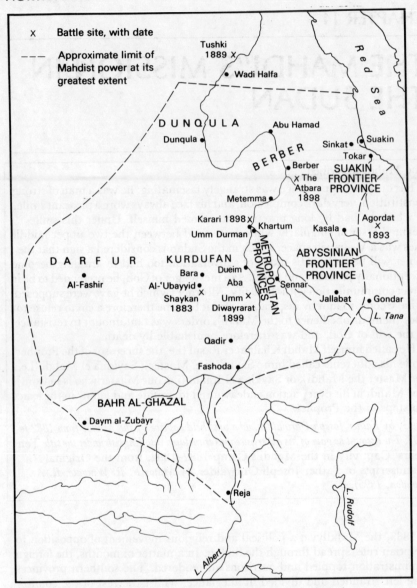

Map 14.1 *The Mahdist state (source: P. M. Holt, The History of the Sudan)*

THE MAHDI AND HIS FOLLOWERS

The man who took the lead in the Sudanese Islamic uprising was Muhammad Ahmad ibn al-Sayyid 'Abd Allah, born on 12 August 1844, in the district of Dunqula. His father, like many other Dunqula tribesmen was a boat-builder by profession, but the family was sharifian and as the young Muhammad Ahmad showed aptitude for learning, he was sent to religious schools in Jezira and later Berbera. Muhammad Ahmad was drawn from an early age to sufism and in 1861 was initiated into the Sammaniyya fraternity. Though he himself became a *shaykh* within the Sammaniyya, he was highly critical of the worldliness of other leaders and preached a rigorist doctrine of his own. At the start of his public career, around 1880, he was living in a hermitage at Aba Island, on the White Nile, and his holiness was already famed far and wide.

From all accounts, the Mahdi was a powerfully built man with a pleasant smile, showing up his widely-cleft front teeth – an admired trait because the Prophet himself was said to have had a similar gap between his front teeth. His lifestyle was ascetic. He sat on matting and lived in a tent. His clothing consisted of loose trousers, a white skull cap round which he wound a large white turban, and sandals. Over his clothes he wore a loose tunic of *dammur* (a locally-made twilled cotton fabric) and a girdle of *goos* (straw). This was to become the Mahdi uniform worn by all his followers and ceremoniously sent by the Mahdi to those whom he wished to convert to the movement. The Mahdi had the traditional air of the Muslim scholar, characterized by a reserved deportment and gentle speech. His life was marked out by the set Quranic prayers, but also by periods of meditation. His relationship with the outside world was essentially through public preaching and private counsel, or through letters and proclamations.

In 1880–1, Muhammad Ahmad had a number of mystical visions in the course of which he came to believe himself to be the expected Mahdi. Belief in the Mahdi plays an important role in Islamic countries. It is the belief that, at the end of time, in a period of darkness and evil, a 'guided one', the regenerator of the Muslim community, would come. He would reestablish the strength of Islam during a short millennium before the end of time. It was also believed that Christ ('Isa in Arabic) would then return on earth. The doctrine of the Mahdi which plays a central role in Shi'a Islam, is not readily admitted by the Sunni-s, and even the idea of an ultimate regenerator is played down by classical scholarship. In spite of this, belief in the Guided One was popular even in Sunni Islam and many were the traditions which developed around the man who was to come. He was to be a *sharif*, to bear the name of Muhammad bin 'Abd Allah and to have certain characteristic signs by which he was to be recognized. Popular belief in the Mahdi is part of the history of oppressed social categories and, as class stratification developed, was also the expression of their hope in an ultimate era of justice.

Who were the partisans who rallied to Muhammad Ahmad when, on 29 June 1881, he launched on his public career by claiming to be the Mahdi? The message had an immediate appeal to the more oppressed categories of Sudanese society. The Mahdi was himself a northerner and it was in such tribes as the Danaqla, Ja'aliyyin or Shayqiya who were hard-hit by economic conditions prevailing in Sudan that his preaching was immediately meaningful. The western nomads, themselves impoverished by the decline of the slave trade, were a somewhat different clientele which nonetheless reacted enthusiastically as early as 1881, notably the important confederated Baqqara tribesmen. Over and above a revolutionary levelling message, traditional manipulation of tribal structures also helps explain the spread of the Mahdi's influence. In the north, he appealed to other sharifian families for support and more particularly tried to win over the fraternities. The Sammaniyya to which he himself belonged was used as a communications network, as was also the Khalwatiyya which, in this period, seems to have played a role in spreading news of rural protest in Egypt and the rise of the 'Arabi Pasha movement. Fraternity response was however not all favourable. The Mirghaniyya, for example, proved hostile and its leaders refused to take the Mahdi's claims seriously in spite of blandishments. Though offered the post of *khalifa* in the movement, 'Uthman al-Mirghani refused and passed into opposition. This is also to some extent true of the Isma'iliyya branch of the Khatmiyya (founded in 1842), since, though the Mahdi won over its leader al-Makki Isma'il as early as 1880 and thus obtained support in Kurdufan, he was unable to obtain favour with al-Makki Isma'il's brother who was an al-Azhar trained *qadhi* and who refuted Muhammad Ahmad's claim that he was the 'Guided One'. He ultimately died fighting the Mahdiyya at al-'Ubayyid. The Mahdi also had recourse to tribal chiefs, some of whom went over to his side. Traditional tribal strategy and a revolutionary message of justice and rigorism upheld the Mahdi's claim to being divinely inspired.

These would not however suffice to explain Muhammad Ahmad's widespread success. One must also take into account economic conditions prevailing and the intellectual climate of the Mahdiyya. Among a depressed population which had for over 50 years suffered from the colonial rule of the Turkiyya seen as foreign, corrupt, and increasingly under European influence, the wild and largely irrational claim that the Prophet's early saga could be re-enacted, spread like wildfire.

The doctrine of the Mahdiyya
The Mahdi claimed a direct relationship with the Prophet:

> I saw the Prophet in a vision. He came to me in the presence of our brother 'Isa (Jesus). He sat by me and he said to our brother 'Isa, 'The Mahdi is your chief'. The brother said, 'I believe in him'.

On the basis of this, blind obedience was required of his followers:

> Be faithful and obedient in carrying out these orders which are the orders of God and his Mahdi, otherwise you will be destroyed.

The inspiring picture he put over was one which derived from the Quran and *sunna* (Prophetic tradition) and which did away purely and simply with time and history, men being called upon to relive Muhammad's time. We thus find him issuing a proclamation forbidding the term *derwish* and saying that his followers were to be known as *ansar* (the term used for the Prophet's companions). Just as Muhammad had had four legitimate successors chosen from among his closest followers, so the Mahdi appointed four *khalifa*-s. They were respectively 'Abdallah bin Muhammad al-Ta'ishi, a Baqqara chief who was his successor designate and was considered as being under the patronage of the Prophet's first successor, Abu Bakr. The place of 'Umar, another of the four *rashidun khalifa*-s, was taken in Mahdist theocracy by 'Ali bin Muhammad Hilu, that of 'Ali, the Prophet's son-in-law, by the Mahdi's own son-in-law, Muhammad Sharif bin Hamid; whilst the fourth place, that of 'Uthman, was offered successively to the head of the Sanusiyya who ignored the suggestion and to the head of the Mirghaniyya who refused it. It ultimately fell to the lot of a lesser man, Wuld al-Uwaysir. The Mahdi's *khalifa*-s had banners bearing their 'predecessors' names.

The urge to ever more total identification with the Prophetic model upheld individual and collective zeal, the Mahdi himself acting as a guide in the process. Among the thousand and one details of daily life which he regulated, we may mention that he forbade the riding of horses except in time of war because 'this is the example set before us by the Prophet and his companions', or expensive wedding feasts because 'your wedding must be simple, like that of Fatima, the daughter of the Prophet. The Prophet has expressed great anger at the extravangances of present goings on'. Though the will to do away with *bida'* (innovations or non-Islamic practices) upheld a collective will which could further see in the rigorist ideal of the Prophet's message a justification and heightened significance of the Sudanese's poverty as opposed to the corrupt luxury of the Turkiyya, a more critical assessment will point to the flaws of the system. The Mahdi himself was not always consistent and though he re-established such practices as slavery, justifying them by Islamic law, he made no attempt to do away with such Sudanic customs as the sexual mutilation of girls, although this had no Muslim tradition to back it up. The logic of rigorism could moreover overstep the limits set by the Prophet himself and in fact contradict the very example it pretended to imitate. This is once again evident with respect to the treatment of women. The Mahdi thus refused to allow women to appear in public. Harsh too were the methods by which these rulings were applied:

> . . . according to God's laws, women should not appear in public places, such as markets, public thoroughfares, etc. A young girl, that is to say one who had not yet reached the age of womanhood, may, however, do so. If a woman venture to go out and be seen in these places three days after the circulation of this order, she will receive a punishment of one hundred stripes, which will be a lesson for others not to follow in her footsteps.

The ideal, in practice, was open to criticism.

At the start, it involved an irrational act of faith: belief that Muhammad Ahmad was, in fact, the Mahdi. This claim was, of course, generally resisted by educated Muslims and notably the *'ulama* and certain fraternity leaders such as the Great Sanusi who, sometimes painstakingly, pointed out that the claim was unfounded. The privileged transcendental relationship between Muhammad Ahmad and the Prophet was moreover of a personal order and could not therefore outlive him or become a principle of social organization. When the Mahdi died, his successor was unable to maintain the pre-eminence of the theocratic stand. Moreover, as a collective ideal, cohesion and militant zeal could only be upheld by constant reference to the evil to be fought against and eradicated. An objectively defined enemy was thus a necessary part of the process of militancy. In an early stage this was conveniently provided by the Turkiyya:

> . . . do not follow the example set by your oppressors the Turks, who live in luxury and exultation, and who fire their guns and rifles through pride and haughtiness. The following has come down to us through the traditions of our Prophet Muhammad: 'Tell my brethren, Live not the way my enemies live, wear not what they wear; if you do not obey this, then you become my enemies as they are my enemies.'

Polarization of Egyptian and Sudanese, corrupt Muslims and true believers was built up by the Mahdi as a channel for the energy of the *ansar*, defining their world view. It was an important part of the Mahdiyya, not only in terms of an armed struggle with the outside world, but within the movement itself, orders being given to do away with everything considered as Turk. Typical of this is a curious letter from the Mahdi asking his clerks to be careful when writing the Arabic letter *sin* to do so correctly and not in the deformed way habitual in the Mashriq.

A clearly identified enemy exterior to the community was necessary in order to limit the destructive tendency which an inturned rigorist tendency might foster. In spite of various improvements to social life that the Mahdiyya introduced (which will be mentioned later), one should not entirely forget that the theocratic state that went with it also implied a permanent system of self-criticism in which spying and public trials were rife and in which, in spite of the Mahdi's own personal gentleness, public scenes of punishment for sinfulness were increasingly necessary to uphold the community's zeal.

The need to set up an enemy as a constant threat on the frontiers of the community went far beyond the initial political criticism which the activities of the Turkiyya could legitimately give rise to. The Mahdi, from the start, had defined the Egyptians as the enemies of Islam: 'the Lord of creation, Muhammad . . . called them infidels, and even worse than that, for they were endeavouring to extinguish the light of God'. Spiritual energies were thus reconverted to outgoing destructiveness for the Egyptians could 'never be reformed except by the sword'. The fight against them was portrayed as a God-given order: 'be it known to you that all I do is by the order of the Prophet. My war against the Turks is by his orders'. It thus implied an ultimate and inevitable victory of the *ansar* over their enemies, even if death or defeat was part of the process: ('are you not fighting a people who have changed their belief, and who have already denied the Prophet'). Hence the desperate courage which characterized Mahdist fighting. Here too, the will to self-destruction became part of the process and acquired a positive significance. The Guided One told his soldiers: 'May God grant that we . . . finally die as martyrs at the hands of the infidels', justifying this on the grounds that 'you have no part in this world, your part in the world to come. This world is for the infidels'.

These elements of Mahdiyya ideology point to the complex nature of the movement which, though it was a forceful social and religious reaction against foreign oppression and an increasingly westernized society, was also a largely irrational reaction against the historical process through which Islam had been realized. It was this aspect of the Mahdiyya which isolated it from other militant Islamic movements, whilst its destructive power not only brought about its defeat at foreign hands but undermined the very cohesion which the movement had aimed at restoring.

THE MAHDIYYA. A POLITICAL AND HISTORICAL ACCOUNT

During the short space of its existence – 1881 to 1898 – the Mahdiyya went through several phases. The initial period of ascendancy culminated in the capture of Khartum on 26 January 1885. It was followed by the setting up of a theocracy, first under the Mahdi and then under under his successor, the Khalifa. The turning point in the so far successful movement came when the Mahdi offensive against Egypt failed and the *ansar* were defeated at the battle of Tushki, on 3 August 1889. The movement then rapidly broke down under the combined pressures of inner dissensions and the attacks of the Anglo-Egyptian army. The actual reconquest of Sudan was undertaken by the Anglo-Egyptian forces in 1896 and ended with the Khalifa 'Abd Allah's defeat and death in 1899.

In the initial phase of the movement, the Egyptian administration indirectly helped the Mahdi by not taking the danger seriously. It was only in 1881 that the governor-general, Ra'uf Pasha, sent a military detachment to take the preacher prisoner. The soldiers were attacked by partisans whilst the Mahdi himself fled westwards and found refuge among the Baqqara with whom he made an alliance and established marriage ties. This he was later to view as his own *hijra*, similar to the Prophet's flight to Madina. The tribal and religious leaders of the region were recognized by the Mahdi as intermediaries between himself and the population and he did not as yet claim absolute authority for himself.

The Baqqara and other nomad and semi-nomad tribes of the Nuba mountain region were constituted into the Mahdi's first official fighting force and their political influence was given official recognition when 'Abd Allah of the Ta'isha tribe was chosen as the Mahdi's representative (*khalifa*). The Mahdi began his triumphant march forward in 1882. That year he and his army marched through Kurdufan and besieged the province's two major centres: al-'Ubayyid and Bara. Though the *ansar* were as yet ill-equipped, their determination was evident and casualties, however numerous, did not deter them. The technique of successive waves of attackers could ultimately get the better of even intense gunfire. Another and no less evident factor was the fact that the Sudanese were obviously sympathetic to the movement. This was shown up at al-'Ubayyid when the inhabitants secretly left the town to join the besiegers, and when the town fell on 19 January 1883, even the 2000 strong garrison joined the movement. The fact that 6000 rifles and £100 000 were found in the town increased the Mahdiyya's fighting capacity. Nor was success that year limited to the west. In the Sennar region the movement had continued to spread in the Mahdi's absence and a number of victorious attacks against Turkiyya posts took place, the most successful being the defeat inflicted in April 1882 on an Egyptian detachment supported by 2500 Shukriyya irregulars under the command of 'Awad al-Karim Pasha Abu Sin. In fact, Mahdist forces were now closing in south of the capital, and Khartum, where desultory preparations to resist were undertaken, was in danger.

Mahdist advance was consolidated throughout 1883. The *ansar* were now organized on a fighting basis. The Awlad al-Balad of the Nile region were placed under the leadership of the Mahdi's son-in-law, Muhammad Sharif, and were given a red banner. The western nomads (chief of whom were the Baqqara) were placed under the orders of their compatriot 'Abd Allah al-Ta'ishi and had a black flag. In spite of a common ideal upheld by the Mahdi's constant reminders that the war had religious objectives, tensions between the two groups were apparent. Moreover men came to the fore because of their military capacities and devotion to the Mahdi rather than for their religious feelings or scholarship. Admirable fighters such as 'Abd al Rahman al-Najumi, a Ja'ali respected by all, were in fact very simple men.

The combination of religious propaganda and attacks on the Turkiyya forces narrowed the area around Khartum which the latter still controlled. The last dashing blow to foreign rule came when the Egyptian government sent out an army of 10 000 men to re-establish government authority in the colony. It was under the orders of a British commanding officer, Hicks Pasha and included many of 'Arabi Pasha's disbanded soldiers. Hicks Pasha's instructions were to reconquer Kurdufan and to this end he left Khartum on 8 September 1883. Progress proved difficult because of dissensions among the officers and the untrustworthiness of guides, although at the time Hicks Pasha did not realise that the latter were in fact in contact with the Mahdiyya which followed close on their heels: the Mahdi's orders were to make the march as difficult as possible before taking the army to a pre-established ambush. When the army realised its predicament, brought home to Hicks Pasha by a personal letter from the Mahdi asking him to surrender and convert, it found itself cut off and entirely surrounded. The *ansar* attacked on 5 November 1883 and destroyed the Egyptian relief force almost to a man.

News of the defeat came as a severe blow to Egypt and Britain. After this, a new impetus would be given to the Mahdiyya, and the Turkiyya, it was felt, was in no position to withstand the onslaught. The Khedive envisaged withdrawing from Sudan and Britain recommended it. The Egyptian prime minister, Sharif Pasha, refused to countenance this and resigned. Nubar Pasha returned to power as prime minister and sent orders to the various governors of Sudan to concentrate their troops in the major centres and prepare for evacuation. The British government decided to send out General Gordon who, after his resignation in 1880, had returned to England, to help carry this out and the Khedive sanctioned the appointment by naming him Governor-General of Sudan. Gordon therefore left for Khartum taking with him a declaration in which Khedive Muhammad Tawfiq announced his intention to 'restore independence to the descendants of the Kings of Sudan'. Among other arrangements made was a provincial division of Sudan excluding the Red Sea zone which was to remain under Egyptian rule. Equatoria and Bahr al-Ghazal were also to be evacuated but from the south, and to this end a relief force under the orders of the explorer Stanley was to be sent out by the British to bring Emin Pasha safely back. This was finally effected by force since Emin Pasha refused to give up his command or take part in an eventual colonial share-out which would have given Equatoria to King Leopold of Belgium, the British keeping for themselves the Victoria-Nyanza region under cover of an East African association.

As Gordon Pasha set up in Khartum, the Mahdist movement, under the impetus of victory, closed in ever more menacingly. The provinces, one after the other, fell under Mahdist control. In Dar Fur, Slatin was forced early in 1883 to concentrate all his troops in the capital, al-Fashir, and even there was not secure, Mahdist influence among his troops being rife. His own officers contested his authority even though he converted to Islam in order to underplay his position as a Christian ruling over Muslims. News of 'Arabi Pasha's stand against the British no less than Hicks Pasha's defeat made his position intolerable and, after consulting officers and officials, Slatin surrendered. By the end of 1883, Dar Fur had passed under full Mahdi control. In the east of the country, and notably in the Red Sea zone, the spread of the Mahdiyya was equally evident in spite of efforts by the Anglo-Egyptian troops of Massawa and Suakin to resist. One of the chief leaders of the *ansar*, 'Uthman Diqna, had been sent to the region and he had won over the population with the help of the Majdhubiyya fraternity. Efforts to consolidate the Turkiyya had led to an expeditionary corps being sent out under the command of General Valentine Baker Pasha. A defeat similar to that of Hicks Pasha, though on a smaller scale, followed when on 4 February 1884, Baker with a force of 3700 men decided to relieve a nearby post, Tokar. A Mahdist attack led to the Egyptian troops giving way and Baker only saved some 1400 of his men in a disastrous retreat. Four Krupp guns, two Gatlings, half a million cartridges, and some 3000 rifles fell into Mahdist hands. The fact that this feat of arms was achieved by a mere 1200 poorly armed men, points to the by now evident superiority of the Mahdiyya in terms of morale if not material. From then on, the coastal harbours alone remained to the Turkiyya, strongly protected and isolated from the hinterland, which remained under the control and command of 'Uthman Diqna until the Anglo-Egyptian reconquest.

The need to organize the evacuation and withdraw from Khartum was more than ever imperative. However events took a different course, essentially because of the personal attitudes of the man who had been sent out to organize the retreat: General Gordon.

In Khartum, the stern god-fearing Gordon took his rank and function of governor-general very seriously. The first fact that comes out, and one which Lord Cromer points out with considerable irritation, is that Gordon, who had been sent out to plan evacuation, no longer showed any inclination to do so once on the spot. There is something typically colonial in the decision-making process by which a European in the lonely conditions of a distant colony, comes to see himself as committed to superior values. In Gordon a certain attachment to the British presence in Sudan – he was after all a Sudanese veteran – combined with the will not to be seen as running away, and this led him to put off the moment when he would carry out his orders. One might go further and suggest that Gordon like other ill-fated imperial heroes, cast himself in the role of a puritan warrior-saint who, for the sake of honour, wanted a fight. The *ansar*, he stated, 'must have one good defeat to wipe out Hick's disaster and my defeat'. Lord Cromer was to comment: 'the truth is that General Gordon was above all a soldier, and, moreover, a very bellicose soldier. His fighting instincts were too strong to admit of his working heartily in the interests of peace'. Gordon in conscience had decided that his instructions meant nothing and that he must stay in Sudan. The pretext that evacuation would have meant leaving some of the garrisons to their fate served to justify his decision 'not to run away from Khartum'. He envisaged his own fate – defeat and even death – with masochistic pride. In November 1883 he wrote:

> I declare positively and once for all that I will not leave the Sudan until every one who wants to go down is given the chance to do so, unless a government is established which relieves me of the charge; therefore, if any emissary or letter comes up here ordering me to come down, *I will not obey it, but will stay here and fall with the town and run all risks*.

This attitude persisted throughout the year 1884. Gordon increasingly shut himself up in his own nightmare. He proffered curt refusals to all offers of communication with others, including the Mahdi. Typical of contrasting attitudes was the exchange of letters which took place between the two men. The Mahdi wrote to Gordon on 10 March 1884, asking him to convert to Islam:

> If you pity the Moslems, you should pity your own soul first, save it from the anger of its Creator, and make it a follower of the true religion by following our Lord the Prophet Muhammad.

The Mahdi followed this up by a lengthy exposition of his doctrine and pointed to the place which would be Gordon's in the Mahdiyya were he to convert: but he also explained that his letter was a forewarning sent to Gordon Pasha, as to Hicks Pasha and other leaders of the Turkiyya in conformity with the Prophet's recommendation, in order that they should have an opportunity to amend their ways before the inevitable attack. With the letter came a suit of clothing – the Mahdist uniform – because, as the Mahdi put it, 'this is the clothing of those who have given up this world and its vanities and who look for the world to come, for everlasting happiness in Paradise'. Gordon's answer is equally revealing: having pushed aside the suit of clothing with his foot, he wrote out the following lines: 'I have received the letters sent by your three messengers and I understand all their contents, but I cannot have more communication with you.' This was as curt a refusal as could be imagined, and probably highly undiplomatic in the circumstances.

The situation in the Sudan was a critical one and Khartum was increasingly hedged in. Communications with the outside world via Berbera could be cut off at any moment. Gordon's reports to Cromer in Egypt remained, however, optimistic, possibly to preclude more pressing orders to evacuate. The refusal to enter into discussion with the Mahdi is all the more illogical in view of the fact that in many other fields, Gordon was quite capable of sacrificing principle to more realistic considerations. Thus he, Gordon, the champion of the fight against slave dealers had made no objection to Cromer's suggestion that Zubayr Pasha, the slave-dealing ex-warlord of Bahr al-Ghazal and Dar Fur, should be sent to Sudan in an official capacity. On 8 March 1884, he even sent Cromer a long letter indicating all the political advantages to be expected of such an appointment:

> It is impossible to find any other man but Zobeir for governing

Khartum. No one has his power ... Zobeir is fifty times the Mahdi's match. He is also of good family, well known and fitted to be Sultan; the Mahdi, in all these respects, is the exact opposition, besides being a fanatic.

This is a curious estimation of the respective weight of material and spiritual values for a man as deeply religious as Gordon, but it also shows up his attitude towards slavery which he was by now quite prepared to accept. The same letter shows him quite pragmatic on the subject:

As for slave-holding, even had we held Soudan, we could never have interfered with it. I have already said that the Treaty of 1877 was an impossible one; therefore, on that head, Zobeir's appointment would make no difference whatever.

Nor was this merely a private view. Believing (as the British generally did) that the sole explanation of the success of the Mahdiyya was resentment at the abolition of slavery, General Gordon soon after his arrival in Khartum, issued a proclamation which if it did not actually allow *trading* in slaves, permitted domestic slavery which automatically implied raiding, albeit in a clandestine fashion. His proclamation is a model of political hypocrisy:

Whereas my sincerest desire is to adopt a course of action which shall lead to the public tranquillity, and being aware with what regret you have regarded the severe and stringent measures which have been taken by the Government for the suppression of the traffic, and the seizure and punishment of all concerned in the slave trade, as provided by the convention and by the decrees, I therefore confer upon you these rights; that henceforth no one shall interfere with your property; that whoever has slaves in his service shall have full right to their services and full control over them without any interference whatsoever.

So much for the humanitarian ideal which was part of the white man's burden!

Level-headed men such as Cromer and Wingate, well-informed as to the situation in the Sudan, were very critical of Gordon's attitude during the year 1884 as the rising tide of the Mahdiyya moved in on Khartum. He proved hesitant and such decisions as he took often proved to be errors. He was over-reliant on the Nile flood to re-establish communications with the outside world. He entertained desultory correspondence with various *ansar* leaders such as al-Najumi, but refused to accept offers for a surrender of the town which would have avoided bloodshed. In summer, when the Nile flood made it possible to send shipping out from Khartum, he attempted an attack on al-Ailafun, some 20 miles south of Khartum. It ended in failure, 800 men out of a total force of 1600 died, and the *ansar* were also able to capture stores and military equipment, including 980 Remington rifles. News of the defeat was sent north to Cairo by steamer. The steamer *'Abbas* set off early in September with most of Khartum's European community on board. It soon became clear that the *ansar* were following the ship and when it ran on a rock, the crew and passengers were killed.

In the meantime, plans for a relief expedition to go out to rescue Gordon were being made, but progress was still slow. The delay which was later to be such a source of guilt to Victorian England, was due to a number of factors. Not only did Sudan lose some of its urgency seen from distant England but the British were very loath to contemplate an independent move by Egypt to go to Gordon's help. On 23 April 1884, Sir Frederick Stephenson, commander of the British army of occupation, and Sir Evelyn Wood, commander of the Egyptian army, opposed the sending of two Egyptian battalions at once to Berbera, considering that an Anglo-Egyptian force had first to be organized. It was not until 8 August, after the British parliament had voted a credit of £300 000, that Lord Hartington, the Secretary of State for War, authorized Sir Frederick Stephenson to take preliminary measures for moving troops south. Lord Wolseley, commander of the relief expedition, arrived in Cairo on 10 September, and instructions were drafted on 8 October, 'more than five months after communication between Cairo and Khartum had been interrupted' as Lord Cromer points out. It was not until the end of December that the march to Khartum was undertaken, one division crossing the desert from Korti, the other moving up the Nile. Progress of the desert division was retarded by fighting, whilst, on the river, it took 24 hours to set afloat one of the ships which had struck a rock on the 6th Cataract. When the Anglo-Egyptian forces came in sight of Khartum, on 27 January 1885, the British flag no longer flew over Government House: the town had fallen during the night of the 25–26th. The relief expedition turned back.

One of the Khartum merchants, Bordayni, has left a full account of events in the besieged city. On 12 November 1884, the *ansar*, after severe fighting, had occupied the outlying ground between Khartum and its northern outpost, Umm Durman. Machine guns had been set up by them to keep up continuous firing; moreover close watch was kept on the river to prevent communications with the outside world. In December, Umm Durman fell to the Mahdiyya and troops concentrated around Khartum, many being tribesmen attracted by *ansar* propaganda. In the middle of January, the Mahdi himself arrived and set up his headquarters in Umm Durman. The situation in Khartum was all the more difficult in view of the fact that no supplies were available. All stores of cereals were requisitioned, nonetheless the population was starving: 'many died of hunger, and corpses filled the streets'. On 19 January, a Turkish officer and his men deserted, going over to the *ansar* who were thus informed of the garrison's problems. Gordon Pasha made preparations for a final stand by placing all available ammunition in the Catholic church which was to be blown up when the town fell, whilst at the same time confidently affirming that the relief expedition would arrive in time. That he himself felt no such confidence was evident to Bordayni:

> I found him sitting on a divan and as I came in he pulled off his tarboush, and flung it from him, saying, 'What more can I say, I have nothing more to say, the people will no longer believe me, I have told them over and over again that help would be here, but it has never come, and now they must see I tell them lies. If this, my last promise, fails, I can do nothing more. . . .' All the anxiety he had undergone had gradually turned his hair to a snowy white. I left him, and this was the last time I saw him alive.

'The fall of Khartoum . . .'
by one of the Mahdi's followers

When the expeditionary force reached al-Matamma, and the Mahdi, with whom be God's peace, heard of it, he consulted his advisers, and they decided to hurry on the capture of Khartoum before the force could arrive. So on the eve of Monday the 7th of Rabi' al-Thani 1302 (Sunday night, 24 January 1885) the Mahdi, with whom be God's peace, came and gathered all the army between the village of al-Ghurqan and the city of Khartoum, and harangued us, mounted on his camel. Part of what he said, before the final oath of allegiance, was that the enemies of God had dug the ditch surrounding Khartoum very wide and deep, and had placed in it iron teeth, each with four iron spikes on three of which it stood, leaving the fourth spike upright to pierce the feet of men or the hooves of horses. Then he said, 'Swear allegiance to me unto death!' and was silent for a moment, when the whole army with one voice shouted three times, 'We swear allegiance to you unto death!'.

Then he said, 'If God grants you the victory, Gordon is not to be killed, and Shaykh Husayn al-Majdi is not to be killed, and Faki al-Amin al-Darir is not to be killed'. There was a fourth man whose name I did not remember, but once when I was repeating this story I heard Ahmad Hasan 'Abd al-Mun'im say that it was Shaykh Muhammad al-Saqqa.

Then he said, 'If a man throws down his arms, do not kill him, and if a man bars his house against you, do not kill him'. Here there came an objection from a man whose voice I heard without seeing who it was, saying, 'Master, in some of the fights we have been in we have seen a soldier throw down his arms and have passed him by, and then he has picked them up again and struck at us or shot at us from behind'. When the Mahdi, with whom be God's peace, heard this, he said, 'Whoever you encounter in the line of fire, kill him. God has said, "Their belief in Me only after they had seen My might profited them nothing." '

Then we swore the accustomed oath: 'We swear by God and his Prophet, and we swear by you, that we will not worship any but God, that we will not steal, that we will not commit adultery, that we will not disobey your lawful commands, that we will not flee from the Holy War'. And finally some words which at the time I did not fully understand, though I did later – 'We swear to renounce this world and to choose the next.' Then the flags were unfurled, and we were on our way to the fortress.

The Memoirs of Babikr Bedri, translated by Yousef Bedri and George Scott, 1969.

The last day in Khartum (25 January) was one of despair for the beseiged as they waited for the final onslaught. It began at about 2 a.m. with the war cry 'God is most great!'. The *ansar* soon overran the ditch and the town's gates broke down (one of them being opened by Faraj Pasha, an officer of the garrison). Government House was then surrounded. After a moment of hesitation, a group of *ansar* rushed in. Gordon met them in full uniform. In spite of the Mahdi's orders he was speared to death. His head was cut off and carried to the Mahdi at Umm Durman.

THE MAHDI THEOCRACY

The fall of Khartum was followed by the setting up of an independent Sudanese state under the Mahdi who established his capital at Umm Durman. It marked a changeover from an outwardly-directed militant movement to one of social and institutional organization.

The Mahdi's first reaction to the victory was made manifest in the solemn prayer in which he praised God and reaffirmed the religious ideal of his community, criticizing those of his followers who had behaved in a way not compatible with Muslim morality. There had been scenes of looting, women had been ill-treated, and the treasury had attracted the greed of some of the leaders of the movement. This was an occasion seized upon by the Mahdi to criticize openly not only more worldly *ansar*, but also members of his own sharifian family.

The Mahdi Condemns the Ashraf

At noon we went to the mosque for the Friday service, and the Mahdi, with whom be God's peace, led the prayers and preached the sermon. Towards the end of it he said, 'Companions of the Mahdi, Ahmad Sulayman (*the commissioner of the treasury*) has distracted the Ashraf with riches. Say after me three times, "We ask the protection of God that we be not like them". And the Ashraf, who were the uncles and cousins and other near relatives of the Mahdi, sat glum and silent, as though birds were flying over their heads. He spoke this as a serious judgement, and not lightly in jest.

The Memoirs of Babikr Bedri

This impressive restatement of the religious ideal paved the way for a new, though rudimentary theocratic state.

The Mahdi at Umm Durman set about organizing a new state as the framework of a regenerated society. This in fact involved eliminating former supporters of institutions which had upheld the Mahdiyya's expansion. This was particularly evident in the religious field where former *qadhi*-s and *'ulama* were dismissed. A new *qadhi al-islam* was appointed. He was a former Dar Furi judge of the Turkiyya called Ahmad 'Ali. However, significantly, the Mahdi himself remained not only the chief judge since he used to hear cases and give rulings, but also the chief lawmaker since he interpreted the Quran or announced rulings by means of proclamations, some of which directly refer to visions in which the Mahdi had personally communicated with the Prophet. Sufi fraternities were now persecuted, not only those hostile to the Mahdiyya but also those which had supported the movement. In 1883, we thus find the Sammaniyya *shaykh* who had helped win the Baqqara over, executed. In fact, religious orders were purely and simply condemned and ordered to disband since it was considered they had now been replaced by the Mahdiyya as the religious force supervising and organizing people's lives and consciences. Even the Pilgrimage was forbidden on the grounds that the Holy Places were under the control of the infidel Turks.

The Mahdi undertook to organize his community and notably camp life at Umm Durman where part of his large army was assembled. There were now over 34 000 men in the army, both black slaves and free men, besides 6000 horsemen and 64 000 spear-bearers. Their zeal and the community spirit were kept up both by prayer meetings and by frequent military parades. Civil administration involved tax-collecting: the regular quranic dues and the taxes paid by those beaten in battle. To oversee tax-collecting and run the treasury (*Bayt al-Mal*), the Mahdi appointed a Nubian called Ahmad Sulayman in whom he personally had confidence. To mark the new state's sovereignty, the Mahdi had the gold and silver taken during the sack of Khartum minted. He also ordained that the new currency should pass at face value. Foreign coins, however, continued to be used especially in view of the fact that the fineness of the Umm Durman-minted coins led to their being hoarded. Local administration was set up on a limited scale and was, in fact, based essentially on the army organization. Chief in command was the Khalifa 'Abd Allah under whom were *amir*-s or commanders who became provincial governors. They could name the officers in charge of the district treasury and the local *qadhi*, but these were responsible to the central government. *Amir*-s were responsible to the Mahdi.

Efforts to extend the theocracy to various parts of the Sudan should not blind us to the fact that the state was in fact concentrated at Umm Durman where the Mahdi and his followers had set up an immense camp of some 150 000 persons, 'a conglomerate of every race and nationality in the Sudan'. Efforts to uphold the theocracy thus increasingly emphasized the person of the Mahdi to whom almost divine veneration was extended. It also had recourse to force to uphold public morality. Spying was rife and public punishments frequent in order to set an example.

In spite of this, it was difficult to keep the unruly flock in order. Political and ethnic divisions among the *ansar* were fostered by close contacts and the rivalry which victory had brought in its wake. Moreover the camp included a horde of newly recruited partisans, tribes who had joined in the last phase of fighting and, increasingly, people who moved in to Umm Durman where opportunities for trade or livelihood were better than in the by now neglected country areas. Commerce was moreover essentially concentrated at Umm Durmann whilst smaller centres such as Berbera declined. There was also an active slave market, slavery having been re-established by the Mahdi. The camp also had its prisoners, over whom close watch had to be kept although they were, to some degree, integrated into the overall pattern of the Mahdiyya. Among those were a number of Europeans. They were priests and sisters of the Austrian Catholic Mission or officers who had formerly been in khedival service. Some of them had converted to Islam and had been recruited into the Mahdist army. This was true of Gustav Kloots, a German newspaper reporter, of Lupton Pasha (who died of exhaustion trying to escape via Abyssinia in September 1886), and Slatin who, in June 1885, became one of 'Abd Allah al-Ta'ishi's bodyguard.

The main danger for the new religious metropolis was not, however, social, but resided in its incapacity to set up adequate conditions of life and sanitation in the face of a massive influx of population. The result, in the months which followed the conquest of Khartum, was the outbreak of epidemics. In 1883, there was an outbreak of cholera. In 1885, smallpox followed.

These difficulties took a dramatic turn when the Mahdi himself fell a victim and died on 22 June 1885, after having confirmed as his successor 'Abd Allah al-Ta'ishi. 'The shock of his death', as Father Ohrwalder, a prisoner in Umm Durman, wrote 'was terrible'. Not only had the Mahdiyya been largely built on faith in one man seen as the community's intermediary with God but in Muslim eschatology the Mahdi was not supposed to have a successor. The Mahdi's death, in effect, deprived the theocracy of its divine sanction.

THE MAHDIYYA UNDER THE KHALIFA

Under Khalifa 'Abd Allah, the political characteristics of the Mahdiyya were more obvious as the overriding religious unity which the Mahdi had provided, disappeared. Though he had been appointed by the Mahdi, 'Abd Allah al-Ta'ishi was a man of the west, supported by the Baqqara and even more obviously by his own group, the Ta'isha. This was resented by the sharifian families of the Nile valley and their clientele. Father Ohrwalder's assessment of the situation is perhaps exaggerated, but nonetheless essentially accurate:

> Before his death, the Mahdi had nominated the Khalifa Abdullah as his successor; he saw that this was the only man capable of holding in check the rapacious Sudanese tribes, and of governing the strange empire which he had raised; but the selection of this 'foreigner' was a bitter disappointment to the Danagla and Jaalin, who, hitherto rulers, had now become the ruled, and from whose hands their authority was transferred to the cruel and tyrannical Baggaras, who henceforth became the conquerors of the Sudan, and who governed its inhabitants with a rod of iron.

The Khalifa was thus, from the start, involved in a struggle for power which resulted in the elimination of the *awlad al-balad* leaders who were replaced by Ta'isha men. By the end of 1886, only two of the former *amir*-s were still in office. This was followed up by a move which had important social consequences: the Khalifa ordered the Baqqara tribes to leave their territory and come to Umm Durman and the Jezira, where they were given lands whilst the former inhabitants were driven out. The Khalifa thus had his followers on the spot to uphold his authority.

The Khalifa's more limited authority was moreover challenged by open revolts. Among more significant uprisings, we may note that of the Rufa'a tribe of the Blue Nile which took to arms in 1887 to prevent the arrest of its chief. Even in the west, the Khalifa's authority was far from effective. Madibbu 'Ali, head of the Rizayqat, one of the more powerful Baqqara tribes, though an early and faithful follower of the Mahdi, quarrelled with his successor and was executed in 1886. Between 1887 and 1889, a man called Abu Jummayza found many to follow him when he claimed to be Jesus (who, it was believed, would reappear after the Mahdi). Severe fighting took place around al-Fashir in October 1888 and the revolt ended in February 1889 when Abu Jummayza died from smallpox or wounds. Moreover, in 1887, a section of the Kababish of northern Kurdufan rebelled and were only crushed after a series of military expeditions in 1888. In 1891, the sharifian families supported by some of the *awlad al-balad*, planned to revolt. The Mahdi's own family was involved in the plot and the Khalifa was forced to come to terms with the *sharif*-s at a meeting which took place at the Mahdi's tomb on 25 November 1891.

Political tensions were fostered by an increasingly difficult economic situation. Agriculture, which had been disorganized by the war, further declined because of lack of rain and in 1889–90 a dramatic situation prevailed. Starving people, 'mere bags of skin and bone' wandered helpless, going to any lengths to get food. People died in their thousands. Khartum and Umm Durman were faced with the added problem of refugees and bitterness increased as incoming stores were reserved for the Baqqara troops. A severe outbreak of typhus is recorded for the period.

Ideology and institutions under the Khalifa

It was perhaps to override social tensions that the Khalifa placed greater emphasis on the state and built up the as yet rudimentary theocracy. Now that the Mahdi was dead, the state was built up around his message and the legitimacy he had conferred on the Khalifa. The latter often withdrew in meditation and on important occasions he would claim he had had visions of the Mahdi and had received his instructions. The Mahdi's central role was further symbolized by the elaborate shrine built up over his tomb soon after his death. It was the most conspicuous building in Umm Durman being some 50 feet-high with a white-painted dome. The Khalifa further recommended visits to the shrine, especially in view of the fact that the Pilgrimage to the Holy Places remained forbidden. He himself does not seem to have equated the two although many of the *ansar* did.

Attempts were made to organize life in Umm Durman where special quarters were assigned to each ethnic group. Large avenues were cut, leading from the city gates to the mosque. As trade developed, northern merchants reappeared on the scene, bringing such commodities as sugar, coffee, honey, perfumes and Manchester-ware which were generally bought up by the state. Institutions became more elaborate with the great mosque as the heart of the new national community. Each social group had its apportioned place at prayers. In the front row, around the *qadhi al-islam* and the Khalifa who acted as *imam*, stood the dignitaries, the *khalifa*-s of the Mahdi's time and the *amir*-s. Behind them came the faithful according to their social groups and, at the back, a special place was assigned to the women. The Khalifa's own house was next to the mosque. The main weekly ceremony was a parade which, as in the Mahdi's time, took place every Friday and was colourful enough to keep up the community's zeal. Besides attending the five set prayers, the Khalifa gave an audience every evening.

Social institutions were established with such functionaries as the *shaykh al-suq*, an officer responsible for honest dealings and order in the market. Punishments inflicted were prison sentences and flogging, but it would seem that the more rigorous sentences of Muslim law were rarely inflicted. Thus the cutting off of thieves' hands was apparently not practised, the only example of this recorded being that of an officer of the mint condemned for false coinage. There is also only one recorded instance of a woman being stoned to death for adultery. Nonetheless the spirit of the community was one of extreme puritanism and it is generally agreed that in the Khalifa's time public morality was on the rise. Not only were Islamic rules respected but, in spite of economic difficulties, roads and commerce were safe. This was further proved by the resumption of the caravan trade with Dar Fur in 1887.

As an independent state, the Sudan also tried to establish relations with foreign governments. Letters were written in this period by the Khalifa to various heads of state including the Sultan of Turkey, the King of Abyssinia, the Khedive of Egypt, and Queen Victoria. The letters were in the evangelizing spirit of the Mahdiyya and were first and foremost an exposition of doctrine and a call to convert. The religious tone of the letters should not blind us to the fact that they were also a political commentary on the prevailing situation. Thus, writing to Queen Victoria, the Khalifa pointed to the defeat of 'one of thy famous men named Hicks Pasha, and with him an army composed of many and diverse sorts of men' as an example of what was to be expected of imperial ambition: 'It was thy own desire alone, without the rest of the nations, imagining thou couldst be victorious over the hosts of God the Conqueror.' Britain had shown the same spirit in Egypt and had there succeeded because, as the Khalifa put it, 'worldly deceit' had entered the hearts of 'Arabi Pasha and his men, 'so that they were turned aside thereby from their faith, and the banner was turned from its victory, so thou wast enabled to gain possession of the land of Egypt'. Imperialism as defined by the Khalifa was characterized by the will to power and the use of perverted Muslims to further it. It also refused negotiated settlements of international problems. Negotiations, of course, could only be on the basis of Islamic law. This was a subjective view, but then so was that of the European powers who applied their own rules to the rest of the world:

> And all this arose from thy error and from following thy own courses, apart from the rest of the nations; for hadst thou taken counsel of them, as it behoved thee to do, they would have shown thee the means to set all thy fears at rest; they would have advised thee to withhold from clashing against the hosts of God, which thou hadst no power to resist, and thou wouldst have confined thyself to the guarding of thine own land and of it alone. But as it is they aid thee with men and arms, and join thee in warring against the troops of God, so in the day of defeat shall the shame not be on thee alone, but shall be shared by others.

The letter ends, logically, with an appeal to the queen to convert to Islam and, should she refuse, to expect the ultimate triumph of true Muslims:

> Thou shalt be crushed by the power of God and his might, or be afflicted by the death of thy people who have entered on war with the people of God, by reason of thy Satanic presumption.

This type of argument, though couched in religious terms, also puts over a nationalist point of view.

Territorial expansion under the Khalifa
Even more fundamentally than his predecessor, the Khalifa was faced with the

problem of diverting his follower's often self-destructive energies to an exterior goal capable of upholding their militant zeal and overriding dissensions. Both religious conviction and political strategy therefore commanded foreign expansion. The Mahdiyya could only expand to a limited degree along its western and southern boundaries. In the south it progressively took over Equatoria which Emin Pasha evacuated in 1889. Many of Emin Pasha's men remained on the spot and took part in the Mahdiyya's efforts to convert the pagan populations of the region. No efforts, however, were made to push further into central Africa. Efforts towards the west were also limited by the growing influence of the Sanusiyya in the eastern Sahara. The Great Sanusi had refused the Mahdi's claim to being 'the Guided One'. Even the Khalifa's own western tribes were increasingly unreliable. The Khalifa was thus led to concentrate on two different projects, both sufficiently ambitious to mobilize the *ansar*: the conquest of Abyssinia and that of Egypt.

Christian Abyssinia, ruled at the time by King John (1872–89), was under dual fire: the Italian invasion in the east, and Mahdi pressures in the west. Skirmishes had already taken place during the Mahdi's lifetime and the war could therefore legitimately be proposed as the following up of the Mahdi's project. A full-scale attack was launched in 1889 and King John was killed in battle at Metemma. Although the *ansar* were victorious, the Khalifa did not capitalize on this, but turned his attention to Egypt.

He wrote on several occasions to the Khedive informing him of the projected invasion. The death of King John which he related in full, was the occasion for another such warning: 'As this has been the fate of the Abyssinians, I now write to inform you, and hope you will take this as a warning for yourself'. Since 1886, the frontier had been fixed at Wadi Helfa and both countries had massed troops on the border. Various skirmishes had taken place in 1887 and 1888 before official orders were given by the Khalifa at the end of 1888 for a march northwards which proved difficult because of obvious Anglo-Egyptian superiority in organization and equipment. The decisive encounter took place at Tushki on 3 August 1889. It was a total defeat for the Sudanese who further lost in the battle one of their most prestigious leaders, al-Najumi.

The defeat at Tushki marked not only the end of the Mahdiyya's ambition to launch a great *jihad*, but a turning point in its history as an independent state. In spite of iron rule, the Khalifa was unable to cope with the economic and social problems of the community. There was growing disaffection among his followers and tribal groups broke away one after the other, preparing the ground for the Anglo-Egyptian reconquest.

SELECTED READING LIST

Allen, B. M., *Gordon and the Sudan*, (London, 1931).
Badri, B., *The Memoirs of Babikr Bedri* (translated from the Arabic by Yousef Bedri and George Scott) (London, 1969) (first published in Arabic in 1961).
Collins, R. O., *The Southrn Sudan, 1883–1898*, (New Haven and London, 1962).
Daniel, N., *Islam, Europe and Empire*, (Edinburgh, 1966).
Gray, R., *A History of the Southern Sudan, 1839–1889*, (Oxford, 1961).
Hasan, Y. F. (ed.), *Sudan in Africa*, (Khartum, 1971).
Hake, A. E., *The Journals of Major-Gen. G. C. Gordon, C. B., at Khartum*, (London, 1885).
Holt, P. M., *The Mahdist State in the Sudan 1881–1898*, (Oxford, 1958).

NORTH AFRICA

Holt, P. M., 'The Source-Materials of the Sudanese Mahdiya', *St. Anthony's Papers*, 4, (London, 1958).

Royle, C., *The Egyptian Campaigns*, (London, 1900).

Sanderson, G. N., *England, Europe and the Upper Nile; 1882–1899*, (Edinburgh, 1965).

Shibeika, M., *British Policy in the Sudan. 1882–1902*, (London, 1952).

Shuqayr, N., *Tarikh al-Sudan al-qadim wa al-hadith wa jughrafiyatuhu*, (Cairo, 1903).

Theobald, A. B., *The Mahdiya*, (London, 1951).

Trimingham, J. S., *Islam in the Sudan*, (London, 1965).

Wingate, F. R., *Ten Years' Captivity in the Mahdi's Camp 1882–1892. From the original manuscript of Father Joseph Ohrwalder*, (London, 1895).

Wingate, F. R., *Mahdism and the Egyptian Sudan*, (London, 1891).

CHAPTER 15

THE SANUSI JIHAD IN THE 19th CENTURY

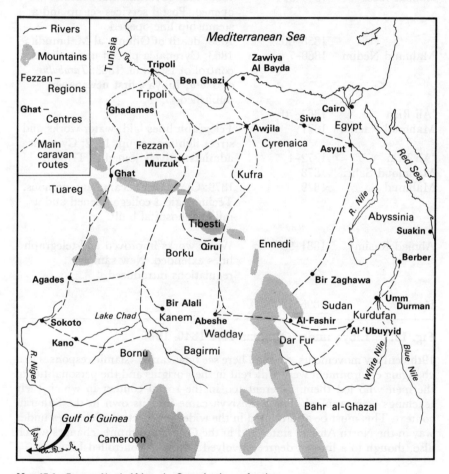

Map 15.1 *Eastern North Africa: the Sanusi sphere of action*

The Sanusi fraternity in Cyrenaica and the Sudanese Mahdiyya are contemporary although the former began earlier and continued effectively to resist European penetration well into the 20th century. Although the term 'revivalist' has sometimes been used to group together these and other

NORTH AFRICA

Pasha-s (List incomplete)	Period of office	Main events
'Ali 'Ashqar	1840–2	1840 The Great Sanusi arrived in Tripoli
Mahmud Amin	1842–47	Modernization of courts of law. 1842: Sayf al-Naser executed by the Turks.
Ahmad Izzet	1848–52	1853: first governmental schools opened. Postal services set up and a steamship line opened.
	1858–60	1858: death of Ghuma al-Mahmudi.
Mahmud Nedim	1860–7	1863: Cyrenaica placed under direct control of Istanbul. 1863: *Tarabulus al-Gharb*, Libya's first newspaper, published.
'Ali Riza	1867–70	
Mahmud Rachid	1871	Telegraph lines laid; water works and street lighting set up. 1872: Cyrenaica administratively joined to Tripoli.
'Ali Riza	1872–4	
Mahmoud Sabri	1878	
Mahmud	1879	1879: Cyrenaica became autonomous. Technological college opened and a military hospital built.
Ahmad Rasim	1881–95	Water works improved and telegraph lines extended. New sanitary regulations introduced.
Hashem	1896–1900	

Fig. 15.1   Libya under Ottoman rule 1840–1900

19th-century movements, we shall here see how varied Islamic responses to a changing environment were, different in their origins and the personalities of the men who led them, different too in the social context in which their teachings were applied. The Sanusiyya came into its own in the Saharan context. This must be appreciated in the wider perspective of changes under way in the North African states and in the Ottoman Empire, changes which also, though to a limited degree, involved Ottoman-controlled Libya.

OTTOMAN RULE IN THE WESTERN PROVINCES IN THE SECOND HALF OF THE 19th CENTURY

The extent and impact of the second Turkish occupation must be measured against a background of persistent Libyan hostility. The armed resistance of major tribal groups described in the context of the Ottoman invasion persisted throughout the 19th century. Though Sayf al-Nasir was beheaded by the

Turks in 1842, his fellow tribesmen of the Awlad Sulayman were not brought under full Ottoman control as is shown by such revolts as those of Ben Ghazi in 1870 and the Fezzan in 1872. This was particularly true of their southern zone of expansion, involving not only Fezzan but the desert area between Fezzan and Lake Chad where they became the dominant group in Kanem and further encroached on Wadday territory. They were thus in strategic command of the trans-Saharan trade which continued to play a fundamental role. The other major tribal leader of the late Qaramanli period, Ghuma al-Mahmudi, had died in 1858 when the Ottoman army had finally crushed Ibadhite resistance in the Nafusa mountains. Sporadic resistance nonetheless persisted bringing to the fore popular heroes. In and around the coastal town of Misurata we thus find the Chetawi family contesting Ottoman power and later passing into open opposition under Ramadan Swahayli (1881–1920). Full control, the necessary prerequisite to Ottoman-promoted social change, was therefore limited to coastal areas and major towns.

Problems of territorial integration were further emphasized by the Sublime Porte's vacillatory attitude. We thus find the administrative connection between Tripoli and Cyrenaica being diversely defined at various times: they were independent one from the other until 1863. Between 1863 and 1871, Cyrenaica was directly administered from Istanbul whilst Tripoli had its own Ottoman administration. In 1871, the two provinces were reunited before being again, in 1879, divided into distinct entities.

The Turks nonetheless undertook to set up a modern centralized government in Libya. This was defined by the 1863 reform which separated Cyrenaica (directly administered from Istanbul), from Tripoli; the latter was governed by a *wali* with the title of *pasha*. The *pasha* had important prerogatives since he was responsible for all local affairs and could also negotiate with representatives of foreign powers. As in Egyptian Sudan, the system was vitiated by Turkish governors' ignorance of local problems, further underscored by a rapid turnover of political personnel: 33 *pasha*-s governed Tripoli from 1835 to 1908.

These facts, combined with general hostility both to the Turkish regime and to its reform policy which included such unwelcome measures as the abolition of secular expressions of *dhimmi* inferiority in the matter of distinctive clothing or protection money paid by them to Muslim Arabs, explain why the social measures taken were on a limited scale and confined to the coastal area or major ports. One should further note that Libya was underpopulated (its population in 1875 was estimated at barely over a million) and that this was not conducive to change. From 1860 onwards, reforms were nonetheless undertaken in order to modernize the country, notably in the field of state education and courts of law. A sanitary service was set up in the ports and the first local newspaper, the *Tarabulus al-Gharb*, was published in 1866. Many of the changes undertaken correspond to European interests in the region. This was particularly so with respect to communications. Though no railway was built, a telegraph was established between Khums and Tripoli and between Tripoli and Malta. Neither functioned for very long. A postal service was organized and shipping lines set up regular services. There was thus a weekly service between Tunis, Malta, and Tripoli, and another between Marseilles and Tripoli, both being run by Rubattino Shipping Lines. The first foreign bank to open a branch office in Tripoli was the Société de Banque Française des Comptoirs Maritimes of Tunis in 1880.

European influence was only getting off to a slow start and the number of foreigners in the country was far smaller than in the other North African states. In 1875 Tripoli had a European community of about 4000. The majority were Maltese and only about 30 families were of other nationalities, French, British, or Italian. Moreover, urban centres were as yet small. Tripoli was the only town of any size and in 1875 it had about 18 000 inhabitants. Ben Ghazi, the capital of Cyrenaica, and Murzuk or Ghadames, the Saharan trading centres, all had populations of under 10 000. The cosmopolitan character of the coastal towns nonetheless tended to increase, especially as foreign invasions brought Muslim refugees to Libya, some on a purely temporary basis as was the case with the majority of the 25 000 Tunisians who sought refuge there between 1881 and 1883. Class stratification on new lines was, however, appearing as Turkish administrators or Tripoli merchants dealt in Mediterranean trade. This also influenced the local Jewish communities which tended to move to the coastal towns where upward social mobility was easier because of Turkish regulations for equal treatment of Jews and of the active interest shown by European organizations such as the Alliance Israelite Universelle. This organization was represented in Istanbul and had set up a local committee in Tripoli in 1866 before extending its activities to other towns of Libya in 1870 at the request of local Jewish communities. Although Jewish schools had existed previously and were indeed responsible for the training of rabbis and judges, their cultural standards were limited as is shown up by the fact that when the Ottomans decided to create the title and office of *Hakham Bashi* or Chief Rabbi in 1874, they were forced to find a suitable candidate abroad. The man they chose, Eliahu Bekhor Hazzan had been Rabbinic emissary in Tunis. As Chief Rabbi, a post he occupied from 1874 to 1888, he promoted educational reform, modernizing methods of instruction and introducing foreign languages. Under later Ottoman rule, the Libyan Jewish community which may have been 15 000-strong (estimates vary considerably) and which specialized in trade, including hawking which was a Jewish monopoly, came to be involved in new sectors of economic activity.

European capitalist interests in urban centres such as Tripoli, Derna or Ben Ghazi was by now obvious, though once again later and on a more limited scale than elsewhere in North Africa. In the 1860s a new export cash-crop production developed, namely esparto grass (locally called halfa) which was used to make ropes, baskets, and paper. Exports began in Tripoli in 1868 and in Khums in 1873. Khums was to become the main centre of production and in 1872 'Ali Riza Pasha organized this on a governmental basis by having special warehouses built, besides markets where taxes on the commodity were levied. In 1881, mechanization was introduced by means of a British hydraulic baling-press.

Turkey was Libya's chief trading partner although this is not brought out by available statistics, especially in view of the fact that trade with Cyrenaica did not classify as import-export. Esparto grass went chiefly to Britain, directly or more often via Malta. In 1869, for an example, £74 000 worth of esparto grass was bought by British traders. The trans-Saharan trade remained considerable. European merchants thus bought £80 000 worth of

Fig. 15.2   Libya: export–import trade in 1875

Country	Imports (in French francs)	Exports (in French francs)
Great Britain	6 295 500	6 200 650
France	947 500	787 959
Italy	244 195	1 607 941
Tunisia	667 900	346 870
Turkey	144 085	306 067

From: P.-F. Bainier, *La Géographie appliquée à la marine, au commerce, à l'agriculture et à la statistique*, (Paris, 1878).

ivory in 1869, figures for ostrich feathers being comparable. Here too Tripoli was not so much a trader in its own right as a purveyor of European merchandise to Sudanic Africa. Goods sent out included colonial products such as coffee and sugar, and the usual Manchester-ware and cheap cottons. Some raw cotton was, however, imported and woven locally. Not only did the Saharan trade remain flourishing but it was to benefit from the disruption of commerce through the Sudan during the period when the Mahdiyya was dominant.

Social change in Ottoman Libya, though similar to that elsewhere along the Mediterranean, was limited in scope. The main focus of interest is, in fact, elsewhere, in the Sanusi movement which in Cyrenaica set up a powerful network of *zawiya*-s which monitored economic, social, and ideological change in Libya and the Sahara.

MUHAMMAD BIN 'ALI AL-SANUSI: SCHOLAR, SUFI, AND MILITANT SAINT

The Sanusi resistance movement of the second half of the 19th century owes much to its founder's personality and teaching. Muhammad bin 'Ali al-Sanusi, 1787–1859, was indeed a remarkable man who combined in his make-up a commitment to higher spititual and intellectual values and a capacity to put them into practice even among unsophisticated groups, a very real awareness of the Muslim world at large and a capacity to adapt his teaching to a more limited specific context. These aspects of his personality are well illustrated by the fact that though he was Algerian-born, his *tariqa* was most influential in Arabia and in Saharan Libya, and that though he was a man of the first half of the 19th century, his teaching came into its own in the latter part of the century and upheld Saharan resistance well into the early years of the 20th century.

Muhammad bin 'Ali al-Sanusi who was born about 1787 in a village near the Algerian town of Mustaghanim, was from a typical sharifian lineage of the west which in addition could claim descent from the Moroccan dynasty of Idris. He was first educated in smaller *zawiya*-s before going on to the university mosque of the Qarawiyyin in Fez in 1805 or thereabouts. He

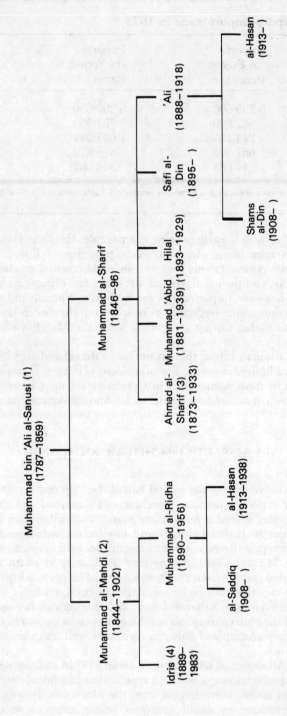

Fig. 15.3 *The Sanusi*

became proficient in the traditional religious subjects: Quranic reading and exegis, and Maliki law, besides showing an interest in more esoteric subjects including astrology and the science of magic squares (*'ilm al-awfaq*). He acquired a number of certificates of proficiency (*ijaza*-s) which made him a teacher in his own right, and he soon had a student following from which was recruited the small group of disciples who were later to follow him in his travels. The supreme council of the Sanusiyya which he later set up included a number of Moroccans. Like other holy men he had shown an early interest in Sufi doctrines and had had contacts with the then expanding Darqawiyya. In Fez he probably came under the direct influence of the fraternity's founder, al-'Arabi al-Darqawi (1760–1823). He also, then as later, multiplied contacts with various *tariqa shaykh*-s, including those of the Tijaniyya.

A student traditionally completed his education by performing the Holy Pilgrimage. This in fact meant a long overland journey with stays in various centres of learning, both smaller *zawiya*-s such as those of Qabis and Misurata where al-Sanusi spent some time, and more famous seats of learning including al-Azhar where he seems to have stayed several months in 1824. In the Holy Places, after the Pilgrimage itself, al-Sanusi like many other devout Muslims stayed on, and it was there that he became one of the very close disciples of Ahmad bin Idris al-Fasi. Al-Sanusi thus became a leading figure in the neo-sufi movement then underway. This had doctrinal aspects derived from the more rigorist of the four orthodox rites, that of Ibn Hanbali, besides following the teaching of the latter's follower, Ibn Taymiya. The movement placed emphasis on imitation of the Prophet (Muhammadiyya) rather than on mystic union with God. It preached very strict adherence to early Muslim practice but also a more active individual responsibility as opposed to *taqlid* or blind observance of religious precedent. The movement, which had already promoted such subversive political ideologies as that of the Wahhabi-s, had a strong impact on the pilgrims who came every year to Mecca and was consequently to arouse the hostility of the religious establishment whose power stand it undermined.

This was demonstrated when, under pressure from more conservative *'ulama*, Ahmad bin Idris and his disciples were forced to leave Mecca for 'Asir, further south along the Arabian coast. It was there that Ahmad bin Idris died in 1836, leaving his disciples divided over the question of leadership. The community broke up, some remaining on the spot, others following al-Mirghani to Sudan, whilst the majority returned to Mecca under the guidance of al-Sanusi. They set up a *zawiya* on Mount Abu Qubays, west of the town, and resumed preaching to incoming pilgrims. Once again *'ulama* hostility came out, upheld by the Turkish governors of the Holy Places who were violently anti-Wahhabi. Al-Sanusi, in 1840, was again forced to contemplate leaving Arabia. This time he decided to return to North Africa.

The kind of opposition al-Sanusi had met with in Mecca was to be no less evident in Cairo where he had stayed on several occasions and where he went in 1840. Doctrinal criticism of his freethinking attitude was rife, upheld by political fears of what was seen as a form of activism. This is well shown up by the comments of a European observer, John Ninet, who in a favourable account of the 'Arabi Pasha uprising, published in 1883, mentioned having met al-Sanusi whom he calls 'a Moghrebbin – I believe of Tunisian origin' and

Muhammad al-Sanusi during his stay in Egypt

. . . the earliest preacher of freedom in North Africa, Mohammed es Senusi, who twenty years ago was a student at the Azhar University at Cairo. He was a Mogrebbin – I believe of Tunisian origin; and though he left Egypt at the early age of twenty-three, he had already sown there the seeds of that society which has since made his name famous among Moslems. His system was a development of freemasonry, but distinctly religious; a religious socialism, in fact, based on those earliest principles of Mahometan teaching which incalculated a universal brotherhood in Islam, a complete religious tolerance. This may have been modified by Senusi later, since his retirement to Tripoli, and in view of the Panislamic movement of modern times with which they had originally no connection; but they have always remained in their early form in Egypt, and account for the language of brotherhood and toleration so constantly held by Arabi and his companions, and which have been thought an affectation by too-learned Europeans. The ideas of Senusi found a peculiarly congenial soil in those *employés déclassés* and their half-enlightened neighbours in the country districts whom I have already spoken of, and were adopted by the mass of the religious professors of the Azhar and by many of the notables and chief merchants of the towns. Es Senusi, however, left Egypt before the modern movement of a distinct Egyptian nationalism began, and so can hardly count as one of its high priests. He was a forerunner rather than an apostle.

John Ninet, *Origin of the National Party in Egypt*, 1883.

'a forerunner' of Egyptian nationalism. Ninet saw al-Sanusi as 'the earliest preacher of freedom in North Africa', a man who believed in the 'universal brotherhood of Islam' and who preached a kind of 'religious socialism'. Official al-Azhar condemnation of al-Sanusi came in 1843 when several *mufti*-s and notably Muhammad 'Ilish, the Maliki chief judge whose name has already been mentioned as a partisan of Arabi Pasha's, criticized al-Sanusi for introducing his own personal doctrinal interpretations.

By then al-Sanusi was no longer in Egypt which he had left in 1840, travelling slowly through North Africa, preaching on the way. He found a ready hearing among the Libyan tribes and even in Tripoli where in spite of *'ulama* opposition, he won over the Turkish Pasha, 'Ali Ashqar who, or so it is said, became a member of the Sanusiyya. In Tunisia, al-Sanusi found the atmosphere less congenial because of French influence on the Regency; moreover he learnt that the colonial authorities in Algeria intended to arrest him were he to cross the border as it was well known that he supported the resistance.

He consequently decided to withdraw to Libya and set up his movement there on solid foundations. To this end he opened his first *zawiya* at al-Bayda on the coastal road of Cyrenaica, half-way between Derna and Ben Ghazi. This typifies his political stand, both the will to live somewhat apart from established authority and hostile pressure groups, whilst not entering into direct conflict with them. This was consistently shown by his acceptance of

Turkish sovereignty. He actively preached respect of rulers and payment of state taxes. He himself in 1856 secured a *firman* from Sultan 'Abd al-Majid I exempting Sanusi property from taxation and allowing the order to collect tithes from its members.

In spite of the successful development of the fraternity, one does not feel that at this stage, al-Sanusi equated his destiny with the Libyan *zawiya*-s. In 1846, soon after his second wife Fatima had given birth to two sons, Al-Mahdi born in 1844 and al-Sharif born in 1846, al-Sanusi once again left for Mecca.

Al-Sanusi's ideas

Al-Sanusi's stay in the Holy Places from 1846 to 1853 probably led him to a wider conception of his role as an ideologue. His residence in Mecca implied interaction at the heart of the Muslim world: moreover he probably felt the need to develop his own research. He was himself a fairly prolific writer and of his 40 or more recorded works, many were written during this second stay in Mecca.

His published works (for many are still manuscript) illustrate his keen interest in many fields of learning. As one of his biographers, B. G. Martin, put it, he was 'a poet, a mathematician, an excellent theologican, and a competent historian and genealogist'. His attitudes are often traditional. His pride in his own sharifian origins was expatiated upon in a work called *al-Durar al-Saniyya* which is also an historical opus. Al-Sanusi is also classical in his account of the 'chain' of masters who through the ages have passed on knowledge, and his own references constitute a typical encyclopedia of North African scholarship. We nonetheless find at the core a more critical attitude based on a fundamental political problem: modern man's relationship with the transcendental model of the Prophet's ideal community. With remarkable consistency, al-Sanusi in this period pursued research on the key concept of *ijtihad* (individual effort) which he opposed to *taqlid* (mere imitation). Al-Sanusi recommended facing up to a changing world which through the intellectual and moral will of True Believers could be mastered and remodelled on the lines laid down by the Prophet.

Like other Muslim thinkers, al-Sanusi believed that this renaissance – he does not himself use the term – was necessarily to be Muslim-wide, and his settling in Mecca, at the heart of this world, the place to which pilgrims came from every part of the *dar al-Islam*, must be seen in terms of an extended militancy. Al-Sanusi and his close disciples made considerable efforts in this period to preach the message and obtain new adherents for the fraternity. In this they were successful since the number of *zawiya*-s increased, spreading over a wider area than formerly: in Arabia, Egypt, various oases including Siwa, and possibly already in Tunis and even Algeria. Division on social lines was, however, apparent, urban populations responding in lukewarm fashion (although such important centres as Medina and al-Tayif now had Sanusi *zawiya*-s) whilst a far more enthusiastic acceptance came from nomad or semi-nomad tribes, both in Arabia and North Africa. An example of this is often mentioned in Sanusi sources: the influence acquired over the Banu Harb, a warlike Hijazi tribe which had up to then lived off the spoils of caravans. Not only was al-Sanusi able to convert them to agriculture but he made peace pacts which effectively protected caravans travelling under Sanusi protection. The same was to be true of the Saharan tribes, some of whom had already been contacted by Sanusi preachers or through pilgrims. Actual political alliances had moreover been concluded, the first being with the Sultan of Wadday, al-Hajj Muhammad Sharif, whom al-Sanusi had met in Mecca as early as 1830 and whom he had won over to his views. The eastern Saharan sultanates were all to pass under Sanusi influence and were to resist not only European encroachments but also those of the Mahdiyya.

During his stay in Mecca, al-Sanusi maintained close links with the Libyan branch of the fraternity, encouraging its expansion. It would seem that an annual conference was held in Mecca every year, attended by delegates from Libya who received instructions from the *shaykh* and discussed local problems with him. Typical of al-Sanusi's approach was his insistence on education which led to a number of students being sent out every year from Cyrenaica to the Holy Places. As soon as his two sons were old enough, al-Sanusi also had them sent to Mecca to be educated.

Al-Sanusi, through information received from pilgrims, was also worried by increasingly emphasized political aggression in the world. The threat of imperialism seems to have aroused in him a sense of urgency together with the will to face up to the danger. Well-established traditions of the mid-1850s depict al-Sanusi as being well aware of the future course of events and of even making startlingly true predictions. He is said to have foretold the capture of Alexandria by the British, of Tripoli by 'the people of Naples', and the invasion of Tunis and other parts of the Maghrib. His decision to return to Libya in 1853 reflects a more radical stand.

The Sanusiyya's development in Libya, 1853–9

Al-Sanusi's hasty return to Libya in 1853 marked a change in the fraternity which now became more actively militant, not only through efforts to propagate the order but also in emphasizing social impact by more effective integration with local society. The traditional spiritually-defined fraternity became a warring order and its *zawiya*-s evolved into *ribat*-s, fortified monasteries such as those which in early times had protected the marches of the *dar al-Islam*. Typical of this change of emphasis is al-Sanusi's decision not to return to al-Bayda but to find a new location for the order's headquarters. This was to be Jaghbub, a somewhat isolated spot some 160 km inland in a desert area near the Egyptian frontier. This limited the inevitable relations with the Ottoman authorities who in al-Sanusi's view were not able to stand up effectively to European pressures, whilst at the same time increasing the order's radius of action since Jaghbub was a crossroad on the caravan routes leading to Egypt from the west and from Sudanic Africa. This further implied a new strategy, one which to some extent turned its back on the Mediterranean and concentrated on the Sahara.

Work undertaken at Jaghbub was on a gigantic scale as wells were dug, access roads cleared, and a town built. Many buildings had a very practical function and point to al-Sanusi's belief that religious zeal should be built up, on and through existing social and economic institutions. Thus holy men who were protectors of tribal groups and regulators of the social order played a key role in promoting affiliation to the fraternity through constant contacts with the *shaykh*-s at Jaghbub where disciples could stay for more or less lengthy periods of initiation. Nomads such as the Awlad Sulayman who roamed as far South as Lake Chad received hospitality at Jaghbub and were thus progressively brought under Sanusi influence. Holy men were also protectors of trade, the safety of which they could effectively guarantee. Not only did al-Sanusi set up his headquarters at a place where merchants involved in extended caravan trading could stop over, but he made special arrangements to promote their activities. Not only were tribal pacts made for the safe conveyance of merchandise but the latter could be stored in the warehouses of Jaghbub. It was indeed by use of these caravan routes both by the order's preachers and by sympathizers won over in the *zawiya*-s and at Jaghbub, that the Sanusiyya in this period was able to expand in the Sahara. Sudanic regions themselves came to be involved as al-Sanusi bought slaves from the Arab merchants. They were educated at the *zawiya* and then freed to go back as missionaries to their native lands. Holy men were scholars and teachers and this was brought out at Jaghbub where not only schools functioned but also a library and university. In the prevalent context of imperialist aggression, the order's fighting capacity was also built up. We thus hear of a store of arms being laid up at Jaghbub. There were, it is said, enough weapons to arm 3000 men, besides four guns brought in from Alexandria via Tobruk. Sanusi mistrust of the Ottoman authorities was here shown by the fact that the cache was a fairly well-kept secret. Al-Sanusi's successful action at Jaghbub made for a fast-developing population, although estimates vary considerably (a mere 1000 according to Evans-Pritchard, some 6000–7000 according to French military sources in Algeria).

Two reasons go some way to explaining this expansion: the strong impact of *zawiya*-s on tribal groups and the independent organization of the Sanusiyya. Better social integration of local *zawiya*-s and integration of the latter into the cohesive pattern of the Sanusiyya based at Jaghbub thus combined to make the order into a new political force.

The opening of *zawiya*-s was effected, taking the existing tribal pattern into account. As Evans-Pritchard put it:

> Starting from the foundation of al-Zawiya al-Baida in 1843, the Order spread itself throughout Cyrenaica until it embraced in its network of lodges the entire tribal system of the country. It seeded itself, as it were, in the crevasses between tribes and tribal sections, and its points of growth were thus also the points of convergence in tribal and lineage structure.

They involved however, a somewhat modified definition of holy men and their tribal status. Scholars and arbiters generally remained aloof from material activities and indeed could, in some cases, be seen as social parasites. This was not to be the case of Sanusi communities made up of the *shaykh* (local head of the *zawiya*), his *ikhwan* (disciples) and sympathizers. Al-Sanusi had adopted the principle of not forcing such a community upon a tribe but of responding to tribal requests for a holy man to be sent to mediate in conflicts and give religious eduation. Land for the *zawiya* was conceded by the tribe or bought by the order, and the buildings which were to have a social function (the mosque, the school, and the *shaykh*'s house) were built by the tribesmen themselves.

The holy men were economically independent and autonomous. They worked their own lands, sometimes with the help of salaried workers, reared cattle or practised various crafts. This system was encouraged at Jaghbub itself where, according to the Arab nationalist leader, Shakib Arslan, the students and even the Mahdi's son used to spend Thursdays learning such trades as carpentry, building, bookbinding or mat-making. Friday was not only a day of prayer but of training in the use of arms. Strict regulations were enforced to maintain the high moral tone and asceticism of these early *zawiya*-s. Spending was strictly controlled. Thus, though traditional hospitality was provided, this was on a moderate scale and no waste was allowed. Students had free board and modest fare. The *ikhwan* who were expected to act as schoolteachers had their keep and two new suits of clothing a year from *zawiya* revenues. The *shaykh* had ten such suits and these also served as traditional presents. He had the right to a wedding feast and upkeep of one wife. Special emphasis was placed on morality. The *zawiya*-s were not only traditional places of asylum and prayer where fighting, quarreling and loud conversations were forbidden, as were also singing and dancing. The collaboration of lay and religious men in community life was further upheld by a common council in which both tribal and *zawiya* representatives took part. Problems concerning the community were debated there and settled, especially since the council also had a judiciary function. The *zawiya*-s thus operated at various levels: by providing a model which the lay community could imitate, by filling traditional holy man functions, by promoting literacy and religious education, and by promoting the *tariqa*'s influence.

The *zawiya*-s also operated at another level, that which was constituted by the centralized network of all the Sanusi lodges of Libya and the Sahara. The Arabian, Egyptian, and Sudanese *zawiya*-s, as also the few recorded Tunisian and Algerian ones, were on the other hand largely independent. The order's capital, in this period, was at Jaghbub and it was there that the annual Council of the order, which has already been mentioned, met. The Sanusi himself took decisions involving the creation of *zawiya*-s, the sending out of preachers and the appointments of *shaykh*-s. Not only were local considerations not taken into account with respect to appointments but the latter were based on the spiritual worth of the candidate and cut across national cleavages. Many Moroccans thus remained in the Sanusi's following and sometimes had rural postings. To help him run the order, the Sanusi had a number of secretaries and close disciples. The annual council gave *zawiya*-s the opportunity to send their *shaykh*-s and delegates to Jaghbub. They would also present their accounts and bring in surplus revenue. General policy was outlined to the delegates on such occasions and local problems were examined.

Al-Sanusi's policy was now clearly turned southwards to the Sahara. This was apparent as early as the mid-1850s by the fact that a strong line of defence was set up at the level of the oases along the 29th parallel. From there Sanusi religious propaganda and political influence spread actively throughout the Sahara in this period, reaching isolated regions such as the Tibesti and Kufra (where the Sanusi-s established a lodge at al-Jawf), and large independent tribal confederacies such as those of the Tuareg. The threat represented by European travellers, who were seen as part of the imperial design, was further brought home by the Sanusi-s, who asked for and obtained tribal cooperation in keeping foreigners out. This policy was well illustrated by Duveyrier's experience, in 1861. Duveyrier was a French officer mapping out Tuareg territory and he had obtained the help of the Turkish authorities in Tripoli who had sent him out with an escort. He was, however, stopped at the Sanusi *zawiya* of Zuwila in the Fezzan and forced to turn back.

Under the strong impetus of its founder and with the support of missionaries and sympathizers, al-Sanusi had to some degree achieved his ambition. His forced exile from his native land, Algeria, and from his spiritual homeland, Mecca – his *hijra* one might call it – had enabled him to set up a social model in conformity with his religious views and to win over to this to a great extent the tribal populations of Cyrenaica and of the Sahara. He had moreover created this in a contemporary context defined by the impending threat of invasion. In the difficult years which followed, his sons were able to build up an effective resistance movement on these foundations.

The Sanusiyya under al-Sanusi's 19th-century successors

When the Great Sanusi died in 1859, his sons who had been called back from Mecca in view of his ill-health, were still young. Muhammad al-Mahdi (1844–1902) was about 15, his brother Muhammad al-Sharif (1846–96) was only 13. The council which had helped al-Sanusi run the order remained paramount whilst at the same time recognizing the joint leadership of the two young men of whom their father had said, 'al-Mahdi holds the sword, al-Sharif the pen'. Al-Sharif as the scholar of the family continued to preside over the order's flourishing university at Jaghbub whilst his brother, who was sometimes seen by his followers as the expected Mahdi, was its temporal leader.

In the 50 years which followed the Great Sanusi's death, the order developed considerably. This was the consequence of earlier efforts which now came to fruition as the number of lodges was quadrupled. The opening of new centres further emphasized the political views of the order's founder. Expansion among urban populations remained limited although a *zawiya* was founded at Ben Ghazi in 1870 or thereabouts and another at Tripoli in 1882. Tribal Cyrenaica on the other hand came almost totally under Sanusi control with the number of *zawiya*-s increasing from 21 to 43 according to Evans-Pritchard. The Sanusiyya's main area of expansion, however, was the Sahara where early missionary zeal now materialized. A number of lodges were created in the oases of Kufra and in the Tibesti, and advance outposts were set up in Sudanic Africa, notably at Bir 'Alali and Kano. More important still was the fact that Sanusi influence was now preponderant throughout the region, as the French military authorities were not slow to note after the failure of Duveyrier's mission. Indeed, Saharan, and more particularly Tuareg, hostility was generally attributed by them to Sanusi propaganda although this to some degree was part of a not necessarily well-founded Sanusi-phobia. The massacre of the Flatters' mission sent to map out the trans-Saharan railway in 1881 is only one of many expressions of Saharan hostility attributed to Sanusi influence; and indeed it is true that European travellers found it increasingly difficult to go into the desert even if, as earlier pointed out, some such journeys were successful, including that of Nachtigal who in 1868 went from Fezzan to Bornu through Tibesti and Wadday. Significantly, however, when in 1876

Gerard Rohlfs was sent out with instructions to come to an agreement with the Sanusi on Prussia's account, the head of the order refused to receive him.

What following the Sanusiyya could command in this period is difficult to say, not only because sources vary in their appreciations according to their assessment of the order's political influence, but also because this to a large degree depended on circumstances: dedicated followers could count on additional wide support in the face of actual European encroachments. Among contemporary estimates we find the Sanusi following put at nearly 3 million. In case of need, the Sanusi, it was said, could turn out some 25 000 armed tribesmen and 1500 horsemen.

The political views of the Sanusiyya and their practical results were further demonstrated in this period, and three problems which had been uppermost in the founder's mind once again came to the fore: the role of Sanusi communities as models of the reformed Islamic way of life, relations with legitimate state authority, notably with the Ottoman regime, and the defence of the *dar al-Islam* against European encroachments.

The Sanusi *zawiya* communities continued to provide a model pattern of behaviour but their involvement in more mundane activities was also increasingly evident, with all that this implied. In the richer coastal areas they acquired considerable property, the latter being given *waqf* status, and by the 1880s the Sanusiyya had become Libya's largest landowner. At the end of the century, it was estimated that the order held some 200 000 hectares, several richer individual *zawiya*-s having more than a thousand. In line with the policy evolved by the founder and successfully practised with the Arabian Banu Harb, these farms promoted the settlement of nomads, who were encouraged to turn to agriculture and cattle-rearing. Considerable efforts were made in more favourable areas to improve methods of production and to introduce new crops. This was particularly successful in the al-Akhdar region where fruit trees were extensively planted. In the drier regions, sheep and cattle-rearing methods were improved.

As the wealthiest and most powerful social group in Libya, Sanusi leaders were faced with the problem of defining their attitudes to various Muslim governments and movements. The Sanusi-s made the Prophet's rule 'to reform Islam through peaceful means and not through bloodshed' theirs, but in the tension-fraught climate of the late 19th century, this implied sometimes difficult decisions. Political movements in the region often tried to obtain Sanusi support. This was the case, as we saw, of 'Arabi Pasha who in 1882 had asked al-Mahdi al-Sanusi to come to his help. Further efforts were made to win over to this project leading *ikhwan*. The Sanusi nonetheless refused, further expressing fears as to the consequences of what he considered an irresponsible uprising. That this view was not entirely accepted by all Cyrenaicans has also been pointed out. Similarly the Sudanese Mahdi's appeals were rejected. Not only did al-Sanusi ignore the Mahdi's offer to appoint him *khalifa* but he condemned the latter's claim to being the 'Guided One' and declared the Sudanese Mahdi an imposter. Pleas both from the Mahdi and later from his successor Khalifa 'Abd Allah were of no avail. The Sanusi gave strict instructions to his disciples in border areas to resist encroachments from the east. In addition he made more political agreements on similar lines with the Sultans of Wadday and Borku. In a letter to the latter he also pointed out the dangers of a civil war which was condemned by the Prophet and which could only weaken the Muslim community.

Peaceful coexistence was also to define the Sanusiyya's attitude to the Ottomans. This to some degree was also the policy of the Sublime Porte, which hoped to have Sanusi help in case of need. Nonetheless relations were distant and increasingly mistrustful. In the latter part of the century, closer watch was kept on the order's doings and in 1890 the Wali of Cyrenaica, Rashid Pasha, came to Jaghbub. He brought an invitation from the Sultan for al-Mahdi to visit him in Istanbul. The Sanusi politely declined. During his tour of the

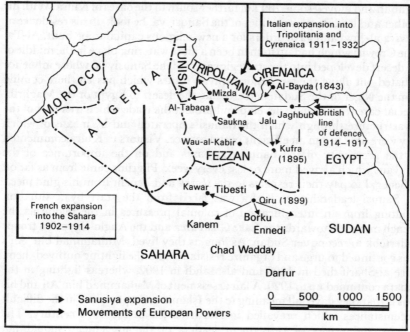

Map 15.2 *The spread of the Sanusi in North Africa (source:* Evans-Pritchard, *The Sanusi of Cyrenaica*

zawiya, Rashid Pasha made inquiries as to the rumoured store of arms. The visitor was put off by being taken to the library and shown the books which, according to his host, were the fraternity's sole weapons. The following year, in 1891, another emissary was sent, this time directly from Istanbul. The Sanusiyya was also to remain aloof from two ideological stands which Sultan 'Abd al-Hamid II (1876–1909) attempted to use as political tools: the Caliphate theory according to which he was the legitimate heir to the leadership of the Muslim community as a whole, and Pan-Islamism as the movement through which this unity was to be re-established.

The defence of the Saharan marches which had loomed so large in Muhammad bin 'Ali's later years, was to be actively pursued by his sons. Not only was al-Mahdi able to win over the Sultan of Borku, but also the regions of Wajanka and Ennedi. This made a powerful pro-Sanusi block at the eastern end of the desert. The order's hold over the region between Fezzan and Lake Chad was developed by an active policy in Tibesti and Kufra to consolidate the results of the activites of Muhammad bin 'Ali's early missionaries there. A no less active policy was carried out with respect to the Tuareg throughout the region extending from Southern Algeria to the Niger Bend. By the late 1870s over half the Sahara was under Sanusi influence.

At the end of the century, Muhammad al-Mahdi was once again to move the order's headquarters so as to be on the front line of defence, since European penetration throughout Sudanic Africa made confrontation inevitable. In 1895 he appointed his nephew Muhammad 'Abid as his representative in Jaghbub and moved some 700 km further south to the oases of Kufra. With his brother and leading personalities of the Sanusiyya, he took up his residence at Zawiya al-Jawf and gave orders for a new religious capital to be built. Al-Taj ('the Crown) which had up to then been a mere watering place in the middle of the desert developed into the strategic centre of the Sanusiyya, whose influence radiated out along the ten major caravan routes which passed there coming from the Niger or the Sudan and crossing the desert to Egypt or the Maghrib. Special care was taken to develop and protect the trade which was part of the infrastructure through which the Sanusi-s operated and by means of which they were able to run an efficient postal service. Visitors to Kufra commented on the prosperity of the Sanusi-run oases and on the importance of the caravans which arrived more or less every week. Pilgrims came from as far off as Senegal to pay their respects to the *shaykh* and benefit from his guidance.

Sanusi leadership at Kufra was faced from the start by a situation resulting from an intensification of colonial pressures in the region as the French moved in towards the Lake Chad area and the Anglo-Egyptian troops undertook to reconquer Sudan. As long as they lived, Muhammad bin 'Ali's sons continued to urge and organize resistance and the fighting outlived them, since al-Sharif died in 1896 and al-Mahdi in 1902, whereas fighting in the Sahara continued up to 1920. A fair assessment of Muhammad bin 'Ali and his sons is that they gave full meaning to the Islamic concept of *jihad* in the difficult circumstances which prevailed in North Africa in the 19th century. The failings and errors of subsequent leaders of the movement should not overshadow their earlier positive contribution to the history and to the defence of the region.

SELECTED READING LIST

I – Libya under the Ottomans
Cacchia, A., *Libya under the Second Ottoman Occupation (1835–1911)*, (Tripoli, 1945).
Goldberg, H., *The Book of Mordechai. A Study of the Jews of Libya*, (Philadelphia, 1980).
Mantran, R. *et al.*, *La Libye nouvelle. Rupture et continuité*, (Paris 1975).

II – Muhammad bin 'Ali al-Sanusi and the Sanusiyya
Dajjani, A. S. al-, *Al-Harakat al-Sanusiyya, nashatiha wa namuwwuha fi al-qarn al-tasi' 'ashar*, (Cairo, 1967).
De Leone, E., *Riformatori musulmani del XIX secolo nell' Africa e nell' Asia mediterranee*, (Milan, 1973).
Duveyrier, H., *La Confrérie musulmane de Sidi Mohammed Ben 'Ali es-Senoussi et son domaine géographique en l'année 1300 de l'Hégire: 1882 de notre ère*, (Paris, 1884).

THE SANUSI JIHAD IN THE 19TH CENTURY

Evans-Pritchard, E. E., *The Sanusi of Cyrenaica*, (Oxford, 1949).

Klopfer, H., *Aspekte der Bewegung des Muhammad ben 'Ali al-Sanusi*, (Wiesbaden, 1967).

Martin, B. G., *Muslim Brotherhoods in 19th-Century Africa*, (Cambridge, 1976).

Nallino, C., 'Le Dottrine del Fondatore della Confraternita Senussita'; in *Raccolta di Scritti Editi ed Inediti*, 2, (Rome, 1940).

Sanusi M. al-, *Al-Majmu'a al-Mukhtara min Ma'allafat al-Ustadh al-a'dham al-Imam Sidi Muhammad bin 'Ali al-Sanusi*, (Beyrut, 1962).

Shukri, M. F., *Al-Sanusiyya, din wa dawla*, (Cairo, 1948).

CHAPTER 16

EXILE AT HOME OR ABROAD

In the preceding chapters special emphasis has been placed on North Africa's will to resist and on some of the more successful movements which upheld this. That at some stage or other they were all defeated has been pointed out, but what must now be stressed is the fact that the common background to these movements was the takeover of North Africa by European powers who set up colonial regimes, transforming the local population into a community in exile, either the kind of exile implied by being a stranger in one's own country, or exile by departure to some other part of the world.

COLONIAL REGIMES IN THE LATTER PART OF THE 19TH CENTURY

It is in Algeria, the earliest and most harshly-administered of the colonial regimes of North Africa, that one can best see what life under foreign rule meant. This was brought out – after the long drawn-out conquest and the somewhat fanciful pattern of coexistence devised by Napoleon III – by the policies of the Third Republic (1870–1940) which well illustrate how a progressive regime at home can, in a colonial context, mean increased oppression.

The Third Republic began by destroying what remained of Algerian identity, doing away with the Arab kingdom and integrating the colony purely and simply into the national territory of France. On the model of the departments or administrative districts which existed in France, Algeria was itself divided into three departments. That Algeria could not, however, be on the same footing was nonetheless shown by the fact that a governor-general was appointed, although attempts were made to curtail his powers by making him responsible to the French parliament. Further efforts to integrate the colony into home administration included decrees in force between 1881 and 1896 placing local administrative departments under the authority of appropriate ministries in Paris. Such measures were to a large degree inoperable because the two active and antagonistic sectors of opinion in Algeria – the Muslims and the colonists – could not or would not accept the pattern worked out in Paris. Between 1871 and 1891, Algeria, 'the smaller French Republic' was to be dominated by some 200 000 Frenchmen or naturalized French citizens who lorded it over 3 million native subjects. As Gueydon, the first governor-general appointed by the Third Republic, put it: French rule 'aimed at satisfying the legitimate aspirations of the colonists'. As for the Arabs, 'they have been beaten and must accept our rule'. The 30 000 or 40 000 Frenchmen, who alone had voting rights, elected six members of parliament whose task it was to promote this policy. The French parliament, which showed little real knowledge of the situation prevailing in Algeria, was largely manipulated by the colonial lobby and was prepared to accept its recommendations so as to secure the votes of the six members for Algeria. Even such measures in favour of native Algerians which passed successfully through parliament were misinterpreted or rendered ineffectual by administrative authorities on the spot, and they themselves were largely cowed by vested interests.

Algeria thus became a territory open to colonist settlement. This implied in the first place constant demands on Algerians to give up their lands. Among laws passed to this effect was the 1873 Warnier Law giving new opportunities for confiscation. European holdings during the last 30 years of the century increased from 480 000 to 1 million hectares, and over 1000 farms changed hands every year. As Algerians saw themselves reduced to farming only small and unproductive land areas, many were forced to become labourers working for Europeans. Colonists received every possible encouragement: grants of land, credit facilities, and help from the administration. The administration, in spite of the massive influx of refugees from Alsace and Lorraine (granted to Germany as part of the 1870 war settlement), continued to ask for more immigrants. The will to build up the foreign community was evident. French responses being limited, a policy of easy naturalization was set on foot with respect to non-French Europeans, mainly Italians and Spaniards. As this itself proved insufficient, children of immigrants born in Algeria were automatically granted French nationality. A further measure in this period, one which was put over to public opinion as being non-racist and promoting equality, but which, in fact, was directed against the national community in Algeria, was the 1870 Crémieux decree granting French citizenship to Algerian Jews. In 1872, there were 129 600 Frenchmen, 115 000 Europeans of various nationalities, and 34 574 Algerian Jews, thus making a dominant community of 279 174. By the end of the century, it had doubled. This did not mean that there was harmonious development within the non-native community, even if privileges acquired at Algerian expense created a common bond: the French despised other Mediterraneans whom they called 'neo-French' and, as Christians, all the Europeans despised North African Jews, anti-semitism sometimes leading to outbreaks of violence.

Every effort was made to develop Algeria into a food-producing area to meet home needs. Early efforts concentrated on cereals, which represented some 76 per cent of the European agricultural sector. In the 1870s an archaic form of farming still survived which differed but little from that of the Algerians and produced a mere 600 or 700 kg a hectare, whereas in France at that time productivity averaged 1500 kg a hectare; but as labour was cheap and prices high, the situation was not unsatisfactory. By the 1880s, however, prices on the international market had begun to drop and by 1894 they reached record low figures. European farming in Algeria reacted by increasing output, not only by more extensive farming as smaller producers dropped out and companies took over, but by introducing mechanization and dry farming. By 1890, the gap between two types of agriculture increased as Algerians were left with only unproductive lands and few credit facilities to enable them to improve their methods. By 1890 European farms were producing on an average 2500 kg of hard wheat and 3500 kg of barley a hectare whilst, in the same period, Algerian productivity dropped to a bare 500 kg a hectare. By 1880 a new trend, moreover, had appeared as European agriculture began to switch to growing grapes for wine which soon became Algeria's major export. Two factors encouraged this: high prices because of the phylloxera disease which had ruined French vineyards in 1880, and local credit facilities available to Europeans (the production of wine and the uncertainties as to quantities produced made credit a necessary condition of success). The parallel development of banks specializing in these operations did much to stimulate colonial optimism and a spirit of enterprise. However, by 1895, prices on the international market had begun to fall as phylloxera-resistant plants were introduced to the South of France. Heavily indebted colonial farms passed under the control of banks and later of companies, thus making for the concentration of property. When the price for Algerian wines began to rise again, a new capitalist farming trend was under way.

Colonial administration evolved to uphold the system by fostering European development and turning the Algerians into a docile labour force. Colonists on the spot and the all-powerful colonial lobby in France made sure the system provided protection and prosperity for the settler community. Two types of districts were created: the mixed communes in which the population was essentially Algerian and which were placed under the full control of the civil and military authorities, and the civilian districts which were organized on the French communal model with responsibility vested in a mayor and a council elected by a minority having voting rights. The budget came essentially from tax revenue, but taxpayers were both Algerian and French; indeed the former far outweighed the latter both by sheer numbers and the fact that they paid proportionately higher taxes, being also subject to Quranic dues and various licence fees. The official Burdeau Report of 1889 shows that Algerians contributed 75 per cent of tax revenue; and yet the money spent was almost exclusively for the benefit of European centres which became flourishing concerns as 19th-century descriptions and postcards show. The colonial boroughs had fine avenues, and public parks with bandstands where well-paid bands would play on a summer evening, whilst Muslim villages could only with the utmost difficulty obtain credits to build a public fountain. Efforts to develop more democratic rule at the end of the century led to such decrees as that of 25 August 1898, which set up an Economic Assembly called the Délégations Financières to advise on public spending. They merely served to emphasize European over-representation, further underscored by the fact that native delegates were chosen for their submissive attitudes (the *Beni Oui-Oui*, the 'Yes-Yes tribe' in colonial parlance). A further distinction between Arabs and Berbers, separately represented in the Délégations Financières, marked the colonial will to break up the national community. Numerically, the Délégations Financières consisted of 24 colonists, 24 non-colonist Europeans, 17 Arabs, and seven 'Kabylies' (Berbers).

As a subject people, the Algerians were submitted to other discriminatory measures. Governor-General Gueydon himself summarized these in an 1877 letter to the French Minister of the Interior as 'the serfdom of the natives'. A law, voted by the French parliament in 1881, codified these measures: the Native Code (Code de l'indigénat) listed 27 (later 33) 'crimes' for which

Algerians could be sentenced. They included refusal to carry out corvée labour, an insulting attitude in the presence of French officials, and travelling in Algeria without a permit. As Schoelcher, the French abolitionist, put it: 'it is a statute of slavery. Only slaves cannot travel without a permit'.

In a more general way, the French administration encroached ever more noticeably on the prerogatives of Muslim institutions. This was particularly true with respect to Islamic law. Efforts to curtail its application and limit the influence of Islamic judges were part of colonial policy. In 1874, the number of *qadhi*-s was reduced from 184 to 80, and in 1886 they were ordered to deal solely in matters pertaining to the family code. French justices of the peace were appointed to deal with all other civil cases and were expected, without any form of training, to apply Islamic rulings in the matter. Criminal cases were tried by popular juries, a democratic measure in France but one which, when applied to Algeria where juries were made up of settlers, led to gross injustice. The governors-general themselves were horrified at the number of death sentences passed in such circumstances: out of 620 Algerians tried in 1872, 71 were condemned to death, often for such crimes as starting forest fires.

An equally grim picture is given by colonial policy in the matter of education. In the earlier period, under Napoleon III, Franco-Arab schools had been opened. In 1877 their number was brought down from 36 to 24 and in 1883 they were all closed. At the same time colonist pressure was brought to bear on the administration to close the three *madrasa*-s where students could be trained in Islamic law. The need to have notaries and a minimum number of *qadhi*-s led the administration to refuse, but standards in the *madrasa*-s continued to decline and half-trained scholars were to constitute an ignorant manipulatable body. Efforts were made to prevent Algerians from sending their children to school: not only were private Arab schools closed but attendance at French ones was discouraged. In 1888, only 2 per cent of Algerian children were getting primary education. The figure was still under 5 per cent by 1914, in spite of the obvious need for a trained labour force. Figures were, of course, even lower in secondary schools – 86 pupils in 1899 – and in the universities, where only one Algerian doctor qualified locally prior to 1914. Even these results were not sufficient to assuage European fears. As *Akhbar*, a newspaper which aired colonist views, put it: 'we are frightened by the sight of so many educated Arabs and we wonder what they will do when they are older'.

At the same time an all-out effort was made to destroy the cultural and religious structures which provided the main guidelines to Algerians' sense of being an oppressed community. The rural *zawiya*-s, which to some degree still upheld traditional literacy and provided for the needs of Algerians for whom they were – even more than before due to the disappearance of urban religious institutions – the core of community life, were closed or generally opposed because they were seen by the French as 'hotbeds of fanaticism, local haunts of Carbonari dressed in ganduras'. The number of mosques was reduced, the local clergy were placed under the control of the French administration, and passports for the Pilgrimage were only granted to a few selected candidates. The justification was that given by Governor-General Tirman: 'were we to do otherwise, we should be working against the consolidation of our interests'. That this implied the moral and even physical extermination of Algerians was a possibility which some colonists sanguinely envisaged. Not only did events such as the 1870 uprising raise a public outcry demanding that the Algerians be 'driven out into the desert', but it was even suggested that their elimination was part of a 'natural law' which led to the 'disappearance of backward peoples'. Statistical evidence was used to back up this theory and the Algerian demographic trend up to the late 1880s seemed to justify colonist optimism. The reversal of the trend and the appearance, here as in other parts of North Africa, of larger families proved that in fact the population as a whole not only survived the shock of conquest but provided an elementary response which dashed European hopes of becoming a numerically dominant community.

Tunisia

In Tunisia, the conquest which was styled a 'coup de bourse' (financier's coup') by a critical Clemenceau, went ahead in spite of the uproar it caused in France where it brought about the downfall of Jules Ferry's ministry. It expressed itself less on the battleground – although some actual fighting took place, notably in southern Tunisia – than in the diplomatic field and was finalized by the La Marsa Convention of 8 June, 1883, which defined Tunisia as a French protectorate.

In a protectorate, the country's own institutions were theoretically maintained. The colonial power was there to 'protect' these, and in addition, to implement the reforms which were put forward as justification for the takeover. On the other hand, the country's armed forces and foreign affairs were in the hands of the protecting power. The Tunisian beylical dynasty was consequently maintained and when Muhammad al-Sadiq died in 1882, his successor was appointed according to normal rules of succession. The country continued to be governed by its own laws with new measures being taken as in the past by beylical decree, the only difference being that these decrees to become law had to be approved and countersigned by the French-appointed resident general. The latter could, however, take such measures as he thought fit with regard to French residents. Although a Tunisian government was maintained in traditional form, French heads of department were appointed, their official position being that of Tunisian civil servants. Various French-staffed departments were created. Local administration continued to be carried out by *qaid*-s (of whom there were 36) but the French named administrators (controleurs civils) to oversee them. As in other colonial regimes the latter gradually took charge. The protectorate did away with consular courts, replaced by French ones. Tunisians continued to be ruled by *shari'a* courts but penal cases were brought before mixed courts.

In terms of international law, the protectorate regime was halfway between national independence and full French sovereignty. Thus treaties which had been signed by the Beys remained in force although foreign policy was now in French hands. That this was an ambiguous situation was brought out in chancery discussions, notably between interested colonial powers (i.e. France, Britain, and Italy). Britain had a favourable, permanently-binding treaty with Tunisia dating back to 1875, whilst that of Italy, which had been signed in 1868, was due to expire in 1896. Among other clauses, both countries benefited from a tariff on imports limited to 8 per cent *ad valorem*. In spite of Italy's will to maintain its foothold in Tunisia where its community was

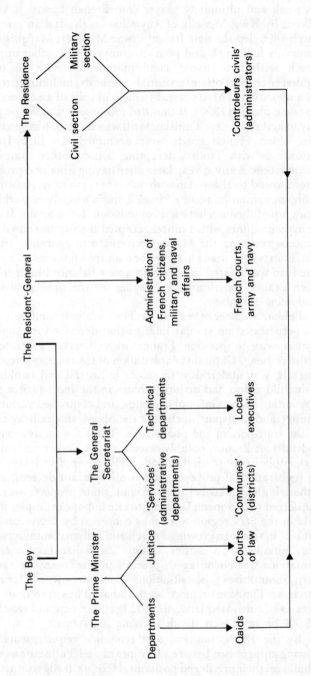

Fig. 16.1 *The protectorate regime in Tunisia*

numerically the most important European group, its international position was weak and ultimately played into French hands. A very severe defeat inflicted by King Menelik of Abyssinia on the Italian army at Adowa on 1 March 1896, led the new Italian Prime Minister, Marquis Rudini, to see his country as 'too weak and poor' to compete with other imperial states. The French wished to avoid confrontation in order to obtain European acquiescence to its other territorial conquests, including projects in the Niger and annexation of Madagascar (which, in spite of assurances to the contrary, had taken place in 1890). It thus had recourse to diplomatic pressures to bring Italy to agree to a new Tunisian tariff which set up high protectionist barriers from which French goods were exempted. In 1896 Italy signed three conventions with Tunisia accepting, among other things, the new tariff. Britain followed suit a year later after having obtained promises that British cottons would be allowed in with only 5 per cent duty. Another internationally ambiguous situation resulted from Tunisia's insolvency which had led to the setting up of the international commission. Once again, Italy and Britain as the main creditors with France, accepted the suppression of the commission, France agreeing in the Marsa Convention to guarantee the payment of the debt. Efforts were made to place the country's finances on a sounder footing. A state loan was floated in 1884 and a new balanced budget was drawn up to which France contributed by paying for the upkeep of the army and by subsidizing shipping.

Behind a veneer of respect for Tunisia's independence, a colonial system was perpetrated on similar lines to that described in Algeria. As a colony, Tunisia was to provide France with Bizerta, a strategic base in the Mediterranean. Capitalist exploitation of the country's resources, notably of minerals, was undertaken by major industrial and banking concerns. The Rothschild group had majority shares in the Jebel Jarissa mines, and in the exploitation of the Gafsa phosphates, and controlled various other sectors of industry and transport, including the Sfax-Gafsa railway completed in 1899 for the transport of the phosphates. Tunisia was also expected to provide foodstuffs for France, notably cereals, olives, and citrus fruits. This, from the start, implied confiscation of lands under cover of such laws as that of 1885 for the registration of property, and two important decrees, in 1888 and 1898, authorizing the takeover of *waqf* land. State property was to a great extent transferred to European farming: to cite but one example, 500 000 hectares of Siala in the Sfax region were thus conceded by decree on 8 February 1892. Tunisia, in spite of a growing French and Italian community, was not however seen initially as a settler colony: capitalist investment in large-scale plantations was encouraged. Jaures's phrase 'many hectares and few men' aptly summarizes the situation. Company-owned farms were run by managers, Tunisian or, more often, Italian. Thus in 1892, out of about 900 000 hectares of cultivated land, 402 000 hectares were in Franch hands, of which 246 000 hectares were divided among 114 farms.

By the 1890s, political and economic requirements were leading to growing antagonism between Europeans and Tunisians as the former sought to build up their privileged positions. Here, as in Algeria, attempts were made to break down the indigenous peoples' personality by an indirect onslaught on religion through the action of the Catholic church (powerful since Cardinal

Lavigerie's time) and through control of education. Foreign schools were encouraged whereas many of the reforms carried out by the Tunisians in the period preceding the protectorate fell into abeyance and the national system of education was neglected. In 1878 a number of Tunisian students had been sent abroad to further their education. In 1882, they were called back and no further grants were made available. In spite of this, we find the same kind of colonial outcry against educated Tunisians and the danger they represented as was heard in Algeria. Efforts to obtain land for European farming were pursued and peasants and nomads had the choice between leaving or settling as farm labourers. Between 1892 and 1914, some 250 000 hectares were thus turned over to the new agricultural sector.

French policy with respect to settlers had, moreover, begun to change and efforts were made to build up a colonist community. Lands were granted to immigrants who further benefited from banking facilities and long-term loans. The response from France proved limited, hence the new interest suddenly shown in the Italian community around 1895. Millet, the French resident-general, who had up to then favoured the French to the detriment of other European nationalities, now declared that 'failing French, who apparently could not be persuaded to come here, the laborious Italian people must be encouraged and promoted'. Whereas in 1890, only 522 Italian immigrants had come to Tunisia, in 1895, there were 1129 and in 1900, 2245. Protectorate or not, the colonial system was underway on a similar pattern to that which prevailed in Algeria, although with less destructive effects on local society, not only because the system only came into its own after 1881 and further had to accept existing institutions, but also because the kind of consolidation of the social fabric to which Khayr al-Din and other reformists had contributed, were themselves to uphold national identity.

Egypt

Egypt, in the absence of any international ruling, was a *de facto* protectorate. Paradoxically no text actually sanctioned this, Britain's position in Egypt being simply an *état de fait*, defined by a circular to the Powers on 3 January 1855:

> Although for the present a British force remains in Egypt for the preservation of public tranquility, Her Majesty's Government are desirous of withdrawing it as soon as the state of the country and the organization of proper means for the maintenance of the Khedive's authority will admit of it. In the meantime, the position in which Her Majesty's Government are placed towards His Highness imposes upon them the duty of giving advice with the object of securing that the order of things to be established shall be of a satisfactory character, and possess the elements of stability and progress.

It is in the logic of imperialism that though men such as Gladstone considered themselves pledged to withdrawal, not only was this not effected but the colonial regime was in fact stepped up and in 1914, when Turkey's entry in the war on Germany's side made the position of Egypt, theoretically under Turkish suzerainty, ambiguous, it was declared a British protectorate.

Indirect and unavowed though it was, British rule was nonetheless as patent in Egypt as in other colonies. The British representative, though officially consul-general and high commissioner, was the real ruler of the country. The man who held this post from 1883 to 1907 was Lord Cromer, an overbearing Victorian who had little sympathy for the East. He himself preferred offstage influence and cast himself in the role of an *éminence grise* acting under cover of what, in a letter to Lord Salisbury, he called 'our native screen'. An Organic Law promulgated in 1883 defined national institutions on apparently more democratic lines since the Khedive was to exercise his authority through a council of ministers who were themselves responsible to a parliament made up of a legislative council and general assembly; but the real government was that of British advisers appointed at all levels of government.

Lord Cromer, who was as yet Sir Evelyn Baring, was a financier by temperament and by family tradition, and his main concern was to re-establish a balanced budget. This he achieved by 1886 in spite of a difficult situation with, on the one hand, the problem of the debt, and on the other, that of defeat in the Sudan. What must, however, be stressed is that the improvement was obtained by a worsening of the peasants' lot. In the years immediately following the British invasion, the peasants were hard hit by poor harvests together with an epidemic of cholera in 1883. This was followed by a fall in world prices of raw materials and by growing Egyptian dependence on imports, not only for manufactured goods but also for basic foodstuffs such as rice. This must be placed in the balance when assessing greater apparent prosperity. Moreover, taxation continued to be heavy, with the peasantry still providing the major part of budgetary resources. In 1892, 50 per cent of these came from land taxes (£5 037 764 out of £9 696 000). Financial and economic measures taken by the new administration included a new Egyptian loan of £9 000 000 in 1885, the setting up of a national bank in 1898, and an effort to extend agricultural areas. Whereas these had not increased during the 1882–5 period, they did so by 10 per cent between 1885 and the end of the century. The increase in productivity was even more noticeable as a policy of barrage-building – Qanater, Asuan, Asyut – extended the areas under irrigation. The Aswan dam, for which plans had been drawn up in 1898 and which became operative in 1902, was one of the major technical feats of the period. The extension of perennial agriculture to Upper Egypt also spread the painful working conditions of the Egyptian peasants to new zones. In spite of the theoretical abolition of corvée labour in 1888, increased productivity was still largely the result of the unpaid workforce of the peasantry.

The authoritarian and colonial nature of British control in Egypt was shown by the excessive development of two branches of administration which were almost totally under British control: finance and security. Cromer, for whom the 'centre of gravity of Egyptian misgovernment lay in the Department of the Interior' began by having a decree issued, dividing Egypt for police purposes into three 'circles' (i.e. districts) to each of which a European inspector was appointed as delegate of the inspector-general. Other changes included prison reforms, efforts to eliminate abuses such as the use of whips by public officials (as inoperable a reform as that undertaken to eliminate corvée labour), efforts to suppress the slave-trade, the abolition of slavery by the 1895 Slavery Convention, and the setting up of new courts of law, native tribunals

(1883) co-existing with *qadhi* courts and the mixed courts. The Department of Justice thus also passed partially under British control. Also characteristic of colonial regimes is insistence on native recruitment for the army, and it was also a protecting power's prerogative to head such an army. In Egypt the army was disbanded on 19 September 1882, six days after al-Tall al-Kabir. The British then set about recruiting new troops, using the peasantry as soldiers whilst the 'cadres of battalions were formed by carefully selecting from the debris of Arabi's army the requisite number of officers and non-commissioned officers' (Lord Cromer). The higher ranking officers and most junior officers were supplied from Britain. The reconstituted army comprised 6000 men formed into two brigades. Typical of this as of other colonial regimes is the fact that in Egypt in 1892, expenses for security on the national budget amounted to nearly 8 per cent (£783 514) whereas under 8 per cent (£91 000) was spent on education.

The last 20 years of the 19th century also marked the opening up of the country to foreign enterprise on a scale at least equal to that in the period

---

An Assessment of Lord Cromer's Policy
by an Egyptian Nationalist, Ahmad Lutfi al-Sayyid

What is the total result of this policy? The result is that if we look at it through English eyes, we can only praise it. But if we look at it as any Egyptian must who seeks the welfare of his country, we cannot drum up the slightest praise for his political accomplishments in Egypt. He has deprived Egypt of the political life for which every living nation yearns. If we cannot but acknowledge that Lord Cromer extended the sphere of personal freedom, we cannot deny that he did just the opposite with respect to the Egyptian officials in the government. He divested them of freedom, authority, and influence, and handed these over to the English officials, and therefore many gifted young Egyptians began to shun the government service. There is no greater proof of this than the current drastic need of the government for officials and employees. We do not think that the ineptitude that Lord Cromer mentions in his report is anything but the reflex of defective education and the poor treatment meted out to officials and employees in the government. Perhaps he thought that the abandonment of decent education was in accord with the best interests of Great Britain, for Lord Cromer seeks the interest of his country above all else in everything – which is the manner in which a zealous patriot will behave towards his fatherland.

Al-Jarida, April 13, 1907

---

which had preceded, when the much criticized Khedive Isma'il ruled. At best one may consider that closer government control limited wasteful expenditure and excessive profits, although even this is not always evident. Moreover major investors acquired political influence in the process. This was true of banks which invested in industrial or agricultural projects, as did the Rothschilds who bought up ex-khedival property, or the Suares Bank which, in 1891, took over 18000 feddans (42857 hectares). Self-made men came forward to take part in major projects, making colossal fortunes in the process. Among examples of such successful careers one might mention Sir Ernest Cassell (1862–1921) who had risen from nothing to become the Prince of Wales' financial adviser and confidant, and promoted the Egyptian barrage policy, or the Belgian Baron Empain whose fortune arose out of Egyptian business deals and contracts, including the building of the famous Heliopolis town. These and similar men were part of the select circle which shared in the occult powers of colonial rule.

EXILE AS A POSITIVE RESPONSE TO COLONIALISM

Exile was in many ways the early expression of faith in nationalism and of religious commitment, a way of rejecting the foreign-promoted order. Once again Algeria as the first and hardest-hit of the North African states, exemplified clearly the importance of emigration as a permanent feature of the colonial age, albeit not one which imperialists liked to mention, thus making it difficult for historians to assess it with any degree of accuracy. Algerians when they left their homeland, generally did so secretly. At the other end of the journey – namely some Mediterranean town under Turkish rule – figures are no less difficult to establish, especially prior to the 1880s, since in the Ottoman provinces Algerians were considered as subjects of the Sultan, the latter never having recognized the *fait accompli* in Algeria. It is in fact through diplomatic skirmishes between France and the Sublime Porte, both claiming jurisdiction over Algerians, and later Tunisians, that some statistical light is shed on the subject. The Algerians themselves could stir up such quarrels since they considered themselves an autonomous national community and sometimes refused integration, notably when 'Abd al-Hamid attempted to force military service on them. They would then sometimes seek the support of the French consul.

Exiles from Algeria

The first Algerian exiles had come in the wake of the 1830 invasion, at first encouraged to emigrate by the French who considered that the departure of the urban bourgeoisie would usefully undermine people's capacity to resist the invasion and would make property available for confiscation. Each military campaign from then on brought its quota of refugees. In 1847, one of 'Abd al-Qadir's *khalifa*-s, Ahmad bin Salam, arrived in Damascus with 442 of his followers, 40 other Algerian families later joined him after having crossed North Africa overland. In 1855, 'Abd al-Qadir himself arrived in Damascus via Brussa with some 85 members of his family. The conquest of Kabylie in 1857 brought more people, as did the repression of the 1870 uprising. In Damascus itself, the Maghribi-s in 1867 were about a thousand; by 1884, they were at least four times as many. Though Damascus was a major centre, other towns, including Istanbul, Aleppo, Tripoli in Syria, and Jaffa all had important Maghribi groups. There were also a small number of rural communities: Syria thus had eight villages of Maghribi peasants, some 3500 persons all told.

The exodus is even greater if one takes into account the fact that many people sought refuge in lands closer by. Thus fighting in western Algeria, notably that involving the Awlad Sidi Shaykh, led many people to seek safety in Morocco. They found asylum not only in related tribal clans across the border but in the town of al-'Uyun (el-Aïoun) near Wujda (Oujda) where the King of Morocco gave them the fortress as a permanent home. When the famous resistance leader Bu 'Amama died and was buried there, al-'Uyun further became the spiritual home of the Awlad Sidi Shaykh. Other Algerians went to Fez where they were progressively integrated into the urban community, some rising to high positions within the *makhzen*, for example the al-Muqri family which was of Algerian origin and rose to ministerial rank. In 1894, for example, 300 Algerian notables in Fez obtained Moroccan nationality.

In Tunisia the same situation prevailed and, as we saw with respect to Khayr al-Din, led to skirmishes over the respective rights of the Regency and the French consul. Here too integration was the rule so that it is well-nigh impossible to delineate the Algerian community, even if major families or leading figures sometimes indicate their Algerian origins. The most famous of the Tunisian nationalists of 1900, 'Abd al-'Aziz Tha'lbi, thus came from an Algerian family which had emigrated in 1830. The trend was later to change when Tunisia in turn became a protectorate and provided its own refugees. After the Bardo Treaty, Muslims in their thousands crossed over to neighbouring Tripoli, although many were to return as a result of negotiations undertaken by the French consul there. A great number nonetheless stayed on and by the end of the century, they were estimated at around 8000, of whom as many as 30000 were in Tripoli itself. The same estimate is made for Egypt where, in 1887, 3000 Tunisians registered at the French consulate. This does not necessarily mean that all were permanent political exiles. In many cases, for example during the 1881–3 period, momentary reactions of panic took place. There was, moreover, a well-established tradition of Maghribi-s setting up in the East in a professional capacity and this continued. Thus, in Istanbul, there were about 200 Tunisians engaged in making and selling *shashiya*-s. In Alexandria, the Tunisians were mostly traders and had their own quarter called the Tunisian Bazar. Some 500 of them specialized in the cloth trade. The fact that many made no objection to registering at the French consulate would tend to prove lack of political commitment.

Nonetheless the presence of an important Maghribi and notably Algerian community, considering itself to be the victim of foreign invasion was a new and important factor in the development of North African self-awareness. This was promoted by the fact that the communities were cohesive. They generally came not individually, but in large families and sometimes actual tribal groups, and continued to live together, sometimes specializing in a particular activity: thus in Damascus there were 95 weavers of whom 45 were Kabylies, most of them from the Ait Iraten tribe. Leading personalities and notably the Amir 'Abd al-Qadir, further upheld émigré self-awareness. It is in fact the presence of 'Abd al-Qadir in Damascus which explains why the latter town should have attracted the greatest number of refugees. Also very striking is the fact that émigrés continued to view themselves as a national community, and this in spite both of Muslim traditions of a common identity and of Ottoman policies of integration. Not only did they refuse to be considered as Ottomans but also kept themselves to themselves – this is shown, for example, by marriage statistics: out of 158 Algerians listed as having married during their stay in the East, 112 had chosen Algerian wives. Solidarity involving a self-awareness of North Africans as the victims of imperialism was thus upheld and led to new associations such as the Society for the Safeguard of Islam founded in 1870 which tried to defend Muslim victims at home and promoted interaction between colonies and independent Muslim communities.

A further fact has to be stressed since it shows that emigration was no mere flight in the face of actual danger: namely that it was a permanent trend and one which far from declining after fighting was over, increased. Important arrivals of refugees from Algeria were recorded in Damascus in 1888, 1890, 1896, and 1898. Many came via Tunisia, thus showing their determination to leave in spite of French efforts to prevent them doing so (returning exiles were commonly thrown in prison). In the 1890s, the main stream of emigration was towards the Holy Places and the French were forced to give way and grant at least some passports to pilgrims who were, in any case, determined to go. At the beginning of the 20th century, the French consul in Damascus complained of the 'horde of Algerians and Tunisians' arriving in the city. A French decision in 1908–10 making military service obligatory for Muslims led not only to demonstrations at home, but to further emigration: the official Barberette commission of inquiry registered 637 cases in Tlemcen out of a total population of 25 000, the local press rating the figure much higher (the *Echo d'Oran*, in 1911, putting it at 1200). Full census figures were established in 1910, and they gave the number of Algerians in Syria and Palestine at 17 500 with a further 1000 in the Holy Town of Madina. Colonial authorities were increasingly worried by what seemed an irrepressible tendency which was not only 'bad publicity and a bad example' as Governor-General Jonnart put it in 1910, but which was economically negative now that agriculture needed a cheap labour force, making Algerians into an indispensable commodity. Even stricter measures were taken to prevent Muslims leaving the country or accomplishing the Holy Pilgrimage, but inquiries were also set on foot to try and understand why people went into exile. In spite of economic pressures and loss of land, answers, significantly, show up essentially cultural and religious grievances. The Algerians explained that they could not go on living in a country where Islam was despised and down-trodden, where they could not practise their religion in peace, where mosques and *habus* property were taken over by the French, and where their children were deprived of schooling. Algerians particularly stressed as the reason for leaving their homelands, the fact that their children could not be taught Arabic or the basic tenets of their faith and civilization.

This points to the role intellectual factors had in the building up of a collective response to imperialism: the *nahda* or Arab renaissance to which successive generations of exile contributed.

THE BUILDING-UP OF MUSLIM IDENTITY IN EXILE

The road to exile also had a positive element in that it gave a common overt significance to the subjective experiences of individuals. It is this process of historical self-interpretation which made the victims of imperialism the tragic heroes of modern times, which we shall now describe. Largely unconscious and implicit though it was, probably more emotional than rational, the historian must nonetheless use facts and concepts to define it. This will lead us to point to successive phases of self-awareness each of which had its privileged symbols: 'Abd al-Qadir, Khayr al-Din, and Muhammad 'Abduh.

'Abd al-Qadir in exile

The image of 'Abd al-Qadir which popularly prevails and which has played so important a role in defining Muslims' awareness of themselves both as victims of imperialism and as champions of Arab values, probably owes more to 'Abd al-Qadir's later years when he was an exile in Damascus than to his earlier political career. His position and prestige in the latter part of his career are indeed something which the historian cannot afford to overlook. As he left France for the Middle East in 1853, settling successively in Brussa, Istanbul, and Damascus (1855), besides spending two years (1863–4) in the Holy Places, we indeed have the impression that a new symbol had come into its own. Accounts of his journey into exile were far more numerous than were those of his surrender, newspapers reflecting general world-wide acceptance of his status as 'a noble, gallant man' in the best Arab tradition of the warrior saint. Recollections of his earlier career which had the pageantry of Arab horsemen in the field, fused with the more contemporary picture of an older man in traditional holy man dress, his rosary in his hand. Age, defeat, and exile turned 'Abd al-Qadir into a symbol of the destiny of North Africa in general and Algeria in particular, but they also made him the champion of destiny reinterpreted, defeat bravely born and mastered by a noble soul. Defeat resulting from the technological superiority of Europeans was of limited significance. Indeed only Islam could provide the ethical guidelines to progress, not only for Muslims but for all the inhabitants of the planet. 'Abd al-Qadir stressed this in a lengthy 'Letter to the French' which was published in Paris, in translation, in 1858, under the title *Rappel à l'Intelligent, Avis à l'Ignorant* ('A Reminder to Intelligent Men, a Warning to the Ignorant').

In Damascus his position can be seen as increasingly influential. This was true with respect to the Algerian refugees, many of whom settled in Damascus to be near the 'Abd al-Qadir and over whom he had absolute authority. Indeed the Ottomans and the French were both to recognize this and carried on their dealings with the Algerians through him. The Amir's appearances in public always caused considerable stir and on his return from the Holy Pilgrimage, he was given an official reception, most of the citizens turning out to welcome him. A further illustration of the Amir's prestige is the fact that during his pilgrimage which had lasted a year and a half, he was, at Madina, granted the exceptional honour of making a retreat in the house of Abu Bakr, the Prophet's first Khalifa who had obtained from Muhammad permission to open a window giving on to the Prophet's mosque. His death on 26 May 1883 was a further occasion for public tribute. More important still, however, is the heightened import of the Amir as a symbol for Muslims the world over. It is indeed striking to note the number of Muslims who went out of their way to call and pay him their respects. The *hajj* itself often involved a detour to Damascus.

Behind the image of the defeated warrior with whom exiles and other victims of imperialism identified themselves, a committed Muslim stance was increasingly evident. 'Abd al-Qadir upheld this by his own holy lineage background and temperament, strongly committed both to learning and mysticism, and by his way of life which was now increasingly taken up by prayers, meditation, and teaching in the mosque. The high sufi tradition to which he belonged was reactivated in this period by contacts with great mystics and with disciples whom he, in turn, initiated. He was indeed considered in this period as *warith al-'ulum al-Akbariyya* ('the heir to Akbari knowledge') and his own works point to communication in vision with the source of this tradition, Ibn 'Arabi himself. The last image we have of 'Abd al-Qadir highlights this twin reference to the grandeur of Islam as a historical civilization and as a spiritual doctrine: when he died, the burial ceremony was carried out in the great 'Ummayad mosque of Damascus, and his tomb was in the cemetery close by where Ibn 'Arabi himself was buried. When Algeria recovered its independence, his body was transferred to Algiers.

The historian, who must take into account symbols, their intensity and the way in which they function, must also examine these in a critical light. This will lead us to conclude that 'Abd al-Qadir's status in exile reflected an early and as yet unsophisticated self-view of Arab values in a tragic mould. It corresponded to a phase in the process of elaboration which, by the end of 'Abd al-Qadir's life, had already taken a new political turn. Not only did the Amir himself no longer adequately fill Muslim aspirations but a more critical attitude to the hero was, here and there, apparent. Not only was his absolute dominion over the Algerian community in exile giving rise to negative comments, but it was also increasingly seen that colonial manipulation was not absent from the Amir's very prestige, which the French tended to further because it promoted their long-term ambitions over Syria and Lebanon. A working partnership between the French consul and 'Abd al-Qadir could, in some instances, be pointed to: after all did he not have a French pension, and did he not provide the guards which effectively protected European quarters during the serious riots which took place in 1860 when the Druze rebelled? The fact that he was granted the *grand cordon* of the French *Légion d'honneur* on this occasion further made the fact public. Moreover the Amir had pledged his word that he would create no trouble for the French in Algeria and he only too scrupulously kept it, even breaking with his son Muhay al-Din, when the latter secretly returned to Algeria in 1870–1.

The political complexity of new times was well brought out at the Amir's death when sincere public homage barely overshadowed political afterthought as the French consul, Gilbert, and the Turkish governor, Hamdi Pasha, headed the 60 000-strong cortège. Hamdi Pasha soon after received instructions (1884) from the Sublime Porte:

> It behoves you urgently to do your best to detach all the Amir's family from France. Promise them rank and distinctions. It is a task of the utmost importance since, should you succeed, we will probably have with us all the other Algerians residing in Syria. It is the sole means by which we can prevent France from having any motive to interfere in this country which, because of its proximity to Egypt, is now the cause of dissension between that nation and Britain.

The careers of 'Abd al-Qadir's sons further bear witness to a fast-evolving situation. Al-Hashmi who became head of the pro-French branch of the family in Syria, ultimately returned to Algeria in 1892 where he died in 1900. One of al-Hashmi's sons, the Amir Khaled, was to play an important though ambiguous role in the development of 20th century Algerian nationalism. Of 'Abd al-Qadir's eight other sons, only two remained French subjects: Ahmad who died in 1911, and 'Umar who was tried by a military court in Damascus during the First World War and executed in 1916. The six sons who chose Turkish nationality occupied high offices in the Ottoman Empire: two of them, Muhammad and Muhay al-Din were senators, a third, 'Abd al-Malek was aide-de-camp to the Sultan. In 1902, he fled from Turkey and went to Morocco where he fought side by side with the Awlad Sidi Shaykh leader, Bu 'Amama, not however against the French but against the King of Morocco. He was to be involved in various other Moroccan uprisings. Another son, 'Abd Allah, stayed in Damascus but applied for French nationality in 1911. The last and best known of the Amir's sons, 'Ali, remained at the head of the Algerian émigrés and lived out a troubled career in the midst of the various protagonists of the international scene to whom he successively gave pledges of amity and sometimes effective help. He thus helped the Ottomans to organize Libyan resistance to the Italian invasion of 1911, but he also paid an almost official visit to France where he was received both by the Foreign Secretary and by the President of the French Republic. Moreover he was a member of the Turkish parliament, representing the constituency of Damascus and he became the parliament's vice-president. Accused by many of being motivated essentially by love of money, and often seen by the Algerian émigrés themselves as having contributed to the break-up of their previously well-knit community, 'Ali bin 'Abd al-Qadir was probably as much a victim of the times and of the international context as of his own weaknesses. The type of nationalist stand taken by 'Abd al-Qadir, in spite of its role in giving shape to Muslim identity in imperial times, obviously had its limits, chief of which was an incapacity to dominate the wider and more subtle issues of confrontation between East and West. Awareness of this characterized a new generation of 'emigrés to whom, in the late 1870s, the Tunisian reformists contributed their own political experiences.

Khayr al-Din and the Tunisan reformists in exile

The Tunisian reformist politicians of the 1870s were driven out of power and into exile in 1878 not by foreign invasion, but by the combined onslaught of the consuls and a corrupt court entourage. They had a narrower social base than the early Algerian community around 'Abd al-Qadir, being socially defined by their ruling class background, whether as *mamluk*-s or as *'ulama*. They were cut off from the masses and the gap was breached neither by exercise of power in 1857–62 and 1869–78, nor by the intervening period of disgrace, the reformists having had little or no sympathy for the peasant uprising of 1864. On the other hand, they apprehended problems in a more intellectual way and it was probably in the period of political retirement – 1862–9 – that reformist ideology in the early Tunisian sense of the term took shape as men such as General Husayn or General Roustam were driven into temporary exile, whilst others, including Khayr al-Din, lived discreetly as private citizens, spending their time alternately travelling in Europe and discussing the wider issues at stake in the Muslim world with congenial visitors.

It was during this period of exile at home that Khayr al-Din worked out the guidelines not only of a new national policy but of Tunisia's stand in terms of the confrontation of East and West. His ideas were defined through personal contacts with leading personalities who included the ageing Ahmad bin Abi al-Dhiaf (1802–74); his exceptional experience of public service and court life is recorded in *Ithaf Ahl al-Zaman bi Akhbar Muluk Tunis wa 'Ahd al-'Aman*, a very full account of 19th-century Tunisia which he was then writing (1862–72). Younger men also contributed to Khayr al-Din's awareness of problems. They included men who were later to be part of his governmental team such as Muhammad al-Sanusi (1850/1–1900) and Muhammad Bayram. The former, at the time a teacher at the *zawiya* of Sidi al-Hayyad and at the Hammuda Pasha mosque, was later to be editor of the *Raid al-Tunisi* to which he contributed a number of polemical articles. He was also to be responsible for the development of publishing in Tunisia. Muhammad Bayram (1840–89) who is generally referred to as Bayram V because he belonged to a long line of famous Hanafi *mufti*-s (and this had helped him to an early start) had been appointed teacher and supervisor at the al-'Unuqiyya *madrasa* in 1861 and later professor at the Great Mosque of the Zaytuna. He was already coming out with progressive views on the type of problem aired in *'ulama* circles. In this period he wrote a short treatise to justify the use of firearms in hunting (traditional views had it that only animals ritually killed with a knife were fit to be eaten). Interest in such subjects was one of the fields in which interaction between East and West was being brought out and Muhammad Bayram's treatise, *Risala Tuhfat al-Khawass fi Hill Sayid Bunduq al-Rasas* written in 1868, was published a few years later, in Cairo, in 1886. Bayram V was to be an efficient member of Khayr al-Din's team. He shared many of the cultural tasks of his friend Muhammad al-Sanusi and presided over the board which managed *waqf* property. It was during this early period of exile at home that Khayr al-Din, probably with the help of his learned friends, wrote a political treatise in which he stated his convictions. *Aqwam al-Masalik fi Ma'rifat Ahwal al-Mamalik* became widely known after its publication in Tunis in 1867. The Arabic edition was followed by a French translation in 1868 and another in 1875. A first English version came out in 1874 and a Turkish one in 1876.

For Khayr al-Din as for all Muslims, whether reformist or not, Islam provided the over-arching intellectual framework of state and society. It is also the conceptual means through which identity is defined. Khayr al-Din in his book addressed himself to public opinion through the *'ulama* whom he tried to persuade that it was necessary and urgent to bring national self-awareness up to date. One of the political conclusions derived from this, which Khayr al-Din's *mamluk* origins may have encouraged, is that this was part of a Muslim-wide stand which should be reoriented toward the Ottoman Sultan who was the descendant of the early unified command of the Islamic world. The modernizing trend which the Ottomans had set on foot further gave them the political lead in an East-West confrontation. Khayr al-Din thus integrated national and pan-Islamic views in a wider world context. A more favourable approach to European technological superiority is a trait of Tunisian reformism apparent in many fields of intellectual activity. Thus the *Raid al-Tunisi* included considerable information about Europe, ranging from practical details on shipping, to translations of political editorials from leading European newspapers. Even traditional literary works such as the classical 'Voyage to the Holy Places' reflected a changing world-view as a detour via Europe and corresponding descriptions were integrated into what was originally a pious rendering of a Muslim's spiritual experience. The relative length of descriptions of Europe in such works as Muhammad al-Sanusi's *Rihla al-Hijaziyya* ('Journey to the Hijaz') are far beyond what the actual fact of travelling on a European ship – by now a common means of transport to Mecca – would warrant. Such accounts further integrate a new form of Muslim political self-awareness and Sanusi's book is no exception: in 1882 he too made the journey to Damascus to pay his respects to the Amir and also gave details of the 'Arabi Pasha uprising in Egypt. One should not underestimate the Islamic commitment of reformists. Once this has been said, however, it should also be pointed out that the new power Europe had acquired, notably through technology, loomed large in Tunisians' awareness of contemporary problems and this can ultimately be interpreted as a secularizing trend upheld by Khayr al-Din's obvious admiration for such feats as the network of railways being set up in the world and the cutting of the Suez Canal. Indeed he himself had the entrepreneurial outlook then prevalent in industrial nations. He defined progress in technological terms and considered this to be upheld by mercantilism, underestimating its negative effects on an underdeveloped economy. The positive features of European society could, Khayr al-Din implied, be purely and simply copied by the Muslims who would thus become competitive and historically active. The type of reforms to be promoted to make such changes operative were themselves seen as purely technical: new forms of state management, infrastructural development, and the switch-over from oriental despotism to enlightened bourgeois rule through parliamentary democracy.

The historical impact of these views must be appreciated in a wider context. This involves a deep-seated and long-term evolution in the Muslim world which has been brought out in various chapters including those dealing with the reformist policies of Muhammad 'Ali in Egypt or Ahmad Bey in Tunis in the early part of the century. Such views increasingly prevailed throughout the Muslim world, including those countries which are generally seen as turning their back on modernity. In Morocco, for example, students were sent to the modern schools of Egypt by Sultan 'Abd al-Rahman and his successors to study modern subjects, and notably mathematics and medicine. Not only were these new approaches introduced at home, but some students became specialists in their own right. A case which might serve to illustrate this is that of the Moroccan 'Abd al-Salam al-'Alami (circa 1834–95) who, after his stay in Egypt, wrote a number of books on mathematics and made a solar clock of his own. In the same light, one might point to signs of change in Sudan, not only evident in the administrative field but in the outlook of a new generation of *'ulama*, some of whom may have been in contact with al-Tahtawi during his four-year exile in Khartum. The political model which Khayr al-Din envisaged was thus integrated into a keener sense of Muslim identity, underscored by increased contacts with Europe and Europeans. One should also remember in this context the role of the modern Arab press, one result of which was a more direct knowledge of events in various parts of the world. Not only were papers appearing in growing numbers in the Middle East and, to a lesser degree, in the Maghrib, but they also had an expanded, if not large circulation. Thus Tunisia's *Raid al-Tunisi* was regularly sent out to Algiers, Tripoli, Beirut, Alexandria, Paris, Marseilles, and Malta.

Though Khayr al-Din's attempt to put his views into practice was brought to a close by the combined pressure of court narrow-mindedness and European obstruction, this should not lead us to think that modernity as a political ideal had been done away with. In Tunisia itself the changes brought about by Khayr al-Din survived his downfall, and indeed continued to be promoted by those of his friends who stayed on in government service. The new cabinet appointed Muhammad Bayram head of the medical service, and he was able to reorganize Sadiqi Hospital on modern lines before he, in turn, broke with the prime minister, Mustafa bin Isma'il, in 1879, when the latter quarrelled with the *Maliki qadhi*-s of the capital, thus leading Muhammad Bayram to leave the country on 14 October 1879, on the pretext of a wish to make the *hajj*. Muhammad al-Sanusi not only stayed on, but continued to run the *Raid al-Tunisi*. General Husayn, another staunch supporter, continued to head the department of education and that of public works.

Exile, however, was, here as elsewhere, the means through which such views were not only upheld but pushed to their logical consequence. Khayr al-Din's place of exile itself illustrates the ex-prime minister's views since he was called to Istanbul by the Sultan. He believed not only that a new political career was open to him but that it was at the political capital of the Muslim world, namely Istanbul, that his policy should be enacted. In September 1878 he was appointed minister of justice in the Ottoman government. He was further asked to preside over a commission set up to inquire into the running of the country's economy. A little later, in December 1878, he was appointed prime minister. However, in Istanbul as in Tunis, Khayr al-Din was made aware of the fact that real reforms were impossible in a context of European pressures and imperial encroachments. He therefore resigned from his functions in July 1879.

Through this second experience of political incapacity, Khayr al-Din was further led to see as contradictory the two poles of political reformism: the pan-Islamic will to unity on one hand, the nation-state on the other. This, of course, had sentimental origins for Khayr al-Din who, as early as 1878, had written to his former colleague on the International Financial Commission, Villet: 'The honours bestowed on me and constant marks of favour will never make me forget that I am a free Tunisian' – but it also implied political stands which Khayr al-Din increasingly came to regard as contradictory:

> Of course, it is impossible for me to withdraw from the scene at present without being accused of ingratitude to the Sultan, but this does not mean that I have abandoned my beloved country. Beautiful though the banks of the Bosphorus be, I will not allow myself to be detained there.... It is in Tunisia, the land of my heart, my adopted mother-country, that I wish to end my days.

The Sultan, whose considered opinion it was that Khayr al-Din had become Turk because of circumstances, but had remained Tunisian first and foremost, envisaged combating growing French infiltration in the Regency by deposing the Bey and, banking on the popularity of the former prime minister, placing Khayr al-Din at the head of the Regency. Tissot, the French ambassador, learnt of the plan in January 1881 and informed his government. He received instructions to energetically combat what the French Foreign Office considered as the 'ambitious aims' of the former Tunisian prime minister. The Sultan in the face of French protest, backed down. This for Khayr al-Din was yet another and more direct experience of the fact that the 'sick man' was in no position to play the necessary role of leader at a time when imperial pressures on Tunisia were at their height. The realistic conclusion he came to, although it was one which shattered his hopes, was that Muslim states were incapable of facing up to the imperial threat because of the weakness and corruption of their governments. At the beginning of May 1881, a few days before the signing of the Bardo Treaty, Khayr al-Din in a long conversation with a French official frankly admitted that he would have wished for the old order of things to have been maintained. He explained his pro-Ottoman stand by the fact that he had hoped Turkey would be able to guarantee Tunisia's independence:

> People think I am Turkish. I am not Turkish. I am a Muslim and I have never had but one idea, one ambition: to save my country, namely that small land of Tunisia to which I owe everything, even my daily bread. I believed the Porte could guarantee its existence. I admit today that I was wrong in believing this.

His appeal to Turkey had subordinated political to religious considerations: 'I believed that a Muslim country should have a Muslim protector'. *Realpolitik* now made it necessary to accept the situation resulting from imbalance: 'Today we have no other choice but between protection and annexation'. He therefore declared himself ready to return to Tunisia and resume his place at the head of the government within the protectorate. However, he made two conditions: his nomination was to be accepted by the Tunisian people and accepted by the Sultan. Nothing, of course, came of this: the French were out to make colonial headway, not to promote Tunisia's welfare, and the time was not yet ripe for a home-based nationalist reaction.

Once again the end of a national hero's life bears witness to an intensification of political isolation. Though Khayr al-Din was called upon by Sultan 'Abd al-Hamid to give advice on several international problems (notably the frontier problem with Greece in March 1881, and Egypt in 1882), he was now in retirement and lived out his last years in a country home on the Bosphorus. He died there on 30 January 1890. Here too, the struggle against colonial rule led to emphasis on the continuity of the national spirit.

Independence recovered led to the transfer of Khayr al-Din's body to Tunis on 28 March 1968, President Bourguiba paying public tribute to the man he called Khayr al-Din the Tunisian. Again in parallel to 'Abd al-Qadir, we find Khayr al-Din's sons illustrating the growing complexity of the age. Though they continued to serve the Ottoman Empire and Tunisia – al-Tahir Khayr al Din, 1872–1937, was a member of parliament in Istanbul in 1911 and head of the Department of Justice in Tunis a little later – they struggled in vain against Oriental despotism which their father had pointed to as the chief cause of weakness of the Muslim states. They indeed tragically illustrated its oppressive power: in 1913, al-Tahir Khayr al-Din and Muhammad Khayr al-Din were deported and their younger brother Salih, executed, as dangerous revolutionaries.

It is my duty to state that the Neo-Destour did not spring out of nothing. It had its roots in the movements which preceded it since Khayr al-Din Pasha, 'Ali Bash Hamba, and the Old Destour.

Speech by President Bourguiba on the 9th April, 1938

Exiles from Egypt

Oriental despotism also underlies the story of the third generation of exiles, namely the Egyptians who were banished by the British-upheld Khedive for their part in the 'Arabi Pasha uprising. Though political criticism of the regime was their starting point, we shall nonetheless see these Egyptians moving to a more intellectual and religious stance as they came to see the moral and cultural reform of the Muslim community as the necessary prerequisite to a firmer attitude which would challenge imperialism and in the process do away with Oriental despotism.

Exile, here again, provided a change of context for men whom we defined in an earlier chapter as strongly marked by common social origins. From the start they regarded the Islamic lands not in the traditional context of the Mediterranean but as world-wide. The road to exile itself showed this up as 'Arabi Pasha was sent out to Colombo, the Qayati brothers going to Beirut where their companions including the Syrian reformist, Rashid Ridha, the Indonesian leader of resistance to Dutch imperialism, 'Abd al-Rahman Pasha al-Zahir, and 'Abd al-Qadir's family. Even those nationalists who sought to make a spiritual retreat in the Holy Places were not out of the field of interaction and indeed confrontation. This was demonstrated by the case of the Tunisian, Muhammad Bayram, who, in the course of the pilgrimage he undertook in 1879, made an ancient ritualized form of Maghribi protest at the Prophet's tomb, reciting a poem of his own çalling down God's justice on his oppressors. In Mecca itself the atmosphere was fraught with political tensions. Not only was an uneasy relationship maintained between spiritual authority represented by the *sharif*-s and the temporal authority which since the beginning of the 19th century was exercised by the Turks, but the Holy Families themselves were involved in plots and conflicts which came into the open when the *sharif* who presided over the Holy Places was assassinated on 14 March 1880. The shock this caused throughout Islam further underscored the fact that religion was no longer a refuge, but something which had to be protected and fought for. European capitals were themselves integrated into the pattern of exile, illustrated, for example, by the fact that Muhammad 'Abduh went to Beirut and from there to Paris where he spent some ten months in 1883–4, besides making a short stay in London.

No less striking is the way in which the pattern of reactions had speeded up. In the five years which followed the 'Arabi Pasha uprising, a new moral leadership was established and the ideology of the *nahda* or Arab renaissance was defined. This owed much to two contrasted personalities, Muhammad 'Abduh and Jamal al-Din al-Afghani whose joint charisma in this period stirred Muslims the world over. It was in fact to meet up with al-Afghani, now in Paris (1883) after a brief stay in London (1882) and a longer one in India where he had opposed the westernizing views of Sir Sayyid Ahmad Khan, that Muhammad 'Abduh went to Paris. Here he met other exiled personalities including the satirist Ya'qub Sanu' and the Persian syncretist Mirza Baqir. Muhammad 'Abduh and al-Afghani together founded a review, *Al-'Urwa al-Wuthqa* which, though short-lived since only 18 numbers were published (1884), had immediate and considerable impact. Rashid Ridha recalls how:

> in our house of al-Qalamun near Tripoli in Syria in 1302 H./1885–6 there were guests who were Egyptians exiled after the 'Arabi affair. One evening the review *Al-'Urwa al-Wuthqa* was brought in. The illustrious shaykh Muhammad 'Abd al-Jawad al-Qayati took it. A petrol lamp was provided and the shaykh began to read in a strong voice as does a preacher for a sermon. He every now and then stopped to express his admiration for certain phrases. He only put down the review after having read it to the end.

Rashid Ridha himself was to be influenced by *Al-'Urwa al-Wuthqa* when, some ten years later, he came across copies of the review in his father's papers: 'every number was like an electric current striking me, giving my soul a shock, or setting it ablaze, and carrying me from one state to another'.

In Paris, however, the two leaders diverged in their appreciation of the situation and chose to follow their own separate paths. Jamal al-Din al-Afghani had a heightened awareness of the geographical extent and social complexities of the Muslim world and he combined this with an infinite capacity for subversive politial activities which took him to London (1884–5) where, with the help of Wilfred Blunt, he put over anti-imperialist views, whilst at the same time contacting Sultan 'Abd al-Hamid and offering to uphold his claims to leadership of the Muslims on pan-Islamic lines. From there he went to Persia and Russia (1887). Back in Iran he helped to organize the boycott of tobacco in 1891 as a form of passive resistance to European economic pressures. This led to yet another expulsion in 1891. A little later we find him in Istanbul where his political plots – including the murder of Nasir al-Din Shah in Persia in May 1896 in which he was involved – made him highly suspect. The Sultan may also have been apprised of the fact that when the Khedive 'Abbas Hilmi had visited Istanbul in 1895, he had paid a secret visit to al-Afghani and the two men had discussed the possibility that the leadership of Muslims be taken not by the Sultan but by the Khedive. Al-Afghani was placed under house arrest and not allowed to leave the country. Curtailment of his boundless energy embittered the end of his life and he died a virtual prisoner in Istanbul in 1897.

Muhammad 'Abduh, on the other hand, considered not only that more limited political objectives were called for but that these had no chance of succeeding unless the Muslim community reformed intellectually and socially and it was this which he decided to promote. He therefore left Paris and briefly re-entered Egypt in disguise in order to visit the Sudan, then under the Mahdiyya. On his way he stopped over in Tunis (6 December 1884 to 4 January 1885). Brief though his stay there was, and marked only by a meeting with the 'ulama, a meeting with the Bey, and a lecture at the Great Mosque, the visit is nonetheless considered to have set on foot an Islamic-based resistance to imperialism in the intellectual milieu of the Zaytuna. Muhammad 'Abduh then settled in Beirut where he lived for three years (1885–88), surrounded by a growing number of disciples to whom he lectured on theology in a school recently founded by a Muslim benevolent society. His Beirut lectures, the *Risalat al-Tawhid*, point to a redirected Islamic militancy promoting knowledge of religion and of the Arabic language. This tried to apprehend and progressively integrate a modern society which, notably in Egypt since Muhammad 'Ali's time, had been artificially recast on European lines and belonged to no historically-founded context except as an easily manipulated imperial tool and as the victim of its own ignorance and inferiority.

By the end of the 1880s, a new stance had evolved which, amongst other things, indicated a deep-rooted urge to reintegrate the society and context where action could become historically meaningful. Several factors contributed to transferring the reformist capital to Cairo. Older justifications of the *hijra* lost their importance as the pillars of emigré society died ('Abd al-Qadir in 1883, Khayr al-Din in 1890). The Ottoman Empire under Sultan 'Abd al-Hamid, who increasingly monopolized pan-Islamism to his personal ends and launched into a policy of tyranny and repression, no longer provided an acceptable political context. Reformists themselves found their activities in Turkey curtailed whilst, at the same time, Egypt was reopened to the exiles. Not only were sentences of banishment lifted but activists, if they were prepared to limit their criticisms to French imperialism, were allowed into the country. In 1888, the Khedive and the British agency granted Muhammad 'Abduh leave to return. Other leading North African and Middle Eastern reformists followed him.

SELECTED READING LIST

I – Colonial regimes in the latter part of the 19th century

Ageron, C.-R., *Histoire de l'Algérie Contemporaine*, Vol. II, *1871–1954*, (Paris, 1979).

Blunt, W. S., *My Diaries, being a Personal Narrative of Events, 1888–1914*, (London, 1932).

Colonna, F., 'Cultural Resistance and Religious Legitimacy in Colonial Algeria', *Economy and Society*, 1974.

Colvin, A., *The Making of Modern Egypt*, (London, 1906).

Laroui, A., *Les Origines Sociales et Culturelles du Nationalisme Marocain (1830–1912)*, (Paris, 1977).

Marsden, A., *Britain and the End of the Tunis Treaties, 1894–1897*, Supplement to the *English Historical Review*, (London, 1965).

Poncet, J., *La Colonisation et l'Agriculture Européenne en Tunisie depuis 1881*, (Paris, 1962).

Ruedy, J., *Land Policy in Colonial Algeria. The Origins of the Rural Public Domain*, (Los Angeles, 1967).

Turin, Y., *Affrontements Culturels dans l'Algérie Coloniale, École, Médecine, Religion, 1830–1880*, (Paris, 1971).

II – The Riposte of exile

Bardin, P., *Algériens et Tunisiens dans l'Empire Ottoman de 1848 à 1914*, (Paris, 1979).

III – The building-up of Muslim identity in exile
1) 'Abd al-Qadir:
'Abd al-Qadir, *Emir Abd el-Kader. Ecrits Spirituels*, trans. M. Chodkiewicz, (Paris, 1982).
'Abd al-Qadir, *Abd el-Kader. Lettre aux Français*, trans. R. R. Khawam, (Paris, 1977).
Churchill, C. H., *The Life of Abd el Kader*, (London, 1867).

2) Tunisian reformists
Abdesselem, A., *Les Historiens Tunisiens*, (Paris, 1973).
Chenoufi, A., *Un Savant tunisien du XIXe siècle: Muhammad as-Sanusi. Sa vie et son oeuvre*, (Tunis, 1977).
Green, A. H., *The Tunisian Ulama 1873–1915. Social Structure and Response to Ideological Currents*, (Leiden, 1979).
Khayr al-Din, *Aqwam al-Masalik fi Ma'rifat Ahwal al-Mamalik*, (Tunis, 1867); trans. into English by L. C. Brown, *The Surest Path*, (Harvard, 1967).
Smida, M., *Aux Origines de la presse en Tunisie. La Fondation du 'Raid'*, (Tunis, 1979).
Tlili, B., 'Kheredine réformateur et homme d'Etat, Tunisien et Ottoman', *Les Africains*, vol VIII, (Paris, 1977).

3) Egyptian reformism and Muhammad 'Abduh
'Abduh M., *Risalat al-Tawhid*, (Cairo, 1942–3).
Hourani, A., *Arabic Thought in the Liberal Age, 1798–1939* (London, 1962).
Keddie, N. R., *An Islamic Response to Imperialism. Political and Religious Writings of Sayyid Jamal ad-Din 'Al-Afghani'*, (Berkeley and Los Angeles, 1968).
Keddie, N. R., *Sayyid Jamal ad-Din 'Al-Afghani', a Political Biography*, (Los Angeles, 1972).
Kedourie, E., *Afghani and 'Abduh: an Essay on Religious Unbelief and Political Activism in Modern Islam*, (London, 1966).
Kerr, M. H., *Islamic Reform: the Political and Legal Theories of Muhammad 'Abduh and Rashid Rida*, (Berkeley and Los Angeles, 1966).
Ridha, R., *Tarikh al-Ustadh al-Imam al-Shaykh Muhammad 'Abduh*, (Cairo, 1931).

CONCLUSION
THE END OF THE CENTURY:

AN OVERALL ASSESSMENT

As the century moved to a close, the imperial order came into its own, even if it involved intense competition in every field and, ultimately, a major world conflict in 1914–18, followed up by an international conference, before a new definition of states in terms of empires and spheres of influence was finally worked out. North Africa was one of the regions where, at the close of the 19th century, a reassessment of the respective power of European nations was undertaken.

INTERNATIONAL STRATEGY AND COLONIAL EXPANSION AT THE END OF THE 19TH CENTURY

In the tension-fraught years at the close of the 19th century, Germany was making good its expansive policy both directly through diplomatic action upheld by its military power, and indirectly through the Triple Alliance. Italy was moving into East Africa. France and Britain's traditional rivalry continued to express itself in conflicts, but growing account was being taken of the need for a new European equilibrium. France more than ever in this period appeared to favour a Russian alliance, and a military convention was signed between the two states in 1892. This did not preclude acceptance of British claims in a future share-out of colonial spoils. Through intense diplomatic activity in Europe and confrontation on the colonial stage, Britain and France were in fact tentatively moving towards the Entente Cordiale. The very fact that colonial claims were being multiplied contributed to this. Germany was now resolutely active in Africa, Holland was upholding its position in Indonesia, Belgium in the Congo, and Spain, in memory of its former *imperium*, was making its Saharan and Moroccan bid effective. Turkey, 'the sick man of Europe', only subsisted precariously. Weakened by successive wars with Russia, the last of which in 1878 had led to the Treaty of San Stefano, confirming the loss of most of the Ottoman empire's Balkan provinces, Turkey was now subject to the autocratic and reactionary rule of 'Abd al-Hamid (1876–1909). The Sultan eliminated liberal and progressive opposition. The

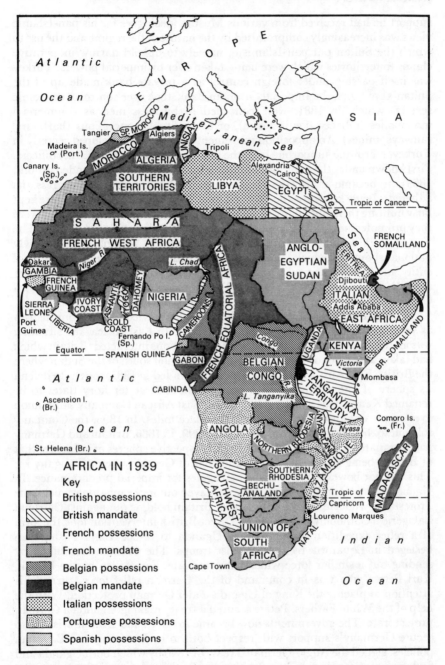

Map 17.1 *The colonial share-out in Africa (source:* M. E. Townsend, *European Colonial Expansion since 1871)*

support he had received from various Muslim ideologues for his pan-Islamic views was increasingly compromised by the nature of the regime and the use to which the Sultan put pan-Islamism, namely to uphold narrow inoperative claims to territories which were being taken over by imperial powers. Turkey was itself passing under foreign control as a private bank made up of the Sultan's creditors, the Imperial Ottoman Bank, took over control of economic sectors, which, in 1881, were conceded to business men as commercial monopolies (tobacco, for instance), or as profitable concessions (harbours, railways, mines). An opposition movement nonetheless developed secretly in Turkey, recruiting supporters from the intelligentsia and among army officers. First known under the name of Committee for Young Turkey (founded around 1869), it became in 1894–5 the Committee for Union and Progress, its adherents being known as the Young Turks. 'Abd al-Hamid's police were kept busy hunting them out; many sympathizers were exiled, notably to Libya were they promoted new and different ideas in Tripoli and other urban centres. The Young Turk revolution was to take place in 1908, leading to a narrowly nationalist outlook which found its political counterpart in the small national entity, modern Turkey, which was all that remained of the Ottoman Empire after the First World War, in which Turkey made the mistake of siding with Germany.

The rival imperial ambitions of the Great Powers led to an all-out rush on as yet unclaimed territories, notably in Africa. In East Africa, the situation was increasingly complex as rival colonial ambitions interacted. Britain which had taken a lead not only in Egypt but in the region south of the Sudan where the British East Africa Company had been founded in 1887, sought to defend its sphere of interest by effective occupation. A large territory (later to be renamed Kenya) was to extend the British East African Company's dominion over an area of approximately 200 000 square miles. In 1895, the Company sold out to the British government for £250 000. In 1886, Britain and Germany had negotiated a settlement defining their respective spheres of influence, that of Britain being Kenya, Uganda, and that of Germany being Tanganyika. This did not however prevent local struggles for imperial predominance. In Uganda French and British rivalry was played out in the missionary field, the Protestants who had come out first from Britain holding out against Cardinal Lavigerie's Catholic White Fathers. Direct British intervention took the form of a relief expedition sent out from Uganda to rescue Emin Pasha then besieged in Equatoria by the Mahdist troops. The Germans retaliated by sending out a similar force which came too late. Forestalled by the British, Karl Peters who was in command of the German relief force, turned his attention to placing the King of Uganda under German protection. With the help of the White Fathers, Peters secured a treaty making Uganda a German protectorate. The governments now became involved and Britain, wishing to secure Germany's support with respect both to its European and Egyptian policies, signed the Anglo-German Treaty of 1890 by which both Uganda and Sudan were recognized as being within the British sphere of influence, whilst Germany, in exchange, was given the island of Heligoland opposite Hamburg. British imperial strategy aiming at control of all the area between Alexandria and the Cape was almost achieved.

France was no less active on the western side of the continent where only

Nigeria, the Gold Coast, Gambia and Sierra Leone, all extensions of early British coastal settlements, had not passed under French control. The extended federated territories of French West Africa and French Equatorial Africa which spread from the Atlantic to the Sudan had been progressively constituted by means of military expeditions and the strong hand of two governors, Faiherbe in Senegal and Savorgnan de Brazza in Equatorial Africa. The French claim now was: 'All Africa above the Equator French'. To promote this, a number of military missions to explore the regions between areas of by now-established colonial rule were undertaken. One of the most famous was Colonel Monteil's 5000 mile journey which took him from Saint-Louis to Lake Chad in 1892. Savorgnan de Brazza was himself an explorer whose *Mission de l'Ouest Africain* led him some 4000 km northwards in 1881–5 to Lake Chad whilst, in 1898–1900, the Foureau and Lamy expedition was to cross the Sahara, from Wargla in southern Algeria, to the Congo, via Chad. In 1899 the Joalland and Meynier mission reached Kanem and, after having beaten Rabih in battle, undertook the effective occupation and colonial administration of the area.

It was inevitable, in spite of the common will to avoid war between European states in Africa, that the two major imperial policies would, at some stage or other, clash. The British line of progression 'from Alexandria to the Cape' crossed that of France 'From the Atlantic to the Red Sea' at Fashoda in 1898.

A French officer, Marchand had offered to make good a French claim on southern Sudan. Time was short but conditions were still favourable since the Anglo-Egyptian campaign against the Mahdiyya was only just getting under way. Italian interests in the Red Sea area were moreover clear since the Bay of Assab had been acquired in 1882 and Massawa conquered in 1884–5. After the establishment of the Eritrean colony in 1889, it behoved France to forestall the Italians who were moving in westwards. Marchand, whose plan was upheld in Paris by the colonial lobby and the then minister of foreign affairs, Hanotaux, suggested that a military detachment and a ship be sent up the Congo from Brazzaville to Bangui, and along the M'Bomu as far as the Bahr al-Ghazal, there to hoist the French flag. The plan having been agreed to, the expedition set off in September 1896 and reached Bangui in April 1897. It was under the command of the fanatical and ambitious Marchand, of a harsh colonial officer, Mangin, and the somewhat more humane Baratier. It comprised 500 Senegalese riflemen and numerous porters to carry luggage and the dismantled ship. The journey proved difficult, especially for the porters conscripted on the road by means of threats and summary executions which Brazza de Savorgnan was unable to prevent. So cruel indeed were these methods that as news leaked out, critical articles were published in the French newspapers. Soueh was reached in August 1897 and Fashoda a year later. The French forces were attacked by Mahdist troops on 25 August 1898 and after the attack was repulsed, a treaty was signed between Marchand and Kur 'Abd al-Fadil, head of the Shilluk tribe at the bend of the Nile. It established a French protectorate from 3 September 1898. The small band of 13 French officers and their Senegalese riflemen settled down to await events. On 18 September Kitchener sailed down from Khartum to Fashoda and beneath a cordial surface a tense situation developed. Both expeditions agreed to submit

311

the case to their respective governments. Kitchener, however, had the advantage of being able to point out to Marchand that the latter was dependent on routes via British-controlled northern Sudan and Egypt for communication with the outside world. On 9 October 1898, an Anglo-Egyptian ship brought a message. It was from the pro-European Delcassé, now French minister of foreign affairs, requesting further information concerning the Kitchener-Marchand meeting. Via Egypt, the French officer Baratier went to Paris, which by now was in the throes of a military scandal: the Dreyfus case. An official message was sent out to Marchand via Cairo on 3 November. It stated: 'Dictated by the general interest of France, the Government's decision is not to remain in Fashoda'.

In France the showdown was considered a national humiliation which rankled for years. It moreover marked the definite limits of France's progression eastwards, on the borders of Sudan, thus leaving the road open for the British to reach the Cape unimpeded. For North Africa, however, the imperial objective, 'From the Atlantic to the Red Sea', had indeed been reached though involving several colonial powers. North Africa was now cut off from Sudanic Africa.

FURTHER IMPERIAL PRESSURES AT THE END OF THE CENTURY

Pressures on Morocco

North Africa was also subject to two imperial powers both of which had strong military forces at their disposal to further drive colonial wedges into the region. In the west of the continent, Morocco and its southern Saharan hinterland were under growing pressures. French military forces were concentrated along the Algerian frontiers and in the last years of the century, encroachments were stepped up. They were carried out by officers of the South Oran military region with the blessing of authorities in Algiers, but were not, however, approved of by the French government which feared European reactions. This did not prevent the invasion in 1899–1901 of a number of Saharan oases, notably In Salah, Tidikelt, Tuwwat, and Gurara which were within Moroccan territory. The incursions continued in the following years until the establishment of the Franco-Spanish protectorate in Morocco in 1912.

French imperialism was also closing in on Morocco from the south. In Senegal, the Gouvernement Général d'Afrique Occidental was established by decree in 1895. It marked a new policy of Saharan occupation and in December 1899, the French Minister for the Colonies announced his intention 'to bring together, in autonomous groups, the different regions inhabited by the Moors from the right bank of the Senegal, Kayes, Timbuktu, up to the south of Algeria, under the name of Western Mauritania'. A policy of religious infiltration of fraternities and zawiya-s, and political manipulation of tribal chiefs and holy lineages was undertaken as a prelude to conquest by Xavier Coppolani (1866–1905), an administrator in French Algeria who arrived in Saint-Louis in 1899 and was appointed French commissioner of the new territory.

That the Moors, i.e. Arab tribes north of the Senegal, and notably the religious leader Ma al-'Aynayn were aware of impending French moves was evident, and the defensive organization set up by Ma al-'Aynayn with

Moroccan government help shows this. Ma al-'Aynayn who had gone to settle further north, at Simara, decided to make this into a brick-built city which would be the spiritual home of the Saharans. He appealed to the Moroccan government for funds which were provided, together with material which was shipped down the coast. Simara was built between 1898 and 1902 but Ma al-'Aynayn was only to occupy it a short time because French military pressures on the region had increased together with the kind of political and religious pressures which Coppolani dealt in. Coppolani himself was to be murdered in 1905 during a tour of the Adrar, and this was attributed to the Saharan holy man although no direct involvement has been proved. It was nonetheless evident that he was behind the resistance, which was indeed to be sustained in spite of the military imbalance, since the region was not brought under full control until 1935.

In Morocco itself, international pressures, notably in the economic field, were leading to the same sort of disintegration as in Tunisia or Egypt a few years earlier. Mulay Hasan had died in 1894 and a young prince, not yet of age, Mulay 'Abd al-'Aziz had been chosen as successor with, as prime minister and regent, Ba Ahmad, an experienced palace servant of slave origin. The latter's prudent policy in the first four years of the reign were chiefly responsible for subdued relations with France whose claims Ba Ahmad preferred to meet rather than see minor incidents develop into full scale attacks on Moroccan sovereignty. By sending messages and royal representatives into tribal and frontier areas, he was able to bring people to accept government strategy. Ba Ahmad was himself personally affiliated to the 'Ayniyya fraternity and he encouraged the close relations between the Saharan spiritual leader and the sharifian royal family. When the young and inexperienced Mulay 'Abd al-'Aziz took effective power in 1898, on Ba Ahmad's death, economic mismanagement soon brought the country to the brink of ruin. This resulted from several converging tendencies: the financial trends studied earlier, including inflation and the growing depreciation of the local currency, well-meaning but inoperative reforms undertaken by the young sovereign with a view to modernizing the country (which included the setting up of a new tax the *tertib* which was massively resisted by the population), the onslaught of European businessmen out to make sales at all costs, who promoted prodigal expenditure abetting a marked taste in the Sultan for costly gadgets, and, finally, here as elsewhere, offers from European bankers to lend money. This led in 1902 to a first loan of 7 500 000 French francs from the Banque de Paris et des Pays Bas in partnership with other banks. Two further loans for the same amount were put up the following year by British and Spanish banks. By the end of 1903, Morocco was insolvent and colonial takeover was openly discussed by the Powers at the Algeciras Conference of 1906.

In a period of intense international strain, Morocco was too important a stake not to make the Powers wary of involvement which might lead to direct confrontation between them. In pursuance of their ends and the final share-out, economic pressures on Morocco were stepped up. Britain consolidated its well-established positions guaranteed by favourable treaties, by the permanent nature of relations between Morocco and Gibraltar and by a foreign community which included diplomatic representation and nationals in Moroccan government employ. The long stays of men such as Sir John

Drummond Hay, Qaid MacLean, or John Harris, correspondent of *The Times*, contributed to British preponderance, further upheld by a growing number of merchants in Casablanca and Tangier, besides a small resident community in the latter town which was becoming a stopping-over place for ex-Indian army officials or members of the gentry who found cosmopolitan Tangier more congenial than Victorian England. The French were also stepping up both their economic and political pressures. The Algerian colonial lobby, actively led by the member of parliament for Oran, Eugène Etienne, were convincing business and governmental circles that Algeria should extend out into Morocco. Various associations (notably the Comité du Maroc) and pro-colonial papers and reviews such as the *Bulletin de l'Afrique française* publicized their views. Germany, which now considered territorial expansion as a way of safeguarding national prosperity, was showing a new interest in Morocco. Missions had been invited to Berlin in 1878 and 1889 and this had led to the signing of a commercial treaty between the two countries in 1890. Though Germany had as yet limited economic interests in the country, with only 35 firms set up there between 1886 and 1901, representing 5 per cent of Moroccan international trade, the German community was growing, increasing from 17 in 1879 to 147 in 1901. Its consular service in Tangier was particularly active. This was to lead to a more direct stand by Germany on the Moroccan problem in the first years of the 20th century. One of its more flamboyant aspects was to be the landing of the Kaiser at Tangier in 1905 as a riposte to the Entente Cordiale by which Britain had 'conceded' Morocco to France. Tangier, to which the main consular services had been transferred and where the sultan's representative (*naib*) acted as official intermediary between the *makhzen* and Europeans, was now a hotbed of intrigues.

Pressures on Libya

In the east of the continent, a similar spirit of competition was on foot with Britain using Egypt as its imperial base. It was in fact in order to obtain a free hand in Egypt that England had been led to give up its claims on Morocco in favour of France. Germany's territorial ambitions in West Africa were paralleled at the other end of North Africa by Italian claims on the east coast where the newly proclaimed Italian colony of Eritrea (1890) served as the starting point for further expansion. Francesco Crispi, prime minister from 1887 to 1896, was himself a staunch advocate of colonial expansion. He had troops stationed along the Abyssinian border and, in 1889, undertook to impose a protectorate on the new sovereign of Ethiopia, Menelik II (1889–1913). Britain in 1891 formally recognized this move in order to win the support of Italy in checking the spread of French influence and new German irredentism.

Under cover of economic infiltration, Italy was also active in Libya, which it saw as a potential colonist settlement for its growing population, notably from the underdeveloped southern regions. Italian emigration had increased from 100 000 in 1875 to 250 000 in 1890. It was there moreover that the national insult to Italy proferred by France when it had taken over Tunisia could, it was felt, be avenged. In Libya itself, Italy was as yet a minor power compared to other empire-building nations. Efforts were nonetheless being made by men such as Manfredo Camperio who promoted exploration of Libya by means of the *Exploratore* which he founded in 1877 and the Milanese Societa d'Esplorazione. Coal, silver, and chalk had been found, and other minerals were believed to exist. Britain was still Libya's major foreign trading power: in 1886 a quarter of Libya's imports came from Britain and only one-sixth from Italy. But from 1890 onwards Italian efforts were stepped up, reflecting its new position as an industrial nation and as an exporter. Italian interests abroad were further stimulated by a favourable balance of trade and a growing population. By 1900, Italian tonnage of shipping sent to Libya was twice that of Britain and four times that of France. Focus on Libya became more evident as diplomatic negotiations led up to the Franco-Italian treaty of 1900 by which France gave Italy freedom of action in Libya in exchange for cessation of its activities in Tunisia. A new influential colonial lobby appeared in Italy to urge annexation of Tripoli. It included members of the nationalist group led by Enrico Corradini and they gradually gained a public hearing both in the press and in parliament. The lobby had the backing of vested financial interests, of the Vatican notably and of the Banco di Roma where a Vatican-promoted director, Ernesto Pacelli, was appointed in 1903. This bank was to come forward as the spearhead of Italian penetration in Libya. By 1907, it was able to open a branch office in Tripoli, followed by others at Derna and Ben Ghazi. It invested massively in economic projects, founded a weekly, *l'Economista di Tripoli*, and obtained support from many leading notables. The stage here too was set for confrontation, this time between Italy and Turkey, and was to lead to the Italian invasion of Tripoli in 1911.

This does not mean that the Libyans themselves were prepared to accept Turkey's decision to give way to Italian claims, as their long resistance was to show, nor that the chief social force of the country, the Sanusiyya, was prepared for unconditional surrender. Sanusi resistance in the last years of the century was increasingly equated with defence of the Sahara. It was itself involved in front line confrontation and underscored this by transferring the order's headquarters still further southwards, the move to Qiru being made in 1899. This must be seen in the light of French occupation that same year of the Lake Chad area. The Sanusiyya attempted to oppose colonial takeover. Tribal contingents made up chiefly of Tuareg and Awlad Sulayman repulsed a first French attack on 'Alali on 9 November 1901, losing many men in the fighting, including Ghayth, head of the Sayf al-Nasir family. But in January the French forces attacked again and conquered the 'Alali *zawiya* of the Sanusi-s. At the end of 1902, the Tuareg and Awlad Sulayman under Sanusi leadership made a desperate effort to reconquer 'Alali, but in vain. Qiru had to be abandoned and the line of resistance re-established at the level of Kufra. Sanusi strongholds fell into colonial hands one after the other, though fighting it out to the end: Wadday in 1904–8, Borku in 1913, Tibesti in 1914–16, the Agades sultanate and the Niger Tuareg in 1916–17. This was the tragic last stand of a very proud, independent people who were not able to look forward to the bright sunrise of nationalism on the historical horizon, as were the Egyptians, Tunisians, and other African peoples, but rather faced humiliating dependency to be carried on, even reinforced after independence.

The Sanusi family after the death of al-Mahdi al-Sanusi, six months after the fall of Zawiya 'Alali, had retired northwards to organize the defence of more exposed parts of Fezzan. Here too the French were active, attempting from their Algerian and Tunisian territories to make contacts in the region and set up trade relations. This was part of a plan to make prior claims on border territories and Saharan trade-routes. Ghat and Ghadames near the frontier of the three countries in particular focused French attention. The Sanusi organization undertook not only to promote local resistance but to bolster up Ottoman authority there. In the last years of the century repeated incidents (including the murder in 1896 of a Frenchman, Mores, who had gone out to make contacts with the Tuareg) were made much of by the colonial lobby and the newspapers. It was generally supposed that France would use such incidents to take over part of the area. Both the British and Italians made efforts to oppose the supposed French move and the Sultan was led to make a number of concessions, including the recall of the governor. Discussions on the actual limits of Turkish sovereignty in Libya were undertaken, leading to a provisional mapping out of the territory in 1898, followed up by an agreement between Algeria (French territory) and Tunisia (a protectorate) in 1901–2 as to the actual frontier.

British expansion from an Egyptian base

Further east, in the Nile valley, British supremacy was an accepted fact since the 1882 landing had made Britain the effective ruler of Eygpt. One of its first tasks was to build up an efficient colonial army of English-officered Egyptian troops in order not only to defend its position in the Mediterranean and with respect to the Suez Canal, but to progress towards the Cape. It met with an initial difficulty because of the rise of the Mahdiyya in Sudan and fall of the Turkiyya. This was a situation for which Britain was only indirectly responsible but which nonetheless directly affected it, especially in view of the fact that loss of control over Sudan was accompanied by national humiliation as a result of the defeat of General Hicks's Relief Force in 1883, the surrender of British officers who were detained in captivity in Sudan, the fall of Khartum and, even more, the death of General Gordon.

Britain began methodically to prepare a campaign to re-establish control in Sudan. This began with the setting up of the new army which was first used for police work. Progressively units were sent out to the border. There non-Mahdi Sudanese volunteers were recruited. At the same time a British intelligence department was set up which, under Sir Reginald Wingate, collected information concerning the Mahdiyya. It found Sudanese agents and even obtained the collaboration of leading personalities, notably the Mirghani family. Captured documents, including proclamations of the Mahdi and his Khalifa, reached Cairo where they were translated and perused by Sir Reginald Wingate's staff. Plans for the campaign were laid. Several factors determined the start of operations in the spring of 1896. There was growing unrest among the Khalifa's followers in an economically and politically difficult situation. The new Egyptian army was now considered ready to face up to the encounter. Imperial considerations were, however, even more important. Not only did Britain thus have an occasion to uphold Italian interests in the region after the defeat of Italian forces at Adowa in March 1896, thus courting the Triple Alliance, but there was also the problem of rival colonial interest on the southern borders of Sudan. Germany was interested in Uganda, and Belgium claimed the Bahr al-Ghazal as part of the Congo. It was indeed to obtain the Lado Enclave which it kept until 1910. The French, as we saw earlier, were making an even more determined effort to stake a claim on southern Sudan. It was thus imperative that Britain get in first. Kitchener received his marching orders on 13 March 1896. The Wadi Halfa frontier was crossed and on 23 September Dunqula was taken. In 1897, another column set out along a more easternly route and conquered Berbera and 'Atbara, whilst the main force progressed southwards. 'On September 4, 1898, the British and Egyptian flags were hoisted with due ceremony on the walls of the ruined palace of Khartum'. Fighting in outlying regions nonetheless continued until Khalifa 'Abd Allah was killed in battle on 24 November 1899. In the process Dar Fur reasserted its independence under the leadership of 'Ali Dinar, a scion of the former dynasty. This was countenanced by the new Anglo-Egyptian government of Sudan in 1901, although in 1916 after fighting in which 'Ali Dinar was killed, Dar Fur was reintegrated into Sudan. Into it was incorporated in 1922 the small, hitherto independent state of Dar Masalit on the Chad border. In the early post-Mahdi period several Mahdi-inspired uprisings took place. In fact, the British in the Sudan were never able to do without a strongly military regime and much effort went into eliminating supporters of the Mahdiyya from social and political activities. That attachment to the Mahdiyya remained strong – in spite of this – was shown a mere quarter of a century later when the development of modern Sudanese nationalism brought back to the fore the *ansar* and their descendants with, as their leader, the Mahdi's son.

The regime set up in Sudan was an ambiguous one from the start. No one quite knew what the exact status of the country was in view of the fact that the Khedive had in principle given up his rights over a colony which he held in the name of the Sultan. In doing so he had not obtained prior sanction from his suzerain. Lengthy chancery debates as to whether Sudan was to be considered *territorium nullius*, part of Egypt, or a Turkish dependency, or even revert to some descendant of the old Funj dynasty, took place and were of interest to specialists of international law – not however to Lord Cromer who set up a no less ambiguous and indeed unique arrangement of his own involving the cooperation of Britain and Egypt under a 'two-flag regime'. The agreement provided that the country was to be run by the British, as illustrated by the fact that on the same day Lord Kitchener was appointed general-in-chief and governor-general of Anglo-Egyptian Sudan. The cost of the operations and of the future running of the colony were, on the other hand, to be paid out of the Egyptian treasury.

The colonial scramble for territory was almost over by 1900 and was to be concluded in the period leading up to World War I and the Treaty of Versailles. In the process North Africa had been shared out and only Morocco and Libya awaited not so much the decision as to their fate, since this had already been more or less taken, as actual takeover, which occurred in 1911 when Italy invaded Tripoli, and in 1912 when Morocco became a protectorate shared out between France and Spain.

STRANGERS AT HOME

In the face of European domination, North African society reacted as a living organism does when a graft is inserted: adaptation or rejection defined people's attitudes.

That a new dominant order was coming into its own is shown by the fact that primary resistance became muted in the latter part of the century. Little actual fighting took place during the takeover of Egypt and Tunisia, and no major revolts were recorded in Algeria after the 1870 uprising. Such armed opposition as there was took place in peripheral zones, along the *bilad al-Sudan* borders. This does not mean that resistance had disappeared but rather that it had become atomized, creating a permanent underlying tension which could now and then break out in largely uncontrolled scenes of violence. The spirit prevailing at the end of the century was largely that illustrated in Algeria by an 'incident' which occurred in the small colonist settlement of Margueritte in Algeria, on 26 April 1901. The peasants there were under considerable strain because of lack of land when they rallied to the call of one Ya'qub ben al-Hajj. For a few hours on the morning of the 26th, rioting was rife. Europeans were stopped, forced to recite the Muslim act of faith and threatened with death if they did not do so. According to contemporary newspaper accounts, eight Europeans were killed. By the end of the morning, violence had petered out and the peasants began trekking home. Troops who had been called in, then arrived on the spot and shooting ensued, in the course of which 16 Algerians were killed. Colonists accompanied the soldiers to tribesmen's homes and pointed out those whom they recognized as culprits; 166 men were arrested of whom 41 were later cleared. Though this can be considered as a relatively minor and in any case isolated incident, it shows well the underlying antagonism of the two communities, and the deep-rooted fear of colonists which expressed itself in a public outcry against the accused, so much so indeed that they had to be transferred to France, no fair trial being possible in Algeria. When the case was heard by a court in Montpellier between 11 December 1902 and 8 February 1903, no death sentences were passed because it was obvious that very real causes of peasant grievance existed. On the other hand in Algeria racial hate was kept up by such apparently minor but nonetheless very significant means as a postcard featuring the accused which remained in popular use in colonist circles for several years.

The suppressed feelings of the Algerians at this time increasingly expressed themselves in minor acts of lawlessness, including arson. That this was a reaction against colonialism in general is shown by the fact that a quite similar picture could be drawn up of rural Egypt where criminality was also on the rise and where latent hostility could, on occasion, create a dramatic situation. Even more than Margueritte, Denchway in June 1906 was to show up colonial relations in their true light. The incident here involved British officers out hunting who accidently wounded a young man. In the fighting which ensued one of the British officers was killed. The trial which followed in Egypt itself further involved the fact that the court was Egyptian and was presided over by Boutros Ghali (a future prime minister, later assassinated by terrorists in 1910). Death sentences were passed on the peasants who were publicly hanged under the eyes of the inhabitants of Denchway. The stir this caused and public reprobation contributed to the resignation of Lord Cromer in 1907.

Against a tension-fraught background in which Muslims constantly had to repress their feelings, people lived out their daily lives under the stress of contradictory urges: adaptation and self-withdrawal. In a general way a compromise was adopted involving adaptation in a public and professional capacity whilst social barriers were not only upheld but emphasized. There was very little social intercourse in colonial society and few Europeans were allowed into the inner sanctum of Muslim lives. A characteristic expression of Muslim feelings was their will to seclude their womenfolk from contacts and it is significant that it should have been in Algeria that the wearing of the veil should, more than elsewhere, have been the rule. This was one way in which Muslims tried to preserve their identity. The breaking of this rule was a cause of considerable scandal. In cases of mixed marriages, families would carry out a pretended burial ceremony to show that they cut off all relations with the culprit, since women were not allowed to marry non-Muslims, and even French wives, though this was allowed by Muslim law, were badly accepted. Even more scandal was caused by conversions or naturalisations. In Tunisia, in the face of public and religious opposition, special cemeteries had to be set up to bury those who had become French citizens.

Nonetheless adaptation was taking place, even in the family and in the home. Adaptation should not be seen as merely giving way to European pressures. It was in fact a well-accepted process of evolution which can be traced back to the end of the 18th century as we saw in the initial chapters of this book and which took very similar forms to changes underway in rural Europe in the same period. New social categories and some sectors of the ruling class had adopted these new standards as theirs and promoted reforms which, in some cases, suffered a setback in the colonial period. The kinds of reforms promoted by Muhammad 'Ali in Egypt or the reformist *beys* in Tunisia showed a will to change and a move to modernity in such fields as parliamentary democracy or education which were slowed down when European powers took over. Nor should the idea of change be limited to state-promoted policies. They also included many aspects of people's daily lives, creating a different set of habits soon largely considered indigenous. This moreover can be seen as applying to North Africa as a whole, irrespective of colonial status. Thus Morocco, though as yet independent, had integrated a great number of imported features into the cultural idiom. This included a status symbol defined by imported goods such as French silks, Italian velvets, Manchester or Sheffield metalware and plated silver, Venetian glass or European firearms. Poorer people were themselves affected by the new trend with far-reaching consequences, as cash-crops were increasingly necessary to pay for now indispensable requirements such as candles, sugar, tea, coffee, household wares and cheap cottons. These brought about changes in people's lives, even in such apparently traditional fields as home cooking where one can point to a decline in the use of such commodities as honey and a lower protein diet, compensated for in taste if not in quality, by the appearance at the end of the century of new varieties of vegetables. In Morocco, tomatoes and potatoes became as indigenous as turnips and onions. These are important facts of social history, though rarely studied as part of the overall pattern of change. The historian generally emphasizes more overt political and economic aspects of this such as greater state control, the development of towns and their new dominant position with respect to rural society, besides a marked tendency to class stratification as people, both in towns and the country, tended to switch over to salaried occupations.

People did not therefore reject change, but rather the foreign non-Muslim regime it brought with it, a reaction further emphasized by the oppression and exploitation characterisic of colonial regimes. It is in this sense that the return to North Africa of former exiles also marks a reintroduction of the struggle for national identity into what was to be the North African battlefield.

The return to Cairo in the late 1880s of Muhammad 'Abduh is of far greater significance than the mere lifting of a sentence of exile might imply. Not only has it its place in a historical development both as a closing comment on early 19th century nationalist uprisings and as an opening sentence on a North African-based reawakening, but can itself be seen as a sign of the turn of the tide as the long process of defeat and withdrawal was reversed.

Muhammad Bayram,
described by Lord Cromer

Sheikh Mohammed Beyram, who is now, alas! dead, was one of my best friends in Egypt. He was, moreover, one of the most remarkable types with which I have met in the course of my Eastern experience. He looked like a thorough gentleman. I have rarely seen a more striking figure than that of this grave Oriental, with his high intellectual forehead, refined features, melancholy eyes, dignified mien, exquisite manners, and graceful costume, who would sit with me by the hour and sing a dirge over the decadence of Islam. Moreover, Sheikh Mohammed Beyram not only looked a gentleman; he was one. In no country have I come across a man of more elevated and refined feelings, or one whose opinons and actions were less tainted with wordly self-interest, than this Tunisian aristocrat.... Pope's fine lines well describe my honoured friend:–

Statesman, yet friend to truth! of soul sincere,
In action faithful and in honour clear!
Who broke no promise, served no private end,
Who gained no title, and who lost no friend.

Lord Cromer, *Modern Egypt*

In perspective, Muhammad 'Abduh's return points to a more general trend. Not only did the Egyptian exiles resume their former positions (the Qayati brothers returning to their home village, 'Abd al-Rahman 'Ilish to al-Azhar) but other men who were to be the intellectual leaders of new times, arrived in their wake. Chief of these was Rashid Ridha (1865–1935) who was to be Muhammad 'Abduh's faithful disciple and mouthpiece. He settled in Cairo in 1897 and his periodical, *al-Manar* published between 1898 and 1935, was to make of 'Abduh's ideas the touchstone of the Arab *nahda* or renaissance. These were moreover to have an international political impact through Rashid Ridha's participation in various organizations and congresses including the Islamic conferences of Mecca in 1926 and of Jerusalem in 1931. The fact that Egyptian prime minister, Riaz Pasha, and the British agency invited other

THE END OF THE CENTURY: AN OVERALL ASSESSMENT

intellectuals over to combat these views (men such as Ya'qub Sarruf and Faris Namir whose influential newspaper *al-Muqqatam* was transferred to Cairo in 1885) was in itself a positive contribution since it made for a greater pugnacity in the nationalist press. Moreover the Arabs invited over to Egypt or made welcome there were not always to provide khedival-colonial rule with the support it expected. Lord Cromer's view that 'Islam as a social system has been a complete failure' was opposed by a Christian Syrian, Dr Shibbli Shumayyil (1850–1917) in his book, *Falsafat al-Nushu wa al-Irtiqa*.

Muhammad 'Abduh's first task in Egypt, even though his activities were curtailed by a close watch kept on him, and his appointment to a minor judiciary function, was, indeed, to contradict another of Lord Cromer's statements that Islam was 'politically and socially moribund'. He first set about infusing a new spirit into intellectual circles of the capital where he encouraged the setting up of associations and where he organized numerous public meetings. These not only helped the spread of new ideas but created a link between the men who upheld them. Muhammad 'Abduh's efforts were more particularly directed towards integrating other North African émigrés into these activist circles. We thus find the Tunisian Muhammad Bayram who had settled in Egypt in 1884, encouraged by 'Abduh. Muhammad Bayram thus played a leading role until his death in 1889. He not only set up his own publishing house (al-I'alamiyya which printed his major work *Safwat al-I'tibar bi Mustawda' al-Amsar wa al-Aqtar*, a comparison of various political systems and their respective merits) but also an influential weekly *al-I'alam* (1885–9).

Muhammad 'Abduh also continued to consider himself as a teacher whose task it was to explain to his contemporaries not only the way in which Islam should rightly be understood but how, through Islam, to accept each aspect of modern life and historical circumstances. It was in this period that his teaching impinged on a wider audience, through his commentaries on the Quran. The fact that at the same time he learnt French, travelled extensively and showed his interest in the works of Rousseau, Spencer, Strauss, and Renan show up wider involvement in philosophical issues of the time. His reputation as the leading Egyptian scholar could not be merely ignored by the Cromer-Khedive administration and he progressively rose to a position where he was able to put his ideas into practice by preparing the new Egyptian code of law and presiding over a committee set up to reform al-Azhar teaching. In 1899, he became mufti of Egypt.

The effect of this on the development of Egyptian and North African nationalism was considerable. Muhammad 'Abduh had already shown his interest in Tunisia and his belief in its capacities to provide a new moral and intellectual leadership by his first visit to the country. His belief was encouraged by the continued impact of the Tunisian reformists in their country. Muhammad al-Sanusi who himself had returned to Tunisia after a brief period of voluntary exile in 1881–2, organized one of the first political stands against the colonial regime of the protectorate by mass meetings, notably at the Great Mosque of Tunis, to protest against the new city regulations the French were trying to impose. We also find Muhammad al-Sanusi playing an active role in the spread of 'Abduh's views among the intelligentsia. In 1888 a first cultural review was founded, regrouping sympathizers, the *Hadhira*, and, in 1896, an association, the *Khalduniyya*.

Bayram's weekly reached these circles in spite of government censure and upheld the movement which now attracted a younger generation of Tunisians who were to become politically active. They included such men as Salim Bu Hajeb, Tahar bin 'Ashur, 'Ali Bushusha, Muhammad Lasram, Bashir Sfar. Muhammad 'Abduh who paid a second visit to Tunis in September 1903 was able to appreciate the progress made. The 'Young Tunisians' were already an active group in society and were soon to be a politically active force. By 1906 they were forcefully making their point both on the national and international scene. Here again Tunisia had taken the lead, but more individual though as yet isolated expressions of the new outlook can be detected elsewhere in North Africa. In Morocco the need for political and cultural reform was being stated by members of the Fasi élite, and a new category of reformist *'ulama* was in the making with such men as Busha'ib al-Dukkali. In Sudan, though the country was hard hit by repression of the Mahdiyya, similar tendencies appear, notably in the views on education held by Babikr Bedri, one of the *ansar* who, in this period, opened a private school.

Just as Egypt had taken the intellectual lead in defining modern North Africa's collective personality, so it took the lead in defining its new political stand as early as 1900. A new militant generation was coming into its own through such men as Sa'd Zaghlul (circa 1860–1927) who was also a connecting link between past and present. He was from the *shaykh al-balad* social stratum and, at al-Azhar, had studied under Muhammad 'Abduh. He was tried after the 'Arabi Pasha uprising, but acquitted. After his release he began to practise law and in 1893 became a judge in the court of appeal. Having married into the ruling class, he was at home both in nationalist and khedival circles and in 1906 he became minister of education, and in 1910, minister of justice. He soon became the principal spokesman of the Nationalist Party and in 1918 demanded Egypt's independence. Sa'd Zaghlul was also typical of his time in believing that public action was called for and that the now powerful media of the press could promote this. It was through journalism that new leaders came to the fore: Mustafa Kamil (1874–1908) notably, who made of *al-Lewa* one of the more influential papers of the early 20th century, together with *al-Jarida* founded by Ahmad Lutfi al-Sayyid in 1906. Ahmad Lutfi al-Sayyid (1872–1963) no less than Sa'd Zaghlul illustrates the development of 19th century into 20th-century nationalism. He too came from the *shaykh al-balad* class and in 1893 he had gone to Istanbul where he had met both al-Afghani and Sa'd Zaghlul. Though he entered public service as deputy public prosecutor in 1894 he also, in partnership with 'Abd al-Aziz Fahmi, founded a secret society for the purpose of liberating Egypt from British rule (1896), following this up by militancy on party lines.

New issues were now being discussed involving national and social problems not all connected with imperialism. Thus Mustafa Kamil called for national solidarity both of Muslims and Copts, a stand later also taken by Sa'd Zaghlul's Wafd Party. Qasim Amin made a courageous stand for the liberation of women in a much criticized book, *Tahrir al-Mara* (1899), and Lutfi al-Sayyid stood up for the unity of Egypt and the Sudan whose inhabitants were 'sons of the Nile'. All were trying to define the stand from which a stronger society having a more forceful personality could launch a unified onslaught on colonial rule. Though more strictly national in its outlook and objectives, the new generation was also more aware of the fact that the same problems were facing other Muslim states. Moreover they were not averse to extending the range of their activities to Europe. This can, of course, be connected to earlier efforts going back to the Moorish Committee in Paris in 1830 and Muhammad 'Abduh's own stay in Paris with Jamal al-Din al-Afghni. New conditions, ranging from easier communications to rivalry among the Great Powers, however, led victims of colonial rule to pay greater attention now to political opinion in Rome, Berlin, Paris, or London. Not only were new relations with government circles in those capitals established, but Geneva was constituted into a political office for nationalist propaganda in Europe. It was Switzerland that Shakib Arslan, a leading nationalist of the Middle East, chose as the rallying point of his movement which included a number of North Africans. No less significantly we find in Geneva in the late 1890s most of the Egyptians whose names have been mentioned: Lutfi al-Sayyid, Sa'd Zaghlul, Mustafa Kamil, Qasim Amin, and Muhammad 'Abduh himself.

By 1900 a new North African Arab nationalist personality had defined itself. An impressive group of Egyptian militants, their public action before and after World War I, and their cultural stand as evolved during the same period, were to make of Egypt a leader both of the Arab world and of the Third World, whilst at the same time providing North Africans with an image with which they could and did identify themselves. Considering later developments, including Nasser's liberation of the Suez Canal from foreign control, we can see 1900 as a turning point when a new attitude became overt, politically active, and largely accepted. The attitude had been in the making through a century-long experience of new problems connected with the rise of mercantilism and industrial capitalism. The will to face up to the threat of imperialism increasingly underlies the history of the period, as warriors or saints, intellectuals or party militants, rulers or ordinary people, all in their own way contributed to forging a new cultural and political self-awareness. This, through varied efforts and much hardship, was to lead North Africa out of self-exile to national self-assertion, out of colonial night into the daylight of independence and reclaimed identity.

SELECTED READING LIST

I – International Strategy and colonial expansion
Baratier, A., *Souvenirs de la Mission Marchand, Fachoda*, (Paris, 1941).
Lowe, C. J., *Salisbury and the Mediterranean 1886–1896*, (London and Toronto, 1965).
Michel, M., *La Mission Marchand, 1895–1899*, (Paris and Hague, 1972).
Miège, J.-L., *L'Impérialisme Italien de 1870 à nos Jours*, (Paris, 1978).
Newbury, C. W., 'The Development of French Policy on the Lower and Upper Niger, 1880–98', *Journal of Modern History*, 31, 1959.
Smith, I. R., *The Emin Pasha Relief Expedition, 1896–1890*, (Oxford, 1972).
Townsend, M. E., *European Colonial Expansion since 1871*, (Chicago, Philadelphia, New York, 1941).
Vignes, K., 'Etude sur la rivalité d'influence entre les puissances européennes en Afrique équatoriale et occidentale depuis l'acte général de Berlin jusqu'au seuil du XXe siècle', *Revue Française d'Histoire d'Outre-Mer*, 48, 1961.

II – Further Imperial Pressures at the end of the century

Burke, E., *Prelude to Protectorate in Morocco. Precolonial Protest and Resistance, 1860–1912*, (Chicago and London, 1980).

Collins, R. O., 'The Transfer of the Lado Enclave to the Anglo-Egyptian Sudan, 1910', *Zaire*, 1960.

Dunn, R. E., *Resistance in the Desert*, (London, 1977).

Gautier, E. F., *La Conquête du Sahara*, (Paris, 1910).

Gerteiny, A. G., *Mauritania*, (London, 1967).

Martel, A., *Les Confins saharo-tripolitains de la Tunisie*, (Paris, 1965).

Martin, G. P. *Quatre Siècles d'Histoire Marocaine*, (Paris, 1923).

Mantran, *et al.*, *La Libye Nouvelle*, (Paris, 1975).

Sanderson, G. N., *England, Europe and the Upper Nile 1882–1899*, (Edinburgh, 1965).

Williamson, F. T., *Germany and Morocco before 1905*, (Baltimore, 1937).

III – Strangers at home

Berque, J., *L'Egypte. Impérialisme et Révolution*, (Paris, 1967).

Charnay, J. P., *La Vie Musulmane en Algérie d'après la Jurisprudence de la Première Moitié du XXe Siècle*, (Paris, 1965).

Lacheraf, M., *l'Algérie: Nation et Société*, (Paris, 1965).

Messali, Hadj, *Les Mémoires de Messali Hadj*, (Paris, 1982).

Vatin, J.-C., *L'Algérie politique. Histoire et Société*, (Paris, 1974).

IV – A new national stand

Ahmed, J. M., *The Intellectual Origins of Egyptian Nationalism*, (London, 1960).

Ben 'Ashur, *Al-Haraka al-'Adabiyya wa al-Fikriyya fi Tunis*, (Cairo, 1965).

Berque, J., 'Lieux et moment du réformisme musulman', *Maghreb Histoire et Société*, (Algiers, 1974).

Sayyid al-Lutfi, A., *Qissat Hayati*, (Cairo, 1962).

Wendell, Ch., *The Evolution of the Egyptian National Image. From its Origins to Ahmad Lutfi al-Sayyid*, (Berkeley, Los Angeles, London, 1972).

Wissa-Wassef, C., 'Saad Zaghloul et la lutte pour l'indépenance et la démocratie en Egypte', *Les Africains*, Vol. VI, (Paris, 1977).

Ziadeh, N., *Origins of Nationalism in Tunisia*, (Beyrut, 1962).

INDEX

Aba (Sud.), island on the White Nile 249

Abada (Sud.), tribe 219

'Abbas Hilmi (Eg.), viceroy (1848–1854) 110, 111, 166–7, 220

'Abbas Hilmi (Eg.), khedive (1892–1914) 110, 305

Al-'Abbasi al-Mahdi, Muhammad (Eg.), rector of al-Azhar 243

'Abbasid, early Muslim dynasty 32, 39, 53, 60

'Abbasid Empire (750–1258) 24

'Abd al-'Al (Eg.); janissary 91
his son, cf. Abdelal, Louis

'Abd al-'Al (Eg.), nationalist 236

'Abd al-'Aziz (Ot. Emp.), sultan (1861–1867) 170

'Abd al-'Aziz (Mor.), 'Alawi sovereign (1894–1908) 35, 313

'Abd al-Hamid (Ot. Emp.), sultan (1876–1909) 281, 294, 303, 306, 308–10

'Abd al-Karim, ruling family of Wadday 60

'Abd Allah (Mor.), 'Alawi sovereign (1728–1757) 35

'Abd Allah bin Muhammad al-Ta'ishi (Sud.), 1846–1899, leader of the Mahdiyya, also known as khalifa 'Abd Allah 250, 253, 254, 261, 262–5, 280, 316, 317

'Abd al-Latif Pasha (Sud.), governor during the Turkiyya (1849–1851) 218

'Abd al-Majid (Ot. Emp.), sultan (1839–1861) 275

'Abd al-Malik (Mor.), 'Alawi prince 35

'Abd al-Qadir (Alg.), 1807–1883, leader of the Algerian resistance 75, 137, 138–43, 150, 152, 153, 188, 230, 231, 294, 295, 297–9, 301, 304, 306
his brother 140
his mother and wife 141
his children, cf. Bin 'Abd al-Qadir
his cousin, cf. Bin Thami, Mustafa

'Abd al-Qadir (Sud.), d. 1857, shaykh

al-mashayikh 127, 128, 129

'Abd al-Qadir Pasha (Sud.), governor in 1882 218

'Abd al-Rahman (Mor.), 'Alawi sovereign (1822–1859) 35, 56, 57, 96, 138, 139, 142, 143, 203, 301

'Abd al-Rahman Pasha, al-Zahir, Indonesian nationalist 304

'Abd al-Salam bin Mashish (Mor.), shrine 95

'Abdelal, Louis, 1815–1882, son of an Egyptian Janissary, French officer 91

Abdel Nasser, Gamel (Eg.), 1917–1970 175, 322

'Abduh, Muhammad (Eg.), 1849–1905, reformist scholar 121, 235, 244–5, 297, 304, 305–6, 320, 321, 322, 323

Abrines, Gregory (Mor.), European resident in Tangier 204

Abu al-Su'ud, Muhammad Bey (Sud.), trader 222, 227

Abu Bakr, companion of the Prophet 250, 297

Abu Bakr (Sah.), chief of the al-Murabitun (11th century) 20

Abu Bakr bin Hamza (Alg.), leader of the Awlad Sidi Shaykh tribe 55

Abu Madyan Shu'aib, d.1197, mystic, tomb in Algeria 25

Abu Nazzara Zarqa, Arab satyrical magazine published in Paris 244

Abu Jumayza (Sud.), d.1889, religious leader 262

Abukir, battle of – (Eg.), 1798 77, 80

Abu Qubays, hill near Mecca 273

Abu Sinn, Ahmad (Sud.), d.1790–1870), chief of the Shukriyya tribe 219
his son, cf. Abu Sinn, 'Awad al-Karim Pasha

Abu Sinn, 'Awad al-Karim Pasha (Sud.), tribal and political chief 253

Abu Widan (Sud.), governor during the Turkiyya (1838–1843) 127

cf. also Taxes

Firman-s 43, 44, 48, 111, 125, 129, 130, 170, 171, 173, 275

Firms (trading or industrial)
European firms 69, 146–7, 148, 150, 314; Cockerill 147, 148; Krupps 147, 148, 206
European firms in North Africa 69, 314; Atlas Co. 215; Compagnie des Chemins de Fer de bone à Guelma 196; Compaña de Pesquerias Canario Africana 215; Compaña Mercantil Hispano-Africana 215; Dussaud Brothers 177; Greenfield & Elliot 177; Foreign Colonial Gas Co. 196; New Gas Co. 196; North African & Soos Co. 215; North-West African Co. 215; Société des Batignolles 196; Shuttleworth & Co. 215; Tunis Railways 196; cf. also Compagnie Universelle du Canal de Suez, Shipping lines
North African firms: Aqqad & Co. 222; Compagnie du Sudan 221; cf. also shipping lines

Fishing rights 98

Flatters, Paul (Fr.), 1832–1881, officer and explorer 212, 279

Flissa (Alg.), tribe 132

Flittas (Alg.), tribe 157

Fort Mackenzie (Sah.), trading post on the Western coast 215, 216

Fort National (Alg.), French military post in Kabylie 158

Foureau, Fernand (Fr.), 1850–1914, French explorer 212, 311

France 27, 55, 57, 69, 70, 71
19th century 72, 73, 75, 77, 87–88, 91, 92, 93, 94, 96, 97, 98–9, 102, 103, 104, 106, 107, 108, 110, 116, 118, 119, 120–1, 123, 129, 130, 131–43, 146, 147, 148, 150–65, 167, 168, 171, 172, 173, 179, 180, 181, 184, 186, 188, 190, 191, 192, 193, 196, 197, 199, 200, 203, 205, 206, 207, 209, 211, 212, 213, 215, 220, 222, 224, 235, 271, 274, 277, 279, 282, 284–91, 294, 295, 296, 297, 298, 299, 300, 303, 308, 310–2, 313, 314, 315, 317, 318, 321
French Imperialism in North Africa 123, 131–43, 150–65, 182, 192, 196, 199, 209, 210, 216, 274, 282, 288, 303, 306, 310–11, 312, 314, 315–16

French Equatorial Africa 311

French West Africa 311, 312–3

Francis I (Fr.), reigned (151–1547) 78

Frankfurt (Germany), town 191

Fraternities, cf. Sufi orders

Fundamental Pact (Tunisian constitutional law) 182, 186, 189

Fundamentalist, Islamic movements 47, 94, 109, 232

Funj Dynasty (Sud.), 16th–19th century 61, 123, 317

Funj, Sultantate of – kingdom of Northern Sudan prior to Egyptian invasion 39, 123, 125, 127, 254

Galla (Abyssinia) 224

Gambetta, Léon (Fr.), 1838–1882, statesman 160

Gambia (Af.) 27, 311

Gao (Sud. Af.), trading post on the Niger 32, 33, 58

Geneva (Switzerland) 323

Genoa (Italy) 49, 72, 189

Georgia, part of the Russian Empire since 1803 49, 81

Germany/Germans 87, 147, 157, 199, 204, 205, 206, 212, 261, 285, 291, 308, 310, 314, 316

Gessi, Romolo (Italy), 1832–1881, officer in Khedival service in the Sudan 224, 227

Ghadames (Sah.), trading centre 58, 59, 63, 100, 130, 213, 270

Ghali, Boutros (Eg.), d. 1910, statesman 318

Ghana (Sud. Af.), kingdom of the Middle Ages 20

Gharbiyya (Eg.), province 244

Ghat (Sah.), trading centre 58, 59

Al-Ghurqan (Sud.), village 259

Gibraltar, British fortress 68, 69, 82, 93, 146, 148, 204, 206, 207, 313

Gilbert, Theodore (Fr.), consul in Damascus (1882–1886) 298

Ginsberg, H. B. Crighton (G.B.), missionary in North Africa 206

Gladstone, William (G.B.), 1809–1898, statesman 245, 291

Gold 31, 33, 34, 55, 58, 61, 125, 127, 147, 210, 214

Gold Coast 311

Golea (Alg.), town 141

Goletta (Tun.), harbour 40, 41, 184, 196

Gondokoro (Sud.), trading post.

Mackenzie (G.B.), traded in the Sahara, founded Fort Mackenzie 215

Mackintosh (Mor.), British missionary 206

Mac Lean, Henry Aubrey de Vere (Mor.), 1848–1920, British officer in the Moroccan army 206, 209, 314

Mac Mahon, Edme, Duke of Magenta (Fr.), 1808–1893, Governor-General of Algeria, President of the French Republic (1873–1879) 155, 163

Macta (Alg.), town 139

Madagascar 290

Al-Madani, Muhammad (Lib.), founder of the Madaniyya 244

Madaniyya, sufi order 244

Madibtu ʿAli (Sud.), tribal chief 262

Madrid (Spain) 205

Maghrib 4, 5–29, 36–7, 38, 47, 54, 65–8, 93, 94, 99, 106, 184, 203, 214, 276, 282, 294, 295, 302, 304
cf. countries of North Africa

Al-Mahallat al-Kubra (Eg.) 113

Mahamid (Lib.), tribe 17

Al-Mahdi, al-Hajj (Mor.), qaid of In Salah 210

Al-Mahdi, real name Muhammad Ahmad bin ʿAbd Allah (Sud.), d. 1885 128, 216, 218, 219, 231, 247, 248–55, 256, 257, 258, 259, 260, 261, 263, 280, 316
his son 317

Mahdiya (Tun.), town 40

Mahdiyya, cf. Sudan

Mahmud (Lib.), Qaramanli Prince 49

Mahmud II (Ot. Emp.), sultan (1808–1839) 110

Mahmud Amin (Lib.), Turkish governor (1842–1847) 268

Mahmud bin Husayn (Tun.), Husayni sovereign (1814–1824) 45, 95

Al-Mahmudi, Ghuma (Lib.), d. 1858, tribal leader 129, 131, 268, 269

Mahmudiyya canal (Eg.) 112

Mahmud Nedim (Lib.), Turkish governor (1860–1867) 268

Mahmud Rashid (Lib.), Turkish governor (1871) 268

Mahmud Sabri (Lib.), Turkish governor (1878) 268

Mahruqi, Ahmad (Eg.), d. 1804, leading figure 90, 91

Mahu Bey (Sud.), governor during the Turkiyya (1825) 127, 129

Maison Carré (Alg.), near Algiers 163

Al-Majdhub al-Sughayyar, Muhammad (Sud.), 1796–1832, leader of a Sufi order 128

Majdhubiyya, Sufi order 123, 126, 128, 255

Al-Makki, Ismaʾil (Sud.), religious leader 250
his brother 250

Makram ʿUmar (Eg.), religious and political leader 90, 107, 116, 241

Malay peninsula 231

Mali (Sud. Af.), kingdom in the early Muslim period 20

Mali (Sud. Af.), modern state 15

Malta (Med.), island 66, 67, 73, 82, 102, 146, 148, 185, 197, 223, 269, 270, 302

Malta, knights of – 41, 44, 66, 67, 73, 82

Mamluk –s 37–8, 46, 66, 78–9, 81, 88–9, 106, 107, 109, 111, 117–8, 119, 120, 126, 127, 132, 184–5, 186, 193, 299, 300

Al-Manar (Eg.), reformist review, 1898–1935 320

Manchester (G.B.) 57, 93, 204, 215

Manfalut (Eg.), village 10

Mangin, Charles (Fr.), 1866–1925, colonial officer 311

Al-Mansur, Ahmad (Mor.), Saʾadi sovereign (1578–1608) 31, 32–3

Maʿqil (West. Sah.) Arab tribes 17, 23, 56

Marchand, Jean-Baptiste (France), 1863–1934, officer and explorer 311–12

Marcuard (Fr.), banker's agent in Egypt 172

Marey (Fr.), officer in Algeria 136

Margueritte (Alg.), colonist settlement

Margueritte, uprising of – (Alg.), 1901 318. cf. also uprising

Marrakech (Mor.), town 20, 31, 33, 56, 92, 95, 209

Marseilles (Fr.), Mediterranean port 70, 71, 73, 93, 108, 134, 189, 204, 205, 215, 269, 302
Marseilles Chamber of Commerce (set up in 1599) 67, 70

Martin, B. G., contemporary historian 275

Mascara (Alg.), town 138, 139, 140, 141

Mashriq, cf. Middle East 5, 36, 44, 53, 135, 138, 148, 150, 167, 208, 231, 252, 302, 323

Masinda (East Af.), 295, 297

Masmuda (Mor.), tribe 20

Massawa, Red Sea port 218, 221, 227,

Shakir Efendi (Ot. Emp.), sultan's envoy to Libya in 1833 and 1835 130

Al-Sharif (Mor.), founder of the 'Alawi dynasty 35

Sharif Pasha (Eg.), statesman in the reign of Khedive Isma'il 180, 251

Sharif-s of Mecca 78, 304

Sharqawi, 'Abd Allah (Eg.), c. 1737–1812, rector of al-Azhar and President of the Diwan appointed by Bonaparte 90

Shaykh al-balad, cf. Society

Shaykhiyya, fraternity of the Awlad Sidi Shaykh 155

Shayqiyya (Sud.), tribe 125, 126, 127, 219, 249

Sheffield, Lord (G.B.), political personality 73

Shibbrekit (Eg.), village 120

Shilluk (Sud.), Southern tribe 127, 311

Shinqit (West, Sahara) oasis 56

Shipping 71, 72–3, 148, 179, 189, 203, 290, 301, 315
  freight 148, 189
  Shipping lines (European) Steamship service between Malta and North Africa 102
    Compagnie Paquet 203
    Italian 189
    London Lisboa & North Africa 203, 204
    Longland & Cowell 204
    Mersey Steamship Co. 203
    Royal Mail Steam Packet Co. 148
    Rubattino 189, 268, 269
    Touache Co. 189
  Shipping lines (North African)
    The Medjidiyé 167
    Nile navigation 167, 221

Shukriyya (Sud.), tribe 125, 126, 219, 253

Shumayyil Shibbli, Syrian author, 1850–1917 321

Siala (Tun.), estate 290

Sicily, Med. island 45, 72

Sidi al-Hayyad (Tun.), zawiya 300

Sidi Brahim (Alg.), place name 143

Sidi Ferruch (Alg.), place where the French landed in 1830 82, 86

Sidi Ifni (Mor.) 215

Sidi Tabet (Tun.), estate 97

Sidiyya (West. Sah.), religious leader, 1775–1868 56–7

Sierra Leone 311

Simara (West. Sah.), holy town 312

Sinan Pasha, Ottoman sea-captain, 16th century 41

Siwa (Eg.), oasis 14, 16, 275

Slatin Pasha, Rudolf Karl von – (Sud.), 1857–1932, Austrian in Khedival service 227, 255

Slaves/slavery 34, 37, 53, 55, 59, 60, 71, 89, 91, 101, 108, 125, 126, 206, 214, 220, 227, 228, 251, 257, 261, 277
  slave trade 31, 38, 53, 58, 60, 62–3, 100, 108, 126, 218, 219, 220, 221–5, 226, 227, 228, 249, 256, 257, 261, 293
  abolishment of 170, 182, 185, 221–7

Sliman bin Hamza (Alg.), leader of the Awlad Sidi Shaykh 155

Smith, Goldwin (G.B.), 1823–1910, historian 145

Society 10, 26–7, 45, 64, 78, 88–91, 111–15, 118–20, 121, 152–5, 158, 159, 186–7, 188, 203, 204, 205–6, 219–21, 223, 228, 235–6, 238–40, 251, 252, 261, 263, 271, 291, 299, 317–20, 323
  ethnic groups (other than Arab and Berber): Haratin 11, 54; Kulughli-s 39, 42, 43, 48–9, 86, 104, 129, 135, 155; Nilots 11
  social groups: Andalusians 45; Beduins 17, 45, 78, 89; nomads 16–7, 22, 23, 27, 34, 46, 49, 52, 53, 58–9, 100–12, 125, 135, 195, 228, 249, 254, 275, 276, 280, 291, 311, 312;
    Turco-Circassian 109, 120, 184, 232, 235, 236, 237, 238, 242
  economic groups: craftsmen 27, 89, 90, 92, 97, 195–6; peasants 23, 36, 38, 46, 108, 111–12, 121, 171, 175, 176, 178, 179–80, 186–7, 188, 190, 195, 228, 236, 237, 291, 292, 293, 318; workers in agriculture 111–12, 121, 285, 286, 291; workers in industry 46, 113–14, 121
  ruling class and notables 36, 37–8, 39, 42, 43, 46–7, 76, 88, 89–90, 91, 93, 94, 97, 104, 116, 119, 129, 135, 154, 161, 169, 173, 180, 186, 189, 190, 237, 299, 315, 319, 322; merchant class 90, 92, 98, 270; shaykh al-balad (Eg.) 119–20, 234, 236, 239–40, 322
  cf. also Arabs, army, Berbers, Copts, Jews, Mamluk-s, religious establishment slaves

Societies, academic or learned,